THE
DREAM
DEATH
OF

A REALITY OF LIFE BASED ON GREED, LOVE, BETRAYAL, MURDER, AND SPIRITUAL REDEMPTION

DIVINE LORD SEKHEM

THE

DREAM OF DEATH

A REALITY OF LIFE BASED ON GREED, LOVE, BETRAYAL, MURDER, AND SPIRITUAL REDEMPTION

DIVINE LORD SEKHEM

ISBN 9781546-576525

sekhemasaru@gmail.com
themanifestword@gmail.com
Facebook: Sekhem Asaru
Instagram: Sekhem Asaru
www.sekhemasaru.com

Cover design & layout by Pharoah Page

This book is dedicated to all the men, women and children whose lives were shattered because of the street life. To all the honorable men and women sitting in prison cages who chased the street dreams. And to all those whose lives were lost due to the blood, sweat, and tears of this cruel world and the street life.

May the wisdom in these pages divinely guide and inspire the seed that I've resurrected myself through; my son Nagi, as well as my nephews and my God-Sun Saru, and all the other young men of the world living in this wilderness.

Introduction

The story you are about to read takes place in Buffalo New York. Buffalo lies at the western corner of New York State on the eastern shores of Lake Erie. Buffalo is 15 miles south of Niagara Falls, NY and right across the river from Fort Erie, Canada. Buffalo is the second largest city in New York right after New York City and the Buffalo-Niagara Falls metropolitan area is the second most populous in New York State. The city of Buffalo's population peaked at over a half of million residents up until the 1960's and 1970's. From the late 1800's to the 1970's Buffalo was a major industrial center which attracted people from all over America as well as European and Asian immigrants who came to work in its many factories and steel plants. African-Americans who were just coming up out of slavery in the late 1800's, fled the racist south for refuge in northern cities like Buffalo which were booming with Industrial plants and factories. The American Dream was to be sought up north where there was the *so-called* promise of equal opportunity.

Despite the achievement of the American Dream by some African-Americans, American society placed many roadblocks which discouraged many African-Americans from pursuing the American Dream by legal means. Racism, mis-education, the lynching's of Black People, police brutality, high rates of unemployment, discrimination and many other social ills caused many blacks to partake in the underworld of crime where Black Men could accomplish what white society doesn't offer.

The Thug Poet and Prophet Tupac Shakur once said, *"There's a ghetto in every city and a nigga in every ghetto…"* Most blacks who fled the racist and dangerous south thought the northern cities were a promised land where racism didn't exist and everyone was living well. To their surprise many blacks from the south found themselves in northern cities living in hell. Plenty of jobs were available but Whites and immigrants would get the available jobs before blacks. This caused many blacks to get involved with the life of crime.

In the early days Buffalo's criminal underworld was ruled by Polish, Irish, and German gangs (Read *Gangsters and Organized Crime in Buffalo* by

Michael F. Rizzo). The Powerhouse of Buffalo's underworld was the Italian Mafia ruled by Stefano Maggadino, who was the first cousin of Joseph Bonanno (The Boss of N.Y.C Bonanno Crime Family). Stefano Maggadino and the Buffalo Mob held a seat on the La Cosa Nostra's national crime syndicate and the Buffalo Mob controlled western NY, parts of Pennsylvania, and Ontario Canada.

Like in most urban cities in America, Blacks in Buffalo found themselves in the midst of this criminal underworld and crime seemed to be the only way for some while others made a way working the steel plants and factories. The Black Community in Buffalo started in Buffalo's downtown area on the east side where many families lived in the 8-10 story project buildings around downtown. As many began to find success they began to flood the east and west side and buy many properties and business establishments where Blacks could provide for themselves and support their own. Black Businesses and nightclubs began to pop up all around downtown and throughout the east side during the 1900's. Blacks became a force in the city of Buffalo from establishing criminal organizations to becoming prominent citizens. In 1905 The Niagara Movement was founded by W.E.B. Dubois and others in the Buffalo-Niagara Falls region. The Niagara movement was the first Civil Rights movement for African-Americans and also the start of the NAACP. Buffalo sits right across the river from Canada so the Buffalo-Niagara Falls region was a main route on the Underground Railroad where the great ancestor Harriet Tubman (Moses) led many enslaved African-Americans to freedom.

Unfortunately, like many great cities where poverty plagues the people, Buffalo has experienced the hardship of crime and violence since time immemorial. President Willam Mckinley was assassinated in downtown Buffalo in the early 1900's. According to national statistics, in the northeast of the United States Buffalo ranks number 3 for the poorest and most depressed city behind Detroit and Cleveland. Forbes Magazine also ranked Buffalo in the top 10 most dangerous cities in America. This story takes place in that ghetto environment where Buffalo native Rick James fell in love with *Mary Jane* (Weed) while partying with a *Superfreak*. This is the depressed place of drama where Stevie J learned them controversial skills he exhibits on Love & Hip-Hop. And this is the soulful environment many watched on Reuben Santiago Jr.'s HBO special *"Lackawanna Blues."*

When the divine light of truth is made manifest it leads one out of the darkness of ignorance into the light of Supreme Wisdom. This story is in no way seeking to glamourize or justify the life of crime. It is only intended to paint a vivid picture and reality of the life of those who pursue the American Dream through the life of crime. The goal of this story is to provide the light of Divine Knowledge and Wisdom for those of us dwelling in the darkness of the street life but yearn for another way out of the spiritual madness of life. While reading this story, if you look deeper than the dark mud of the sex, money, drugs, and violence, you will see that every beautiful flower springs forth from the dirt and if we look deep into our dark souls of ignorance, we will discover a divine light of God which is greater than the thug, gangster, hoe, and the many other negative images we identify with in todays world.

In memory of my childhood friends who were murdered on the streets of Ruff-Buff: To my best friend and co-d, Baby John. I miss you Sun. R.I.P Tre, Heavy Sed, L. Bell, Boogie Brown, Chill, Pooh (Karon), 2-Inch, Tone Alexander, Big D Love, Dolph, Lil Bubbles and all the others who inspired me to write this book while they exist in the Duat (Spirit Realm) with the Ancestors.

Peace, Divine Lord Sekhem.

CHAPTER 1
Spring of 2000

Beams of sunlight sparkled on the emerald green Range Rover creeping thru the congested traffic on Grant Street where car horns screamed at the slow-moving traffic. It was mid-day and school kids dashed thru the bumper to bumper traffic while crossing guards flailed hand signals directing traffic. Pedestrians and consumers along with college students from Buff State strolled the strip crammed with its international grocery stores and retail shops.

All eyes were glued on the Range Rover stuck in the traffic jam. It wasn't only the custom-made paint job on the truck or its clear acoustic sound system blasting Beanie Sigel which captivated everyone's attention, it was the two occupants inside the Range. To the onlookers it appeared the truck was navigated by remote control as Zulu and Cream reclined in the plush leather seats like they were lounging on lazy boy sofas.

Zulu's left arm dangled out the driver window, displaying his 14-carat gold Figaro bracelet as he softly stomped his ACG Nike boots on the gas pedal. And with hazel hued eyes and hands dark as the armor all tires on the truck, Cream fiddled thru a stack of dead presidents faster than a bank teller.

"Big Walt need to lower these prices yo." Cream blurted leaning forward in the passenger seat wrapping rubber bands around the large stack of money. "We only profiting $550 off each Big eight (4 ½ ounces or 125 grams) we knocking off for this dude.

"Yo instead of selling Bigs for the Tre-duce ($ 3250)," Zulu twisted his neck checking for passing traffic as he swerved into the clear passing lane to his right side, "I think we should raise the price to thirty-five."

"Come on Zulu you know these dudes not gone pay no more than thirty-two.

"We do need lower prices to make a better profit…but you know Big Walt not lowering the price." Zulu remarked sliding thru a clear intersection and mashing the gas pedal, accelerating the Range Rover to about 45mph zooming down Grant Street passing Buff-State College. "Either we raise the price or we gotta start cutting it."

"Hell no Zulu check it out," Cream rolled up his window shutting out the breezing wind as they slid onto the Scajaquada Expressway, "I know Big Walt getting each big for like $ 2, 200. It would be stupid and against the whole object of hustling if he not making a profit. We the damn fools only profiting the shorts and taking all the risks. Dude got to lower the price because we the ones who moving the work."

"You right yo. Either he lowers the price or we just gone continue busting everything down and moving our shit on the blocks. We make more profit breaking everything down anyway. And being that we taking all the risks, we better off pumping the work where we can make more profit because we selling weight for this dude to keep him off the street."

"Word up. Let's go holla at this dude."

Zulu pushed it down the Scajaquada expressway heading east. He raced thru the traffic on the expressway as thoughts flashed like lightning in him and Cream's mind while they pondered the situation at hand.

Along with their childhood friends, they were two young men with aspiring futures of street dreams ahead of them. Like many ambitious young men in this capitalistic society of American Dreams they not only wanted a piece of the American Pie, they desired the whole pie. Big Walt was the gourmet chef who had all the ingredients and skills to bake the whole pie, but Big Walt worshipped his own desire to stay on top and want everything for himself.

Zulu and Cream operated their own business serving the wretched of the earth with smaller amounts of crack cocaine. From nickels, dimes, to fifties and grams they profited tremendously, but selling large weight for Big Walt was fruitless since the profit was short as a mosquito. Big Walt on the other hand figured they were satisfied with just a slice or two of the pie. Big Walt should've known better. These young men were ambitious and dedicated to the game and it was time they achieved and enjoyed the success they were due.

Besides the music playing in the Range Rover they cruised down the expressway listening to their individual thoughts. The expressway took them to the east side of the city where they skated off the exit at Humboldt Parkway. Along the Parkway well-groomed and sharp dressed members of the Nation of Islam flashed bean pies and Final Call Newspapers. They blew it pass the brothers and headed to their destination which was a few stop lights away on E. Ferry street. After rolling thru a yellow light at an intersection they rolled smoothly into a potholed filled parking lot on the corner. The lot served a pizzeria on one side and a soul food restaurant on the other side. The Range Rover dipped into the only parking space which was in front of the pizzeria.

Zulu and Cream exited the truck and straddled across the parking lot to the soul food restaurant where a group of men lounged outside in front of a table covered with Cd's, socks, incense, and other items.

"Fuck took yall niggas so long?" A man named Tam barked at Zulu and Cream. Tam's light brown eyes hid behind the golden yellow dreadlocks suffocating his albino pigmented face. "Yall never handle business and come right back…what yall was out joy riding…and stunting in Big Walt truck like its yall shit?"

"Yeah," Zulu and Cream screwed their faces at Tam while approaching the door to the restaurant. "We ran train on ya baby moms in the back seat you pink pussy face looking ass dude."

"Violate me again I air both of you lil niggas out."

"Fuck you leprechaun face," Zulu and Cream slid inside the restaurant glancing while the men who stood with Tam spit out laughter.

"Welcome to Gigi's sugar!" An older lady with streams of sweat drizzling down her chocolate face greeted Zulu and Cream. "Are yall eating in or taking out?"

"We gone eat in…our party already here." Zulu and Cream then slid pass the stools along the counter and passed a jukebox where the mellow sounds of the Whispers breezed out the speakers. The clinging noise of dishes and sizzling grease clashed over the chattering of patrons seated at the tables, while the music created a soulful atmosphere tasty like the soul food people munched on. Zulu and Cream entered the rear section of the restaurant, filled with its white cloth tables and wood colored walls covered with framed pictures of famous African Americans, who once sat in this ancient greasy spoon joint and blessed their stomachs with the good food.

"You can drive around the whole city in like 45 minutes," Big Walt tapped the diamond encrusted bezel on his Movado watch as he sat at a table near the back wall. "Yall been gone for over an hour and yall only had to run to the Langfield Projects."

"What you always tell us?" Zulu and Cream dropped into their seats and began whispering since people who should've been eating their food were being nosey, "You always tell us to make sure we not being followed before we hit the spot to pick up and before we drop off any work."

"Yeah yeah…yall better put gas in my truck too. But anyway, everything good right? Yall got that bread?"

"Of course we got the bread…but everything not good."

"Oh boy," Big Walt leaned back in his seat while stretching his arms. "What's the problem now?"

"Alright check it right…we respect everything you doing for us…when the Feds snatched the A-Squad from the hood you was the only one to come thru for us. You took us off the corners and got us to moving weight for you…we respect that…but we not making no profit at the price you charging us for the weight we move for you. If you could lower the--."

"Whoa whoa whoa," Big Walt interrupted now folding his large hands across the table. "Yall tryna say yall not making no gwop. Come on now. Before I put yall on yall was on the corner pumping dimes, copping garbage from niggas, rocking slum gold chains and driving hooopties."

"If the A-Squad was here we would really be eating."

"Yeah whatever. Quiet as it's kept, when they was here they had yall young asses on the corner with pebbles and yall little guns like yall was little Soldiers, I got yall living like young bosses."

"Living like bosses…" Zulu and Cream glared at each other unbelievably. "You can't be serious yo. How you figure we on some boss shit when off every big eight we sell for you we only profit a nickel and change ($ 550). If you get knocked with four and a half ounces that's at least three years up north. Five hundred dollars not worth a couple years upstate. Nigga you got us living like immigrants or some shit. This not us. Boss shit run in our blood."

"Ungrateful little niggas." Big Walt mumbled to himself massaging his forehead thoughtfully.

"Come on yo, all we saying is just how the A-Squad put you in a position to bubble when they left, we need you to do the same with us…if you got knocked we aint got enough bank to step it up and keep things moving on a major level. We would be back to square one like we was when the A-Squad left. No connect and shortchange. You gotta step it up with us before yo time come yo."

"Oh so yall praying on my downfall?" Big Walt asked rubbing his neatly trimmed goatee.

"Come on yo…of course not. We just saying we need you to step it up with us. You know you can trust us but what good is we to you if you keep us at this level?"

"Just be patient. I'm gone step it up with yall in time. Everything good and bad in life has its time and place."

Big Walt trusted Zulu and Cream without a doubt. They were young, loyal, and dedicated to the game of hustling. This is what Big Walt needed at this stage of the game. Now if Big Walt was to slip and fall in the bottomless pit where most hustlers unfortunately ended up, Zulu and Cream was sure to take Big Walt's throne and live like kings while Big Walt rotted away in a 6x9 cell, just like Big Walt took the throne from the A-Squad when Feds snatched them.

The A-Squad (Assassination Squad) started off in the early 80's as a hip hop break dancing crew, but when the demon of crack cocaine began terrorizing the hood, the A-Squad became capitalist and murderous black youth who unknowingly sold their souls to the crack god for riches and power. The A-Squad flooded their E. North street neighborhood with crack for years until a few criminals got caught up and found them selves trapped in federal interrogation rooms, and began revealing secrets to federal agents like devout servants of the church revealed secrets to the priest. These snitching criminals informed the federal government on how the A-Squad's narcotics business was pouring in cash by the hundreds of thousands and how the A-Squad was also responsible for bloodshed rivaling U.S. troops in Iraq. With this information the feds rushed the E. North street neighborhood and the A-Squad's destiny was to be locked behind steel bars in federal prisons for life.

Big Walt then seized the throne and took over the drug flow around the E. North street neighborhood. He began eating like the big bear he was and started blessing his 375lb appetite with the exquisite lifestyle the A-Squad left for him. So with Big Walt being king of E. North and Tam as his only trigger finger, Big Walt had to shield himself with an army of gun clappers because Tam was not Terminator by himself. This is where Zulu and Cream along with their conglomerates known as the Young Assassins came in at.

The Young Assassins were criminal offspring of the A-Squad and not only had a lust for money but they were just as blood thirsty as the A-Squad. Big Walt needed the Young Assassins so he utilized them to be the ponds that would shield and protect him from the misfortunes of the game. To Big Walt's advantage, the Young Assassins were loyal 110%. But lately, one ultimate fear and worry that began adding stress to Big Walt's mental galaxy was the Young Assassins dissatisfaction. Big Walt's soul was enveloped in fear and he dreaded having to suffer like the A-Squad while the Young Assassins took his throne and lived like kings. Big Walt felt the throne was only for him. He was the last man standing for a reason. All those who came up before him and with him had fallen. He was still here and been through it all. The throne of success belonged to Big Walt. It was rightfully his and no one else's. This is what Big Walt felt deep inside the recesses of his greedy soul and at the present moment of the here and now, while sitting in the restaurant between Zulu and Cream, Big Walt realized they desired the next level but Big Walt wasn't ready to take them to that level.

There was only room for one king and if Big Walt wanted to stay king, he would have to devise a crafty plan to keep the Young Assassins from taking his throne by force. They were loyal young men but they also had blood on their hands, and within the blink of an eye their loyalty could turn to betrayal and they could murder the king and take the throne, the same way many young hustlers treacherously murdered their drug connects who put them on. Big Walt was a great thinker and he hadn't made it thus far without Supreme Intelligence, he knew how to use the art of seduction like he knew how to breathe oxygen. He was a master manipulator who knew how to keep these young wolves under control.

"Ok listen to me fellas," Big Walt's game face took over as he gulped his glass of ice cold lemon water. "Yall know I will front yall whatever yall ask for. It's just prices high right now. I'm paying $21,000 for each brick and I'm only profiting a couple geez off each brick I sell…but check it right, if yall just give me a little time I can holla at this other plug I know who got bricks for like $ 17,500. Just hold tight and by next re-up we should be good and on deck with my other plug, then I can hit yall with the big eights (4 ½ ounces) for $ 2,200."

"Fronting us not the problem because we eating on our blocks hitting the feigns…but if you want us to keep moving the weight for you, your gonna have to lower the prices…you want us to risk our freedom selling all this weight for you but the profit short as fuck…we make a crazy profit hitting the feigns and the risk is real low."

"Trust me I'm gone make sure yall good…And for good faith so yall know I aint playing…I got three bricks left and I'm gone bless yall with one brick and yall can break it down to hit the feigns. The other two bricks I need yall to push for me in weight but check the math. By time yall knock everything off my other plug should come thru and we gone get the work for the low low. All I ask is that yall throw all the money back in the pot for the re-up. Put everything in the pot so we can cop the mother-load and get rich. Come on I know yall feeling me."

Zulu and Cream skeptically gave each other the eye before deceitfully agreeing to Big Walt's game. If Big Walt had any tricks up his sleeve, they had one too. Tam then rudely bum rushed the table and plopped himself into a chair as Zulu and Cream arose from their seats.

"Yeah make moves and bounce when yall see bosses ready to politic." Tam muttered eyeing a menu after seating himself.

"You know what...we not even gone entertain you because you aint shit but Big Walt flunky and shadow you ugly muthafucka."

"Listen fellas," Big Walt gestured his hand to stop Tam from responding, "Get with the crew and let them know it's come up time. Let's make it happen fellas."

"Yeah whatever yo," Zulu and Cream left the restaurant vexed at how Big Walt thought all he had to do was flash a little gold to get them to jump. He was insulting their intelligence. If it wasn't for their loyalty and respect for the game they would have been knocked Big Walt and Tam off and took the throne. Big Walt was their plug, so respecting the game, they gave him that respect by being patient and dealing with his selfish greed. Now with this opportunity Big Walt was proposing, what did they have to lose by seeing if Big Walt would fulfill his word.

"Check it out Tam," Big Walt spoke in a hushed tone after Zulu and Cream left the restaurant, "You got to watch them because they starting to become dissatisfied...You remember what them young boys from Sycamore and Woltz did to Old Man Jacob?"

"Man fuck them little niggas I murk every last one of them niggas if they even get slick out the mouth with you. Old Man Jacob trusted them little niggas from Sycamore and Woltz a little bit too much."

"Listen Tam...the only people who can ever hit you where it hurt is the people you trust...and I gotta trust the Young Assassins to move this work for me...you can't move the work because you gotta watch my back, and I'm too ahead in the game to be on the streets moving work."

"Old Man Jacob would probably still be alive if he got up off his ass and moved that work himself instead of having them young boys move the work for him. He showed them young boys those bricks and they killed him. I'm telling you Big Walt, fuck these little niggas...them Young Assassins would murder they own mama to get rich."

"Why you think I keep them on the level I keep them at...but this the plan I got for them boys...I'm gone have them knock off the last three bricks I'm holding and get them to bring all the money back for the re-up. I'm gone tell them I'm copping from a cheaper plug and then say the plug snaked us for all the bread."

"Man them niggas really gone get on shit if you have em throw all they bread in the pot for the re-up and then you say we got robbed." Tam shook his head disagreeing. "Man I'm gone have to murder all them little niggas then."

"Na, come on Tam you know I know how to play this…once we get all they bread they gone be broke and fucked up and then I know how to hit they young asses where they will never bounce back. It's more than one way to sit a nigga down and make sure he can't get back up. I just need you to watch them and make sure they don't have no other connect that could supply them and knock me out the box…we can't put nothing pass them…they might be planning on beating me for them bricks…just find out what's up with them because I definitely need them to move this work for me and bring all that gwop back."

"I got you…don't even worry."

CHAPTER 2

She stood above the earth's surface with her Fendi pumps on at around 5' 6", and the one piece Fendi pantsuit embraced her 36-27-45 physical form like it was tattooed on her. She was a vision for the eyes of man and her beauty impulsively aroused man's most lustful animal instincts. Her name was NyJewel and she was flaming hot like her fire red Nissan Maxima she swerved about two feet from the curb on Loepere street. And like the passionate creature she was, NyJewel crept out of her vehicle feeling the lustful eyes of men undressing her as they depressingly sat on battered porches playing cards and drowning their lungs with 40 ounces of malt liquor. She stepped onto the block crammed with its two and three story dilapidated houses squeezed tightly together along the narrow one-way street. The street had a few dozen decaying houses lining the block amongst a few houses which still displayed their architectural beauty due to routine maintenance. The few well-kept properties belonged to the Queen of Queens, NyJewel. After bouncing from tenant to tenant and collecting her rent, NyJewel sashayed towards the middle of the block where a group of men huddled between two parked cars on the street playing a dice game of Cee-Low.

"Yo I'm hearing everything," a short chocolate Pillsbury doughboy looking young man named Dolla shouted as he rattled three dice in his gold ring flooded fist, "Just drop the dough on the ground and yo bet heard…money on the wood make the bet good…come on let's go."

"Gimme a ball ($100). I want a C-note too…I got 50…I want 20…Lemme get a half of bill ($ 50). Come on and roll the dice fat boy I want 40," were the numerous bets thrown at Dolla.

"Let's get em girls," Dolla blew a breath of good fortune on the dice before he sent them scrambling across the asphalt where they banged the curb. After spinning the three dice revealed the numbers 2-2-3. "Ok that's Tracy and Tracy burning with that chlamydia…yall niggas don't wear condoms so yall fucked…and I'm hearing side bets nobody gone beat Tracy."

"I got a dub ($ 20) everybody smoke that hoe."

"You heard," Dolla responded to the side bet.

"Nigga you stupid thinking I'm gone let Tracy burn me…I wouldn't fuck her with yo dick," a gambler spit at Dolla scooping up the dice from off the ground then rolling.

NyJewel neared the dice game but kept her distance and stood across the street on the sidewalk. NyJewel was born and raised on the notorious streets of the east side, but she was too much of a lady to be caught dead at a street dice game. On the other hand, the Casino was her second home.

"Dolla." NyJewel impatiently yelled over the blasting music of a car stereo with her hand cuffed on her curvaceous hip. "I know you see me standing here Dolla."

"Hold on Miss Bossy lemme make this money real quick," Dolla responded glancing at NyJewel then returning his focus back on the dice. It was hard for most men to keep their eyes off NyJewel, but after everyone at the dice game let their eyes behold her beauty for a few seconds, they all focused back on the dice game knowing it was only a tease to lust over a woman none of them could even dream of sexing.

"Dolla you holding me up come on now."

"Come on Ny stop knocking my hustle," Dolla responded keeping his eyes on the dice.

"Negro you knocking my hustle," NyJewel stepped into the street and slowly waltzed towards the dice game.

"Come on Ny you breaking my concentration…give me a minute." Dolla blurted while crouching over the rolling dice.

"Negro I'm gone break yo hands and take that money you owe…come on Dolla."

"First off Ny," Dolla snapped while dishing out money to two gamblers who beat his point. "It's not the first of the month yet and Big Walt cover half of the rent for the spots in the hood anyway…go see Big Walt Ny." Dolla then observed the next two gamblers beat his point. He went on an emotional fall into sore losers' world. "See Ny you causing me to lose…now you see why I can't pay you yo rent money…fucccck."

"Boy please…I'm going on a cruise and I need mine."

"I get with you later Ny you fucking bad luck," Dolla brushed NyJewel off and snatched the dice from off the ground then announced, "Come on what yall want my bank still popping…da hustle don't stop…whatever yall want I'm hearing."

"See that's why you don't got mines Dolla because you a degenerate gambler…you lucky you like family to me boy." NyJewel spun from the dice game and pranced back down the block unintentionally swinging her sumptuous hips.

Then out of nowhere, the street began to vibrate with the force of a 7.0 magnitude earthquake as a Silver Chevy Blazer zoomed down the block with thunderous bass booming out of its speakers. The Blazer then came to an abrupt halt as NyJewel took her bold stance in the middle of the street. It was Zulu and Cream.

"What I tell yall about coming thru my block with this loud music?" NyJewel stood at the passenger side of the Blazer and folded her arms on the passenger door. "I'm taxing and giving out fines for this type of ruckus on the block."

"Come on Ny stop playing we gotta park we dirty as hell," Cream informed her easing his foot on the brake. This was no time for jokes and games riding with a stash of drugs that carried a mandatory prison sentence.

"Yeah we gotta hit the spot a.s.a.p before we get stretched by the boys…move yo sexy ass out the way Ny." Zulu jokingly added from the passenger seat.

"Shut up boy," NyJewel playfully tapped Zulu on the head, "Go take care of yall business because I need to see yall as soon as yall finish." NyJewel stated easing away from the truck and heading to a house on the block where she chatted with some ladies sitting on a porch.

Cream cautiously squeezed the Blazer down the narrow street lined with parked cars on both sides. With two pair of eyes, they both scanned the area from left to right for unsupervised kids darting across the street before they slowly eased up on the dice game.

"Yo Dolla dice game over," Zulu leaned halfway out the passenger window as they slowly crept by the dice game. "Come to the spot a.s.a.p yo."

"Alright lemme smash these monkeys real quick…gimme a couple minutes I be right there," Dolla responded before rolling the dice.

"Nigga you need to leave with yo mans and stop losing yo re-up money lil nigga." A gambler joked.

"Winners don't quit," Dolla shot back rolling the dice and unable to hit a point. After a few rolls and acing out, Dolla accepted the fact that today he was a sore loser and king of the degenerate gamblers. He paid everyone and then jokingly warned everyone that tomorrow he was taking everyone's money at the dice game. Dolla then bounced his chubby physique up the block to the house where Zulu and Cream was entering. "Yo yo yo," Dolla hooted catching the door with his body before Cream shut it close.

The three then entered the house thru the front door and stepped into a gloomy hallway. In front of them to the left was a staircase which led upstairs. The trio then jogged upstairs to the upper apartment with Zulu in the lead. Zulu jammed a key into the dead bolt lock on the door, twisted the key and shoved the door open. Zulu took one step inside and stopped in his tracks when he observed thru his peripheral the flash of a swift moving figure charging at him with a baseball bat.

"Romp romp," was the sound of the aluminum bat smashing the soft but callous skin on the palm of Prince's hand. "Yall dickheads know yall supposed to call or at least page a nigga before yall come to the spot...make yall selves known when yall come in the spot," Prince growled in his half sleep state while softly pounding the palm of his hand with the bat. "I could've busted yall melons wide the fuck open and it would have been a honest mistake." Prince groggily headed back to the couch, tossed the bat on the floor, then fell onto the couch with shut eyes.

"Go back to sleep Prince." Zulu shot back stepping into the apartment.

"Yo ass would have got clapped by an honest mistake," Cream snatched the chrome Glock 380 from off his waist and carefully sat it on the dining room table.

Dolla had just slammed the door. "I keep telling yo Lennox Lewis looking ass Prince…this is 2000, the new millennium and niggas is blasting chrome…not fighting and swinging baseball bats." Dolla ranted while locking the door.

"Yeah whatever… just don't interrupt my sleep or I'm gone knock one of yall niggas to sleep." Prince muttered tossing himself around on the couch and falling back to sleep.

"Yo lets divide this shit up," Zulu opened a book bag then pulled out two Ziploc bags full of bagged up cracks and tossed them on the dining room table near a box of sandwich bags.

"So Big Walt reed niggas up huh?" Dolla asked before sliding into the kitchen in search for some munchies to appease his 300lb appetite. He found some double stuffed Oreos on top of the microwave then snatched some milk from the refrigerator and slid back into the dining room and sat at the table with Zulu and Cream.

"Hell no Big Walt stingy ass didn't re niggas up." Zulu sharply replied emptying the cracks from the Ziploc bags onto the maple wood dining table. "This our profit from the last batch."

Spread out across the table was a huge pile of an assortment of colorful 12x12 and 38x38 baggies containing light peanut buttered colored rocks inside. And while Prince lay on the couch snoring, the trio began dividing the huge pile of bagged up cracks into several orderly piles. Each pile belonged to a Young Assassin and would be delivered to the blocks around the E. North street neighborhood where the drugs would be sold to the feigns for the almighty dollar.

After the trio divided the drugs and packaged them up, Zulu and Cream gave Dolla a replay of their meeting with Big Walt. Dolla, and all the other Young Assassins shared the same emotions as Zulu and Cream when it came to Big Walt.

"Yo we never gone reach our full potential with Big Walt," Dolla threw in the air while splitting a Garcia Vega blunt. "He want it all for himself…he think we supposed to be satisfied with him because we ain't got no other connect. If that double whopper head ass nigga give us those bricks, we gotta walk that nigga. Word up." Dolla boldly stated emptying the blunt tobacco in an ashtray then crumbling some lime green weed into the blunt.

Cream shot a leery look while shaking his head, "If we walk Big Walt—yo," Cream sighed deeply and peered intensely at Zulu and Dolla, "If we walk Big Walt...we gotta----body Tam--we got to."

"I knock Big Walt ass out," Prince grumbled in his sleep. "I put him in a coma." Prince finished sleep talking and went back to snoring with his large nostrils on vacuum mode sucking up the oxygen in the room.

"What the fuck?" everyone was shocked and surprised at how Prince overheard their conversation while sleeping. Prince ventured from the sleep world of the subconscious to the reality at hand and back to sleep instantly. "Yo this nigga Prince is weird is fuck. Word up yo."

"Keep yo fake boxing ass sleep while gangsters building," Dolla blasted hurling two Oreo cookies across the room at the sleeping Prince. After the cookies hit Prince in the face, Prince dapped himself in the face a few times like he felt a fly buzzing on his face.

"Anyway right," Dolla continued on the subject of Big Walt. "All we gotta do is get them bricks and find a new connect while we knocking them things off. And then we just tell Big Walt fuck him." Dolla explained while passing the lit blunt to Cream.

"I'm telling you Dolla," Cream inhaled the blunt deeply from his gut, "If we walk Big Walt we gone have to body Tam. Tam gun go off and we not just gone be able to walk these niggas with no repercussions."

"Yo fuck that pink panther looking nigga...what Tam gone do against our team...besides us...Tam the only shooter Big Walt got...what the fuck is one shooter against a whole crew of clappers...that nigga not Steven Segal."

Zulu finally cut in, "Big Walt sitting on cake so he can pay for more shooters...but on some real shit this not a decision just the three of us can make on our own...we need the whole crew here. So until we all together to make that decision let's just make this bread and get them bricks from that nigga...and no matter what, once we get them bricks he not getting paid…we just gotta decide how we gone walk his ass and what we gone do about him and Tam."

"No doubt." They all reached across the table and slapped hands. Zulu then dipped into the bedroom and stashed one of the packages. A few moments later Zulu appeared back in the dining room clutching a 38 Special and a Mossberg shotgun. Dolla and Cream were stuffing their packages in their boxer briefs.

"Yo Prince wake up," Zulu slid into the living room pumping the gauge on the shotgun before nudging Prince awake. "Yo get up and lock the doors we out."

"Come on yo yall niggas got keys…yall let yall selves in so let yall selves out," Prince hollered rubbing his blurry eyes and sluggishly lifting his tired body up. "I'm tryna sleep what the fuck yo."

"Nigga why you sleeping so much? You got one of these freaks pregnant?"

"No nigga." Prince barked seated on the sofa allowing his mind to fully awake before he stood on his feet. "I hugged the block all night and today…I just went to sleep before yall came." Prince began to feel alive and awakened. He snatched the shotgun from Zulu then followed the trio into the hallway then downstairs. "Zulu it's yo turn to play the block. I'm too tired."

"Yo I'm gone be out here for a minute but I gotta get up with Destiny…just hold it down for the late night flow and I play the block all day tomorrow bro." Zulu stated stepping downstairs into the hallway and then easing backwards out the door with his eyes on Prince.

"Fuck you Zulu I'm going back to sleep," Prince shot back before saluting Cream and Dolla who flew out the house, jumped in Cream's Blazer and peeled off in a hurry.

"Damn Prince it's like that," Zulu asked standing in the doorway with his back to the street. "I gotta get up with Destiny and swing downtown yo…I aint been home in a few days and Destiny bugging…just hold it down for the night you know we can't miss no money."

"Fuck you and that money Zulu, my rest more important right now,"

Prince massaged the bags drooping under his pear shaped eyes. "Go downtown and play house with Destiny…its money over bitches' nigga…I did what I had to do now you need to get on yo grind…I deserve to relax and that's exactly what I'm gone do…I'm gone rest up so I have my energy to do it again." Prince stated peeping pass Zulu onto the street before snickering, "Watch yo back Zulu." Prince pushed Zulu outside then slammed the door in his face.

While sensing someone creeping on him from behind, Zulu spun around but it was too late. A pair of soft hands gripped his neck and shoved him into the door Prince just closed in his face.

"Where my money Zulu," NyJewel yanked one of her hands off Zulu's neck then began tapping his pockets bulging with money. "So you holding huh?"

"You know it sexy…I'm holding like a tyrannosaurus rex," Zulu squeezed her tightly against his body and grinded on her mid-section. He felt his testosterone pulsating thru his libido causing an instant erection. "Yeah you know I'm holding what can give you more pleasure and satisfaction than money," Zulu boasted with his arms wrapped around NyJewel's waistline.

"Ugh…get off me you pervert," NyJewel slipped out of Zulu's hold and grilled him with contempt in her eyes. "Yall men so nasty and disrespectful…I can't even play and joke with you like I used to without you thinking like a nasty dog."

"Come on stop it…I'm not a kid no more Ny…you can't be all up on a grown man and expect him not to get aroused…you bugging."

"Cut it out freak I was just playing with you not tryna get you aroused," the fresh scent of winter fresh gum blew off NyJewel's breath as she eased down the steps on the porch.

"Yeah whatever," Zulu slid down the steps behind NyJewel then posted up on her Maxima while NyJewel sat in a chair by the steps. "You just scared of what people gone say about us."

"Scared." NyJewel rolled her eyes at Zulu then snatched a Newport from the pack stashed in her top pocket. "Boy I'm a grown woman and do as I please and I could care less about what anybody has to say about me and what I do," NyJewel then flamed her cigarette and inhaled with a feminine gesture.

"But I tell you what I don't do and that's you and all the gangsters that came before you. Even the gangsters that will come after you…I don't do you thugs in the streets. I don't do you doggish men period."

"Ah…I knew it," Zulu got excited, "You like the cat huh. You don't like that beef. I knew you liked that twat because you haven't been with a man in how long?"

"Oh my God." NyJewel's mouth opened wide in disbelief. She couldn't believe Zulu with his mannish and disrespectful ways. Letting the light of the Truth shine, he was only a being a man, a young man at that who was innocently attracted to her sex appeal like all the other men who ever laid eyes on her. Zulu was no longer the young boy she once looked at like a little brother.

"I can't believe how you turned out Zulu. You used to be a sweet little boy who loved me like a big sister."

Zulu frowned while scanning up and down the block at the passing cars. 'I can't believe you Ny. You need to stop playing with me. I'm not a little kid no more I'm a grown ass man and I only play with women I get sexual with. You too sexy to be playing with a grown man, and think he not gone get aroused. Plus we not blood Ny."

"Wow." NyJewel tooted her face up at Zulu, "You lost yo damn mind you fool and the respect I had for you…you becoming just like these assholes out here who think money and street fame can get them any and every woman on earth."

"You bugging."

"Oh I'm bugging." NyJewel leaped out of her seat and stormed up into Zulu's face. "Ok grown ass man. No more treating you like the little brother I never had. That relationship is over. It's strictly business now and I'm gone treat you just like the grown ass man that you are. So don't come crying to me for advice when it comes to yo little girlfriends, and I want my rent when it's due." NyJewel roasted Zulu then began to storm to the driver door of her car.

"No no no ok Ny," Zulu skated right behind her. "Come on I'm sorry Ny. I got a little carried away…but you know I love and respect you to the fullest…you like a sister to me…you was always there for me." Zulu embraced

NyJewel with an honest brotherly hug.

"And you know I love you too Zulu. All that babysitting I did for your moms back in the day I probably only got paid once or twice. You was a mannish little thing back then," NyJewel and Zulu both shared a memorable laugh.

"You know I aint mean that," Zulu stood beside NyJewel on the driver side of her car. "You just too sexy Ny and it's hard for a man to resist you unless he gay."

"It's called control boy. Keep yo thoughts and body to yo self like I had to tell you when you was younger," NyJewel shook her head while smiling.

"Ok sis I got you." Zulu took both her hands and softly held them.

"Now where my money Zulu? I need rent early because I'm going on a cruise," NyJewel demanded with that I mean business look in her eye. Zulu hit his pockets and retrieved his bread. He counted out $350.00 and handed it to NyJewel.

"This my half Big Walt gone pay you the rest."

"Awww come on Zulu." NyJewel whined flicking the bills in her hand. "All that money you got you can pay me in full and get it back from Big Walt."

"Nyyyyy...you don't understand...this nigga Big Walt on some shit and strait raping us...it's like the money we make just disappear...we be knocking bricks off for that nigga...we caking thousands for that dude and we don't make shit...that nigga tight as wolf pussy...word."

"Listen Zulu," NyJewel reached into her car and placed the money in her Fendi pocket book, "Big Walt was always selfish...yall was all too young to understand and know what was really going on...but when the feds snatched the A-Squad, I had to chase Big Walt all around town just to get lawyer money from him for the Squad...then he had me tell the Squad that he needed their connect in order to keep things going and to help pay for their lawyers...he did just enough so the Squad wouldn't get mad at him...but after all the Squad did for him they basically had to sell their connect to Big Walt in order for Big Walt to help them out...they were the ones who showed Big Walt the game and they even protected him."

"Grimy ass nigga."

"You find out people true colors when they got the upper hand and you need them Zulu…but God don't like ugly…and how he turned his back on the Squad wasn't right…yall was too young and wasn't ready for that level of the game, if only yall was a little older yall would have been the ones running everything but it is what it is…and now that yall up and coming Zulu I want you to be careful out here." NyJewel set her gaze upon Zulu steadily without blinking before she became teary eyed. "Please be careful out here Zulu…besides the squad you like the only family I got out here…I don't wanna see you and none of yo friends end up like the squad…the squad was the only family I ever had."

Memories flashed across NyJewel's mind of her childhood with the A-Squad. Her heart was massaged with joy and pain. Back in the day NyJewel was the sister of the A-Squad. She was one of the most gorgeous but roughest girls raised in the E. North street part of town, and all the thugs in the A-Squad viewed her as a sister, not a piece of flesh for sexual gratification. She was highly respected and earned it from day one with the A-Squad. From the sandbox days they played together, grew up together and as adults they lived a lavish and luxurious life together. NyJewel's monopoly on the real estate market in town was mostly due to the A-Squad financing her ventures when she graduated from college. The rest is history.

"I love you Zulu," NyJewel fell into Zulu's arms as he leaned against her car. And like a heartbroken woman she cried on his shoulders as they embraced under the streetlight. "I don't wanna see you and your friends get caught up in anything with Big Walt…please Zulu promise me."

"Don't worry Ny," Zulu softly cuffed the back of her bobbed hair du as she buried her face in his chest.

"We gone be good but that nigga Big---," Zulu was cut short by the screeching tires of a car zooming towards him and NyJewel as they stood in the street by NyJewel's car. Zulu swung NyJewel behind him and eased between her car and the one parked in front of her car. He then gripped the steel hugging his torso as the flashing high beams blinded him.

Destiny jerked the gear in park before the car even stopped and she jumped out the car in a rage. She snatched her ear rings off while storming over to Zulu who shielded NyJewel behind him. "So this why I haven't seen you in two days Zulu." Destiny flared rushing over to Zulu tryna discover who was the big booty slut she seen him hugging from way down the block. Destiny wanted to put a beating on the freak Zulu was shielding behind his back. "I'm tired of you disrespecting me out in these streets fucking with these bitches Zulu."

"First off Destiny," NyJewel stepped from behind Zulu and began approaching Destiny. "I aint no bitch little girl and you know I don't want Zulu...you need to stop being insecure...real women not insecure because they keep they men satisfied...I don't want yo man sweetie."

"Oh my fucking God yall bugging," Zulu grabbed his head in frustration.

"Well I aint know it was you NyJewel," Destiny calmed down only enough to acknowledge her insecurity. And just like that, she flared up again replaying the scene over on her mental screen. "But bitch you can kick rocks with all that yin yang shit you popping...I aint no little girl...I will whip yo old ass bitch...you all up on my man talking shit."

"No no no please chill," Zulu jumped in between them with his arms extended like a referee in a boxing match, "It's a misunderstanding Destiny it's not what you thinking chill out."

"Zulu you better control yo girlfriend," NyJewel stated with no worries calmly stepping back and sliding out of her pumps. She then unsnapped her bamboo earrings and slid them around her fingers like they were brass knuckles. "You better control her Zulu because you not gone be able to look at her once I'm finished with that pretty little face of hers."

"Bitch come on," Destiny screamed dipping around Zulu and lunging at NyJewel.

"Yo *stopppp*," Zulu snatched Destiny and rushed her to the other side of the street. Zulu peeped the swarms of people coming to spectate the action then told Destiny, "Yo chill the fuck out you making the block hot and I got my banger on me...you gone make the fucking cops come."

"I'm not making shit hot it's that old bitch who hot in the ass all up on my man…get yo own man bitch."

"I don't need a man little girl. Zulu you supposed to have her under control because this is bad for yall business."

"NyJewel you couldn't have said it any better," Prince was hanging halfway out the second floor window of the house. "Zulu you supposed to be handling business out here…what the fuck up yo…you interrupting my sleep with all this drama." Prince shouted pulling himself back into the house.

"Fuck all yall muthafuckas," Destiny skated to her car which was blocking the street and holding up traffic. Before she jumped in her car she grilled NyJewel and shouted, "I'm gone see you bitch."

"Lil girl you know where I be and if anything happens to any of my properties I got insurance so that's gone be money in my pockets…and money on yo head…now try me."

About 20 minutes later

While screaming at the top of her lungs and cursing Zulu out, Destiny stomped on the gas pedal like she wanted to do NyJewel's face. Destiny pushed her Dodge Neon to the max across the skyway overpass heading towards downtown. With her left hand she recklessly gripped the wheel while her right hand swung violently at Zulu. Zulu found himself bopping and weaving under the passenger seatbelt trying to avoid her blows. He came to realize he was a suicidal fool for jumping in the car with a raging Destiny. After several minutes Destiny then ceased beating on Zulu as the expressway curved itself around a cluster of skyscrapers peering down at the moving vehicles. Destiny now whipped the wheel with both hands while planting her foot on the brakes, vehemently swerving the car around the bend before she sped down the exit ramp.

Destiny zoomed down the exit ramp and made a reckless left turn through a light switching from yellow to red. Flocks of rowdy fans pouring out of the Coca-Cola Baseball Stadium had to dash across the street as she turned the corner in a rage.

She then blew it pass the Buffalo Sabres hockey arena and turned onto a strip stacked with bars and food vendors grilling hot dogs and burgers on the street. After driving several blocks, she turned onto Marina Drive where there were a group of high rise buildings facing the Erie Marina Basin. She pulled onto the service road and banged her tire on the curb parking in front of her and Zulu's building.

"*Ewww*," with both hands Destiny aggressively pounced on Zulu who curled up in his seat. "I'm tired of yo lying, cheating ass. You was hugging her like she was me."

"No stop you don't understand." Zulu released his seatbelt, sprung forward, grabbed Destiny's swinging arms and climbed on top of her. He softly pressed his lips on the tear streaks drizzling down her face. "I love you Destiny, I wouldn't dare cheat on you."

"Get off of me I seen yall," Destiny snatched her face away from Zulu while struggling to push him up off her.

"I swear it's not what you thinking...you know me and Ny like family...she like a big sister to all of us."

"She not yo blood and I don't care how close she is...I hate you...just leave me alone."

"Destiny believe me she was just ventilating about some serious issues...that's all it was."

"Fuck you and her...she was ventilating her face in yo chest like you was her man...I seen yall...just get out my car."

Zulu pleaded and begged Destiny to believe him but his pleas went on deaf ears. He climbed from on top of her and opened the car door.

"Well fuck it then...you don't wanna believe me that's yo problem...you know NyJewel aint been with no man long as any of us can remember...and you know me and her aint got nothing going on...she don't want me...she was just crying on my shoulder."

"How you know she don't want you unless you already tried her with yo dirt bag ass...get away from me," Destiny screamed pushing Zulu out the car.

"Well fuck you too." Zulu slammed the car door shut and began pacing along the service road towards the benches at the marina. He stopped under a streetlight and pulled a thin pack of crisp bamboo papers from his back pants pockets. His eyes then explored the dimly lit surroundings as he knelt down and snatched a small bag containing Hawaiian skunk weed from his sock. There wasn't a soul around beside the mosquitos buzzing under the lights of the high rise buildings and the tall street lights. Besides the roar of vehicles whisking by on the overpass freeway, the atmosphere was serene as the calm waters of Lake Erie were slowly swishing into the basin where two colossal warships floated nearby at the pier. Zulu crumbled the sticky bud into tiny pieces on the paper and then like a pro, he twisted the paper and rolled it into a fat cigarette. He then dug in his pockets searching for a lighter but he came up empty. He headed back down the drive to where Destiny still sat in the car.

"Open the damn door Destiny." Zulu shouted breaking the night silence yanking on the car door.

Destiny sat in the car with her face buried in her hands against the steering wheel. She was in her own world of emotional heart ache and oblivious to Zulu's presence outside the car. Destiny loved Zulu and Zulu loved Destiny. The joy is what kept them together but there was so much pain in the history of their relationship, the thin line between love and hate was often crossed. It was always Zulu cheating on Destiny, and then Destiny kicking Zulu to the curb and searching for a shoulder to cry on, only to find out that most young and older men were sexually weak creatures who allowed their lusts to overpower their love.

Destiny's beauty alone was heavenly and would make any man desire her and her only, regardless to how many beautiful and sexy women there were. Destiny's beauty was molded by three exotic gene pools. Her father was black and Indian, and her mother was full blooded Vietnamese. Her skeletal frame was clothed with a reddish yellow skin tone like peaches. She had wavy jet-black hair with beautiful chinky black eyes. She was paradise in the physical form. And her self-esteem was higher than the 12-story building her and Zulu lived in. And no matter how much of a dog Zulu was, she couldn't love no other man like she loved Zulu. Just like her mother loved her doggish daddy.

"Earth to Destiny." Zulu stood at the driver window which was cracked open. "Come on love…let's get our mind right with this nice spliff of Hawaiian skunk." There was still no response from Destiny. Zulu knew exactly what to do. He slid the spliff between his ear, busted a Puff Daddy move and spun around singing *112's hit song "Only You."*

Destiny heard Zulu trying to harmonize the vocals but he was a mess. "Boy…you know you can't sing…stop it." Destiny lifted her face from her hands and smiled at Zulu's comical performance.

"I can do anything for you love."

"I wish you can stop cheating on me."

"I love you Destiny."

"I'm still mad at you Zulu," Destiny unlocked the door before dabbing her wet face with some Kleenex she snatched from the arm console.

"I know I done things in the past that make you not trust me," Zulu opened the car door for Destiny and gave her his hand, gently leading her up out the car before embracing her and softly caressing her face. "But it's not what you thinking…me and the crew got a serious situation going on in the hood and Ny just got a little sad because she don't wanna see us go down like the Squad."

"What's the situation baby?" Destiny cuddled her head on Zulu's chest.

"You know I don't like putting you in my business." Zulu then reached into the car and snatched the lighter from out the cup holder. Zulu then clutched Destiny by her waist and they strolled over to the benches on the marina.

"You don't want me in yo business but you got NyJewel all up in it."

"Naaaa," Zulu leaned back on a railing with his back facing the cool breeze blowing across the waters from the Canada side of the Marina. "You know the role NyJewel play in this…she just be giving advice because she been around for a long time…that's all it is…she seen a lot out here in these streets and just be looking out for us."

"I bet she did see a lot…did she see this?" Destiny seductively whispered in Zulu's ear while massaging his throbbing penis bulging in his jeans.

"Noooo. Come on love you have to trust me…what good is we without trust…I'm only concerned with making a bankroll for me and you…cheating not on my agenda."

Destiny pecked her thin lips on Zulu's lips. "I trust you...you just better not give this to no bitch." Destiny passionately gripped Zulu by the balls and squeezed tightly.

"Ahhhhh." Zulu quietly groaned. "You know I'm not. I'm all yours."

"You promise."

"With all my heart." Zulu blew palming Destiny's soft and tender apple bottom booty under her tennis skirt.

"You think you deserve this." Destiny grinded against Zulu while letting her moist and pierced tongue slide around Zulu's ear lobe.

"Hell yeah." Zulu moaned noticing a light flicker off above the tenth floor of their building.

"Then let's go upstairs my king."

CHAPTER 3

Criminal Defense Attorney Antonio Leonetti leaned back in his deluxe red leather office chair examining the neatly stacked files spread across his large office desk. His eyes focused on one file. It was a manila envelope and it was thick in size and read *Federal Courthouse for the Western District of New York*. Leonetti lifted his eyes from the file then reminiscently peered across the room at the poster sized picture hanging on the wall above the office printer. It was a picture of him and his family cuddled together under a blue sky on a luscious green hill in Sicily. Those were the good old days Leonetti thought to himself. The days when he made lots of money representing some of the richest criminals in the city of Buffalo, vacationed with his family overseas, and enjoyed wild nights on his yacht with promiscuous women.

"So long for chasing old dreams old Man. Live in the future but remember the past." Leonetti mumbled to himself while opening the thick manila envelope on his desk. Thru the medicine filled lens of his Armani spectacles he read the cover letter from the head *United States Attorney for the Western District of New York.* "You gotta be fucking kidding me." Leonetti felt his heart rate increase. His throat became dry and his palms became moist and sweaty as he slid the cover letter behind the thick file he held. He couldn't believe what he was reading let alone holding in his sweaty hands: *United States of America v. Sean Livingston, David Pruitt, et al INDICTMENT # 99-345878-055.*

This was unbelievable he thought to himself leaning back in his chair reading the superseding indictment. The indictment was throwing numerous charges of conspiracy at Sean Livingston b.k.a. Sun-Z, and David Pruitt b.k.a. Hawk, who were known members of the A-Squad. They were being charged with *conspiracy to possess and distribute 5 or more kilograms of cocaine, conspiracy to commit the murder and the attempted murder of two confidential informants, conspiracy to intimidate a government witness, conspiracy to traffic narcotics across interstate lines and continuing a criminal enterprise.*

"Kiss my Sicilian ass." Leonetti angrily tossed the indictment onto his desk. Leonetti sprung from his chair and began pacing the plush Burberry carpeted floor in his office. In deep thought, he strolled along the bookcase lining the wall. Blindly, his eyes scrambled across New York Supplement and Federal Digest Case Law books but his mind's eye was focused elsewhere.

"A confidential informant...unsolved crimes of the past." Leonetti stopped in his tracks thinking deeply as he journeyed back almost 10 years ago. Sun-Z and Hawk were two of the founding members of the A-Squad, and when the A-Squad began moving large quantities of drugs throughout the E. North Street neighborhood and the rest of the city, Sun-Z and Hawk hit the highway and took their show on the road. From Jamestown New York to Erie Pennsylvania Sun-Z and Hawk was infamous for seizing small towns and hypnotizing the white residents with the white crack demon. They introduced crack cocaine to numerous small towns where the only addiction problem was a drink at the local honky tonk bars. While the feds had the A-Squad under investigation back in Buffalo, Sun-Z and Hawk was busy on the road so they escaped the Federal Government's investigation which took down rest of the A-Squad. It wasn't long before the snitches began telling and narcotics detectives from numerous drug tasks forces in New York snatched Sun-Z and Hawk for flooding the small towns with crack. So while the A-Squad was locked up and fighting a battle with the feds, Sun-Z and Hawk was locked up in a county jail fighting drug charges in the state. The feds wanted to pull Sun-Z and Hawk right into federal court with the rest of the Squad, but they figured they would let the two slide since they had everyone else from the A-Squad. Leonetti with his thorough knowledge of Jurisprudence knew the feds was going to bang the A-Squad with astronomical football numbers. The human race would become extinct before the A-Squad was released from Federal Prison. So Leonetti with his skill of Legal Persuasion made a deal with the U.S. Attorney, that if the members of the A-Squad who were currently charged and in federal custody plead guilty to the federal charges, the federal government would at no time in the future go after and charge other members of the A-Squad like Sun-Z and

Hawk who were not a part of the A-Squad's federal indictment. Nor could the federal government go after and charge known associates of the A-Squad like Big Walt, or NyJewel who was believed to launder money for the A-Squad.

So even though the A-Squad would plead guilty to life sentences, Big Walt was still free and would keep business flowing. The feds didn't seize none of the properties and accounts NyJewel had in her name. And Sun-Z and Hawk would be released from state prison in 10 years. The A-Squad would be in a cage for eternity but they would have the support they needed on the outside to make their time comfortable on the inside.

Leonetti breathed deeply while thinking of the matter at hand, before stepping away from the bookcase and sliding over to the large window of his office, capturing the view of the 60 story H.S.B.C building hovering above several smaller skyscrapers downtown. He thought about most of the professional figures of society who sat in their plush offices up in the sky along the downtown skyline. It wasn't only the power structure of the city which vexed him, but the bureaucracy of the whole country was out of tune with checks and balances. Leonetti felt betrayed by the US Attorney who made an honorable deal on the A-Squad case. Leonetti then wondered where was the dignity and honor the torch holders of society made oaths to keep and honor when they signed up to work for society and the country. It seemed the power structure didn't honor their own commitments.

Leonetti then ventured from his thoughts and scrambled through the rolodex on his desk searching for NyJewel's phone number. "Come on NyJewel where's your number," Leonetti asked himself before finding her number. *"Bingo."* Leonetti dialed her number and it shot straight to voicemail.

"Hello world...I hope your call is the one I been waiting to hear, I'm so sorry I'm unavailable and unable to take your call, if your call is the one please leave your name and number and I will be pleasured to return your call...goodbye world."

NyJewel wouldn't be returning any calls for the next few days because she was pampering herself on a stress free vacation in the Caribbean. Leonetti then scrambled for Big Walt's phone number only to learn that his number was out of service.

There was only one last solution to this problem for Leonetti and that was to journey deep into Buffalo's drug infested east side and search the notorious E. North street section for Big Walt and the Young Assassins.

....

"Hey hey what's up Buffalo it's ya girl Pleasure Sounds."

"And you already know it's ya favorite D.J. Mic Rocka."

"And we gone rock the city live today from E. North Avenue...it's Summer Bash on the Ave...come on down and bring the whole family...it's bbq everything and plenty of food...it's plenty of gifts for the kids...school supplies, games, and bounce houses...it's everything here come on down and enjoy...come have fun...it's WBLK 93.7 jamming live from E. North avenue."

Big Walt may have played the Grinch who stole Christmas most of the time, but since the A-Squad been missing in action, Big Walt carried on the A-Squad's Summer Bash on the Ave tradition and the local Hip-Hop & R&B radio station WBLK always came out showing support and live broadcasting the event.

Flaming grills, picnic tables, bounce houses, entertainment games, and booths offering artistic face painting, portraits, and air brushing crammed three blocks of the Avenue which was blocked off. Numerous businesses on the avenue supported the event, but the two businesses which sponsored the event was NyJewel's Creative Expressions Hair and Nail Salon and Big Walt's New Millennium Entertainment.

Creative Expressions was situated on the avenue in the midst of the festivities. And every year NyJewel had her employees give out free hair products and do nail designs for the young girls. Directly across from Creative Expressions sat Big Walt's New Millennium entertainment. Big Walt made sure the young boys weren't forgotten. He made sure they were given books, DVD's and other items. All businesses kept their doors open to the people during this neighborhood gala, but at the present Summer Bash event, the doors to New Millennium were locked while Big Walt and the Young Assassins sat behind the tinted windows of the store.

New Millennium was decked with bookcases flaunting the newest urban literature and magazines. Display cases housed the latest movies and shelves along the walls displayed the latest hip-hop, r&b, and gospel music CD's. At the rear of the store where a thick glass display case advertised urban crime movies and documentaries, a small computer monitor, cash register and numerous party flyers sat on top of the display case. Also on top of the display case sat America's favorite appetizer; 3 kilos of cocaine.

The money machine sitting on the display case rattled as Big Walt tossed fifty bills in it at a time. The Young Assassins were seated on the large leather money green circular sofa in the back corner, counting and stacking dividends in orderly stacks of a thousand dollars each on a long rectangular coffee table.

"Yo you act like we can't fucking count," Dolla tossed a stack of money onto the display case near Big Walt. "I know niggas dropped out of school and all that…but we can do simple math yo."

"Word up," Prince nervously scuffed the floor pacing in circles swinging a motorcycle helmet. "Big Walt we counted the money before we came here, and now you got us counting it again and then you triple counting it with that annoying ass money machine…this shit a waste of time…the money correct." Prince swung the helmet halfway over his impressively designed French braids.

"Quiet as it's kept," Tam sat at a display case shoving down his throat chili dogs drenched in spicy chili sauce with ketchup, mustard, and onions. "I'm finally happy yall lil niggas copping a whole key with yall own money. It's about time yall on a come up."

"At least we copping a brick nigga," Dolla shot back. "What the fuck is you copping? Oh I forgot…yo broke non hustling ass live off of Big Walt."

"Shut yo fat ass up."

"Yo yall two stop it," Big Walt cut in snatching bills out of the money machine then wrapping rubber bands around them.

"Pssst." Tam hissed while thinking to himself, *"You got a whole crew of these niggas putting all they money together just to cop one fucking brick. Wow. They really big time. Get the fuck outta here."*

The Young Assassins then finished counting the money they knew was correct from the jump. "This $ 22,000." Cream stated while standing up, stretching his arms and wringing out the numbness of his fingers from counting the money.

"And this $ 1, 200 for Summer Bash," Zulu tossed Big Walt their contribution for the event. The Young Assassins then slid over to Big Walt who sat next to the three kilos on the display case. The scene looked like Santa Clause and the elves on Christmas.

"Now yall paying for one kilo," Big Walt placed a kilo in a Helly Hansen bag. "Now being that I'm fronting yall these two, I need $ 25,000 for each brick."

"Damn yo you always grilling us…you taxing the hell out of us."

"Beggars can't be choosy," Tam rambled swiping his sauce covered face with a paper towel. "Yall niggas need to be thankful we fronting yall two bricks."

"Fuck you, you aint fronting nobody shit."

"Listen fellas," Big Walt waved his hand intervening, "I gotta make a profit…if I sold these keys myself I can make way more than a $ 3,000 profit per key…but I'm doing this for yall so we can hurry up and holla at my other plug who got bricks for the $ 17,500." Big Walt deceitfully winked his eye.

"Yall made almost $ 25,000 off of ten ounces…so imagine what yall about to make with these bricks yall got…just do the math…y'all do numbers on these blocks hitting the feigns…and all yall gotta do is make that bankroll and bring everything back so we can cop with my other plug…the way yall do numbers…I guarantee yall we gone be millionaires after the two re-ups…trust me yall…I came thru for yall this time so yall can step up…trust me I got yall." Big Walt dropped his seductive game.

"Yo just let me get the fuck up outta here," Prince nervously stuffed the rest of the bricks in the Helly Hansen mountain gear style book bag. "We should've took care of this shit earlier…it's too many people out there…it's cops everywhere this shit is ridiculous…got me riding with three bricks and it's hot as fuck out there."

"Breathe easy Prince." The Young Assassins walked Prince to the door while assuring him, "This the best time to move because it's mad shit going on out there so they not focusing on you."

"That shit sound good." Prince yanked the helmet down over his face then slid his chiseled arms through the book bag straps and threw the book bag on his back while trekking out the door, "Yall niggas just hurry up and get to the spot."

"We got you bro…be safe and we see you in a minute."

Big Walt was still stationed behind the display case placing the money in a bag when the Young Assassins bounced out the store.

Tam then stated, "You had to front them those bricks."

Big Walt then mischievously glared at Tam while nodding his head with a sly smile on his face. "I'm always two steps ahead…better believe that."

....

With three bricks in the book bag strapped on his chiseled back, Prince stepped outside of New Millennium with a keen eye focusing on the scene as he skipped to his GSX-R-750 Motorcycle. With the alertness of one doing wrong, he looked around the environment letting his five senses take in the mixed cacophony of loud music, boisterous chattering, hyperactive children scrambling around, and the roasted smell of sweet barbeque saturating the hot air.

Prince jumped on his GSX-R-750 and swiftly hit the ignition. He kicked the clutch in neutral gear and gripped the throttle, awaking the monstrous engine. The thunderous growl of the bike sent swarms of people clearing a path for him as he used his feet to propel the bike through the crowd. Scantily clad females felt their insides throbbing at the sight of Prince's muscular frame hugged tightly by his clean white tank top. The ladies in their intoxication could taste the sweetness of his glossy skin tone the color of sweet potatoes.

Prince neared the wooded planks marked *"DO NOT ENTER,"* where two middle aged African-American Police Officers stood burying their faces in the soul food stuffed on their Styrofoam plates. If only the officers could see the fear in Prince's eyes which hid behind the tinted visor on his helmet, the officers would have dropped their plates and snatched Prince off his bike and found in the book bag what would give the officers a decorated promotion. Instead, the food was too good and the dancing women had the officer's attention kidnapped.

Prince slid pass the police and away from the barricade and told himself with relief, *"Let's make moves and bounce up outta this bitch."* Prince then clutched the bike into gear and used his 18-inch python sized arms to lift his bike three feet into the air and sped off doing a wheelie down the avenue and away from Summer Bash. In a flash of seconds, Prince zoomed several blocks down the avenue before whipping down a side street and checking his rear-view mirror.

"Who the fuck is this?" Prince spotted a burgundy Expedition truck with tinted windows spin the corner behind him. Prince switched gears and like a rocket the bike blasted down the block at lightning speed. The Expedition truck accelerated and went after Prince but Prince had a lead on the truck halfway up the block. Prince gripped his brakes and slowed down as he bent a corner, leaning his bike inches from the ground before maneuvering the bike upward. He glanced back at the corner behind him before turning onto the next street over and spotted the truck ready to turn the corner behind him.

"What the fuck," Prince thought to himself, *"Ok I got something for you muthafuckas."* Prince zoomed down the residential street crammed with brick homes dressed in reddish brown bricks. He glanced back noticing the truck hadn't turned onto the street yet so he slowed down and dipped between two parked cars and rode onto the sidewalk. He glanced back down the block and still didn't see the truck turn the corner.

"Yo I be bugging the fuck out…I need to chill I'm too paranoid." Prince told himself vrooming the bike up into a vacant lot between two buildings. He cautiously sped across the dirt filled lot cluttered with old furniture and car parts before pulling into an alleyway. Prince then dipped behind a building once tucked in the alleyway and covertly peeped out onto the street to see if the truck was coming down the block. While waiting he snatched his cell phone from the bike compartment and dialed the Young Assassins.

"Yo what's the deal where you at?" Cream answered in excitement.

"Yo why I thought I was being followed by some niggas in a

truck…niggas aint following me I was just----oh shit," Prince felt like his tongue was swallowed by his throat when he peeped the burgundy Expedition stop in front of the vacant lot. Prince quickly spit into the phone, "Yo niggas in a burgundy Expedition following me…meet me at the laundry mat on Main street, yall know what to do…I think Big Walt got niggas tryna rob me for them things hurry up yall know what to do it's the burgundy Expedition."

"We on it."

Prince slammed his flip phone shut, hit the gears on his bike and blew it down the glass filled alleyway before sliding out onto E. Ferry Street where the traffic was light. He peeped the Expedition spin onto the avenue two blocks behind him. Prince had no time to obey traffic laws so he blew it thru two red lights. When he approached a green light he swung around a car stopped at the light making a left turn. He swerved his bike to the right and made the mistake of leaning while braking. The bike skidded several feet along the street before hitting a pothole, hurling Prince several feet in the air.

"Fucccck." Prince tumbled across the rugged and scorching asphalt before he sprung to his feet. His adrenaline flooded his bloodstream so his senses didn't feel the stinging sensations of the brush burns plastered on his bare arms. He gripped the book bag straps on his shoulders feeling blessed the bricks were still on his back while he aimed his dizzy vision at his bike which lay two cars ahead idling in the middle of the street. Prince dashed to his bike and felt his heart flutter faster than the wings of a scared chicken when he heard the sound of sirens. He snatched his banged up bike from off the ground and then became frightened at what he seen next. It was police lights flashing in the headlights and on the dashboard of the burgundy Expedition.

"The fucking cops." Prince blurted feeling ripples of fear race through his system. In the middle of the street he stood motionless and frozen in time while holding his bike. His mind was absorbed by what just happened and what could transpire in the next few minutes. He was so absorbed in his own mental galaxy he was unaware of the people racing out of the Chinese restaurant, dry cleaners, and corner store to see if he was okay. Thoughts weighing heavy as the earth itself flashed in his brain forcing him to realize that he had to make a

decision at the present moment that would determine his future and the future of the Young Assassins.

"Yo fam you good?" A man guzzling a 40oz of Old English snapped Prince back into the present moment.

"Hell yeah I'm good," Prince yelled from under his bike helmet. Prince tapped his helmet feeling blessed for the helmet staying on and preventing injuries to his head. In that split second Prince felt his energy stimulate his flight response to make moves as the police in the Expedition got closer.

"Young man stay and talk to the police baby," an elderly lady stepping out of the cleaners shouted as Prince steadied himself on his bike. "You need some medical attention look at yo arms child," the lady and everyone else observed the scrapes and brush-burns on Prince's arms.

"*Fuck that I'm not going to jail.*" Prince quietly shouted cranking up the bike and throwing it in the air while glancing back at the lights flashing on the burgundy Expedition. *"I can't believe this shit…the fucking cops yo…they can't be cops…hell na."*

Prince scurried off thinking how he unknowingly put a hit out on police in an unmarked vehicle. He had to call it off or stop it. His first option was to call it off. His foot smashed the clutch into gear while twisting the throttle and revving the engine. He upshifted the bike as it spurted forward and blew it down the strip leaving the unmarked police truck several blocks behind. He then felt his pockets for his phone and then like a revelation it hit him—his phone was in his hand when he fell off the bike.

"Fucccck." Prince yelled over the thunderous motorcycle engine as he neared an intersection. The intersection was too congested so he dipped through a gas station parking lot and headed to the destination on Main Street. *"I can't let that shit happen…hell no."*

If Prince could make it to Main Street on time he could give the bricks to the Young Assassins and let them know it was undercover cops who were in the truck. He would make sure the Young Assassins got away and then he would surrender to the cops and take the criminal obstruction of justice and fleeing police charges with comfort. He jumped the gun too quick thinking Big Walt was setting him up. That wasn't a worry because that situation would be dealt with the G-Style way. But this situation had to be rectified a.s.a.p.

Prince's first choice of calling it off was impossible since he lost his phone. And his second and only choice left would have to suffice. He even thought of not going to Main Street and leading the cops elsewhere but how would he get rid of the bricks. Even if he was able to lead the cops elsewhere and get rid of the bricks, the Young Assassins would shoot up every burgundy Expedition truck they seen. He had to get to Main Street a.s.a.p and do the only thing possible to prevent an ambush on police.

When Prince flew onto Main Street there were swarms of summer school students and white-collar workers rushing to the train stations on the strip. It was mid-day and people were moving in and out of the diners and stores sitting underneath the old tenement buildings with their chipped bricks being strangled by trails of vines on their exterior surface.

Prince slowly rode up onto the sidewalk whipping his bike around the people who dodged out of his way. He looked back down the busy street and spotted the burgundy Expedition several blocks down racing with its lights on making traffic pull over. Not sure if the cops observed him in the midst of the people crowding the sidewalk, Prince dipped into an alleyway right off the street. The alleyway was narrow and sandwiched by two buildings which led to a back parking lot saturated with the odor of dumpsters against the back wall.

Prince cruised slowly thru the parking lot packed with a few cars and food delivery trucks before he came out onto a side street. He peered down the side street looking onto Main Street peeping for the Expedition. The coast was clear so he zoomed across the side street into the next parking lot. That's where he spotted Cream and Dolla sitting inside Dolla's Cadillac STS beside a Rent-A-Center truck. Prince zoomed over to the car and jumped off his bike speaking fast like an auctioneer.

"Yo yo yall aint gone believe man the red truck man yo yall can't—." Prince had to slow himself down to catch his breath as he slipped the book bag off and began retrieving the bricks. "Listen… listen oh my fucking god yo—yall just take—just take—the bricks—just take the bricks and leave I'm gone—whoa whoa—."

"Yo slow the fuck down we can't even understand you," Dolla grabbed the bricks and handed them to Cream who threw them in a bag then jumped out the car and stashed them in the trunk.

"Yo Prince what the fuck happened to yo arms yo?" Cream asked slamming the trunk then jumping back in the passenger seat. "And where them faggots in the truck at?"

"No no don't shoot—yall can't," Prince kneeled with his hands on his knees breathing deeply. Exhaustion and hyperactivity had him unable to think and speak properly. "Yall can't shoot—the cops yo—they coming—yo yall gotta bounce." Prince couldn't help but notice the confusion on Dolla and Cream's faces.

"Prince what the fuck is you talking about yo?"

Instantly, Prince began to feel his mind untangle itself from the tension and his thoughts became clear as his lungs absorbed more oxygen. "Yo I fucked up yall I'm sorry…give me the bricks back…yall gotta leave before the cops come." Prince skated to the trunk of the Cadillac feeling like a low down dirty piece of shit. Prince thought he was preventing an ambush on the police, but he was leading the police to his friends whom were in possession of guns and he just gave them three kilos of cocaine. How file was that Prince thought. Why did he even come to Main Street he wondered during this moment of truth?

Being caught with guns and three kilos was a mandatory 15-year sentence in New York at the order of Governor Pataki. The Young Assassins would never forgive Prince for this decision which was like snitching. Prince stood at the trunk of the Cadillac analyzing these thoughts within a millisecond. He had to stand up and face the music. This was all his fault and he had to man up and take responsibility for his actions. He then banged on the trunk so Dolla could open it.

"Open the trunk Dolla…I can't let yall get caught with these bricks."

"Prince what the fuck is you talking bout?" Cream jumped halfway out the car.

"The red truck—it's not Big Walt setting us up it's the fucking---."
Prince stopped in mid-sentence as gunshots rang out in the parking lot across the street.

....

The two detectives in the unmarked truck could barely keep up with Prince as they trailed him from several blocks behind. When they peeped Prince dipping onto Main Street they anticipated he was racing to a hangout of the Young Assassins. The detectives swerved into the parking lot with the numerous dumpsters searching for Prince's motorcycle but it was nowhere in sight. They rolled thru the parking lot heading to the one across the street, and as they slowly eased the truck out the parking lot onto the side street, a black car which was parked on the side street before the parking lot's entrance recklessly peeled out in front of the detectives' truck. The black car blocked the detectives from proceeding across the street to the next parking lot, so with a sharp reflex the detective slammed on his brakes and pounded on his horn at the reckless driver. Disregarding the detectives, the black car didn't move from in front of the truck. The detective wanted to flash his police lights so the car would move but that's when both detectives realized this was a decoy only to give Prince enough time to get rid of the evidence within the backpack.

The two detectives pondered at each other without words saying Prince and the Young Assassins would suffer for this. Then in a flash that's when the gates of hell opened. The front and back passenger doors of the black car swung open and two shooters cloaked in black hoodies gripping a submachine Cobra Mac-11 and a Kalashnikov AK-47 opened fire on the two detectives in the burgundy Expedition.

Swiftly, the detective at the wheel shifted the gear in reverse and mashed his foot on the gas pedal, launching the truck backward thru the parking lot at full speed as slugs from the rapid spitting assault weapons banged the metal exterior of the truck. Ear popping gun blasts resonated thru the air sending echoes clashing with the buildings enclosing the parking lots. Fearful screams of women exiting the laundry mat could be heard amidst the sounds of screeching car tires.

In a race for their life the detective zipped the truck thru the parking lot in reverse several yards from the bloodthirsty shooters. The two shooters were squeezing their triggers like they were trying to empty their clips. The detective whipped the steering wheel in a 180-degree motion, smashing the truck's rear into a dumpster. He threw the truck in park and climbed out snatching the pistol from his holster as his partner followed and did the same. Both detectives then took cover on side of the truck and between the dumpster and shielded themselves from the raining firestorm.

The lightweight sized detective was Mexican and in appearance favored the lightweight champion Julio Caesar Chavez. He clasped his rosary beads then kissed them with shut eyes mumbling a prayer to God he didn't die in this rotten smelling parking lot as bullets tore thru the truck. The black detective clutched his 357 Magnum thinking to himself how he was going to rip the eye sockets out of Prince's head if he survived this ambush.

"Let's bounce yo." Zulu shouted sitting behind the wheel of the black car as the get-away driver.

"Yeah we let them niggas have it," the one shooter jumped into the car after the truck spun out of control and banged the dumpster.

The second shooter fell into the back seat snatching off his hoodie, "Niggas should know by now they playing with death trying to rob us."

"Hell yeah yo," Zulu murked off, "Lets get back to the hood…hit summer bash…and get Tam and Big Walt…fucking faggots."

"First let's dump these tools on the tracks and grab some more heat."

In a rage the detectives spun from behind the dumpster upon hearing the car murk off. They aimed their guns towards the street where the shooters stood moments ago only to see Prince zooming out of the parking lot across the street.

"Let's get him," the Black detective yelled in a rage jumping back in the shot up truck.

When the shooting erupted moments ago, Dolla and Cream skated out of the parking lot with Prince following behind on his motorcycle. When Prince exited the parking lot behind Dolla who almost hit a Rent-A-Center truck, Prince heard them sirens on the truck again. Prince turned his head and gazed back into the parking lot as he wheeled his bike into the street. Prince never seen it coming but he felt a tremendous force racing at him full speed. It was like a locomotive freight train came at him and his mind and spirit flashed a feeling that told him this was the moment he was to die.

"*Boooom*," Was the sound of the two-ton Expedition truck slamming into Prince. The truck mangled Prince's 210lb solid physique and the 300lb bike throwing them both rumbling across the street.

"Back up we're Police," the two detectives jumped out the truck flashing their badges at the onlookers. A blue and white police cruiser then pulled onto the scene.

"We got calls of shots fired." The uniformed officer jumped out the police car eyeing the madness of this crime scene. There were bullet holes painted all over the truck, the banged-up motorcycle lay in the street and then you had the discombobulated Prince lying in the street squirming in pain.

"Yeah there was shots fired as you can see." The black detective stood over the groaning Prince. The black detective then fabricated the incident, "Some perps were shooting at this guy who was on the motorcycle and we got caught in the crossfire."

"Were you guys able to I.D. the shooters?"

"Yeah," deceit flashed in the Mexican detective's green eyes. "It was a light blue car…a sedan…a Ford I believe…they headed down towards Leroy Avenue…more than likely they were shooters from the Rodney Street Gang…3 suspects."

"Responding to it now." The uniformed officer flew back to his patrol car while yelling into his dispatch radio.

Prince struggled trying to sound his vocal chords and get the uniformed officers attention. It felt like Prince had a stone stuck in his throat and he couldn't speak to save his life. If only he had enough energy to speak he would've confessed right on the spot to the uniformed officer that he was responsible for shooting up the unmarked police vehicle, because the two detectives who were now snatching Prince from off the ground and shoving him into the back of the truck were two of the most crooked and dangerous detectives on the east side of Buffalo. Prince would rather have been arrested and thrown into a cell than to face the soul wrenching terror he was about to be dealt by Black Bull and Gonzalez.

CHAPTER 4

About an hour after Black Bull and Gonzalez was ambushed by the Young Assassins, Leonetti was flashing his yearly parking pass at the new parking attendant before sliding out of the parking ramp in his bumble bee yellow BMW convertible. To the grooving sounds of Frank Sinatra, he cruised thru the heavy downtown traffic before jumping onto the 33 east expressway which took him to the east side of town.

Exiting off the expressway he headed down the ramp to the Avenue. He swung thru the green light and headed several blocks down the avenue towards Summer Bash where he spotted a few police officers posted by the barricade. Besides their uniforms the officers didn't appear to be on duty the way they discreetly swayed to the music while jovially conversing with the people.

Leonetti searched for a parking spot on the avenue but was unlucky. He turned down a side street right before the barricade and spotted a few cars pulling out of parking spots. In the middle of the block he found a parking spot but felt timid parking there due to the slum infested environment he found himself in. Leonetti was well known and respected by some of the most dangerous criminals in the city but that didn't erase the fear he felt being in the ghetto. Nor did it deter him from securing his luxury car as he parked on this gloomy side street where tall trees blocked out the sun-rays lighting the blue sky. His eyes scanned the decrepit surroundings as the convertible roof unfolded and enshrouded the car. Devastation swept thru this community long ago and hadn't received any relief Leonetti observed feeling chills creeping inside him. Abandoned houses boarded up with graffiti splashed on them sat guarded by knee high grass and trash filled yards.

Leonetti began rolling his windows up feeling the negative thresholds of misery that the people felt who lived in this depression. Leonetti shook his head feeling sympathy for the unfortunate when all of a sudden and from out of nowhere, an arm reached inside the car stopping the window from going up. A hard stiff object was forcefully jammed behind Leonetti's neck. It was a robbery.

"Don't move you Irish mick." The robber shouted drilling the hard object on Leonetti's neck.

"O-o-o-ok." Leonetti felt his heart thumping and a lump form in his throat. "I-I-I."

"You what…you gone give me that Rolex watch and this car."

"P-P-P-Please," Leonetti stuttered, "You may know m-m-my clients— the Y-y—young Assassins---B-B-Big Walt----they---might not like this."

"Fuck what they don't like I like this muthafucking car and yo watch."

"Please please I'm a lawyer and I'm Sicilian."

The would be robber burst in laughter and removed the cell phone from off of Leonetti's neck. "Calm down Leonetti and stop being so scary."

Leonetti cautiously twirled his neck around and fearfully gazed into a pair of cloudy grey eyes that seen more bloodshed than a butcher. "Jahtu." Leonetti's terror vanished instantly. "Hey. How are you and how have you been? Where's your twin?"

"He right there." Killa, whose government name was Jahtu, pointed to a driveway where his twin brother whom everyone called Terror stood with Zulu curled up laughing.

"Yo come on Leonetti you look shook as hell," Zulu and Terror bounced out the driveway laughing. "Man you supposed to have that Gangster ass Sicilian blood in you...what the hell you scared for…you know you safe whenever you come to these parts…we run this."

"I sure didn't feel like I was safe," Leonetti straddled out of his BMW smoothing the wrinkles on his cream silk button down shirt then tugging at the brown leather belt holding up his beige slacks. "You guys sure had me there. How you doing Zulu?" Leonetti and Zulu embraced after a handshake. Leonetti then stepped to Killa and Terror with a sly smile on his face. "Well if it isn't the infamous Kadari Twins."

BACK DOWN MEMORY LANE WITH THE KADARI TWINS

Jahtu and Sahku Kadari. Twin brothers who fought their way out of their mother's liquor and cocaine flooded womb minutes apart. Jahtu, known on the streets as Killa, was a few minutes older than Sahku, known on the streets as Terror. Their mother was a beautiful Creole woman with light skin from Louisiana. Her name was Sadiya. Sadiya made a living frequenting the brothels in New Orleans and using her beauty and passionate skills in the bed to empty married Men's pockets. Sadiya had one customer where a love developed between them. The customer was a rich Nigerian businessman by the name of Abadu Obatala Kadari. Sadiya fell in love with Abadu's care and concern for her life. He was different than most men who only lusted her beauty. When it came to Sadiya, Abadu seen more than a beautiful whore, he discovered the divine beauty of her soul. To Abadu, Sadiya was like a lovely flower he could spot blindfolded in God's luscious paradise. It was beyond the sex they had together because Abadu desired Sadiya completely, not just sexually. He wanted her whole existence to be united with his life. Sadiya wanted to be saved and Abadu was the captain to rescue and save her.

Sadiya had a sister named Sabrina who was very attractive but wasn't as beautiful as Sadiya. The emotion of jealousy had always forced Sabrina to unsuccessfully compete with Sadiya when it came to certain customers, mostly those with big bankrolls. So when Sabrina found out that Abadu had fertilized Sadiya's egg with two seeds, the grimy Sabrina let the devilish seeds of jealousy, hate, and envy drive her to commit an atrocious act that would cost her, her life in the future.

Deep in the swamps of Louisiana Sabrina conjured up spirits and negative energies to attack the minds of Sadiya and Abadu. Sadiya began to lose her mind and charming beauty. Abadu felt possession but he consulted the Orisas (Divine Spirits) before it was too late. Through consultation with his ancestral spirits he was advised to bring the pregnant Sadiya to the holy ancestral land of Ile-Ife in Nigeria. By taking the pregnant Sadiya to the holy land, the twins would be blessed and protected by the Orisas and not harmed by the demons of the white man's land of America. The twins were born in the strange and mysterious land of Nigeria. They were healthy, strong, and beautiful babies unaffected by the roots their aunt Sabrina had put on their mother while they were in her womb. The Orisas blessed and protected the seeds, but for some reason, Sadiya's mind began deteriorating slowly as the years went by. Sadiya may began to lose her mind, but she still had enough sanity and awareness to desire dying back home in Louisiana with her relatives.

Abadu insisted on Sadiya not going back to the wilderness of America. He even warned her that his twin sons were unwelcomed in the white devils' land. America may have represented a lot of bad things to Abadu, but America was Sadiya's home and that's where Sadiya would die before her mind completely shut down, and the twins would be with her if Abadu didn't want to come back to America with her. Abadu did all he could to stop Sadiya but even the Queen Mothers of his tribe ruled that the mother has sole authority over the children. So back to the devil's civilization Abadu journeyed with his family and like the prediction of the Orisas foretold, the demons would attack.

Sabrina, still dealing with her inner demons of jealousy and hate, and still not satisfied with the harm she had already done, worked roots again and this time poisoned Abadu and caused him to die a mysterious death. The Orisas couldn't help Abadu this time because he failed in heeding their divine order. He died from mysterious causes. Sadiya became sicker and began punishing the twins and blaming them for their father's death. Child welfare found out about the abuse and took custody of the twins. Sadiya was admitted to a mental institution, never to regain her sanity.

Sabrina was the twins closest next of kin in America, so they were released to her. Around this time Sabrina ended up in the clutches of a Pimp from the Buffalo-Niagara Falls region. Since it was all about the money, this is where Sabrina ended up getting splashed by the semen of tricks she provided services for in Niagara Falls.

The twins were well aware of their father's sickly death and how it ill-affected their mother since they endured ferocious beatings by their mother. They were too young to understand the spiritual wickedness of their aunt Sabrina which made their young lives a living hell by destroying both their parents.

Unfortunately, when the twins got older and reached puberty, nightmares and visions of bloodshed began infesting their dreams. When most adolescents experiencing puberty had wet dreams about nude women they watched on T.V. and seen in playboy magazines, the twins had violent dream after violent dream.

They went to their aunt Sabrina and asked her about the horrors they were experiencing mentally since Sabrina was a spiritual hoodoo lady. Sabrina would just brush them off and tell them to stop eating candy late at night and stop watching gangster and horror movies. The twins then consulted a real dark skinned Cuban lady whose name was Yemaria. Sabrina always went to Yemaria for advice, so the twins felt comfortable telling Yemaria their problems. Yemaria was a Santeria priestess who provided readings for many people in the hood. And to find the solution to the twins' problems, Yemaria sought the divine oracle deep within the core of her African Ancestral genetic intelligence to receive the utterance.

Yemaria and the twins sat on the floor in a triangle holding hands. A clear green onyx bowl with clean water sat in the center of the trio with a tarot card floating in the bowl. With flickering candles and frankincense lighting the dimly lit room, the three closed their eyes and meditated as Yemaria began chanting in an African language the twins were familiar with.

"*Elegba…Oludamare…Babalu-Aye,*" Yemaria tightly squeezed their hands while speaking in the African tongue. After she received the séance (spiritual meeting with the ancestral spirits) and learned the source of the twins' dread, she uttered, "Jahtu and Sahku Kadari…royal seeds of Abadu Obatala Kadari…descendants of divine Yoruba Ancestors of Ile-Iyin…warriors of *Ogun* who is master of the metal…may *Odudwa* open the eye inside of the Kadari Twins and show them the way into the darkness with no fear…*Orisa Ogun* and *Shango* will guide and protect them…have no fear."

The twins opened their eyes and peered into the green onyx bowl. The clear water began to stir and whirl around and their mother and aunt's history reflected on the water like they were watching T.V. They even glimpsed the evils their aunt Sabrina committed against their parents. Vengeance raced thru their young hearts as they fled Yemaria's abode and took flight to their grimy aunt's house.

Once inside the house which was dark and gloomy, the twins discovered their aunt and her pimp boyfriend sleeping butt-naked in the bed. The twins grabbed kitchen knives and went to work. Fear and pain stretched Sabrina and her boyfriend's eyes wide open as the twins punctured knives into their guts.

"Stoppp...noooooo," were the screaming pleas reverberating thru the apartment. A neighbor upstairs heard the screams and thought the Pimp was beating his hoe as usual, only this time the screams were louder and longer and that of a man and a woman. The neighbor usually minded her business but not this time.

The two Niagara Falls Police Officers responding to the call never thought of walking into a crime scene that would flash in their minds whenever they seen pasta. It was horrible. When they arrived at the apartment the door was ajar. They stepped inside and observed the twins playing Double Dragon for Nintendo like two innocent boys.

"Where's your parents?" One officer asked receiving no response from the twins who were absorbed by the violence on the video game. The officer stood there focusing on the video game while his partner began stepping through the dark apartment. He slid pass the bedroom and noticed a bloodstain on the bedroom doorknob. He flicked the dining room light on and cautiously pushed the bedroom door open. He found the bedroom light on the wall and flicked it on, feeling the organs in his body freeze up and the dinner digesting in his stomach hurl up onto the floor upon seeing what he saw. With a mouth full of throw up he yelled to his partner stumbling out the bedroom into the dining room. His partner dashed to the bedroom with his pistol out and pumped the brakes on his feet when he peeped the horror.

Blood soaked the blankets and dripped onto the bedroom carpet. Reddish pink and white ligaments were shredded and hanging out of the stomachs of Sabrina and her boyfriend. A large kitchen knife was protruded into Sabrina's left eye. Her right eye was wide open and peered into a dimension living souls couldn't see while another knife was rammed into her neck. It was gruesome crime scene and no one could believe two young boys reaching puberty could do this. The high profile and big shot lawyer Leonetti was called upon to represent the juveniles and Yemaria served as a character witness in favor of the twins, the judge sentenced the twins to 5 years in a Juvenile Detention center. The judge was a middle aged Hispanic lady who understood the mental forces that roots had on the human psyche. The judge felt sorry for the twins and was lenient and granted them youthful offender status.

Besides Yemaria, the twins didn't have much family in the states, but during their time at juvie hall, the Kadari Twins developed a bond with the Young Assassins that would last until the sun burnt out. They were brothers for life.

Now back to the present moment.

"So what bring you to these parts Leonetti?" Zulu and the Kadari Twins curiously asked as they all lounged around Leonetti's BMW.

"Well guys," Leonetti sighed with a breath of tension while removing his sun-blocker shades. "I got good news and bad news…what do you guys want first?" Leonetti asked noticing a vibe of worry cover their faces. They took a deep breath then asked Leonetti if the bad news had anything to do with Prince, Dolla, and Cream since they hadn't seen or heard from them since the shooting earlier. Leonetti replied no. They all then decided to go bang out on some grub at Summer Bash.

In his brown Bruno Magli reptiles Leonetti stepped onto the Avenue and up into Summer Bash with the Young Assassins. Leonetti swayed with such a hip demeanor he appeared more like a wise-guy than a lawyer. All eyes beheld the sight of Leonetti's well conserved professionalism as he strode thru the crowd with three of E. North's most dangerous Young Assassins.

In lawn chairs they lounged and caressed their stomachs with the nutritious elements of the soul food. When their full portions were emptied into their stomachs, a young lady wearing a chef's apron on top of her booty shorts and halter top approached the fellas with her eyes enticingly focused on Leonetti's glistening oyster perpetual Rolex watch.

"Hey yall…yall want seconds?" The young lady collected their empty plates and tossed them in a trash bin close by. Zulu and the Kadari Twins told her they were full, but they couldn't help but notice how Leonetti's eyes were magnetized on her sumptuous thighs. Like a juicy rotisserie chicken glistening with its juices over the fire, the young lady's shiny thighs were a glossy brown pigment and oh so healthy. Even under the apron her voluptuous breast looked like they needed to bust out and be munched on like the food she been serving.

"You know what baby girl," Killa snatched the thick young lady by her waist and pulled her onion booty onto his lap. "Leonetti want you for seconds."

"Boy stop who the hell you talking about?" The young lady blushed trying to jump out of Killa's lap, "You play too much boy."

"I'm not playing." Killa kept her planted on his lap and blew in her ear. "That's our lawyer right there...Leonetti...and I want you to bless him for me...I'm gone look out for you like I always do."

"How much you gone bless me with? Because I hate doing white men...they be smelling funny and they dicks' look like baby rats and be all pink and little."

"Yo I don't need to know all that shit...that's too much info...but he Sicilian and like I said that's our lawyer so you know I'm gone bless you...I got a ball ($100) for you."

"Un un...I need a duce ($200) pretty boy."

"Alright I got you...just do what you do."

"Just for you." The young lady sprung up off of Killa's lap and snatched her apron off. Killa pulled out some bills and gave them to the young lady before she prowled over to Leonetti.

"Look like Trick Daddy Killa done got you some dessert." Zulu and Terror chuckled as the young lady stepped to Leonetti extending a seductive handshake.

"Hello sweetheart." Leonetti was pleasured. "But oh no I'm a married man and plus I'm too old," Leonetti stated accepting the young lady's hand and softly kissing it while staying seated. "Definitely in my young days' allure, you'd be all mines."

"That's what I'm here for," the young lady peered down into Leonetti's eyes twirling her hips to *Eve's* hit song *"What yall niggas want."* The young lady then flirtatiously said, "I can make you feel young again."

Leonetti felt more testosterone than a young healthy athlete stimulating his penis. He may have been older, but he still had the drive. Leonetti observed the crowd at Summer Bash realizing he wasn't the only professional society figure there. He wasn't the only white face there either. As much as he desired to throw this young tiger in his BMW and zoom down to the harbor, climb in his yacht and let her give him his youth back, it couldn't happen.

"I'm sorry sweetheart…but I'm older and don't party like I used to…you grow out of that type of fun and become happy with just living life…but I tell you what…if you ever need any legal advice feel free to contact me." Leonetti stated reaching in his wallet to retrieve his business card.

"You don't know what you missing Leonetti," Killa jumped up and threw his arm around the young lady. "Life aint happy without women…and this all the fun I need." Killa then turned towards Zulu and Terror, "Yall get the good and bad news…I'm about to have some good sex with this bad bitch…Ashay ashay (Peace.)."

"So what do you guys want first?" Leonetti asked sipping his ice cold Loganberry.

"Give it to us whichever way you want," Zulu and Terror demanded watching Leonetti remove his shades then rub his eyes before swiping beads of sweat off of his forehead. Leonetti then explained how Sun-Z and Hawk from the A-Squad was set to be released from Elmira State Prison, but the Feds was gonna be there at the gate to arrest them for federal charges.

Leonetti observed a puzzled look on Zulu and Terror's faces so he explained in more detail and told them how there was a superseding indictment stemming from the initial charges the A-Squad plead guilty to and was already serving time for. The bad news was the fact that a confidential informant came out of the closet revealing info about Sun-Z and Hawk right before their release dates.

"Listen guys," Leonetti gestured for Zulu and Terror to move closer to him. They all scooted their chairs closer and huddled under the loud music.

"Lord knows who this rat is...and being that this rat is coming out of the grave with this...it's no telling what this rat knows...and God forbid this rat has something on you guys too...it seems whoever this rat is, is scared of Sun-Z and Hawk coming home and don't want them out here."

"What the fuck." Zulu and Terror sat at the edge of their chairs jittery hoping they weren't next to be included in an indictment.

Leonetti then rubbed his hands together, "I need you guys to let Big Walt know what's going on, tell him to think of who else knew about the hits on those witnesses...and you guys have to bring $ 25,000 to my office asap...for a high profile federal case like this fees can run up to $ 75,000, but your my guys so I can handle Sun-Z and Hawk for $ 50,000 and provide the best legal representation my firm can guarantee."

"Ok we gone take care of this." Zulu and Terror stated before giving Leonetti a farewell. Zulu and Terror then stood amidst the crowd at Summer Bash analyzing the bomb Leonetti just dropped on them. Half of the day had just passed but considering all the tragic events of the day they been through, their minds felt an exhaustion that weighed on their minds like a lifetime experience. They were still in the dark knowing that it was the cops they shot at and how Prince was snatched by the cops. They were still under the impression that Big Walt sent the stick up kids to rob Prince. They still hadn't heard from Dolla and Cream, and now with Leonetti and his delivery of bad news, they felt trouble and something horrible was heading their way.

"Yo what the fuck we gone do Zulu?" Terror ranted tapping Zulu out of his mental absorption.

"We need to see what up with everybody first," Zulu motioned for Terror to step onto the sidewalk where it was less crowded. Zulu pulled out his cell phone and began dialing everyone. No answer from no one.

"That's crazy niggas not answering the phones Zulu."

"That's what I'm saying yo...we need to find out where everyone at...we should've heard from the crew by now...what if niggas got knocked with them bricks?"

"Psssss." Terror blew steam as him and Zulu eyed each other not even trying to consider the worst.

"Listen before we jump the gun let's just hold on because we need Big Walt to put up that bread for Sun-Z and Hawk."

"I'm telling you Zulu fuck that nigga Big Walt…he tried to have niggas rob us so we should just rob that nigga and blaze him…we just gave that nigga over twenty stacks…and I bet you them stacks still up in the store right now…them stacks is the bread we can give Leonetti for Sun-Z and Hawk…if we wait we might miss this opportunity…what if Cream and them did get knock…this our only chance to stay afloat."

"Fucccck." Zulu began pacing in circles thinking deeply. Terror had a point. Getting at Big Walt was mandatory and necessary, but when to get at him was the key. "Ok listen it's too many people out here for us to get him at the store. We gone have to wait."

"I can't wait for whenever you think the right time gone be Zulu."

....

When Zulu and the Kadari Twins hit Summer Bash with Leonetti, word had spread that the Young Assassins was rolling with a mobster who looked like a Soprano. Big Walt and Tam was sitting up in New Millennium politicking while Leonetti and the Young Assassins were at the bash eating. As soon as Big Walt heard the news he prayed the Young Assassins wasn't spitting in his face. Big Walt just gave them two kilos of coke on consignment with the intentions of having them knock the bricks off and bring everything back so he could walk them. Now according to what Big Walt just heard, the Young Assassins just returned to Summer Bash with a Soprano who was probably their new drug connect. Big Walt became furious but before he would run into a situation blindly without knowing the facts he had to do some fact finding first. If the rumors were true, then Big Walt knew that without words the Young Assassins was saying he wasn't getting paid because they had a new connect.

Big Walt prayed this wasn't the case because if it was, none of his plans were working as planned. As Big Walt and Tam sat inside New Millennium analyzing these probabilities, Big Walt snatched the bag of money he had sitting behind the counter and slid to the back room where he stashed it in the safe. He bounced out the back room then him and Tam stormed out of the store to see if the Young Assassins really had the balls to spit in his face. They stepped outside and began asking people where the Young Assassins and the Soprano was. Someone pointed them in the direction about two blocks down.

Big Walt began creeping behind Tam through the crowd and as they neared the section, they spotted Killa embracing the young lady who was trying to sexually seduce Leonetti. Big Walt then pumped the brakes on his Clarks and spun around hoping the Young Assassins and Leonetti didn't see him.

"Tam come here." Big Walt snatched Tam and pulled him to the side before they slid on the side of a bounce house. "What the fuck is Leonetti doing here?" Big Walt asked. At first Big Walt was ready to unleash the vicious Tam on the Young Assassins according to the rumors he was hearing. But now the truth was making itself manifest and Big Walt's emotions went from anger to fear. "What the fuck is Leonetti over there talking to them about Tam?"

"It's only one way to find out." Tam tapped the gun hiding under his Ice-Berg shirt.

"Ok listen," Big Walt looked around the crowd in fright. "See what Leonetti want…then go find Dolla and them and try to get them bricks back." Big Walt began pacing in small steps on side of the bounce house. "Just try to get them bricks back because it's only a matter of time before shit blow up."

"I told you not to front them those bricks." Tam rambled moving out of the way for children dashing in and out of the bounce house.

"It's too late to complain about the past…you know what you gotta do…I be downtown at the Hyatt Hotel just get the shit done." Big Walt broke out not looking back. Tam then dipped from the side of the bounce house and headed towards the area where the Young Assassins were now huddled with Leonetti. Tam noticed Killa and the young lady had disappeared as he shuffled through the crowd with his eyes locked on Leonetti who huddled with Zulu and Terror.

Tam continued bumping thru the crowd towards his destination before a rump shaking mama planted her butt on his mid-section and began twirling.

"Oooh I turn you on like that Tam?" She was mistaking the chrome barrel of Tam's gun for his penis. She then spun around and ran her fingers thru his dreads. "I wanna kiss all over yo albino ass."

"Not right now." Tam brushed her to the side continuing thru the crowd. His view was now blocked by a group of people and he couldn't see the location of Zulu and Terror. He continued shoving thru the crowd finally bumping heads with Zulu and Terror.

"I should let my heater burn yo ass up since the sun aint burning yo pink ass up." Terror ranted inching his hand close to his waist.

"Let's see who can draw first and get burned by these hot slugs." Tam tapped his waistline.

"You can't hit both of us at the same time," Zulu added petting the handle on his back, "So you got no wins."

"Yeah whatever yo…what did Leonetti want?"

Zulu and Terror mischievously glanced at each other out the corner of their eyes. "He wanna holla at Big Walt. Shit don't concern you."

"Big Walt leaving town," Tam noticed Zulu and Terror tighten their faces suspiciously. Tam was gonna rock them to sleep. "He going to holla at that plug who got it for the low and he wanted me to get them bricks back from yall because he got a lick that want them right now."

"Haaa." Zulu and Terror busted out a laugh.

"Nigga we aint giving shit back." Terror let his anger flare.

Zulu disappointedly shook his head at Terror then told Tam, "What he mean to say is we not giving you shit back because you aint give us the bricks…Big Walt gave them to us and that's who we gone give em back to."

"Oh my fucking God yo." Tam thought to himself. *"I hate these niggas…I swear I'm losing my patience and I'm gone kill these niggas."* Tam then let his large nostrils suck in the BBQ soaked air before he exhaled the frustration in his system. He then told Zulu and Terror, "Listen…get them bricks back to me at the store by midnight or have that fifty thousand." Tam warned spinning off.

"Muthafucka." Terror let his rage take over. Terror snatched the pistol off his waist and began to aim it at Tam.

"Yo chillllll." Zulu yelled grabbing Terror and standing in front of Terror so people couldn't see the gun but a few people already peeped it and felt the energy.

"So you gone shoot me in front of all these people Terror?" Tam turned around and faced Zulu and Terror. Tam then glanced at the people close by who stood fearful of what might happen.

"You lucky Zulu jumped in the way…but next time I see you it's on and that's not a threat I promise you that." Terror gripped his pistol slowly placing it back on his hip.

"It's about who got the drop on who first."

"Yo listen fuck all of that we gone see yall tonight and just make sure Big Walt with you," Zulu yelled to Tam while easing Terror back. "And you aint gotta worry Tam because I'm not bringing Terror."

"If you wanna keep him alive don't bring him." Tam stated breaking out.

As Zulu and Terror stormed away from Summer Bash they felt nothing but death towards Big Walt. They felt so insulted at Big Walt's audacity. They thought he sent the stick- up kids to rob Prince for the bricks but the Young Assassins stopped that and now he was asking for the bricks back.

"Yo who the fuck this dude think he is…and who the fuck do he think we is?" Zulu and Terror asked each other. A short while later they met up with Cream and Dolla and learned they was three kilos ahead in the game and they were ready to take Big Walt off the throne. As to Prince, everyone was unaware of his tragic dilemma.

CHAPTER 5

Prince awoke from his state of unconsciousness feeling dizzy and unaware of his surroundings and the tragic events of earlier. Through squinting eyes, Prince strained his blurred vision struggling to make out the group of individuals circling around him. Besides the rays of light beaming on his lumped up face, the room was like triple darkness. Prince struggled rising up off the floor he lay on as his consciousness began to resurface. His body was aching with severe pains all over and as he struggled to get up, pains shot thru his limbs and upper body.

"*Ahhhh.*" Prince groaned leaning against the wall and using it for support as he stood on his feet. He stood up against the wall in the dark peering at the flashing lights, finally becoming aware of who and what was creeping around him in this hellish environment.

"*Arggggh...what the fucccck.*" Prince yelled a terrifying holler before almost passing out from the force of fear. Huge rats swiftly crawled over each other devouring slices of steamy steak and cheese pizza scattered on the floor around him. "*Noooo.*" Prince yelled swinging his hands which were handcuffed to a rusted radiator pipe. "Please noooo...no." Prince pleaded as the two flashlights flickered light on the swarms of rats savagely tearing and clawing at the pizza near his bare feet.

Black Bull and Gonzalez stood across the room laughing at the trembling Prince who jumped up and down raving. After they captured Prince earlier they shipped him to this abandoned house which sat in the Lackawanna section of town. The abandoned house was close to a waste site and old steel plant so the rats in this area were humongous and scrapped with the stray cats and dogs for the trash on the streets of this neighborhood.

Prince's consciousness was still blurry so he couldn't recall all the events from earlier. After they captured Prince, they beat him unconscious before throwing him in this hell like house and handcuffing him to the radiator pipe then stripping him of his socks and shoes. They bought a large steak and cheese pizza but only ate a few slices, the rest was for the creepy crawlers back at the house of hell. Black Bull and Gonzalez were going to put Prince through a test of terror like they done several so-called thugs and gangsters on the east side. It was only a few thoroughbreds who left these bowels of hell still ready to play the streets.

"You must be hungry Prince?" Black Bull shined the light in Prince's bloody face. "You haven't eaten all day and you been through a lot of physical pain...you got to be hungry and dehydrated...you wanna eat?" Black Bull jokingly asked.

"Come on mannn...why y'all doing this to me?" Prince muttered trembling inside with so much fear. He wanted to cry but he couldn't. He felt so helpless. This was horrible and made the illest gangsters cry for mama.

"Oh...why you have your friends try to kill us earlier?" Gonzalez shot at Prince.

"Man I don't know what y'all talking about please...I don't remember anything."

"Oh so you don't remember." Black Bull stated with intimidation. "Ok go ahead Gonzalez." Black Bull then flashed his light on Gonzalez who whipped out a bottle of syrup from a plastic bag.

"You know mi amigo." Gonzalez hopped over the feasting rats and moved closer to Prince. "The Apache Indians were some mean sons of bitches...they would tie their enemies to a cactus tree...smother them in syrup and let the ants eat them to death before the vultures finished the feast," Gonzalez stated unscrewing the top to the syrup bottle then squirting drops of syrup near Prince's bare feet.

"Come on man stop y'all bugging...please stop...*pleeeease*." Prince shouted grabbing the pipe and raising his feet in the air when a few rats scrambled to the syrup near his feet.

"We will stop if you take us to E. North to see your friends."

"Why y'all wanna see my friends I'm the one that y'all got here...please stop."

"He wanna play tough Gonzalez."

"Oh really." Gonzalez splashed some syrup on Prince's feet.

"No no ok ok…what y'all want me to do." Prince unconsciously submitted to their plea. Anything to get him away from hell he thought. "Whatever y'all want me to do I will do, please just get me away from here, please?" Prince just needed to get away from hell and once they took him from hell and onto the street, Prince would run and hopefully they would shoot and kill him. Death would be beautiful at this point because he would suffer no more. He just needed to get away from hell. This was ugly as it gets.

"I'm telling you and I swear to God," Black Bull kicked a rat out of his way as he stormed over to Prince. He shoved his 357 Magnum up in Prince's face. "If you try anything I'm gone blow yo fucking head off."

"Ok ok ok just please get me out of here please man please." Prince pleaded jumping into his shoes after Gonzalez threw them at his feet. While Black Bull was un-cuffing Prince, Prince heard his conscience whisper, "Please God…please let them kill me when we leave out of here God…please…please."

                ....

The raining shower sprayed on Big Walt's clean shaven dome where numerous thoughts raced along his brain circuits. He stood under the shower letting the water beat on him like it could wash away his stressful thoughts. He then stepped out the shower and slid into his bathrobe before moping into the cool air of the Presidential Suite.

The mellow and jazzy sounds of *Sade* created an atmosphere in the suite filtered by depression. The bottle of Johnny Walker Blue lounging on the mini bar seemed the only escape Big Walt could find in this time of turmoil. He snatched the bottle of Scotch and wandered to the balcony overlooking Pearl Street and the surrounding downtown area. The people below on the streets looked like cockroaches racing in and out of the night clubs lining the strip.

Despite the big bankroll and lavish life Big Walt lived, he would trade everything from his past, present, and from the way his future was looking, he would trade it all in just for the happiness and joy the people on the street below were experiencing as they partied. He gulped the smooth Scotch which ignited a fire in his chest. He then peered up at the full moon wishing he could flee to its realm and escape the hell on earth. It looked so quiet and peaceful up on the moon. With his eyes magnetized to the moon, Big Walt turned the bottle up to his face and splashed his throat with the Scotch again. The huge dose of liquor he just gulped burnt his insides forcing him to let out a loud growl into the night air.

"Why the fuck me?" Big Walt's intoxication made him yell at the moon. He may have contributed to the devastation of his community by supplying the white death of crack to its users, but he only played the cards he was dealt. Big Walt never asked for the street life. Back when all he knew was misfortune and poverty, the street life appeared to be the only good fortune which made the circumstances get better. His history then flashed across his mental screen like he was watching a Blu-ray movie on a LED screen.

Fourteen-year-old Walter Mims was just another poor kid growing up on the impoverished East Side of Buffalo. He was very smart and a young genius when it came to math and numbers. Many nights he went to bed hungry and woke up hungry, and despite this hunger and misfortune, he still stomped his way to school and focused hard on his education like a disciplined disciple of knowledge. It wasn't easy at all. Most young kids weren't overweight and they were either breakdancing, rapping, or they had artistic graffiti skills. That's what earned respect and attracted the girls. The girls went crazy for the B-Boys and those hustling back in the days. The smart kids like Big Walt were whack and was only good for giving up answers during exam time. Even when the legendary hip-hop trio *The Fat Boys* busted out on the B-Boy scene swagging, Big Walt was still being clowned by everyone for being a sweaty fat kid. Many nights he cried because of the ridicule and wanted to hurl himself off of one of the 8 story buildings of the Ellicott Mall Projects. His intelligence was supreme but it wasn't making life any easier because everyone called him a fat nerd.

As fate was destined, one day while walking home from school everything would change. Members of the A-Squad were having a heated argument about their drug business and it appeared a serious fight was about to go down if not a homicide. Big Walt never expected to happen what would change his life when he jumped head first into an argument that could have cost him his life. He was only trying to prevent violence.

"Nigga," A member from the A-Squad was barking at another member,

"You was supposed to make at least $ 85 dollars off every gram…and you had 56 grams so you was supposed to make?" Members of the A-Squad began digging in their book bags and pulling out notebooks and pencils trying to calculate.

"$4, 240 dollars is the answer." Big Walt interjected after quickly calculating the math in his head.

"Who the fuck asked yo stinky fat ass…mind yo business before you get dealt with fat boy."

Big Walt just wobbled on with his head down as everyone laughed including the females walking along. After the A-Squad members scribbled the numbers on the paper and came up with the answer Big Walt had just given, everyone's smiles turned to frowns and they all looked awestruck at Big Walt.

"Yo Walter." The A-Squad ran up to the crying Big Walt. "Yo how the hell you can calculate like that? You aint use no calculator or nothing…what the fuck fat boy?"

"I don't know," Big Walt lifted his head while wiping his eyes. "I just picture the numbers in my head and it's like I'm writing on paper and I just calculate."

"Yo you wanna make some money calculating for us and keeping records?"

"Yeah I do anything for yall." Big Walt agreed finally feeling a part of something bigger than his overweight self. He was finally liked and admired and people respected his intellect after all. As the A-Squad's drug business got bigger and increased, so did the money Big Walt was clocking just from being the hood accountant. At first all Big Walt did was keep the money count and keep records, but then he began to learn about everything else in the drug business. And when the Feds snatched the A-Squad, it was either go to school for 4-8 years to become a certified account, then get a job and bust his brain for some measly paycheck as an accountant, or get out there on the streets and take over the drug business and keep living the lavish life he became accustomed to.

"So this is what it all comes down to." Big Walt took his eyes off the moon and slid back into the Presidential Suite. He grabbed the phone, made a quick call and had a conversation for a seconds before hanging up. He then called Tam.

Tam sat inside New Millennium scoping the hands of time on his gold Timex watch. It was midnight and Summer Bash on the Ave was over. There were still a few people on the Ave cleaning up. Tam had the doors to the store locked but he kept the lights on while he was waiting to see if the Young Assassins would sign their death certificates or return what wasn't theirs.

Getting the bricks back from the Young Assassins wasn't for financial needs. Not at all. Big Walt was paid. His bankroll had been stacking for years with no interruptions. His money was super heavy like he was. Big Walt could lose $ 50,000 at the Seneca Niagara Casino, then hit one of his safes where he had hundreds of thousands stashed, lose more then do it again. Big Walt was heavy in the game.

Getting the bricks back from the Young Assassins was about control to Big Walt. Because now that he finally realized it, a couple of bricks in the hands of the Young Assassins meant the Power to take Big Walt off his throne of rulership. Big Walt harbored a grudge from his youth that made him insecure about seeing others equal to him. No matter how much money he made and how respected he was, the memories of being a poor kid whom everyone once clowned lingered in the front of his consciousness like the events of the present moment. When he put the Young Assassins on, he never intended for them or anyone else to ever have the upper hand on him. He would never again be in a position where people could down him. He had the power to use people like tools, and that's what he did with the Young Assassins. If a tool couldn't be utilized to his benefit, it was time to get rid of the tool, there was no repairing it.

Tam lifted his eyes from his watch and glared at his ringing cellphone which sat on the counter next to his gun. *"These niggas not stupid."* Tam spoke in reference to the Young Assassins while snatching the phone from off the counter. He glanced at the number displayed on his phone then glowered at the phone seeing it wasn't the Young Assassins. Tam took a deep breath then answered the phone.

"Big Walt I'm still on the fucking clock for these niggas?" Fury rode on

Tam's voice.

"Ay yo listen…if they don't come thru don't even worry I just talked to them people and we up…Just sit tight I be right there…we got the upper hand no matter what…I'm going to meet with them people then I be right there…get the bread from out the safe and be ready when I call you."

"No doubt I see you in a minute." Tam ended the call gazing towards the front of the store outside, peeping a car pull up in front of the store. A woman in a fitted sundress then hopped out the car and approached the door. She seen the lights on so she tried opening the door but it was locked. She then peered thru the tinted windows of the store seeing Tam at the back of the store behind the counter. She knocked on the glass like she was in a rush.

Tam snatched his blue steel 9mm Taurus from off the counter, cocked it and placed it in the small of his back before swooping to the front of the shop where the curvaceous lady stood outside the door. 'I wish I could help you Ma but we closed…we be open tomorrow at 9 am." Tam yelled standing behind the closed the door.

"Awww come on boo," the lady became jumpy and began begging. "I'm going out tonight and I wanted to hear that new *Ruff Ryders* album…please." She begged holding her hands together like a child asking for candy.

"*Well damn.*" Tam gave in enticed by her charm. "Alright hold on ma. Give me one minute." Tam ran to the C.D. section in the middle of the store and grabbed *Ruff Ryders Vol 2*. He zoomed back to the front of the store with his eyes focused on the C.D. cover as he knelt down and began sliding the C.D. under the door. "This yo lucky night ma…it's on me just make sure you come back and--." Tam glanced outside while he was still kneeling and sliding the C.D. under the door. He froze up at what he saw next.

The lady had skated from the door to the shop before she even got her CD. For some odd reason, she was standing at the driver door to her car and giving Zulu a hug. Tam told the lady the CD was on the house but he figured she was at her car to grab the money. It didn't matter because Zulu was there and that's the only reason Tam was at the shop. Tam knew the Young Assassins played with death and liked busting their guns, but they weren't stupid enough to want death by disrespecting Tam. Zulu came exactly when he was supposed to come and return the bricks. Tam smiled still kneeling at the door. That's when things got weird and Tam began scratching his head still kneeling at the door. After giving Zulu a hug, the lady didn't come back for the CD but instead she jumped in her car and peeled off.

In confusion Tam peered thru the glass at Zulu who began stepping to the store door. Tam's face was inches from the glass door as he began standing up eyeing Zulu who was smiling. Tam could see his own reflection in the glass while observing Zulu walking to the door. Tam gripped the gun on his back while returning a devilish smile at Zulu. Zulu's smile now disappeared and his eyes opened wide at the sight of Tam's hand behind his back. Tam seen the fear in Zulu's face and that's when out of nowhere what sounded like an explosion erupted in Tam's face. A brick was smashed into the glass door shattering the glass in Tam's face.

"You wanted some bricks pink panther." The Kadari Twins shouted before rushing thru the broken glass door and shoving Tam onto the floor covered with thick shards of sharp glass. It happened so quick. Tam had his eyes focused on Zulu the whole time and he never peeped the twins creep from the side and smash the glass door. He was caught off guard watching Zulu and the sudden eruption of glass bursting into his face caused him to drop his gun from the shock as the twins rushed him to the floor. He was still trying to register what happened as Terror stood over him.

"What's up with that shit you was popping earlier faggot." Terror shouted hunched over Tam who lay on the floor in shock. Tam seen death flashing in Terror's bottle green eyes. "Get yo bitch ass up and take us to the safe."

*"Mannnn…*fuck y'all niggas." Tam felt breathless as they snatched him up off the floor and walked him to the back room where the safe was located. Zulu was the last one in the store after surveying the empty street and making sure no witnesses were lingering around. Once inside the store Zulu pulled the blinds down over the broken glass door and shut off the lights in the front of the store. Zulu then dashed into the back of the store.

"Call Big Walt nigga." Zulu entered the back room observing the Kadari Twins holding Tam and aiming their pistols in Tam's face.

"Fuck y'all—y'all might as well--," Tam shook his head feeling defeated. This was it and he knew it but he would stand his ground like the man he was. "Y'all might as well kill me...word up." Tam gazed deeply into all their eyes as they surrounded him at gunpoint. "I'm not calling Big Walt or opening the safe...just get this shit over with." Tam shut his eyes and sunk his head low.

"Muthafucka." Killa busted Tam in the forehead with the butt of his gun causing a knot to form on Tam's forehead. Tam grabbed his forehead and fell into the chair near a desk. "Keeping this tough gangster shit up only gone get you killed quicker you faggot."

"Word up tough guy." Terror then took his gun and slapped Tam across his face with the gun. "Open the safe you bitch ass nigga."

"Listen Tam," Zulu raised his hand stopping Terror from shoving the gun in Tam's face. "You already know you gone die and you can't take the money with you...just open the safe and call Big Walt...let's get it over with like you said."

With blood drizzling down his head and shards of glass pierced into his face, Tam let the windows of his soul look into the faces of his undertakers. What did he have to lose besides his life? In his lifetime, Tam took a couple lives and had an appointment with Karma. Live by the gun die by the gun. But every man controls his destiny, and maybe Tam could save himself he thought to himself.

"The code to the safe--," Tam couldn't believe this. "It's...it's... 28-74-47-15."

"Ok." Killa punched in the electronic codes and heard the door unlock. "Wow...you not that much of a dickhead after all."

"Got damn...what the fuck!" Zulu and Terror peered into the 3ft x 3ft safe and felt like they hit the lotto. Their $ 23,000 was in the safe plus another $ 70,000. "Oh we back yo for real."

"Listen y'all," Tam sensed opportunity at their excitement over the large sum of money, "I got the combination to two more of Big Walt's safes. It's way more than this...y'all can have it all...I give y'all the combinations now."

"And call Big Walt."

"Yo just let me go and I do it...that's my word."

"You is a dickhead...you know you dying tonight right." Killa smirked snatching the money from out the safe. They had no time to chance any tricks up Tam's sleeve. Right at that moment Tam's phone began ringing out in the store area on the counter where he left it earlier. Zulu and the Kadari Twins glanced at each other in shock thinking maybe someone crept in the store. That couldn't be because Dolla and Cream were outside across the street between two buildings in the cut watching everything.

"That's my phone I'm telling the truth," Tam did his best to calm the trigger-happy trio.

Terror dipped from out the back into the store area and snatched the phone from off the counter. He then slid to the door at the front and peeked out onto the street seeing nothing or no one. He then skated into the back room and gave Tam the phone which wasn't ringing anymore. Tam called back the missed call which was Big Walt. Big Walt picked up on the first ring.

"What's the deal Tam, them boys come yet?"

"*Mannnnnn...*"

"Tam you alright?" Big Walt could sense the trouble in Tam's tone of voice. "What's wrong Tam talk to me."

Tam dropped his head in defeat before he blurted into the phone, "Don't come yo...it's over...just leave while you can...it's not good."

Big Walt removed the phone from his ear and glanced at the number re-checking it not believing it was Tam he was talking to. He sensed a sound of fear in Tam's voice, something the fearless Tam never displayed. "You know that's not gone happen Tam."

"I'm good Walt—I can handle this on my own."

"Yo if you still at the shop I'm coming."

"Don't come just grab the bread and break out...it's my time Walt...I can't escape this but you can."

Big Walt couldn't believe Tam let the Young Assassins get the drop on him. Tam was an original gun clapper compared to these young shooters. How could Tam let them do this Big Walt wondered. Tam was a cold-blooded Killer who played the angel of death many times when he took the lives of others and now he acknowledged his karma and was willing to bite the bullet just to save Big Walt. Tam was willing to suffer for his own Karma and Big Walt's. Big Walt couldn't let Tam go out like that, Tam was too loyal. Black Bull and Gonzalez was the ace in the hole that gave Big Walt his negotiating chips.

"These little bastards." Big Walt thought to himself before he yelled into the phone, "Yo tell them dirty little niggas if they do anything to you I'm gone have Prince killed...yeah they got you but we got Prince so what it's gone be?" Big Walt asked.

Zulu and the Kadari Twins couldn't believe it. Big Walt still had the upper hand. Now they wondered how the hell did Prince got caught slipping. Silence captured everyone's attention as they mentally tuned into each other's thoughts.

"So what it's gone be fellas?" Big Walt yelled thru the speaker phone breaking the silence.

"Give us Prince back and we return yo shadow." Zulu hung up the phone then dialed Cream and Dolla who was still across the street behind the building. Cream and Dolla couldn't believe it and spit out, "This nigga Big Walt win again and stay mad steps ahead of us...what the fuck is we gone do with this dude?"

....

Prince rocked around in the back seat of the Chevy Impala as the corrupt detectives drove him to the east side of the city. Prince couldn't believe it. This wasn't a dream this was a real life nightmare. It was no way he was gonna take the cops to the Young Assassins. The only light Prince could see at the end of this dark tunnel was being away from the rats in hell and then having these cops take him downtown where he would be willing to confess to a few unsolved homicides. He'd rather live in a cage for the rest of his life like a Man who stood up than to live knowing he took his friends down.

"Yo listen y'all," tears began streaming down Prince's face, "I don't want no more trouble with y'all…and I'm not tryna be tough…but I can't take y'all to my friends…I can't…but I can…I can tell y'all about a few---."

"Tell on what?" Black Bull cut Prince short looking into the rear-view mirror at the shook up Prince. "What you gone tell a lie…that's what you gonna tell…a few lies…dudes like you a needle in a haystack…you passed the test."

Prince was so absorbed by the mental, physical, and emotional pain he didn't hear anything Black Bull said but test. "I don't have to take a polygraph test…I'll confess to a couple of shootings and bodies I took part in but I'm not telling on who I was with…please believe me I just want this to be over."

Black Bull and Gonzalez burst out in laughter knowing the fatigue was wearing Prince down. They been on the police force for years and they arrested, brutalized, tortured, and interrogated some of the toughest criminals. The majority of criminals broke down and told on others while some confessed and told lies on others. Only a few withstood the soul breaking pressure that made many Thugs tell just hearing about the torture. The detectives knew from their training and experience that beatings and hours of interrogation mentally exhausted and drained criminals, forcing them to break down and either confess or tell on others due to duress. But when criminals withstood the pressure and kept their dignity and loyalty to silence, honor and respect had to be given from both sides of the law.

"Listen bro," Gonzalez spun around in the passenger seat and leaned towards Prince, "You don't have to confess to anything…your solid and if most of these guys out here on the streets were like you we all would make a lot of money and our jobs would be a lot easier."

"That's right," Black Bull confirmed gripping the steering wheel, "These snitches help us get more arrest but they make our jobs harder because we got more work to do…but what we don't know about we don't give a fuck about…you understand."

"Exactly," Gonzalez added still turned around in his seat facing Prince, "We're all brothers Prince…*somos hermanos* and were gonna go to E. North and finish this."

Prince was so consumed mentally and in his own world he was unresponsive and when he heard *E. North* and *friends* he began trembling. He had no clue to what the future would hold, he just hoped it would be death real soon because he wasn't gonna take them to his friends.

Black Bull whipped the Impala onto Best Street and drove pass an armory where military tanks and trucks sat in front of the armory on display. They then rolled by the white brick face of City Honors high school. Across the street from the Armory and City Honors High School sat a parking lot for the Johnny B. Wiley stadium which was once home to the Buffalo Bills. Now it hosted track and field events and semi-pro football games. The parking lot to the stadium was empty except for a White Land-Cruiser trimmed in gold. Black Bull pulled on side of the Land-Cruiser and Prince couldn't believe his eyes as he watched Big Walt jump out the Land-Cruiser.

"They got Tam." Big Walt leaned on the passenger window of the Impala looking at Gonzalez. Big Walt fearfully avoided eye contact with Prince who was in the back seat on fire biting his lip in anger. "Just get Tam back for me, y'all can do whatever with him," Big Walt nodded his head at Prince after tossing a bag of money onto Gonzalez' lap. "Just get my homie back and I got more money for y'all."

"You fucking piece of shit," Prince yelled at Big Walt who jumped back in his truck and pulled off. "So y'all doing all this for this fucking dude?" Prince barked as they followed behind Big Walt.

"Na listen Prince…even though yo friends almost killed us…we not gone kill you or get y'all asses locked up like Big Walt wanted us to."

"What the fuck is y'all talking about?" Prince inquired wishing he was just dead. This was getting too complicated and too heavy for his 22-year old mind. Black Bull and Gonzalez then explained what was going on.

Since the beginning and way before the A-Squad, Black Bull and Gonzalez been biting big chunks of the cake hustlers on the east side was making. Everyone knew they was dirty and shook down hustlers, but they stepped their game up with Big Walt. Big Walt officially put them on his payroll and he was eating peacefully not worrying about the police since Black Bull and

Gonzalez was his eyes and ears downtown at headquarters narcotics and homicide departments. Even though the Young Assassins were taking all the risk, Black Bull and Gonzalez would make sure Big Walt stayed eating so they could continue taxing him. But with Sun-Z and Hawk from the A-Squad coming home and the Young Assassins dissatisfied with Big Walt and wanting to take over, Big Walt felt like a fat rat trapped in a corner and he acted out of fear. He planned on setting the Young Assassins up and having them locked up since Tam couldn't kill them all. Then he was gonna snitch to the Feds about numerous homicides and drug trafficking that could keep Sun-Z and Hawk incarcerated for life. This was the only way he felt he could keep the throne.

Black Bull and Gonzalez agreed with snatching Prince and taking the bricks from him, and then having him locked up for some bogus charges, but earlier at headquarters when they found out about Big Walt snitching to the Feds about everyone, Black Bull and Gonzalez knew they couldn't trust Big Walt anymore. If Big Walt was turning on his fellow Thugs, then two crooked cops didn't stand a chance and if given the opportunity Big Walt would tell on the cops if need be. That couldn't happen and that's why Prince was still alive and free, because Black Bull and Gonzalez needed thorough Thugs like Prince and the Young Assassins running the show, not weak links like Big Walt.

"So that piece of shit sent y'all to arrest me earlier?" Prince asked feeling his energy of fear transform to rage and vengeance.

"No not exactly...let's just say that's what he wanted but when we found out how he was gonna sell you guys out to the feds...we knew we could no longer do business with him because if you can't stand by your own people...you have loyalty to anyone."

"I'm gone kill this muthafucka with my bare hands." Prince balled up his hand cuffed fists and stomped his feet repeatedly on the floor of the backseat.

....

Cream and Dolla hid themselves between the hair salon and the two-story row house across from New Millennium while Zulu and the Kadari Twins were inside with Tam. The Young Assassins was ready for whatever, but they they weren't ready for what they were about to witness.

The Land-Cruiser rolled in front of New Millennium and stopped its tires. Thru his rear-view mirror, Big Walt observed the Impala parking a few blocks down. Big Walt then cautiously stepped out the truck with his gun in hand eyeing the surroundings and peeping in between the buildings on the avenue. It was quiet and lifeless outside.

Dolla and Cream chirped Terror on the walkie-talkie letting him know that Big Walt was creeping into the store through the front door. Dolla and Cream then slithered across the street as Big Walt stepped through the broken glass door. Big Walt tip-toed over the glass covered floor while softly crunching shards of glass and trying to be silent as he could be.

"Drop it muthafucka." Cream shoved a sawed-off shotgun into Big Walt's back.

"*Fuck*." Big Walt mumbled to himself. He knew if he dropped his gun he had no defense but Black Bull and Gonzalez would be coming thru the door any minute to rescue him, so he dropped his gun anyway.

"*Ku-Ku.*" Dolla alerted sounding like a bird as him and Cream walked Big Walt thru the dark store at gun point.

"*Ku-Ku.*" Killa signaled back flicking on the lights. Zulu and Terror then slid from out the back room with Tam. "Throw them niggas right there," Killa ordered.

"Y'all not gone leave here alive." Big Walt threatened after he was shoved onto the sofa next to Tam.

"Shut the fuck up." Cream smashed the barrel of the shotgun into Big Walt's nose, causing blood to drizzle from his nostrils. "You a fucking snake…you sent niggas to rob Prince for the bricks…you dirty muthafucka."

"Yeah," Dolla then ran behind the counter and snatched a baseball bat. "You thought you was gone have niggas rob Prince for the bricks and then blame us for getting robbed." Dolla banged the bat on Big Walt's knee cap. Big Walt howled in pain clutching his knee.

"Na he ain't send nobody to rob me." Prince limped into the store with Black Bull and Gonzalez and shocked everyone, "He sent them…he a snitch and working with the feds to keep Sun-Z and Hawk locked up and he was tryna get us trapped off." Prince observed everyone eye each other in shock.

"Man yall niggas shut the fuck up believing these cops." Tam blurted while Big Walt sunk his head low feeling the truth of his file deeds come to light.

Prince then snatched the gun from Killa and aimed it at Tam. *"Blam-Blam."* The slugs pierced Tam's face and cranium, slumping his head back onto the head rest of the couch where red jelly like brain fragments splattered.

Big Walt shivered from the blast ringing in his ears and the blood splattered in his face. Prince then leaped onto Big Walt and began ramming his knuckles into Big Walt's face. Pound for pound Prince was smashing Big Walt's facial cranium as his knuckles punctured the flesh and cracked the bone lining his facial structure.

"Get off me." Big Walt screamed while raising his arms in defense between punches. Dolla then stepped in and banged Big Walt on his shin bone with the bat. The combined pain began gnawing at Big Walt's energy and he felt weak. He gave up defending himself feeling his consciousness slowly fade away as Prince continued pounding Big Walt's face.

"I can't believe this nigga a fucking rat," Someone roared. The word rat transformed Prince.

"Muthafucka." The word rat made Prince's mind flash the scene of the rats in the abandoned house, making Prince strike Big Walt with the gun gripped in his right hand. Prince now used both his hands to pulverize Big Walt's face. The sound of chrome and knuckles caving Big Walt's disfigured face in was unbearable to everyone watching except the Twins. At that moment no one knew about the excruciating pain thrashing at Prince's mind and soul. This one day in Prince's life was like a thousand years in a bottomless pit of hell.

"Yo Prince just stop and shoot him." Everyone yelled but Prince heard no one and could see nothing but blood. He completely blacked out.

"Na don't stop." The Kadari Twins smiled with their green and grey eyes gleaming with excitement. They loved this and could bust off a billion sperm cells of pleasure for this. "Keep on Prince…make this coward suffer while he still conscious…shooting dudes is too easy…real killers do it like this…we never knew my boy Prince had it in him like this."

"Hey enough of this sick shit," Black Bull couldn't bear this savagery anymore. "One of y'all kill this piece of shit and get it over with…this shit is un-called for."

"Fuck that y'all kill him…y'all cops and y'all can tell on us anytime…y'all not gone hold this shit over our head." The Young Assassins barked while Prince was still viciously beating Big Walt to a pulp.

"For one Prince wouldn't be here if we wanted to be good cops…and two y'all black asses would be going down for attempted murder on police…yeah that was us y'all tried to kill earlier…now if y'all wanna be bigger than the A-Squad and Big Walt…kill this snitch and let's get down to business."

With that guns were drawn and dozens of slugs were pummeled into Big Walt and Tam's lifeless bodies. Big Walt was gone and the Thugs on the street didn't care to remember him. For the children who were too young to understand the reason for his death, they would miss Big Walt.

CHAPTER 6

Spending years and years in rural upstate New York prisons was harsh on the minds of prisoners locked far from home. Imprisonment was like slavery and brutal on the soul. However, being locked up north in the country could be nurturing to the soul and natural on the senses because the air was cleaner and free from the pollutants of city life. The sky was bright and clear. The green color of the earth was beautiful. And despite being caged in like animals, the natural country environment gave Prisoners a degree of peace and solitude urban city life couldn't offer. Back to the world meant back to the drama.

NyJewel sat behind the wheel with Hawk in the passenger seat while Sun-Z held his wife Iyana in his python sized arms in the back seat. It was a nice day outside in the city and the sun bathed the city with its eminent radiance. For some reason to Sun-Z and Hawk everything appeared gloomy and dark. The buildings and houses had a dull glow. Everything appeared crammed together and ready to crumble. The east side of Buffalo looked like a hurricane swept thru it. Abandoned buildings once housing brand name department stores on avenues were now lifeless tombs where drug addicts and prostitutes dwelled. Nice colorful homes once sheltering families were now dilapidated and battered and others demolished to rubble where little kids had rock fights. The scenery hadn't changed much since they left the streets. What had changed seemed to be the energy. It seemed like death hovered over the east side and no one smiled in this depressed place forgotten by society.

"Would y'all cheer up," NyJewel broke the silence. "Yall free stop looking sad."

"Ain't nobody sad," Hawk let his eyes take in the unfamiliar faces and surroundings, "This shit just look fucked up out here…it look like Bagdad or some shit."

"Word up," Sun-Z added. "It look like dudes in prison doing better than people out here."

"It look the same as it always looked." Iyana replied. "Y'all just been in them mountains too long."

"Right," NyJewel tapped her lips with some gloss while stopped at a streetlight, "This the same place y'all was born and raised so stop acting scary like some strangers."

"You know what's gone make me feel good and at home sis?" Hawk stated letting his eyes undress the skimpy dressed females strolling the strip. NyJewel tilted her head to Hawk for his answer. "One of these nice tenderonis out here…I need to get laid," Hawk moaned feeling his testosterone rise at the sight of the lustful flesh.

"Yeah please get my boy some trim," Sun-Z shot from the backseat laughing, "Because that's all my dude been thinking bout."

"Why is sex all men think about?" Iyana threw in the air.

"When you been locked up as long as we have…looking at black tail, black video illustrated, and flicks…of course a man like me gone only want the real thing all day everyday…I deserve it," Hawk stated lighting up a Newport.

"Hawk yo ass probably can't even handle one of these thick young dames," Sun-Z stated amazed at the development of the bodies gracing the young ladies.

"Watch your mouth and your eyes Sir," Iyana playfully slapped Sun-Z on his shoulder.

"Well y'all can worry about breaking y'all virginity again later on," NyJewel pulled up at B.O.S.S. (Buffalo Original Steakhouse and Seafood). "Why don't y'all tear up this delicious food like y'all did those porno magazines and Vaseline in prison?"

"*Ewww*, Ny you ain't right girl." Iyana busted out laughing for the first time in a long time.

"Damn sis you still act like everybody mother," Sun-Z and Hawk smiled feeling the pleasure of freedom.

....

Destiny stormed thru the apartment recklessly pacing thru every room cursing, fussing, and yelling at the walls while Zulu showered.

"You not going to that damn stripper party Zulu." Destiny ranted bursting into the bathroom.

"Baby girl why you bugging?" Zulu asked lathering soap on his body. "I'm going to see Sun-Z and Hawk...I'm not going for the strippers."

"Well I'm going with you then." Destiny seductively gazed at the soap suds bubbling on Zulu's fudge chocolate physique glistening under the water. The strippers at the welcome home party wasn't going to taste her whipped cream brownie she thought to herself.

"Baby girl we got business to discuss."

"How y'all discussing business at a party with a bunch of nasty ass strippers?"

"Come on Love," Zulu began rinsing the soap off his body. "Why you don't trust me."

"It's not you I don't trust."

"Come on you mad insecure always worrying about some other females...I love you and you the woman who I'm with." Zulu rinsed the soap from his eyes. "You ain't got nothing to worry about."

"Yes I do," Destiny slid off her silk gown then stepped into the raining shower water. "Whenever you around bitches who ain't got a man like this at home...I'm gone worry about mines." Destiny began softly kissing Zulu's wet lips. As their tongues wrestled under the shower, Zulu's fudge colored body and Destiny's peaches and cream flavored skin looked so edible together.

Zulu held her head while they kissed, then he slid his hands down her slippery curves before gripping her plump butt. He squeezed her body close to his. Destiny's mouth was watering for Zulu and it wasn't from the shower water drizzling into their mouths as they kissed. Zulu pressed her body close to his and Destiny could feel his erect penis grinding on her clit while he gripped her butt-cheeks and spread them, letting the steamy shower water drizzle down the crevice of her butt. It opened her flood gates of creamy love.

Destiny then slid her tongue out of Zulu's mouth, slithered it down his neck making him tingle as the steamy water beat on their naked bodies. She then glided her tongue down and across the wet surface of his chest. She took her hands and placed them on both of his shoulders as she began to kneel. The water soaked her loose hanging curly black hair, straitening it as she held onto his shoulders while lowering herself. She then let her hands discover the smoothness of his wet body. Her tongue swam thru the waters trickling down his chest and stomach before his erect penis pounced into her face. With her chinky eyes closed, she clutched it with both hands adoring the snake like veins racing thru his long john silver. She began to softly kiss it before inserting it between her lips.

"Oh shit...hell yeah." Zulu tilted his head back into the water as Destiny slurped away. With her mouth she passionately stroked his penis while gripping his lower back with both hands. Zulu groaned in ecstasy as he rammed his love stick in and out of her mouth. She moaned in enjoyment as his love stick massaged her throat. "Oh...oh...oh bay I'm cumming." Zulu's legs began buckling. *"Stop...stop...stopppp."*

Destiny sucked up all the future seeds he had in him when he exploded in her mouth. No stripper would have a chance of receiving any of his seeds tonight she figured as she spit the glob of sperm cells and saliva into the draining water.

"You love it baby." Destiny asked letting the shower water rinse her mouth before grabbing a toothbrush.

"Hell yeah." Zulu wobbled out the shower. "You make me feel so good love...the only thing that ever matter is getting money...fuck all that other shit my love."

"Yeah...just like fuck going to that stripper party tonight...you can handle business another time...stay home baby." Destiny spoke softly scrubbing her tongue with a toothbrush.

"Huh...what?" Zulu's eyes opened wide and his mouth hung. "Here we go again."

....

The roaring sounds of *Ja-Rule* blasted out the booming speakers inside of Natasha's Cabaret. Yellow and white strobe lights flashed on the plexiglass stage where topless strippers erotically swung their glossy toned legs around the poles on stage. Waitresses in mini-skirts skated thru the club carrying trays cluttered with liquor, beer, and saucy Buffalo Wings. Men and Women sat at tables tipping waitresses, throwing money on stage while others enjoyed lap dances.

The welcome home celebration for Sun-Z and Hawk was invitation only and the club was packed. Everyone was there. It took Zulu some serious sensual seduction for Destiny to let him go without her. After Destiny blessed him with her shower loving, it took Zulu about twenty minutes of letting his tongue massage her loving, then it took him another half an hour of ramming her vaginal walls until he exploded inside her and she passed out. After showering a second time then dressing, Zulu was finally ready to attend the welcome home celebration for the O.G.'s of the hood.

Zulu stepped thru the doors of the club feeling *"Fresh dressed like a million bucks."* He was decked from head to toe in a hunter green and gold valor ENYCE outfit with cheddar and broccoli Timberlands. The flashing lights swirling around the dimly lit club caught the radiance of the jewels gracing his neck and fingers as he shook hands with the two linebacker sized bouncers at the door. All eyes focused on Zulu like he was the one everyone waited on.

"It's been a minute lil bro." Sun-Z stepped to Zulu and squeezed the life out of him with a brotherly embrace. "Damn, look at you baby boy." Sun-Z gazed up and down Zulu who was no longer the shorty Sun-Z had raised. "You a man now sun...a true G."

"Don't let this nigga fool you Sun-Z," Cream yelled over the blasting music while standing next to Sun-Z and Zulu. "This nigga a sucka when it come to Destiny and Destiny the man in the relationship."

"Fuck you too dick." Zulu smirked slapping Cream's hand. With admiration, Zulu then scoped out Cream's heavy Rolex chain with a bull-dog charm draping his neck. "But fuck what you talking bout Cream...let's get this party started...I'm ready to get saucy and celebrate, yall home."

"Hell yeah we back sun...let's have a few drinks then get down to business." Sun-Z threw his arms around Zulu and Cream heading to the bar.

"Na big bra we not doing the bar…this you and Hawk party so yall get King treatment." Zulu stopped in his tracks.

"Hell yeah big bro…strait V.I.P status with the bottle service…let's get it popping." Cream added leading Zulu and Sun-Z over to the V.I.P section a level up.

"No question baby boy…I just prefer business before pleasure… this party shit could have waited." Sun-Z stated as they plopped down into the cushioned V.I.P booth in the upper corner where they could observe the whole club.

"Relax big bro." Cream waved a young waitress over once they were seated. Cream then ordered bottles of Dom Perion, Hennessy, and Thug Passion Alize. "You been gone for a minute get yo nuts out the sand and enjoy the party…plus we caked up so yall aint gotta jump right back into the streets…we got a bankroll for yall so yall good…business can wait…as a matter of fact," Cream motioned across the circular table to Zulu and asked, "You brought that right?"

"You already know." Zulu reached into his pocket and pulled out a thick bank envelope and tossed it to Sun-Z.

"Damn." Sun-Z received the envelope and fiddled thru the crisp hundred dollar bills wrapped in a $ 10,000 bank band. "Ok…me and Hawk can split this…good looking."

"Na na…that's yours," Zulu pulled out another envelope, "This Hawk's right here."

"And it's more where that came from too," Cream stated as the waitress returned with their bottles. "Thank that uh--," Cream glanced at the waitress who popped the Champagne. Cream then whispered to Sun-Z, "Thank that fat rapping nigga…feel me."

"What's understood aint gotta be verbally manifested…mind detect mind…but fuck that snitch," Sun-Z held his glass up for Zulu who was pouring shots for everyone.

"Yo where the fuck Hawk at around here?" Zulu asked once he finished filling their glasses.

"Where you think Hawk at?" Sun-Z gestured towards the section way on the other side in the far corner where two strippers clobbered Hawk. Hawk was sprawled out on a table stripped down to his tank top and boxers while he suffocated his face in the thong laced butt of a dancing stripper. Another stripper grinded on Hawk while the Kadari Twins stood on side of the table raining dollars on the two strippers bouncing on Hawk.

"Salute." Zulu, Cream, and Sun-Z threw their glasses in the air and sipped.

"Yo I'm honored to be here with yall…every last one of yall." Sun-Z stated after smoothly sipping his champagne and savoring the taste. "Yall don't know how much I thank yall…me and Hawk…that was a Supreme Power move yall made happen for us…if it wasn't for yall we would be under the jail…I know yall look at me like the big brother, but yall Supreme in my eyes and I owe my existence to yall…word up…Salute once again."

"Come on big bro stop it…you don't owe us shit," Zulu was chasing his champagne with Hennessy.

"Hell yeah…yall held us down when we was little niggas," Cream shouted rolling a blunt stuffed with some chocolate Kush after he guzzled his glass of champagne. "And yall showed us the game…yall the reason we move like the unit we is…we owe our existence to yall."

"Word up big bro…if you wanna return any favors…go have fun and let one of these sexy ass strippers we spent all this money on get rid of them blue balls you got," Zulu stated.

"No question my G's," Sun-Z guzzled a double shot of Henny feeling the spirit stimulate him. They then dipped out of V.I.P and got involved with the action.

Fat Boy Dolla was the pleasure God who took everyone in the party to a higher dimension of mental ecstasy as he sat up at a round table in a V.I.P booth all by himself.

Cluttering the table he sat at was a bucket of blazing hot Buffalo wings, a few dragon stout beers and a stack of singles several inches high. And sitting by his side in the booth was a book-bag filled with lime green weed, bright colored ecstasy pills, and pearly white cocaine bagged up in half grams and whole grams.

Strippers, party goers, and even employees of the club raced back and forth to Dolla's booth chasing that flight of euphoria thru the narcotics he supplied. Dolla lived up to his attribute. No matter the time and place, he was all about a Dolla.

Sun-Z spotted Prince sitting front row by the stage clutching a liter of Grey Goose. His bloodshot red eyes spoke of his intoxication but his emotion was blank. Ever since the ordeal with Black Bull and Gonzalez, and Big Walt's death, Prince started becoming withdrawn and absorbed into his own world but tonight he had to have some fun to block out the agony and pain of his tormented soul.

"Big bro what's good?" Prince acknowledged Sun-Z drop into the seat next to him but kept his eyes glued to the stage. "So what's yo bench press?" Prince asked with his expressionless face after he glanced at the vein busting arms bulging out of Sun-Z's Lacoste Polo shirt.

"Like 415." Sun-Z boasted eyeing the two strippers working it on stage. "I could go heavier with a spot...but ain't nobody got the power to hold that kind of weight to spot me." Sun-Z indirectly challenged Prince winking his eye at him with a smile.

"Yeah you think so huh?" Prince slightly smiled with a competing tone before yelling to one of the strippers on the stage. "Come here sexy." Prince waved the 5'4" 160lb stripper over to him as he flashed a wad a singles. She crawled over to Prince lusting his strong muscular frame.

"Yes Daddy." The stripper climbed on top of Prince and began massaging his muscle swollen arms. "I love to give you a lap dance."

"Na I don't want no lap dance sexy."

"So what you want daddy?" The stripper asked grinding on Prince. They were face to face inhaling each others breath. Prince took a swig of his bottle of Grey Goose, sat it on the floor, then slipped his hands under her thighs then onto her juicy rump. He gripped both her butt cheeks with both hands then lifted her up in the air as she spread her legs in a split position. He lifted her up and down, catching a sweet whiff of the aromatic scent of Victoria Secret body spray on her vagina.

"How much you weigh sweetheart?" Prince asked while lifting her up and down and ice grilling Sun-Z out the corner of his eye.

"I don't know," the stripper snickered at Prince and felt awkward and embarrassed as he lifted her, "You not supposed to ask a female her weight and put me down."

"Come on lil bro she light weight." Sun-Z then waved the amazon looking stripper over, whispered in her ear and began doing the same thing as Prince.

Hawk was on a coke wave high as the clouds. He was the only person in the party who could get Dolla to move from his V.I.P booth. Dolla bounced over to Hawk who was getting a lap dance by two strippers and Hawk was still in his underclothes. Dolla slid over to Hawk while shaking his head at Sun-Z and Prince. Dolla was confused.

"Yo Hawk," Dolla was handing Hawk some coke, "Is that what prison do to some niggas?"

"What the fuck is you talking about Dolla?" Hawk asked despising the little flaky chunk of powder.

"Do prison make niggas wanna lift the bitches like they weights…they supposed to be licking the bitches not lifting them."

"Man I don't know about them niggas because I'm licking these hoes and living the life with em…but what the fuck is this?" Hawk ungratefully tossed the coke back to Dolla. "What the hell I'm gone do with that little shit…give me an 8 ball (3.5 grams) nigga…I'm the Hawk…and me and these hoes gone fly high into the sky where the Hawk gone pulverize them thighs…give me a 8 ball nigga."

"You a crazy nigga Hawk," Dolla tossed Hawk a chunk of coke weighing about 5 grams before skating back to his post up in V.I.P.

The celebration was live and the 15 strippers had the crowd sensuously aroused and entertained but the night couldn't end without *"The Baddest Bitch"* putting on her exotic performance. She clacked her high heels on the stage with long silky legs. She was tall but not as tall without the heels. Her body was slender but plump in the right places. She had the body of a model and perfect coordinates for a stripper. She had pumpkin pie skin tone and crinkly black hair with matching cat eyes. She was gorgeous. Her name was Desiree, but on stage she was Desire. And the way she seductively swung her body around the pole, strétched her plump petite body like a pretzel, and erotically bounced around with a dildo inside her loving made men and several women desire her. She was Zulu's girlfriend Destiny's sister. They reflected each other face wise but not body and character wise.

Being that Hawk desired having the instant gratification of the insatiable pleasure of beautiful women, he was blessed with the pleasure of Desire's arousing sex appeal. While everyone crept to private rooms to get their sexual appetites satisfied or got lap dances, Zulu sat alone at a table near the stage watching Hawk and Desire entertain each other.

"So all this ass floating around in here and you sitting here looking lost," NyJewel staggered over to Zulu's table talking with a slur of intoxication.

"What the fuck." Zulu let his eyes roll up and down NyJewel's well-proportioned body blessing her silk skirt with the slit sides revealing her thick thighs. "I'm just chilling Ny…this shit don't turn me on," Zulu responded feeling his ignition turn on his sex drive while gazing up and down NyJewel.

"Nigga please." NyJewel stated disbelievingly as she fell into the seat next to Zulu. She then crossed her legs up on the table. Her shiny brown thighs were in Zulu's face looking like tender meat needing to be eaten with their juicy form. "Talking bout you not turned on…you a man that get horny like the rest…oh I guess you just smart because yo girlfriend sister here."

"What." Zulu screwed his face at NyJewel while struggling hard not to gaze upon her thick thighs let alone her voluptuous cleavage sitting under the skimpy straps of her dress. "For one I done fucked most of Desire's friends up in here…and two I do what the fuck I want."

"Really."

"Of course," Zulu poured himself a shot.

"Well I wanna see you get a lap dance."

"Lap dances don't turn me on and I already had these hoes…they don't turn me on."

"Is that so," NyJewel snatched Zulu's glass of liquor, threw it back, and seductively asked, "Well who turn you on?"

"Yo come on stop playing with me Ny." Zulu stated feeling his testosterone go from 0 to 100 instantly.

"I'm not playing with you." NyJewel jumped on Zulu's lap. Zulu could smell the sweet wine reeking in her moist mouth as she whispered in Zulu's ear. "I had a dream about us Zulu."

"Oooooh." Zulu felt a tingle shoot down his spine as her breath filtered his ear. "Tell me about it."

"How bout I show you." NyJewel grinded on Zulu.

"Come on let's break out now," Zulu let his hand caress the curvature of her waist before he gripped her soft and tender ass.

"Damn sis you done became a cougar." Hawk yelled from the stage as him and Desire sat cuddled up sniffing the coco.

"And it's about time Zulu." Desire stuffed Hawk's face between her small perky breast. "Sow your royal oats baby boy."

"Oh my God…" NyJewel came to her senses realizing the liquor took control of the moment. She jumped up feeling embarrassed.

"Yo Ny what's wrong, what you doing?" Zulu sprung to his feet and embraced her. "Come here."

"No Zulu I'm sorry." NyJewel snatched her purse from off the table and stormed to the door looking back at Zulu before leaving the club.

"That fucking broad get on my nerves," Zulu growled watching NyJewel's jumbo booty bounce through the door. "She always playing games like a fucking kid."

"Yo my bad lil bro," Hawk shot at the evil looking Zulu. "At least she gave you a lap dance."

"Yo fuck all dat shit…it's all about the money we bout to make…fuck these hoes…" Zulu poured another shot and raised his glass to Hawk who was still entwined with Desire on stage.

"Salute...let's get this money...party time over."

. . . .

"Click...click...click...click." Were the sounds of the stove igniting before the ether blue flames lit up the eye on the stove. A huge pot which been around since great grandma days was then filled with water and placed on the flaming stove.

"How many grams y'all want me to chef up?" Hawk asked tearing open a box of baking soda. He was told 500 grams by the Young Assassins. "Ok...I'm gone turn a half a key into a whole key."

"What...How the hell you gone do that?" The Young Assassins asked unbelievably while seated at the kitchen table.

"Just sit back and watch." Hawk dumped the whole box of baking soda into a huge Pyrex bowl. "Just strap on y'all seatbelts while the Hawk make the work fly high and do wonders." Hawk slid to the sink and let the faucet splash just enough water into the Pyrex bowl to liquefy the baking soda. He then placed the Pyrex on the stove and dumped the Ziploc bag full of the crystalline powder into the Pyrex bowl and began whipping the liquid soda and powder together like it was mashed potatoes.

"Whew." Hawk's nostrils inhaled the vaporous odor of the raw cocaine as he whipped the thick clump until it oiled. "Where that fat possum ass rat was plugging this shit from?" Hawk asked referring to the deceased Big Walt while fanning the fumes from his face.

"Yo we don't even know...but we know we gone need a new connect before we knock the rest of these bricks off."

"Don't even worry." Hawk assured taking the pot off the stove and stepping over to the sink. "Sun-Z got us a plug that's gone get us right...Supreme hustler status."

After using a blender to stir the light oil into a vanilla pudding looking glob, Hawk filled the sink with ice cubes and set the Pyrex bowl in the ice. After twenty minutes or so had passed, Hawk spread newspaper on the kitchen table, sat the Pyrex bowl on top of the newspaper but upside down, softly tapped the bottom of the pot knocking the hard round cake out the pot onto the table.

"*Damnnn.*" Everyone was amazed as the hard round cake banged the table.

"Hard as a brick right!" Hawk then placed the cake on the scale. The digital scale read 1, 027 grams. "This what you call a one on one." Hawk then placed the cake in a large Ziploc bag and wrapped it in newspaper. He then began smashing it with a hammer before unwrapping it and taking out a nice size chunk of the glistening white rock. He yelled into the living room and within seconds a man who looked like *LL Cool J* stepped in the kitchen rocking a blue suede Adidas suit on top of white and blue shell toe Adidas with a blue brim Kangol resting on top of his head.

This was Old School Al. He was still stuck in the B-Boy days of his youth and while everyone was rocking Pelle Pelle and Rocawear, he stayed true to the gear of his B-Boy days and sported Adidas, Nike, and Puma suits. He was no longer the hustling B-Boy who flaunted his drug money by rocking dookie ropes and four finger rings with gold teeth, now he was just living for a blast of the rock. And even though he was a crackhead, he was still Sun-Z and Hawk's brother, friend, and conglomerate from the A-Squad.

"So you ready for me to rock the bells homeboy?" Old School Al asked doing the cabbage patch dance as Hawk gave him the boulder. Old School Al then whipped out his pipe and began to torch it right in the kitchen in front of everyone.

"Yo Al." Hawk stopped him. "Take that shit in the bathroom yo…show some respect…don't nobody wanna smell that shit."

"Word up yo." Everyone agreed.

"My bad homeboys." Old School Al slid to the bathroom and shut the door. He was happy just to be given the job as a tester for the new cooked crack. About three minutes had passed and Old School Al hadn't come out yet. Hawk then worriedly yelled his name, hoping Old School Al didn't try smoking the whole rock and bust his heart open.

"*Homeboooy.*" Old School Al swung the bathroom door open, spun around like he was Michael Jackson in thriller then did the wave from arm to arm. *"Rock the bells homeboy...yeah homeboy...this shit the flava...uh oh."* Old School Al's mouth began twitching and he began biting his lips annoyingly. *"This that butter...my m-m-mouth nummmb...hell yeah homeboys...y'all got flava."*

"What the fuck you done cooked up and gave this damn fool?" Everyone laughed but couldn't believe how Hawk took 500 grams and turned it to over 1,000 grams and it still had its potency. The Young Assassins would cook their coke into free base form or what they called strait drop. If there were any additives in the cocaine they would cook it out. 500 grams would be cooked and come off the stove probably weighing 550 grams. What Hawk just demonstrated was like magic. Hawk even showed them how to take the raw cocaine and mix it with cocaine derivatives like procaine and lidocaine. Hawk would take 125 grams of coke and add 62 grams of the cut and they would serve it to the coke sniffers. The sniffers loved it and said the coke wave was a 10 strait off the Richter scale. It was time to blow. Sun-Z and Hawk couldn't have come home at a better time. It was time to elevate their level of hustling to a higher level of supremacy in the game. They were no longer scrambling for shorts and making big money for someone else. They were bosses working for their own benefit. And now they were working with Sun-Z and Hawk who blessed them with a higher hustling philosophy that gave them a great advantage in the game.

With Hawk's magical knowledge of cocaine chemistry, they were not only flooding their E. North street neighborhood, but now they were able to flood hustlers all throughout the city with larger amounts. This was perfect timing. It was the year 2000, the New Millennium. Society was technologically changing and Man's life was progressing on a level great as the stars. The Young Assassins were progressing and changing for the better as well. They were now aligned with Sun-Z and Hawk and they became a force moving thru the city. It was all about money and power, but what is power without respect.

CHAPTER 7

It was the first of the month, and children who were smart enough and old enough rushed to stores to purchase food for the house before their drug addicted parents spent them welfare checks on that white demon; crack. Throughout every ghetto in America this was the activity for the first few days of every month. Hustlers filled their pockets with dead presidents the government dished out while some welfare recipients filled their lungs and brains with the powerful blasts of the rock. The drug flow around E. North was like always but more fast paced since the Young Assassins had more work and was giving out more in quantity for the same price to the feigns.

Zulu started his day early on a block called Planet Rock. This block had history beginning with the A-Squad and this is where the first crack houses in E. North were operated back in the 80's. There were more abandoned houses and vacant lots lining this block than there were occupied houses. In position to handle business, Zulu posted up at the mouth of a walkway between two houses on Planet Rock. One house had occupants who lived inside and the other house was abandoned but occupied by a couple of early morning crack heads starting their day with the activating blast of the crack. The sun was just opening its orange eye as the darkness evaporated when a lady crept up on Zulu from out of nowhere.

"The early bird gets the worm huh baby?" Candy greeted Zulu moving fast as lightning into the walkway.

"You damn right Candy!" Zulu focused on the bright lipstick splashed on her fat lips. She had on more make-up than a clown. "Why you moving so fast?"

"My tricks here from Canada, and please baby I know you don't like selling me eight balls but come on baby I'm spending," Candy dipped her little hands into her one-piece spaghetti strap dress and whipped out three crisp hundred dollar bills and three twenties smelling like her cheap perfume and new money. "Lemme get three baby."

"I got you Candy." Zulu snatched the money then dipped down the walkway between the houses. He slid to the back of the abandoned house and removed a piece of the vinyl siding from the house and retrieved the three eight balls. He slid out the yard and told Candy as he handed her the eight balls, "Let's gets this day started."

"You know it baby." Candy ripped open one of the eight balls and broke a piece off. She then grabbed the pipe from her purse, threw the rock in it and blasted off. Her eyes enlarged like golf balls. "Umm huh baby...I'm gone get you rich today nigga."

"And you know I got you...you the only smoker I sell eight balls to...so let's make it happen."

"See you in a minute baby." Candy sprinted away on her pretzel sized legs heading up the block to sexually satisfy one of her customers.

The morning rolled in slow with a few stragglers copping ten and twenty dollar rocks. With his stomach grumbling and feeling a little hungry, Zulu became furious when two crackheads approached him with thirteen dollars and a toaster.

"What the fuck I'm gonna do with a toaster out here...did y'all muthafuckas cash y'all checks yet?"

"Yeah we spent it on Moselle Street last night because you wasn't out here." The two feigns gave the wrong response.

"Get the fuck out my face." Zulu barked whipping out his cell phone and dialing Destiny to bring him some breakfast. As soon as Zulu hung up with Destiny a red Porsche swerved over to the curb where Zulu stood.

"Hey sweetie!" an attractive lady softly chanted from the driver seat of the Porsche.

"You must be lost?" Zulu slowly stepped to the passenger window inhaling the *Carolina Hererra* perfume emanating off her sun-tanned skin tone.

"*Nooooo*." She smiled flaunting her pearly white teeth. "A friend of mines told me to come here."

"For what?" Zulu asked letting his eyes follow her auburn striped hair dangling on her melon sized breasts.

"I need an 8 ball of coke."

"Huh…what?" Zulu shot a confused look like he was dumb. "It's a pool hall like two blocks down where they play 8 ball and its soda pop machines that might got Pepsi and Coke up in there." Zulu sarcastically directed her with suspicion in his tone.

"Aww come on," the lady whined while flashing her money.

"I don't know what you talking about miss." Zulu swiftly eased back onto the sidewalk looking up and down the block. "As a matter of fact you need to break out before someone try to rob you for your car."

"Well I'll take my money elsewhere," the lady murked off angrily.

"Go ahead you fucking cop." Zulu slid back into the walkway, dropped onto a milk crate and observed the block. The morning rush was slow like the sun travelling across the eastern horizon. After Destiny brought Zulu his breakfast, Zulu displeasingly dug his fork into his Styrofoam tray filled with salmon patties, grits with cheese, scrambled eggs and jelly toast. He wondered why the morning flow was so slow. It was now afternoon and his digits hadn't increased much. Zulu then pulled out his cell phone and hit the rest of the crew up. When he dialed everyone, this is he what he heard.

"Yo Zulu I gotta call you back it's bleeding with no band aids bro." Dolla answered and hung up.

Zulu then dialed Cream. "Yo Zulu hold on yo…what y'all want…yo hold hold…yo Zulu I gotta get off this line this shit getting too hectic with all these buddies surrounding me…I hit you in a minute."

Prince was the next one Zulu dialed. Prince answered with a dry tone of voice. "What you want Zulu?"

"Damn yo I'm checking up on you seeing how you doing on that side?"

Prince got hyper yelling, "Zulu I can finally take a fucking break and eat my pizza and wings from High Spot and you interrupting me…I ain't been able to sit down since last night and you calling me like you my grandmother checking up on me…I talk to you in a minute Zulu."

"What the fuck." Zulu mumbled upon hearing Prince click on him.

When Zulu called the Kadari Twins Terror answered the phone while yelling at the crack feigns, "Yo yall gotta back the fuck up and form a line or yall not getting served…no no…everyone get in line the order yall came or we taking yall money and yall not getting served," Terror then spoke into the phone, "Zulu what it do yo?"

"Ain't shit doing on the Planet…ain't nothing coming thru here…what the fuck going on?"

"Yo don't even worry yo we sending some of these fools over to the Planet because they bum-rushing us yo."

"Damn good looking yo."

The Kadari Twins sent a flock of feigns to Zulu's block and they swarmed Zulu with "I got 60, 30, 15, 40, 75, 20, and even I got 7 dollars." This went on for the next hour or so thanks to the Kadari Twins. This was only a minor increase for Zulu's pockets compared to everyone else's flow.

It was around 4'oclock and Zulu was just finishing his morning package while everyone else was on their third and fourth packages. *"Something not right…I know all the feigns on this side of the hood didn't go to rehab."* Zulu thought out loud to himself hearing his cell phone ringing inside his car.

"What the hell you want NyJewel?" Zulu answered his cell phone sitting halfway out of his car. He was still fish grease hot with NyJewel for playing with him at the welcome home party not to mention this slow first of the month.

"Wow, why you so rude Zulu?"

"Wow…why the fuck you play so many games NyJewel? You act like a little girl."

"You still mad Zulu? I was drunk and got a little beside myself. I hope you understand."

"Yo who give a fuck…what the fuck you want…and I hope it's not about rent…because if it is you not getting shit right now because it's slow as fuck…and if you got a problem I go rent somewhere else."

"Damn." NyJewel heard herself say. Zulu never treated her so cold. Even if NyJewel was wrong and a Man had the balls to tell her she was wrong would diss a woman as lovely as NyJewel. *"Umm um um Zulu…*you must really want me if I get to you like that."

"No I want some fucking money."

"Well that's why I was calling you…my girlfriend came through there to see you earlier and you dissed her." Zulu asked who was her girlfriend. "The lady in the Porsche…that's my girl I went to Buff-State with…she good peoples and she married to one of the Buffalo Bills. They love partying."

"Ok tell her to come back through here."

"Only if you apologize for yelling at me." NyJewel demanded so sweet and softly.

"You know what NyJewel," Zulu bit his lips thoughtfully. NyJewel, like many other women knew how to seduce a man and grip him by the balls and play with his mental. Zulu felt himself falling into her submission. "I'm—I'm—so--." Zulu then remembered the words of a Pimp ring in his head.

"You make her submit to you and then you show her some love…but as long as she rebellious and don't follow protocol…kick her to the curb and show her it's yo world…if she wanna live in it she better act like it."

"Zulu is you still on the phone." NyJewel broke the silence. *"Zuluuu."*

Zulu smiled seeing he was getting to her. He hung up the phone telling himself he wasn't submitting to NyJewel or no other woman. NyJewel called back several times but he just ignored her. His focus was money and he wondered what was going on with this first of the month flow. He would soon find out.

"Homeboy." Old School Al came thru Planet Rock styling in his red and white shell toe Adidas. "How you caking it on this first of the month homeboy?"

"Mannnn." Zulu stressed his words as he stood up out his car and stood toe to toe with Old School Al in the street. "It been slow all day…I don't know what the fuck going on…but what's good with you though? What you need? You know I'm gone bless you since it's slow."

"Zulu." Old School Al shot Zulu a surprising glare. "I don't get high no more." Old School Al poked his chest out smiling before he reached into the pockets of his Adidas pants and flashed a bankroll with a gold money clip. "I'm getting back on my feet homeboy…it's back to the money now… Sun-Z and Hawk home…I gotta get right and get in place…no more rocking the bells homeboy."

"I hear that shit." Zulu felt happy for Old School Al's recovery but Zulu just became more depressed. Zulu then dragged his feet over to the milk crate thinking how everyone was doing numbers this first of the month. Even the rehabilitated Old School Al was adding on.

"Man I been on the block all day Old School and I barely made a gee (thousand dollars)."

"Man Zulu I'm all around the hood and the city…I used to get high so I know where to go and who to see…but check it homeboy," Old School Al began counting out some money. "I wanna cop two ounces from you."

"Hell yeah I got you." Zulu spit in excitement sprinting into the backyard to hit his stash. After retrieving 16 eight balls from out the stash he called Old School Al in between the houses where they made the transaction.

"Yo good looking homeboy…you know I'm bringing all my money to you…I aint fucking with nobody else." Old School told Zulu while throwing the eight balls in a paper bag then stuffing them in his drawers before they slid back out onto the street. "Word Zulu…you the only one who gone get my money, fuck these other niggas."

Zulu was happy Old School Al would re-up with him but Zulu was puzzled and didn't understand. "You supposed to keep it all in the fam…but what you mean fuck niggas…you got problems with anybody."

"Yo homeboys Zulu…the Young Assassins…they acting real funny yo…they on some hating shit…they not happy to see me getting money…they rather see me out here rocking the bells," Old School Al stated disappointedly shaking his head while peering into Zulu's face.

"Yo hold on what the fuck is you talking bout?" Zulu flailed his hands angrily like it was about to go down.

"Aw man come on now…I hope Zulu aint gone flip on me too." Old School Al began to whimper and raised his hands for Zulu to calm down. Ever since Sun-Z and Hawk been home, Old School Al dug deep into his soul and found his will power to kill that temptation for the blast of the crack. He didn't wanna settle for being the tester who was gonna smoke the crack. Old School Al

said it was time to bring the old school glory days back and it was time for him to get money and shine with his old school crimes. He'd rather sell the crack instead of smoking it. Old School Al was moving thru E. North like a thief in the night taking all the money in the hood. Since he used to get high with most of the feigns in the hood, he knew where all the smoke spots were in the hood. Old School Al didn't have to sit on a block and wait for the feigns to come to him, he went to the money. With his will power at 360, he had no problem sitting around feigns while they got high because he was only around them to get their money. He was all around the city capitalizing with this strategy. And on this first of the month when he hit E. North, he attempted to move like a Jew and continue colonizing the hood. That wasn't happening today he would learn.

When he slid thru Cream and Dolla's side of the hood, they told Old School Al that he lost his stripes from the 80's and early 90's and he was still a crackhead trying to be a hustler and he was only gonna end up smoking his own product.

Old School Al then found himself sliding thru the grounds Prince had an iron fist on. Prince told him, *"In this ocean, I'm the only shark eating fish around here."* And if Old School Al had a problem, he could test Prince's knuckle game.

Old School Al did his best to avoid the Kadari Twins, but as fate would have it, he bumped into them on the Avenue. The Kadari Twins stepped to Old School Al and before he could even say a word they warned him, *"If we catch you in any of the yards on or near the block and you tryna steal a stash with yo crackhead ass we gone slump you there and leave you for the rats...and if you even dare stealing any of our licks you not gone live to spend the money."*

Old School Al couldn't believe it. It was him and the A-Squad who started the first gates in the hood. He was there riding shotgun when the A-Squad had gun battles on the streets of E. North. When the Young Assassins was kids stealing money from the collection plates in church Old School Al made bankrolls in the streets.

"I can't believe this shit Zulu," Old School Al shook his head disbelievingly. "Yo friends just cold dissed me though...like I ain't even from around here…then they judging me because I used to get high…you know what it's cool though because I'm gone show everyone…watch…I did it once and I'm gone do it again," Old School Al looked so deep into Zulu's face it was like he seen through Zulu. "Watch how I get this money Zulu."

"Hell yeah I wanna see you getting money…and I'm gone holla at them boys…even though you got high you still like a big bro and yall paved the way for us in the hood."

"I ain't stressing this shit Zulu…I can go all over the city and hustle…this shit aint stopping my flow even though it's fucked up niggas in my hood on shit and don't want nobody getting money but them." Old School Al would soon learn that was the deadly truth. "No matter what you my homeboy Zulu and I fucks with you…and like I said I'm gone re-up with you." Old School Al stated shaking Zulu's hand as they both eyed the red Porsche pulling up. "Watch Zulu…give me a year or two and I'm gone be pushing something exotic just like that…watch…I'm gone show these suckas…Peace out Home boy." Old School Al skated to his girlfriend's Honda Accord and peeled out.

Zulu slid over to the Porsche feeling a motivation he hadn't felt all day. "What's up miss?"

"Hey sweety…so were gonna try this again." The lady ordered Zulu pulling her money out of a leopard colored wallet. "I need an 8 ball of powder…raw and uncut sweety."

Zulu told her no problem before he disappeared and returned within two minutes. "This so raw they call it that nosebleed." Zulu stated leaning on the passenger door then handing her the powder.

"Well I'm about to find out sweety." The lady untied the bag and dug her long air brushed nail into the pearly white flakes. She crushed up the flakes before she sniffed some off her fingernail. She glanced in her mirror while dabbing her nose with a tissue. "Umm…its strong…give me another one," she told Zulu feeling the cocaine drizzling down her throat.

"For sure," Zulu told her. She would turn out to be a good customer who bought 8 balls of coke like she bought shoes at the McKinley Mall.

It was almost nightfall, a little past 8'oclock, and Zulu was starving so he decided to take a break and go onto the avenue to grab some grub. Thus far, Zulu's digits did some nice multiplying due to Old School Al, the lady in the Porsche, and Candy who came thru to see Zulu more than once. But according to the usual first of the month flow, Zulu knew his pockets weren't holding what they should be.

Zulu pulled up in front of Uncle Johnny's steakhouse peeping two young teenagers in front of the Red Sea Deli which sat next to the steakhouse. The two young teenagers were in front of the deli slanging weed like they were selling candy bars for their high school charity.

"Yo Lil Flip go grab a Dutch and roll me up a dub (20) of that Northern Lights yall got," Zulu shouted to one of the young teenagers as he jumped out his car and slid into Uncle Johnny's to place his order.

"Got you big bro." Lil Flip responded heading into the store to snatch a Dutch.

About two minutes later Zulu stepped out the steakhouse and posted up in front of the deli with Lil Flip and his man Crumbs. "So what's good with yall lil niggas?"

"You know us big bro…we tryna get it like you." Lil Flip stated as he split the Dutch and began to roll the weed up for Zulu.

"Hell yeah," Crumbs added placing the twenty dollars Zulu had giving him on his nice size knot. "This weed selling like crack for us…word up yo."

"These lil niggas do not wanna be like me right now," Zulu told himself, *"It's so fucking slow I should've got a job today…yeah fucking right…picture that."* Zulu thought to himself admiring the ambition and diligence of Lil Flip and Crumbs. They were young teenagers but their souls been traveling the earth for eons. They were grown men in little boys' bodies and they had a desire to make tons of money slanging their weed like corporate tycoons on Wall Street.

"Come on and get yo melon busted Zulu," Lil Flip handed Zulu the fat blunt once it was rolled then slid over to the arcade game sitting outside the store. It was Capcom's Marvel Superheroes vs. Street-Fighter. "I aint mangled you in a minute Zulu…can't nobody in the hood fuck with me."

"Lil nigga," Zulu lit up the blunt stepping over to the game, "I taught you how to get busy in this…you will never whip the master my student."

"Nigga pick Wolverine and I'm still gone smash you."

"Yall like playing these video games and shit," Crumbs sat on the newspaper cart next to the game observing the cars cruising the strip and the people pacing the sidewalk. "It's about money…fuck games…the only game I'm playing is hustling."

"Don't rush to be grown lil nigga," Zulu stated realizing life could be so stressful games were needed to ease the mental strain of the everyday struggle.

While Zulu and Lil Flip got busy on the arcade game, several people popped up copping weed. Lil Flip kept his eyes on the game while the customers placed the money on the game near the controls. Crumbs then led them inside the store where he served them. When a few older people began pulling up for weed but didn't want to get out of the car for fear of being seen, Crumbs would skate over to the car and serve them.

"Come on Flip you got me doing all the work while you playing that fucking game," Crumbs wiped the perspiration off his high yellow forehead. He was shirtless and all skin and bones. His little body looked kind of famished, but he was far from starving with his neatly trimmed curly afro.

"Alright because I'm tired of smashing Zulu anyway…you aint playing like yo self Zulu."

"That's because I picked Beast slow ass and you had Blanca."

"Come on Zulu you had Wolverine and I still smashed you…yo mind aint there big bro…you must be hungry or some shit." Lil Flip's comment hit it right on the nose.

Zulu's mind definitely wasn't there. His mind was wondering where was the money he was missing. This first of the month sucked. It sucked just like it sucked getting pulverized by Lil Flip on the video game. After the game Zulu then went and grabbed his chop burger and French fries from Uncle Johnny's. He then posted up at his wheel busting down his grub while Lil Flip and Crumbs slung there weed right on the spot. As Zulu gobbled his chopped burger and washed it down with his kiwi strawberry Mistic, he observed the tan Honda

Accord swerve in front of the Red Sea Deli. It was Old School Al.

"Zulu you not gone believe this shit homeboy," Old School Al hysterically jumped out and stormed over to Zulu. "Homeboy I know why you been starving all day…check it right…I was just over dope feign Charaine crib right…and why some niggas over there from Walden avenue…they pumping that demon (crack) and boy (heroin)…they giving out double ups on the crack and they dope stamped the Formula."

"What…hold on…slow the fuck down…let me see if I heard you right." Zulu's mouth dropped revealing the mushy food inside his mouth. Zulu held his hand up to Old School Al gesturing him to stop talking while he tried chewing his food, because Zulu felt like throwing up. Zulu slowly chewed his food struggling to let his mind understand what his ears just heard. Zulu couldn't have heard what he thought he just heard as he swallowed without chewing. It felt like trying to swallow raw chicken.

"Old School…did I just hear you say Dope feign Charaine got niggas at her spot pumping? And it's some niggas from Walden?"

"Yeah Zulu." Old School Al got hyper and began pacing in circles flailing his hands. "I seen crackhead Stacy and she told me to swing thru Charaine's because some niggas was pushing garbage demon in there…yo I went thru there and these niggas was selling double ups and the whole nine…they dumping at that…ain't none of they crack bagged up…Stacy said that's why everyone from this side of the hood spent they checks over there even though them niggas got garbage."

Zulu felt an outburst of anger flood his bloodstream. His fingers began twitching and unconsciously he began shaking like a volcano ready to erupt. "Go find out how many niggas up in there because I'm going to kill them niggas," Zulu barked dashing to the driver side of his car then jumping in.

"Yo Zulu let us roll with you," Lil Flip and Crumbs ran over to Zulu's car flashing a 32 semi-automatic pistol.

"No sit yall little asses out here and don't tell no one about what yall just heard." Zulu yelled igniting his engine.

"Damn big bro." Lil Flip and Crumbs looked disappointed like Zulu told them they couldn't go to a party with him. "Just be safe big bro…we love you."

Zulu murked off and swerved into the oncoming traffic before blowing it thru a red light heading to Planet Rock. Zulu reached the block and jumped out the car in a rage. He flew into the backyard and retrieved his stash from the back of the house then slid into a tool shed in the yard. He dipped inside and stashed his package in the empty gas tank of a broken lawn mower. He then turned to a shelf and snatched two Twin Beretta 9mm's from out of a toolbox.

Zulu's mind was so clouded and in a rage, he flew out the backyard clutching both guns and hit the street not caring who seen him. He ran to the trunk of his car and placed the guns on the bumper then popped the trunk. He dug his hand on side of the 15-inch bass tube in his trunk and pulled out a black hoodie. He then slammed his trunk shut feeling a car creeping up on him from behind. He turned his head just enough to peep out the corner of his eye to see if it was the police. It was a red car. Zulu discreetly snatched both the guns from off the bumper and concealed them under the hoodie he held as he stood at the trunk of his car hearing the car slow up and mash on its brakes.

"I know I can get my rent money now Zulu?" NyJewel yelled pulling alongside Zulu while checking herself out in the lit up mirror on her visor. "My friend spent that N.F.L money with you…can I get a referral fee."

"Listen you fucking cunt," Zulu spun around facing her at her driver side while placing one of the pistols on his waist and the other one on his back. "I aint got time for yo games and none of these niggas who taking my fucking money…as a matter of fact," Zulu attempted to reach in his pocket but stopped short when Old School Al ran up frantically yelling.

"Zulu you not gone believe what the fuck just happened homeboy. These niggas violated and pulled a roscoe (gun) out on me and stretched me when I pressed them for getting money in the hood, they straight robbed me Zulu…Stacy said they from Walden and Harmonia…that's them G.F.L niggas right?"

"Nigga what." Zulu bit his lip so hard he could taste blood. He tasted the same blood the Young Assassins and the Gangster for Life crew been spilling for years. The G.F.L crew was notoriously bold and known for always dipping their hands in someone else's pot of gold. They were a crew of stick up kids who would rob hustlers for their drugs and then go wherever the drugs could be sold, even if it meant trespassing on dangerous grounds like they were doing now in E. North. "Come on we over there." Zulu told Old School Al while snatching the pistol from off his back then giving it to Old School Al.

"No Zulu please don't do nothing stupid," NyJewel jumped out of her car and dashed over to Zulu. "You gotta think Zulu don't risk yo life for money or hurt anyone for money, I'll give you money if that's what you need, I don't wanna see you---."

"Get the fuck out my face," Zulu snatched half the money out of his pocket and threw it in NyJewel's face. "Here yo rent money and more you fucking cunt...come on Old School we out." Zulu and Old School Al jumped in Zulu's ride and sped off.

NyJewel felt so belittled. Zulu just dropped an atomic bomb on her world where she was the Queen Goddess above all. He made her feel so down. She watched Zulu grow up but it seemed his male chauvinism and gangster ways had him thinking he grew above her. NyJewel felt a tear drizzle down her cheek. The sweet young boy she once knew no longer existed. She slowly picked up Zulu's money from off the ground feeling hurt. No man ever made her feel this way she realized as she rose up from grabbing the money.

"Please God...make sure he safe and don't let anything happen to him...please God...if not for anyone please for his mother." NyJewel heard her conscience utter as she jumped into her car and pulled off. As much as Zulu crushed her soul, she still couldn't find one inch of hate or unconcern towards him while feeling the pain of his disrespect.

....

Zulu stopped at a store and snatched a black hoodie for Old School Al before they pulled two blocks from dope feign Charaine's house. The two Grim Reapers clothed in black hoodies then hit the darkness under a full moon and dipped into the backyard of an abandoned house. They trekked thru knee high grass before stepping thru a huge hole in a wooden gate which lead to a trash filled vacant lot.

"Yo Zulu man," Old School Al stopped Zulu in his tracks as they came out onto the street. "I don't wanna kill nobody homeboy."

"Nigga what?" Zulu barked sprinting across the street and up into another backyard. "Them niggas robbed you...and they disrespecting the hood by coming thru here taking my fucking money...them niggas gotta die...if you wanna get money in the hood and be respected by the Young Assassins you gotta put this work in with me."

"God why?" The quiet voice in Old School Al's head spit out as he followed behind Zulu into the dark backyard. *"I'm just tryna get my shit together...this nigga bugging...I don't wanna kill nobody...I put my work in when the squad was here...why do I gotta prove myself...come on God please don't let him kill no one."*

They crept slowly thru the dark yard and passed a raggedy looking garage with no doors and broken windows. They slid alongside the garage swiping a broken down car. Behind the car a small pathway led thru a group of bushes which led to dope feign Charaine's gloomy and creepy backyard.

"Yo we gone lay behind these bushes until someone come out the side door," Zulu cocked his gun throwing a bullet in the chamber.

"Zulu it's not that serious," Old School Al whispered while eyeing the cats purring on top of the garbage cans behind dope feign Charaine's house. "People can go anywhere they want to get money Zulu...I been all around the city getting money."

"Muthafucka don't no one make money in my hood unless they eating with me...you acting pussy as hell and that's not the Old School Al from the A-Squad...if you wanna get down with us you better act you like know." Zulu shot back keeping his eyes glued to the side door and walkway.

"Oh my fucking God." Old School Al thought to himself. *"I helped this hood get its stripes and now I gotta prove I'm not a burned out hustler turned crackhead...this some bullshit...I'm from this hood and I can't get money over here but you got some niggas from another hood over here eating...fucccck."*

Old School Al then had a reality check when gunshots rang out several blocks away. Hustling and violence didn't mix, but you couldn't have one without the other. And if Old School Al wanted a license to get money in the E. North of the New Millennium, he had to earn his stripes all over again dealing with the young and dangerous Young Assassins who were worst savages than the A-Squad. The fruit don't fall too far from the tree and generation after generation it gets worse.

"Yo get ready." Zulu alerted Old School Al upon hearing the locks twisting at the side door. "Let's go." They sprinted behind the dark house covering their faces up with their hoodies and scaring the cats away from the trashcans. A tall slim man stuck his head out the side door holding a shotgun. He peeked up and down the gloomy walkway on side of the house before he leaned back inside and sat the shotgun by the door in the hallway. The man then stepped outside and began to quietly shut the door. That's when Zulu spun from behind the house and rushed the man before he closed the door.

"Shut the fuck up and don't say nothing," Zulu smacked the man in the face with the pistol. "Take us inside." Zulu shoved the man back into the dark hallway.

"Yo fam aint no one in there but feigns with no money." The man pleaded being shoved inside while holding his face stinging with pain from the chrome.

"Shut the fuck up." Zulu whispered loudly now striking the man on top of his head with the barrel of the gun. Blood began trickling from the gash in the man's wave cut. "Grab that yo." Zulu motioned for Old School Al to grab the shotgun sitting by the door as he walked the man up the backstairs and into the dimly lit kitchen. They entered a disgusting kitchen cluttered with dishes and rotten food with buzzing flies everywhere. They crept swiftly and silently thru the trashy smelling kitchen forcing mice to scramble behind a greasy and filthy stove. They exited the kitchen and slid down a dark hallway where a woman lay unconscious on the floor with a needle dangling out of her arm. They passed a pissy smelling bathroom with no light before passing two rooms crowded with drug addicts of all kinds.

When they neared the living room, clouds of weed smoke lingered in the humid air. A huge floor model T.V. showed *Master P's movie "Bout It."* Sitting on a sofa in the living room were three females with more weave and jewelry on than a Chinese store in Manhattan. They were hunched over a coffee table with rubber gloves on using McDonalds coffee spoons to bag up heroin. Relaxing on a love seat with a semi-automatic Tech-9 on his lap, a Ziploc bag full of crack beside him while choking on a blunt was an individual who seen just as much bloodshed as the bloodthirsty Kadari Twins. His name was Keyshawn Sparks, a gun blasting money getter from the Gangster for Life crew.

Keyshawn Sparks peeped more than one shadow creeping down the hallway so he quickly aimed his Tech-9 towards the entrance of the hallway ready to fire. Keyshawn Sparks wasn't a scary individual so he kept his blunt clamped by both his lips still toking when his friend flew into the living room head first. Keyshawn Sparks didn't fire when Zulu shoved the man in the living room, causing the man to trip over a foot stool in the middle of the floor. But when Zulu and Old School Al stormed in the living room behind the man, Keyshawn Sparks squeezed his trigger sending bullets spraying as he leaped off the couch towards Zulu and Old School Al who dipped back into the hallway.

"*Rat-ta-tat-ta-tat-tat*," was the sound of the numerous bullets being spit from the Tech-9, ripping into the door frame and walls of the hallway, splintering wood shreds and drywall in the air.

"*Fuck, come on*." Keyshawn Sparks rambled trying to unjam the bullet lodged in the chamber of the Tech-9 as he stood in the center of the living room near his friend who was pulling himself up from off the floor.

"*Muthafucka.*" Zulu blasted two shots into the living room before rushing in and chasing the fleeing Keyshawn Sparks who dashed thru the living room heading to the front door while still trying to unjam his gun. His friend jumped behind the couch and took cover as Zulu opened fire.

"*Boom boom boom,*" thundered throughout the house as Zulu ran thru the living room blasting at Keyshawn Sparks who now flew out the front door. Zulu flew outside and leaped off the front steps blasting at Keyshawn Sparks who zig zagged into the street then behind a car on the sidewalk.

"*Watch out Zulu.*" Lil Flip and Crumbs ran from out of a yard dumping shots at Keyshawn Sparks who sprinted from behind the car and jetted down the block then disappeared.

"Get the fuck outta here…I told yall to stay on the block." Zulu yelled racing back into the house where Old School Al had Keyshawn Spark's friend and the three females lying face down on the floor.

"Where the money and all the work at?" Old School Al declared aiming the shotgun and Beretta at the man and three girls.

"Yo it's some boogie (heroin) right here." Zulu slid over to the coffee table where the light grayish powder lay on a plate with some stamped wax paper bags that read *"The Formula."* One of the girls then fearfully cried out and pointed to the boulders of crack in the Ziploc bag on the love seat.

"And where my money at yall robbed me for?" Old School Al kicked the man in the back as he lay on the floor.

"And where the money yall made? That cheese mine." Zulu added bagging up the heroin and crack. One of the girls began pulling money out of her bra then pointed to the purse on the couch. "Hell knaw this can't be all the money yall got?" Zulu barked throwing the small bankrolls into the bag he held with the drugs.

"She got some too," one girl pointed at her friend who lay on the floor shaking. Upon searching her Zulu noticed she was bleeding from a gunshot wound to her stomach.

"Damn she got hit yo." Zulu glanced up at Old School Al while snatching the rubber band knots from her bra.

"See this what I'm talking bout man…I told you I didn't want nobody to get hurt." Old School Al felt his conscience began to eat him.

"Shut yo punk ass up and kill this nigga." Zulu ordered leaving the living room and hitting the rooms looking for dope feign Charaine. The feins were so high they were stuck and couldn't move upon hearing the gunshots in the house. When Zulu stormed into the room they were terrified with large eyes and trembling bodies. Zulu noticed the bedroom window was open. A few feigns who wanted to live another day to get high had jumped up and broke out when the gunfire erupted. And amongst the group of feigns in the room, Zulu spotted dope feign Charaine nodding while she sat against the wall.

"*Heyyyyy.*" She spoke to Zulu like he was there to bless her. Dope feign Charaine was on cloud 9 as she rubbed her arm with fluttering eyes.

"You a grimy ass bitch," Zulu put the gun to her chin and lifted her head up. "After all the look outs I gave you bitch…this how you repay me?"

"Huh…noooo." Dope feign Charaine nodded off.

"Disrespectful bitch," were the last words yelled into her ears before Zulu put a slug into her head. The boom made a few dope feigns shake terribly as they covered their heads in fear while Zulu stormed out the room.

"Yo what the fuck is you doing yo?" Zulu stepped back into the living room only to see Old School Al standing over the man hesitating to pull the trigger. "Shoot this nigga we out."

"I-I-I-can't."

"Come on man yall aint gotta kill me," the man pleaded attempting to get up off the floor and beg for his life. "I get high please don't kill me I wasn't with--."

"Fuck you nigga," Zulu rushed over to the man and pumped three slugs into the man's body. Zulu then turned to Old School Al yelling, "Give me my muthafucking heat you scary ass nigga…we out," Zulu shouted as they broke out the house thru the side door hearing sirens a few blocks away.

CHAPTER 8

Sun-Z hunched over the flaming barrel grill flipping steaks, chicken, and burgers in his spacious manicured backyard out in suburban Amherst, N.Y. Even though this event at Sun-Z's crib was a meeting of the minds, everyone was invited to his plush house with their ladies in attendance, and the ladies fulfilled their womanly duties for the cookout. The ladies shared a hand in the kitchen and had their own gathering on the back patio over daiquiris and margueritas while the fellas huddled around Sun-Z who cheffed on the grill in the yard.

After Zulu sent the wrath of death on that bloody night of the first of the month, Sun-Z had to re-structure and lay the law down in regards to the drug flow in the hood. With one person shot dead and two people seriously wounded in a drug house on top of Big Walt and Tam's murder was only bringing unnecessary heat on the hood. After filling Black Bull and Gonzalez' pockets with a nice bankroll, the two crooked cops made sure the heat didn't point at the Young Assassins. As far as Sun-Z was concerned, violence had to be avoided or intelligently executed in order to get lots of money with a smooth flow and no pressure from law enforcement. It was time for Lil Flip and Crumbs to step up with their young crew and control the blocks. The Young Assassins were advancing their game and didn't need to be on the streets. After discussing these issues and others, Sun-Z asked if there were any other issues needing to be addressed while he stood over the grill.

"Yeah I got an issue," Old School Al spoke up taking in a breath of courage as he exhaled from his queasy stomach. "When me and Zulu took care of that situation… Zulu gave me my loot back they stretched me for…but he aint bless me with any of that loot or work he came up on."

"Nigga you aint put that work in." Zulu spit tightening his jawbone. "Be happy you got yo bread back because if it wasn't for me you wouldn't even have that…Lil Flip and Crumbs got busy on that mission…they deserve some of that come up."

"See what I'm saying Sun-Z." Old School Al explained shaking his head shamefully.

"Hell knaw Old School," Sun-Z stepped close to Old School Al and spoke in a low and calm tone, "How you couldn't get busy on a nigga who put chrome in yo face and stretched you...you ain't the same and them drugs done took yo heart and made you soft." Sun-Z stated as him and everyone else observed Old School Al looking defeated with his head low.

"Yeah you was a thorough nigga from day one Old School," Hawk spoke while lounging in a lawn chair next to the picnic table, "I don't know what the fuck happened to you...but Zulu handled that situation so he call the shots on that...it was his move and you was basically in the way."

"But if we got knocked we would be co-defendants and sitting in a cell together." Old School Al felt he deserved a piece of the prize Zulu collected.

"We wouldn't be co-d's because I would tell em I kidnapped you and forced you to come with me as my hostage," Zulu joked stirring a moment of laughter amongst everyone. "But since you tryna get on yo feet Old School, you know I got you...you know I'm gone bless you off."

"See that's why I fuck with you Zulu and you my favorite lil bro," Old School Al let his grudge be known to the others.

Once finished building about their street business, the fellas then hit the back patio where the ladies were lounging amongst the sides of delicious foods stuffed in aluminum pans on a table on the patio deck. The fellas stepped onto the patio along with Sun-Z who carried the roasted and tender meat from the grill. The meat completed the cookout and the ladies got busy and made plates for their men.

Once the plates were served everyone lounged on the back patio and the picnic tables in the yard digging into their plates. Zulu and Destiny sat at a picnic table and while Destiny nibbled at her plate, she raised her gaze up only to lock eyes with NyJewel who sat on the patio conversing with Sun-Z's wife Iyana.

"This bitch wanna get clocked in her eye the way she keep looking over here," Destiny hammered to herself focusing her eyes back to her plate where she picked at her Tilapia.

What's wrong sweetheart?" Zulu swallowed some orange crush washing down his BBQ turkey wings. He then softly caressed Destiny's back waiting for her response.

"Nothing." Destiny glanced back at NyJewel who was still shooting darts at her. "Oooh this my song Zulu." Destiny grabbed Zulu's hand and jumped up when *Murder Inc's hit song "Down Ass Chick"* blasted out the bombastic Peavey speakers on the patio. Destiny led Zulu by the hand to the well paved concrete in the yard and began coordinating the curves on her body like a snake sliding up and down on Zulu.

"Psst." NyJewel extinguished her steam thru her clenched teeth as she snatched her empty plate from the table and slid inside to the kitchen. *"That little girl so insecure thinking I want Zulu."*

"Go head sis," Desiree shouted to Destiny while she sat with her plump rump shaker in Hawk's lap as they sat at a picnic table.

Destiny was moving and sparked the mood for grooving and several couples blessed the atmosphere with dancing as the hit songs played on. After working her hips like she was hula-hooping, Destiny had to rest her body and relieve her insides of the intoxicating wine stimulating her so she skated into the house to hit the bathroom.

After emptying her bladder, Destiny stood at the marble sink rinsing her hands while beholding the reflection of her beauty in the mirror. As she scoped herself out in the mirror, the envy of NyJewel crept into her mind.

"That bitch cute…but she just jealous she not as gorgeous as me," Destiny smiled at herself erasing the thought of NyJewel's envy. *"She lucky we here at Sun-Z and Iyana's because I would step to her and check her for looking at me like she want it."*

Destiny then slid out the bathroom switching the gears to her emotions back to party mode. As soon as Destiny stepped out the bathroom and began bopping down the hallway, NyJewel popped out and began heading Destiny's way.

"Listen Destiny," NyJewel stopped a few feet away with her hand on her hip. "I aint got time to be beefing with you…I'm too grown for that…and just so you know…I don't want Zulu…you know me and him like family so cut out the insecurity."

"Bitch you cut out the bullshit because y'all not blood related…and it's hard to tell you don't want my man," Destiny was itching to leap forward and put a beating on NyJewel who stood like she was 10 feet tall. "You been watching me like it aint nothing else to look at."

NyJewel snickered amusingly. "Listen lil girl…stop being full of ya self." NyJewel then dipped her hand into her purse and began to retrieve something.

"Come on bitch and try something," Destiny snatched a small oriental statue from off the glass octagon shelf in the hallway. "I will bust yo head wide open bitch now come on."

"Lil girl please I ain't worried about you," NyJewel yanked out of her purse a sandwich bag full of money. "I'm being nice and returning yo man's money.

Destiny stood frozen, measuring NyJewel with a look of confusion. Destiny didn't understand and NyJewel could see it painted all over Destiny's face.

"Me and Zulu had a disagreement about something," NyJewel sat the money on the shelf giving an open-ended answer to Destiny's puzzled look.

"About what?"

"Ask him."

Destiny now felt her heart pump rage. "Oh let me guess…you either fucked him or sucked his dick and now you feel like a whore and wanna give him his money back."

"Ewww you little bitch," NyJewel felt herself leap forward but caught herself. She took a deep breath as Destiny braced herself ready to swing the statue. "If I wanted to fuck him or suck him best believe it wouldn't be for money…I got all the money I need sweety."

"Whatever bitch," Destiny ranted snatching the bag of money from off the shelf then placing the small statue back in its place before storming pass NyJewel and slightly bumping her.

"You better watch it Destiny." NyJewel threatened.

"Stop watching me and mines." Destiny rushed back outside where everyone was having a good time. She spotted Zulu sitting at a table with Dolla and the others laughing. She then snatched Zulu's hand and led him away from the gathering after making an excuse to everyone why she had to leave early. Destiny kept her composure under control until her and Zulu got inside the car. Zulu didn't have a clue about the thunderstorm about to be unleashed on him as he ignited the engine.

"Why the fuck did that bitch have your money?" Destiny screamed slamming the passenger door shut.

"What bitch?" Zulu responded pulling off, "Fuck is you talking about?"

"Stop acting stupid and tryna play me Zulu." Destiny snatched the money from her purse and ferociously banged the dashboard with the bag of money.

"*Ummm.*" Zulu was clueless. He couldn't forget about the shootout with Keyshawn Sparks but he forgot about the incident with NyJewel moments before the shootout.

While Destiny repeatedly banged on the dashboard like it was Zulu and kept asking why did "*she*" have his money, Zulu's cerebral awareness sparked his mind with the realization of what Destiny was talking about.

"*Fucccck.*" Zulu needed his cerebral cortex to think quickly and come up with an excuse as to why NyJewel had over $1, 500 dollars of his money. "Ooo." Zulu's mouth dropped opened like he remembered once his brain created the perfect response. "Oh yeah that's from NyJewel right…yeah I paid her for a few months of rent in advance so she wouldn't keep bugging me…you know how she is."

"Stop lying to me she wouldn't have giving it back."

"Destiny that's my word I swear it w--."

Destiny sprung from the passenger seat and clawed into Zulu's face like a fierce feline as she screamed, "Stop lying to me you fucking her and I know you is."

"*Stopppp.*" Zulu raised an arm in defense while steering the wheel with his other hand. He then abruptly pulled over struggling to shield himself from the scratching and punching Destiny was attacking him with. "I'm not fucking her."

"Yes you is I hate you." Destiny now began pouncing on Zulu with the bag of money. "I hate you—I hate this money---you a liar." Destiny ceased beating on Zulu then opened the car door and jumped out before kicking the door shut. She began strolling down the residential street with its neatly landscaped yards and two-story houses and flats nestled with two car garages attached to the side.

"Sweetheart come here I swear I'm not fucking her." Zulu jumped out and dashed after Destiny who was striding down the block like the tears sliding down her face as she cried into her hands. Zulu ran in front of her and hugged her tightly.

"Get off me I hate you."

"How you gone accuse me of something I ain't do." Zulu squeezed her tightly as she struggled to wiggle out of his grip.

"Because you always doing something with her just like when we was kids…I don't trust you and her."

Women and their emotional attachments to past memories and grudges that they never let go of. Destiny couldn't let go and neither could NyJewel let go. It was back in the day. Back when NyJewel, Destiny, and Zulu all stayed in the McCarley Gardens apartments. Zulu and NyJewel stayed in the same building next door to each other.

Zulu and NyJewel's parents were both single mothers and good friends who downed their depression by drowning their lungs with liquor in bars with flirtatious men. NyJewel was 7 years older than Zulu, so she was forced to play baby sitter to the young Zulu while their mothers were busy entertaining themselves at the hole in the wall bars. Many nights, Zulu and NyJewel stayed up late watching shows like *Goodtimes, The Jeffersons,* and many other memorable sitcoms. Their mothers didn't have much money for food but NyJewel made Peanut Butter and Jelly sandwiches, sugar toast, oodles and noodles, and Vienna sausages seem like a luxury. Many mornings Zulu and NyJewel awoke only to find their mothers sprawled out in bed with some strange men. NyJewel would then take Zulu on bus rides throughout the city so they could get away from the hell at home.

The years passed and it wasn't long before men and teenage boys alike began lustfully desiring the teenage NyJewel. She loved Zulu like a little brother, but she was a very attractive young girl who had an outgoing spirit and she didn't want to spend her blossoming youth babysitting Zulu. So when NyJewel started dating, she would take Zulu over to Ms. Cookie's house. Ms. Cookie was the neighborhood nanna who tenderly cared for all the young children. This is where Destiny sometimes found herself while her mother worked.

Zulu didn't mind being at Ms. Cookies because this is where his future wife Destiny was. But one thing Zulu never liked was the men and boys who took NyJewel away from him when they took her out on dates. Zulu would fuss and throw tantrums and even hurl rocks at the guys' cars when they came by to pick up NyJewel. The only thing that would calm Zulu down is when he would reach Ms. Cookies and Destiny would be there.

To cheer Zulu up, Destiny would have the young mannish Zulu play house with her. As Zulu and Destiny grew older, they began playing real house and they broke their virginity with each other. They found a love that would last forever like the stars, but as adults Destiny was made to remember the emotion Zulu felt towards NyJewel and how possessive Zulu always been over NyJewel. Destiny felt the connection Zulu and NyJewel once shared was deeper than what everyone thought, because most men are dogs and there's even some with no restrictions.

"You was always protective over NyJewel." Destiny screamed at Zulu still in his grip. "You never wanted her to leave you or have boyfriends when we was kids…and now it's like she don't want you to have me now that we older."

"No no you got it all wrong," Zulu gazed into Destiny's tear filled eyes while pressing her body close to his. "That's when we was kids…I'm a grown man now…all I care about is you."

"I don't trust you…yall men love with yall heart but let yall penis control yall minds."

"Baby I love you and I'm here for you…sex not stronger than my love for you." Zulu pried one of his hands from off Destiny's waist and went to wipe the tears from off her moist cheeks. "I love you sincerely Destiny."

"Don't touch me Zulu." Destiny slipped out of his hold. "Just take me home and you sleeping on the couch…don't touch me or come near me," Destiny eased back to the car."

"Come on I'm all yours don't do me like this." Zulu opened the passenger door for Destiny. "I'm not having sex with no one but you."

"I don't know where that thing been," Destiny's eyes beckoned towards his genital area as she dropped into the passenger seat.

"I'm telling you I'm faithful and I belong to you," Zulu stated once he jumped in the driver seat. "I promise I w--."

"Shut up and take me home. And you sleeping yo cheating ass on the couch…dream about NyJewel."

. . . .

West End Communications sat in the heart of *Tiera Boricua* (Little Puerto Rico), home to Buffalo's Hispanic community on the west side of town. Sun-Z was inside West End copping two sky pagers and two burn out cell phones which couldn't be traced to any subscriber. Sun-Z stepped out the store peeping Zulu and Hawk gluing their eyes on the mami's dancing in front of the bodega a few stores down.

"Let's hit the *Can* my boys," Sun-Z stated as the three jumped inside the wheel.

"What side of Canada we going to?" Zulu asked driving south down Niagara Street heading towards downtown.

"Go to the Peace Bridge…we hitting the Fort Erie side." Sun-Z informed.

Zulu turned off Niagara Street onto the west side highway which directed him to the Peace Bridge. He pushed the wheel up onto the colossal bridge amongst 18-wheel tractor trailer trucks, tour buses, and an assortment of foreign and American made vehicles slowly squeezing thru the toll booths flanked with toll booth attendants and border patrol officers.

"Hello...what is your citizenship and your reason for coming to Canada?" A middle aged blonde toll booth attendant quickly asked the three men. Once everyone replied they were U.S. Citizens and said they were going gambling and shopping, the lady wished them a nice stay and let them pass.

Zulu slid thru the toll booth and eased onto the bridge separating the two countries. Travelling across the bridge in either direction offered the panoramic view of the skyline of downtown Buffalo and its many condominiums and lofts dotting the waterfront. And streaming below the Peace Bridge Lake Erie poured its forceful waters into the flowing Niagara River which flowed north into the mighty Niagara Falls.

Zulu slid off the first exit on the bridge and hit the town of Fort Erie. He rolled into the town's shopping district famous for its bingo halls, duty free stores, and landmark Tourists destinations. Zulu whipped the wheel onto a main thoroughfare crowded with tourists and shoppers. The street was clean with small trees lining the strip amongst French style buildings rising two and three stories sitting side by side squeezing trash free alley-ways.

They found a French coffee shop and bakery located next to a parking lot by a cathedral. They pulled into the half full parking lot and exited the car with Sun-Z carrying the bags with the communication devices. They entered the coffee shop where the soft harmonic sounds of Opera music warmed the environment. About a dozen or more tables filled the center of the shop. About 7 booths were by the front window giving patrons a perfect view of the street outside. On the left side of the shop was a lounge section where magazines, newspaper stands, and a bookcase caught the attention of patrons who desired mental soothing while sipping on their *Crème au lattes*. Across the shop on the other side was the counter which at one end displayed the numerous warm and delicious breads, cakes, and donuts the shop offered.

"Zello gentlemen," an elderly lady greeted the three men with a heavy French accent. *"Howz may I zhelp yous?"*

"Bonjour Madam," Sun-Z placed both the bags on the counter but held onto one of the bags. "We like to try three crostini's and three cappuccinos..your best flavor."

"Ok lads," the lady gripped the bag with one hand and snatched the cordless phone from the counter behind her and began to dial a number before whispering, "Have a seat and he za be with you shortly."

The lady then slid into the kitchen as the three stepped to a booth by the front window. A middle aged man with a light tan complexion and curly oily black hair stepped from the kitchen and posted behind the counter waiting to take orders from arriving customers. The older lady then returned from the kitchen speaking French to the man. The man then motioned for Sun-Z and the others to follow him. They slid from the booth and followed the man thru the kitchen inhaling the sweet warm oven baked breads and pastries coming out of the oven. They then went thru a door which led downstairs into a basement. The air in the basement was cool and ventilated and stacked with boxes in neat rows. They slid down rows of boxes and passed a huge door to an ice cold walk in freezer. They then walked down a narrow hallway with old castle like bricks before they approached another door. This door was a three-inch-thick steel door and the man used a set of keys to unlock the heavy door. He used both hands to swing the heavy door open and to everyone's surprise a luxurious one room flat was on the other side of door.

Thick aqua green carpet covered the floor from wall to wall. A bathroom sat to the left not far from the entrance. Pass the bathroom was a small kitchen area with bright colors. A king sized bed sat against the back wall where an old French rifle trimmed in gold sat on the wall above.

"*Sunny...myza boy,*" an older man with a head full of curly gray hair sitting atop his freckled face shouted as he sat in a rocking chair petting a feisty *Patter Dale Terrier.*

"Mr. Francois," Sun-Z stepped into the center of the room where Mr. Francois was rocking. Sun-Z patted Mr. Francois' shoulder before Mr. Francois lowered the dog onto the floor. "So how you doing Mr. Francois?"

"Wuz can I say." Mr. Francois achingly stood up and embraced Sun-Z. *"I'ze still have my vision and myza mind and hands to make ze fortune I said I'ze do."* Mr. Francois stated happily before the introductions were made amongst the five men as they all sat at a table.

The elder man's name was Marcel Francois. He was a veteran of the French-Algerian war and the French-Vietnam battle which initiated the U.S.-Vietnam war. After France brought her troops home after the wars, Marcel found himself in his hometown of Corsica, France. Work was slow and he had mouths to feed. Being a trained killer honorably discharged from the French army had to pay off somehow. He ended up becoming a contract killer for the *Corsican Mafia* in his hometown. He carried out hits all across France and southern Europe for his hometown mob. The money was good, but it was even more money to be made in the drug business. So upon capitalizing on the drug trade, Marcel found himself in Canada establishing a drug empire that would flood the northeastern states of the USA. From France the drugs would find their way into Canada. And from Canada through Buffalo and Niagara Falls was just one of the many shipping routes that Marcel and his French Connection utilized to get drugs into the states.

Marcel Francois made millions upon millions shipping his large cargoes into the states until a new border patrol commissioner took office and began inspecting more and more vehicles driven by Frenchmen. Marcel then crossed the Peace Bridge and took a trip to the border patrol office in Buffalo where he tried to bribe the newly appointed official. It would be 10 years before Marcel set foot back in Canada. He was charged with bribery and conspiracy to distribute narcotics into United States territory. He was giving 10 years in the New York State Department of Corrections. That's where he met Sun-Z whom he took a liking to. The rest is history.

Over French cuisine the five men sat around the table and engaged in casual conversation. Marcel then showed them photos of France where mountainsides, green pastures, and nice blue lakes reflected in most of the pictures. He then showed them pictures of the city of lights; Paris.

"So zpromise me," Marcel closed his photo album, "That you will visit my country and zbuy a house there with ze tons of money youz bout to make?"

"No question…for sure Mr. Francois." Everyone responded happily and determined.

Marcel had tons of heroin available, cocaine, hashish, and his son added a boatload of ecstasy pills to their product supply. The business relationship was consummated when Sun-Z gave Marcel $125, 000 dollars' straight cash. Marcel's distribution was perfect and secured. He used his bakery trucks and tourist shuttle buses to deliver product across the Niagara River into Buffalo. The operation was sweet.

Sun-Z would only have to drive the money across the bridge into Canada which wasn't a problem considering the numerous casinos and bingo halls along the Buffalo U.S.-Canada border. There was no real crime in having money. And Marcel would handle all the rest with his secret compartment equipped bakery trucks and tourist shuttles.

The New Year was fast approaching and with Marcel Francois as The Connect, the New Year would be one of prosperity and the achievement of lavish street dreams were soon to become real.

....

Flocks of party goers crowded the two floor levels of the Pearl street bar and grill in downtown Buffalo on New Year's Eve. Zulu and Destiny double dated with Hawk and Destiny's sister Desiree on this New Year's Eve night. The couples settled themselves at a table by the second floor patio feeling the icy chill of the Buffalo winter air amidst the sardine packed bar.

Over drinks and dialogue everyone let their minds do a 360-degree reverse and thought of their lives and the events of the year behind them. The future is what mattered to most while some lived only for the moment. For Zulu and the crew, they desired the success of the past year to roll into the New Year but on an elevated level of more money and power.

As for the love life of Destiny and Zulu, Destiny wished for a new and improved Zulu whom she could trust like her sister Desiree trusted Hawk. Ever since Hawk and Desiree intertwined themselves at the welcome home party they were inseparable. Their attraction was natural and pure but extremely aroused by their indulgence of coke sniffing and partying. They lived life to the fullest and partied like *Prince's* hit song *"1999"*. Destiny only wished her and Zulu could be under each other's arms like Desiree and Hawk. Well this was New Years and maybe Destiny's resolution would come true as they watched the hands of time tick towards bringing in the New Year.

Bottles popped. Glasses were raised high. Kisses and hugs were exchanged and wishes for a Happy New Year were shouted. After the ball dropped the party went on. Zulu and Hawk then courted their wine fine ladies to the many New Year's parties jumping off downtown. The ladies were pleasured and took this as a gesture for bringing in the New Year as couples happily in love and living life.

Up in Niagara Falls on the Canadian side the rest of the crew brought in New Years in the sky tower overlooking the mighty Niagara Falls. Hawk advised Zulu it wouldn't be a good idea to go since NyJewel was in attendance at the party. So to avoid Destiny and NyJewel bumping heads and letting grudges flare up on New Year, Hawk and Zulu stayed back in the city and was having one helluva night.

They hit the city barhopping all around town, gratifying their souls with the intoxicating liquors before ending up at a New Year's party where the energy was out of control like the sensual emotions pulsating thru the people. The energy moving the people at the party was stimulated by the ecstasy pills, cocaine, and liquor which had people tearing the roof off the party. Booty bouncing females with G-Strings and thongs swallowed in the crevices of their butts sexually pranced around the party in six-inch heels hugging piles of dollars on their bare breasts. Men getting lap dances passionately grinded champagne bottles in the hot and steamy vaginas of the strippers. It was off the chain.

"*Ugh*, couldn't be me girl, no way," Destiny twisted her face with disgust. She detested the promiscuity and immorality of the atmosphere. She couldn't understand how some beautiful women treated their treasured bodies and let men misuse them. Destiny then tugged at Desiree's arm, "I can't believe you do this Desi…what the hell make you like doing this besides the obvious reason of money…men putting bottles in girls' vaginas…that's disrespect sis."

"First off ain't no nigga ever put nothing but dick in this vagigi…and second…I took care of me and you by stripping…but that life is over because I don't have to strip no more," Desiree was held in Hawk's embrace so lovely, "I only strip for my man now…ain't that right daddy?"

"That's right," Hawk shouted before softly caressing Desiree's ear with his lips while whipping out a stack of singles for him and Desiree to tip the strippers. "Yo sister will never strip again unless it's for me Destiny."

"I hope so Hawk." Destiny shot back slowly grinding her backside on Zulu's manhood while observing Desiree pull out a small ring box from her purse. The ring box was full of cocaine and Desiree dug her long nail inside of it, cuffed the pearly white powder in her nail and stuck her nail in Hawk's face. Hawk took a sniff with each of his nostrils then Desiree did the same.

"Oh my God Zulu," Destiny was still grinding on Zulu when she reached back and grabbed his head and whispered into his ear while eyeing Desiree and Hawk sniffing, "Why my sister gotta be so wild and loose Zulu."

"Destiny calm down yo sister a vet at this shit," Zulu responded squeezing Destiny's onion booty on his erect wood. "Just worry about this pole I'm gone lay on you tonight."

"Boy whatever."

Desiree's best friend and used to be tag team dance partner Chocolate then sashayed her ebony complexioned body over to the couples. Chocolate was so black she was beautiful as the night sky and her hot pink lace stripper outfit fitted well with the curves of her sumptuous body. She possessed all the curves of a big booty stripper. Chocolate and Desiree were the complete opposite and they offered the best of both worlds. Chocolate was a thick stallion with the majestic charm of the night sky and Desiree had the lustful form of a petite supermodel with her pumpkin pie skin tone.

Chocolate stepped over to the couples dancing and happy to see her bestie but a little shook when it came to Destiny. Chocolate was bi-sexual and had a crush on Destiny until Destiny threatened her and told Chocolate she bet not ever come at her sexually again. Chocolate gave Destiny a friendly hug before spinning over to Desiree and gyrating her heart shaped hips in front of Desiree. Desiree was sandwiched between Hawk and Chocolate as they all danced to the sounds of *Juvenile's hit song "Back dat ass up."*

After watching Desiree, Hawk, and Chocolate sniffing and getting loose with each other like they were warming up for a threesome, Destiny had enough and was ready to leave the freaky atmosphere. Destiny was no angel, she was a freak behind closed doors and that was for Zulu and Zulu only.

About an hour later and at home Zulu and Destiny was ready to go half on a baby.

"Come on baby," Destiny slid to the bedroom with Zulu following closely behind. "I love you so much Zulu," Destiny stated stepping into the bedroom.

"I love you too." Zulu followed her like a hungry dog. Destiny wasted no time when they entered the bedroom. She rushed Zulu tongue first while they stripped each other of their clothes.

"I want you all to myself," Destiny fell back onto the bed with Zulu on top of her, "I don't want no one but you Zulu."

"And I don't want no one but you Destiny," Zulu lay on top of her aiming his flesh of steel on the moist lips of her vaginal paradise. "You mines always and forever."

"Yes, I'm all yours Zulu," Destiny gripped him tightly and dug her nails into his back as he slipped his rod inside her loving. He stroked her wet and tight warm loving with a long thrust and a focus she could feel with him. Time and the world around them was non-existent as their energy intensified with a pleasure that only paradise know. As Zulu thrusted him self deep inside her, Destiny wrapped her thick legs around his waist and they humped in sync. The vibrations of their moans and groans were deep, deep as the climaxing orgasm Destiny felt as her insides unleashed her juices.

"*Oooooo...Zulu...ooooo.*" Destiny felt joy shake her body tenderly as Zulu went full speed ramming her while she came.

"*Ahhh...*I'm bout to cum too bay," Zulu fell on top of Destiny and gripped her moist butt cheeks as he exploded his seeds of life inside her. They both climaxed together feeling ecstasy envelope their minds as they drifted off to a peaceful realm of triple darkness from the heated exhausted sex. They were both knocked out and sent to sleep.

....

"Welcome to urban styles fashions…how can we help you guys?" The middle-eastern sales attendant greeted the crew as they stepped inside the clothing store at the Galleria Mall. All day they been all around town shopping and spending bankrolls on exclusive garments. They hit up several malls and clothing stores in and around Buffalo. From the Boulevard Mall, to the Main Place Mall downtown, the Fashion outlets in Niagara Falls, and now to the Galleria Mall, the crew was cashing in for them garments. The summer of 2001 was blazing with new flavors and many new fashion brands. From *Moschino to Akademiks* it was all about styling. The Galleria Mall was their last stop and the purchases made there would complete their summer wardrobe. Dolla and the Kadari Twins were up in Urban Styles Fashions battling each other with jokes while shopping, they been at it all day with the joking.

As Killa scoped out a burnt orange LRG track suit, he spotted a sexy young fox over in the ladies' section. She was so hot and attractive she magnetized Killa and he couldn't keep his eyes off her. She wore red Capri jeans made by Pepe with the matching halter top. She was petite and gorgeous like a doll. She had the same butterscotch complexion as the Kadari Twins and she looked Creole with her crinkly jet black hair and almond shaped eyes. As Killa beheld the beauty of this foxy doll her pure beauty was reminiscent of the only beautiful woman he had ever known and loved; his mother. This wasn't lust this was a natural attraction which sent an impulse surging thru Killa making him humbly step to the foxy mama.

"Excuse me gorgeous…my name Jahtu." Killa made his introduction as he approached the young lady who had her eyes glued to the garments on the rack. She paid Killa no mind. "I don't mean to interrupt you or waste yo time ma but you mad beautiful, you so appealing to my eyes…the only woman I ever seen with so much beauty is my moms." Killa's mother was his heart and the only woman he never lied to, but this was straight game.

The young lady now raised her gaze to Killa and thought to herself, *"Oooo he fine as hell."* He was a pretty boy but his grey eyes had the gleam of power and he approached her like a gentleman even though she could tell he was a thug. The eyes didn't lie. "Oh I'm sorry my name is Jessica," she responded gazing into Killa's face now giving him her full attention. "I wasn't tryna be rude I'm just frustrated because these clowns keep tryna talk to me, distracting me and I can't find anything to match these champagne colored shoes I just bought. I want a dress that will match."

"Hmmm…let me help you then," Killa thoughtfully touched his chin while scoping out the dresses on the wall. After a minute or so of checking the assortment of dresses on display, Killa gently pulled from the back of one of the racks a turquoise Guess dress with gold embroidering on it. "I think this will compliment you my sunshine."

"Aww," Jessica blushed holding the dress up to her chest. "You got taste."

"Yeah I got that eye…but listen I'm not tryna be too pushy…I know we just met…but how bout we exchange digits and after some good convo you let me take you out?"

"I'm down Jahtu," Jessica tossed the dress over her shoulder then snatched her phone from out of her purse and the digits were exchanged. "You seem real nice and I would love to go out with you."

"Ok so check this out sunshine." Killa turned his head and snuck a glance at Dolla and Terror who were on the other side of the store in the men's section. Killa made sure no one was watching him and did what he always did, got his trick daddy on. "I'm gone cop this dress for you so you can rock it for me when we go out."

"You don't have to."

"Don't worry sunshine…yo beauty alone make me wanna give you the world."

Dolla then peeped Killa and Jessica heading to the counter. Dolla tapped Terror as they compared different outfits. "Yo whut up with yo trick ass brother…he give his bank away to every broad he rock with."

"That nigga a sucka just like yo fat marshmallow ass," Terror responded matching a Pelle Pelle outfit with some Uptown Nikes. "Both of yall niggas aint got no game so yall drop that bread for these bitches."

"You sound stupid you baboon face," Dolla slurped his large slushy, "All I do is smile and rub my belly and the ladies go crazy and give to me…Big Poppa is the shit now…not you little 2 Pac niggas."

"Yeah whatever." Terror found the right match then slid to the counter where Killa and Jessica stood.

"Oh my God you got a twin?" Jessica's mouth dropped upon seeing Terror. You could only tell the difference between the Kadari Twins by their green and grey eyes, and Killa wore a pony tail most times while Terror rocked a wave cut.

"Yeah that's my physical a-alike." Killa glanced at Terror before he handed them dividends to the cashier for Jessica's dress and his LRG track suit. "But I'm the older one sunshine."

"Since you the older brother and you buying people clothes…pay for my mines as well trick daddy." Terror threw his outfit and sneakers on the counter.

"Yall niggas only minutes apart and yall was born at the same time…neither one of yall is older…that's some stupid ass logic," Dolla stated leaning against the counter emptied handed since they didn't have what he wanted in his size.

"I came out the womb first and I was breathing air before him…I was on earth first…therefore I'm older than him." Killa explained.

"Who give a fuck trick daddy." Terror added. "Just pay for my shit."

"Right…it don't even matter because this lovely lady Jessica right here make me happy with her sunshine…I buy her and all yall whatever yall want." Killa counted out the money to pay for Terror's possessions as well.

"Yeah make sure you keep him happy ma," Terror snatched his bag from the counter speaking to Jessica, "Because I won't have to spend none of my money since you got him feeling so free hearted."

"Yo brother a damn fool, *The P is still free*" like *KRS-One* said," Dolla spit at Terror as they bounced out the store and left Killa and Jessica to themselves. When Dolla and Terror stepped out the store, Zulu and Cream were bouncing out of Sterling Optical across the concourse where they purchased *Cazal* frames. Prince lounged on a bench with a bunch of shopping bags around him.

"Yo is yall ready or what?" Prince impatiently asked as everyone lounged around the bench Prince was seated at.

"Yo let's hit *Against All Odds* then we out," Cream tossed two more bags into the pile of bags all around the bench. It was so many bags just from the Galleria Mall it looked like they were Christmas shopping.

"I'm sitting my fat ass down," Dolla plopped onto the bench finishing a slice of Buffalo Chicken pizza he just bought. "I sit here and watch the bags."

"Cool I'm going to get the truck," Prince stood up as everyone but Dolla headed to *Against All Odds* clothing store. "Yo Zulu come roll with me to get the truck."

"Alright," Zulu stated walking beside Prince. As they strolled thru the mall Zulu noticed Prince's angry demeanor. "You alright bro…what's up?"

"No I'm not alright Zulu." Prince sharply replied as they approached the elevator.

"What is it…that shit with the cops?"

"It's everything Zulu," Prince stated as they neared the elevators to the parking levels. Prince then hit the elevator button and said, "I'm tired of this life yo…word up…I'm really tired of this shit."

"Nigga we just getting started," Zulu responded as they stepped into the elevator. "We ain't never had this much money and balled out like this…how you tired of this."

"We can't take none of this with us when we die…and what good is this shit if we locked up Zulu…we can't sell drugs all our life…I want something different in life…I want peace…this shit doesn't make me happy anymore."

"Nigga this money we making give a nigga peace of mind. With all this money we got we can get any bitch and anything we want…we can go anywhere we want and do whatever we wanna do…that's all the happiness a nigga need."

"You crazy," Prince shook his head at Zulu's misunderstanding as they stepped out the elevator into the parking ramp. "Sometime I wonder Zulu, being a thug can't be the only life for us…we too smart to think the streets is all we got."

"Hold the fuck on Prince," Zulu stopped in his tracks disturbed at Prince's statement, "You got amnesia now or some shit...or you just scared...because last I remember we was wards of the state when we was kids...we spent half of our early teens in juvie hall and group homes...and we been taking care of ourselves because of the streets...shit...you been taking care of yo self since you was 11 years old...yeah don't forget if it wasn't for you selling weed back then you would've starved and wouldn't been able to buy a Triple Fat Goose jacket when it was freezing outside...I don't wanna hear that shit...maybe we should kill them cops...maybe that will make you feel better," Zulu shot at Prince before they moved out of the way for a passing car.

"That's not gonna erase my pain of living this fucked up life we living."

"This the only life we ever knew and shit getting better. We about to be," Zulu's vocal chords went silent and his eyes opened wide. His breath was snatched away when he spotted KeyShawn Sparks and another Thug stepping thru the parking ramp a few rows of cars over. Zulu snatched Prince by the arm and they both ducked behind a parked car. "Fuck...I aint got my hammer on me Prince."

"See what the fuck I mean Zulu," Prince muttered while cracking his knuckles and balling up his fists, "We can't even go nowhere without guns on us...I'm tired of this shit."

"You an asshole Prince...you can't change because for one we got too much murder beef to change...*fuccck*...I ain't got my gun on me I can't believe this shit."

Keyshawn Sparks stepped thru the parking ramp with a thug named K-Drop. When K-Drop was a young teenager he was destined to become a 7th degree black belt master in Tae Kwan Do and Ishin-Ru karate but Killa destroyed that aspiration when he clapped K-Drop in the leg. Even though K-Drop had a permanent rod in his leg he could still swing his kick 5 feet into the air with enough force to knock whoever or whatever down like gravity. That's why he was called K-Drop; his Kick could drop anyone.

The beef between the Young Assassins and the Gangster for Life crew was ancient and inevitable. Nobody even cared how it started and who started it.

It seemed like only death could finish it. They all had the reminder of the war wounds, scars, and the many months spent in either juvie hall or the county jail because of this beef. Just like the shootout between Zulu and Keyshawn Sparks on the first of the month. It was murder on site.

"Yo Prince I know Keyshawn strapped so check it…I left my strap in the wheel…we gone have to creep to the wheel and then I'm gone call the crew to put them on point."

"Fuck that I'm not creeping nowhere."

"Well we just gone have to hide here," Zulu whipped out his phone, "I'm gone call the crew and tell them to come out right now."

"Fuck that I'm not hiding here either," Prince began creeping low and easing towards Keyshawn Sparks and K-Drop. "I'm gone handle this myself and my way…I'm tired of this shit."

"How the fuck this shit gone get handled and we not strapped…I bet my life on it Keyshawn strapped and you tryna get us killed," Zulu stated trying to hold Prince back as they knelt behind a car.

"Look," Prince spotted a glass bottle under a car and handed it to Zulu. "You gone rock K-Drop with this bottle and I got Keyshawn…who give a fuck about him being strapped…I'm gone knock his ass out before he gets a chance to reach for his shit…you know how I go," Prince punched his hand forcefully and continued creeping.

"You bugging dude," Zulu gripped the bottle creeping behind Prince. "You got a fucking death wish with yo tired of living this life ass…and I'm stupid as fuck following you to a gun fight with a fucking Snapple bottle."

"Shut up Zulu." Prince muttered as they crouched low moving in closer. They were about four cars behind Keyshawn Sparks and K-Drop.

Keyshawn Sparks was spitting a rhyme while K-Drop bopped his head and was beat boxing with a nice beat Keyshawn Sparks spit to. Keyshawn Sparks stayed on point at all times and while they walked thru the parking ramp he kept twisting his head around checking the surroundings as they neared the elevator. There were too many cars circling the ramp looking for parking spots and too many people scrambling thru the ramp searching for their cars for Keyshawn

Sparks to be relaxed.

"On the count of three let's go Zulu," Prince was timing Keyshawn Spark's rotating head and peeping for a distraction. Prince then spotted a few kids dash out of an elevator ahead. Good distraction because Keyshawn Sparks glued his eyes at the kids. "1-2-3." Prince and Zulu sprinted from behind the car and rushed their enemies. They were a few feet away from being within reach of striking when a lady stormed out of the elevator yelling and cursing at the kids for running thru the parking lot. She then peeped passed Keyshawn Sparks and K-Drop and screamed at the top of her lungs at the site of the dangerously looking Zulu and Prince about to attack.

With the natural reflexes of killer instinct, Keyshawn Sparks snatched the pistol from off his waist and swiftly spun around looking to where the lady's fearful eyes focused; behind him and K-Drop.

"*Bonnnng.*" Keyshawn Sparks turned right around into Prince's pound for pound right hand. Keyshawn Sparks stumbled backwards still gripping his gun and ready to raise it. Prince swiftly trailed him and followed up with a left hook then a strait right hand. Keyshawn Sparks dropped, butt crashing into the pavement before he rolled onto his back.

While Prince sent Keyshawn Sparks to the canvas, K-Drop spun around and Zulu hurled the bottle smacking into his face. K-Drop shuffled back raising his arms in front of his face as the bottle shattered upon hitting his face. K-Drop stumbled backwards tripping on Keyshawn Spark's right hand which held the gun. K-Drop's trembling foot slid on the gun and sent it sliding under a car several cars away.

"*Muthafucka.*" K-Drop fell back but used his hands to stop himself from falling on his back. He thrusted himself up onto his feet while Zulu was charging at him. K-Drop lunged a power kick in the air which collided with Zulu's chest. "Come on muthafuckas." K-Drop's yelling could be heard under the screams of the lady who gathered her kids and skated to her van.

Prince observed Keyshawn Spark's hit the ground then peeped Zulu stepping back and painfully clutching his chest from K-Drop's kick which knocked the atmosphere of air out of Zulu's chest. Zulu then charged K-Drop a second time and Prince did the same. Prince loved fighting so much he knew the science of fighting and he knew to beat K-Drop who was ill with his feet, he had to get up close on K-Drop so he couldn't use his feet.

K-Drop jumped up and got in his stance ready to blast the charging Zulu again. He then spotted Prince rushing at him as well thru his peripheral vision. K-Drop was so deadly with his legs he could hit both of them with one kick. K-Drop's timing was precise because he took a deep breath then jumped about two feet in the air and shot a round house kick as Zulu and Prince came within his kick's reach. Zulu seen it coming and with quick reflexes he ducked feeling the swift and forceful breeze whisk pass his ducking head. K-Drop's kick continued traveling in Prince's direction with a rapid force and speed. Prince had to get a hold of K-Drop's feet so he couldn't use them. So instead of ducking, Prince threw his arm up in block mode as the kick swung inches from his face. The kick banged Prince's arm and then Prince snatched K-Drop's foot with his other hand.

"This the only kick you had," Prince smiled now using both his hands to hold K-Drop's foot which was on Prince's shoulder. K-Drop's free foot was still in the air and Prince broke his balance in mid-air by holding his kick foot. K-Drop came crashing down on his tippy toes and landing on his hands in a push-up position while Prince still held onto his one foot. K-Drop peeped Zulu rushing toward him upside down so he used his free foot to bang Prince in his nuts.

"*Arrrrgh.*" Prince groaned letting go of K-Drop's assault weapon foot. "Get him Zulu." Prince cried out curled up holding his excruciating painful nuts.

"I got him I got him," Zulu dived at K-Drop before he could get up off the ground. K-Drop was quick and swift. He pushed himself up off the ground and kicked Zulu right in the face as Zulu flew at him in the air. K-Drop then rolled out of Zulu's way as Zulu landed on the ground on all fours. K-Drop then charged at Prince blasting a double kick, hitting him in the knee cap and then his chest. Zulu was painfully raising himself from off the ground while holding his face only to be kicked in his shoulder by K-Drop. K-Drop was just warming up and ready to do some damage until Zulu and Prince were saved by who Thugs hated the most; Law Enforcement.

"Freeeeze...stopppp." Three security guards rushed to the scene rescuing Zulu and Prince from *Bruce Leroy*. The security guards drew their pistols on K-Drop and restrained him since he looked like a black Shaolin Master mercilessly crushing Zulu and Prince.

"I'm gone kill yall niggas," Keyshawn Sparks awoke after a minute or two of rest. He jumped up yelling with his mind in a daze. His face felt like cement and it was hard for him to talk. "Ewww it's over for yall watch...I'm gone kill yall niggas."

"It's about who catch who first you faggot," Zulu shot back as him and Prince limped away feeling sharp pains shooting thru their bodies.

"Hold on do you guys wanna press charges and wait for an ambulance?" A security guard asked while another security guard was shuffling K-Drop away.

"Hell fuck no." Zulu and Prince barked wobbling away while helping each other walk.

CHAPTER 9

"*Ay yo yo dealer*." Dolla shouted across the crap table at the craps dealer. "Lemme get a thousand across the board." Dolla then tossed a stack of chips onto the table and rubbed his hands as the dealer used his stick to swoop up the chips then place them on each of the numbers. "And yo here go fifty for the house." Dolla tossed a fifty-dollar chip to the dealer once all bets were made.

"Yo Dolla you bugging." Cream whispered as him and Zulu stood beside Dolla. "We only here to change the money up not lose it…you know you a degenerate loser yo."

"Hell yeah you never win and all you do is chase yo money and keep losing," Zulu added.

"Come on chill yall fucking me up I got this I got this." Dolla waved them both away. The trio were only at the Seneca Niagara Casino changing up the dirty drug traced cash. Their job was basically done and now they were killing time waiting on NyJewel but Dolla decided to hit the crap table.

Secreted in a stash compartment near the gas tank under the Nissan Pathfinder NyJewel was driving was $ 275, 000.00. And Zulu, Dolla, and Cream had in their possession a little over $ 50, 000.00 all in small bills they were changing up for bigger bills that were clean.

"Yo this that broad paging me right now," Zulu referred to NyJewel whom he was still mad at. Zulu and Cream then stepped away from the crap table telling Dolla to cash out immediately.

"Hold on let me hit this point…I'm bout to win chill."

"NyJewel here we gotta break out."

"Yo why yall gotta--," Dolla watched the dice roll a 7. "Come on man," Dolla shouted crapping out. "Yall niggas bad luck." Dolla stated as the dealer swooped up everyone's chips. "Yall niggas always fucking my flow up…I was bout to cash in on these Indians."

"Nigga the only flow you got is a loser's flow." Zulu stated as they watched Dolla throw a fuss at the crap table. They then skated thru the table game section housing dozens of craps, blackjack, and poker tables. The Casino was fluttered with the loud shouting of gamblers surrounding the tables and the pinging electronic sounds of the slot machines.

"I can't believe you Dolla…you gambling with re-up money…that's fucked up dude," Cream squawked as they dipped thru the slot machine area then neared the cashier's cage.

"Dude it's my fucking money and I can always make it back."

"Save that shit you degenerate." Cream responded stepping in line.

After handing the cashier their trays of casino chips' and tickets they were giving fresh stacks of money and told to have a nice day and come back. They stepped out of the Casino's gaming area and hit the casino's huge concourse surrounded by restaurants, bars, and souvenir shops. NyJewel was seated on a group of benches at the center of the concourse by a set of small waterfalls imitating Niagara Falls.

"Hey fellas." NyJewel greeted the trio while rising to her feet and holding the truck keys in her hand.

"Ny what's good." Cream responded taking the truck keys from NyJewel then handing her a hotel room key.

"Yeah the room number 619," Dolla informed. "Zulu will be more than pleased to escort you up to the room Ny…wont you Zulu."

"Why you gotta joke so much," Zulu blasted at Dolla while refusing to gaze upon NyJewel. "Come on let's go across the bridge and do this."

"Yo only two of us need to cross the border with all this money." Cream stated twirling the keys around on his finger.

"So you know what that mean Zulu." Dolla began cheesing standing beside Cream. "You gotta let NyJewel babysit you like back in the day baby boy."

"Fuck you you fucking clown." Zulu was vexed at the thought of being around the teasing NyJewel. Cream then tossed Zulu the keys to his car before him and Dolla left the casino and headed across the bridge to Canada.

Zulu shot a displeasing gaze at NyJewel before stepping over to a bar in the concourse. NyJewel stood still like the Indian statue by the bench she was standing near. She watched Zulu skate to the bar paying her no mind like she didn't even exist. Zulu hit the bar and downed a double shot, feeling the intoxicating liquor stimulate him and open him up a little.

"Come on let's break out I drive you home," Zulu stepped back over to NyJewel avoiding eye contact with her. "I need some fresh air anyway."

"Stop it Zulu." NyJewel grabbed his hand as he slid by her. "Stop acting childish Zulu…we need to talk…we too close for this."

"Exactly." Zulu finally put his gaze upon her. NyJewel was so gorgeous. Her shiny brown hair cascaded down her smooth cinnamon flavored skin complimenting her tone while her cat like eyes were so seductive looking.

"We know each other too well for you to act like I'm a stranger," Zulu didn't even realize it because he was caught up in her rapture. Right there in the middle of the concourse where tourist snapped photos and purchased souvenirs, Zulu pulled NyJewel close to him and peered deeply into her eyes. "Stop playing games with me…you know I want you but I need you…you know I do."

"His heart may need me but his penis wants me." NyJewel thought to herself feeling a quiver pulsate along her spine while being held in Zulu's embrace. He was much younger than her, but she felt so protected in his arms and his masculinity turned her on.

"Stop playing with my emotions Zulu."

"I'm not playing Ny…give me a chance to show you I'm serious." Zulu intensely stared into her lonely eyes.

"I'm…I'm just scared--."

"Scared of what?"

"Of you hurting me and playing with my feelings…you already in a relationship."

"I'm not tryna--," Zulu was cut short by an Asian tourist who held a Nikon camera around his neck.

"Perfect Picture." The Asian man held the camera loving the view of Zulu and NyJewel embracing in front of the neon lit waterfalls in the concourse. "May I take your photo…please its perfect."

Zulu and NyJewel glanced at each other surprisingly before NyJewel shouted, *"Sure you can."*

"You are a beautiful couple." The Asian man stated snapping two photos of them.

"Come on we upstairs," Zulu led NyJewel to the elevator with his arm around her waist. As they rode the elevator up silence took a hold of the mood as they both entertained the thoughts flooding their hearts and minds.

Zulu on one hand was dealing with his lust for NyJewel while another part of him cared for NyJewel. And then he hated the fact that NyJewel gave Destiny the impression her and Zulu had something going on. The way Zulu in his lustful mind thought, he would rather lose Destiny for having an affair with NyJewel than to lose Destiny and he hadn't even tapped NyJewel's good loving. That would suck losing on both ends.

NyJewel on the plane of her womanhood knew Zulu was a strong and determined young man. She loved that about Zulu. Since he was a young youth he was always protective over her and made her feel loved. NyJewel never had a man to truly love her. She never even knew her father. And even though Zulu was some years younger than her, it was a time he made her experience a feeling of protection little girls and women felt with their fathers. NyJewel was never the one to love another woman's man, but as tempting as it was, NyJewel refused to be a piece of flesh or a jump off to any man no matter who he was and no matter how lonely she felt.

"I wish you loved me now like you did back then." NyJewel stated when the elevator reached their floor.

"I'm not a kid no more Ny...I can love you better," Zulu responded following NyJewel out of the elevator and down the hall to the room.

"How can you when you love Destiny too?" NyJewel paused and studied his face as they stood at the door to the room. "You only have one heart but you trying to love two women."

Zulu was at a loss for words as he stood frozen watching NyJewel slide the room card into the door. He followed her into the room digging deep into his mental archive searching for some game to hit her with. This was the real deal and this was no time for games Zulu then realized watching NyJewel sashay over to the large panoramic window.

"I know you love Destiny Zulu and I'm not here to mess up what yall have with each other," NyJewel turned from the window and peered across the room at Zulu who stood at the foot of the bed. She then slowly slid over to Zulu and hugged him as he stood frozen in the Glaciers of his thoughts. "And I know you care for me Zulu…no one ever gave me the attention you used to give me…no one ever made me feel appreciated and wanted like you…I miss that so much Zulu," NyJewel's voice began to falter and tears began gleaming in her eyes. She lay her head on Zulu's shoulder as they embraced. "I get lonely Zulu having no one…I been lonely for as long as I can remember…only when we were younger did I feel happy…just me and you…we was all we had when our mothers left us to fend for ourselves…but we both grew up and you fell in love with Destiny…you just forgot about us and what we had."

"What the fuck!!!" A flashback triggered a nerve in Zulu's system. He threw NyJewel's arms from off him and stepped back, shooting an unforgiving look at the teary eyed NyJewel. Zulu now felt she was playing some sort of reverse psychology. Zulu felt she was the one who was dead wrong and selfish and she deserved to be lonely. Zulu now felt like a cold sucker trying to game her and show her some love. Now he was going to smash her with the truth and let her know how he truly felt.

"You got some fucking nerve yo," Zulu was in flip mode. "When they sent me to the Masten Street Boys Home you wasn't there for me…you only wrote me like three times and you only came to see me once…you didn't give a fuck about me…you was all I had and you knew my mother just died…and you the one who promised her on her death bed you would always be there for me…get the fuck outta here."

"But Zulu I went away to College…what was I supposed to do with my life…I told you once I finished college I was gonna come back and get you so we could move outta town so you could get away from these streets."

"But you didn't."

"Because you went to Destiny and her family like you didn't need me…and you wanted the streets more than anything."

"Well the streets is how I was taking care of myself…when I came out of the boys home I had no one or nothing but the streets…I was only 15…no family or no one…I had to live in them fucked up group homes until Destiny and her family came thru for me and took me in…you left me out here in this fucking jungle and this is what I become…if you can't accept this then oh well…you one of the reasons I'm like this."

"But Zulu I'm sorry." NyJewel tried hugging Zulu but he pushed her hands away and stepped over to the window overlooking the splashing waters of Niagara Falls pour into the mouth of the river.

NyJewel stood close behind Zulu wishing she could turn back the hands of time. Truth be told, what happened back then was meant to happen and there was nothing no one could do because the Creator wrote it that way in the book of life. When Zulu's mother was called back to the essence of the earth, the streets became Zulu's guardian and he loved the streets. NyJewel was striving to elevate herself in life so she went off to college. This was the destiny they chose and no one was to blame or could change it but them.

"Please Zulu you gotta forgive me…I love you and I need you to know that I need you…I'm sorry I wasn't there when you needed me," NyJewel stood behind Zulu and wrapped her arms around him while planting her face in his back.

As Zulu gazed at the falls he wondered what would his life had been like if the Masten Street Boys Home would have released him to NyJewel instead of the group homes. Would him and NyJewel have ended up out of town in a nice environment where Zulu could've finished high school, learned a skilled trade, went to college and had a nice life with NyJewel. He pondered about the possibilities of that fantasy life before his cell phone rung and brought him back to reality. It was Cream and Dolla calling, a reminder and testament to the real world Zulu was born and raised in; a world where adolescents were forced to be men as soon as they reached puberty.

"Please don't leave me Zulu." NyJewel squeezed him with all the strength she had as Zulu whipped out his cell phone. "Please let's stay here Zulu…please."

"Let me answer this," Zulu smiled like a happy child before answering, "Yo."

"It's all good bro...the raft made it across the river."

"Holla."

"Peace."

Zulu hung up his cell phone, spun around and gazed into NyJewel's face. He began to speak but she placed her index finger on his lips stopping him from opening his mouth. They kissed slowly, squeezing each other tightly before finding their way to the bed. It would be two days before they jumped out of the bed and left the room. They lay cuddled wrapped in each other's arms opening their hearts and rekindling a fiery love they always knew would surface.

Zulu was waiting for this moment longer than a Christian was waiting on the return of Jesus Christ. His day came and now he felt unstoppable and thus far, he'd accomplished almost everything he set out to accomplish. Street Dreams were real.

....

A few days later up in Creative Expressions Hair Salon it was the usual weave sewing, hair curling, roller setting, hair braiding and the everyday gossip about who's who, what's going on, who balling, who sleeping with who and *blah-zay-blah*.

At one moment NyJewel aroused everyone's curiosity about who and what was responsible for the glow of love on her face. NyJewel was all smiles and even while getting her roller set and reading the latest issue of Essence Magazine, she kept blushing.

"Come on Ny I'm yo best friend," Lashelle stated pulling the rollers out of NyJewel's hair. Lashelle then whispered, "I know you too well girl...you met somebody and got you some didn't you girl?"

The thought alone of how Zulu worked her insides sent tingles throbbing thru NyJewel's body causing her to squirm around in the salon chair she sat in. NyJewel wasn't young and quick to go blabbing about her personal business so she decided to keep it to herself until she knew for sure Zulu was gonna play his cards right.

"*Nooo* Shelle I haven't met no one." NyJewel turned a page in the magazine not interested in Lashelle's inquiry.

"Girl you had to get something up in between them thighs the way you moving and smiling...I aint seen you like this in I don't know how long," Lashelle looked into NyJewel's face and whispered, "You can't stop cheesing girl...and if you wanna be secret squirrel you need to stop blushing like you got a nut."

NyJewel lifted her gaze from the magazine and peered into Lashelle's face, "Girl I'm not smiling."

"You smiling like a little girl in Barbie Dream Land." Lashelle pulled the last roller out of NyJewel's hair and began twirling her mahogany brown hair into ringlets that cascaded down her shoulders and rested on her collar bone. Lashelle caught a sight that revealed it all. "Un un girl...what's that on yo chest heffa." Lashelle just now peeped the bright and fresh ink of a leopard's head tattooed on NyJewel's cleavage. The leopard was growling with the word *"Zulu"* barking from its mouth. Lashelle took her hand and covered her wide open mouth in shock. "No Ny...it can't be."

"Damn girl would you finish my hair." NyJewel inched around in her seat and pulled her blouse up to cover up her cleavage. "Now you know could we move on."

"Um huh girl...go head you heffa...you a old cougar on the low low...I always knew it was something deeper with you and Zulu...but ain't you like 10 years older than him?"

"First off age don't even matter...and two...you got some nerve you cradle rocker...you screwed Dolla how long ago?" NyJewel tooted her lips and rolled her eyes at Lashelle.

"Ok ok I can't lie...Zulu and his friends got it going on and they way ahead of they time...they better than all the guys our age...it seems like all the men we grew up with either dead, in jail, or on drugs...or if they got they senses they already taken...a sister can't find happiness with these men out here for nothing girl."

"Sometimes happiness and love can be right in yo face but you will never know it unless you give it a chance."

"I hear that girl," Lashelle finished NyJewel's hair and spun the chair around so NyJewel could face the mirror. "Look at you Ny…you look like a new woman with a new love…go head with yo Zulu."

"Stop it girl."

"Well I wanna celebrate with you," Lashelle stepped to the sink to rinse her hands, "I got a nice cold bottle of some Pinot Minor in the fridge just for us."

"Ok well let me call Zulu to bring me something to eat…I don't wanna drink on an empty stomach." NyJewel stood up out the chair and grabbed her phone from off the work station. NyJewel and Lashelle was unaware of who the lady was sitting two stations over getting her own hair done. It was none other than Desiree's best friend and tag team dance partner Chocolate. The whole time Chocolate was air hustling and the info she just scooped up was right up her alley of bisexual attraction. She was gonna expose Zulu's double life with NyJewel to Destiny and hopefully she could play the shoulder to cry on for Destiny. Hopefully Destiny would thank Chocolate and they could share some feminine loving which Destiny might love better than the love of a doggish cheating man.

....

Zulu and the crew posted up on Terror's Ocean Grey *Mitsubishi Diamante* and Prince's Forest Green *Bonneville* on the avenue in front of Pristine Kuttz; a new barbershop establishment owned by the Young Assassins.

"Prince what they got you reading over there with yo illiterate ass," Dolla was being his usual self and clowning like always. Prince just ignored Dolla and continued breezing thru the *F.E.D.S magazine*. He was zoning into an article about a Man known as the Father Allah.

"Ay yo check this out yall," Prince shouted with his eyes still glued to the article, "What yall think about the Black Man being God…all religions teach that the Creator created the first man as a Black Man who have power over all things…we made in the image of the Creator and we got the power to control our destiny and we the ones who direct the course of our life…the power and spirit of God is in us to bring about whatever reality we want…the reason why we in this fucked up situation as Black people is because we made it like this for ourselves…we the Creators of the situations we experience in life…and we the soul controllers and rulers of this universe…that's why man the one who make all things happen…what yall think about that."

"I think you bugged out Prince and you going crazy now." Dolla responded taking Prince's spiritual quest lightly and started joking. "I think the Blackman a fool…and the Whiteman just a wicked and racist dude who wanna hate everybody and own everything for himself…you need to stop reading whatever you reading because that shit gone fuck yo mind up worse than it is Prince…you already act possessed and shit…being all quiet like you see dead people." Dolla aroused a little laughter in everyone.

Everyone knew Prince was going through a psychological dilemma and it wasn't often Prince would engage in any type of conversation. Prince was silent most times because he didn't know if he would explode or shut down. But the article that Prince was reading about the Father Allah seemed to have Prince's attention and open him up.

"Yo Dolla chill out and let the man speak his piece," everyone cut the joking as Prince continued focusing back on the article.

The article explained the life of a man known as The Father Allah, aka Clarence 13X. Clarence 13X was in the Nation of Islam with Malcolm X. And through the Divine teachings of the Honorable Elijah Muhammad who was the leader of the Nation of Islam, Clarence 13X experienced Spiritual Enlightenment and realized the Divinity of himself as being God as all religions state is the true nature of Man. Clarence 13X left the Nation of Islam and became known as the Father Allah. He hit the streets of New York City and went on a divine mission to save the lives of thousands and thousands of black, white, and Hispanic youth who were caught up in the street life and rejected by society. He taught black and Hispanic youth that they were more than thugs, dope boys, bitches and hoes, and that their true nature was to be Supreme Beings who had the Power and Intelligence to be Great Builders and Universal Architects that could build a righteous civilization instead of destroying themselves. The Father Allah taught the youth to acquire knowledge of all things in existence which would activate their minds and make them great. The thousands of youth whom he enlightened became known as The Nation of Gods and Earths, aka The 5 Percenters, or The Gods and Earths. The wisdom manifested by The Father Allah captured Prince's attention and made him look at himself in a whole different light. And while Prince read the article, Prince was in his own realm visualizing himself as being a God of his own universe who could destroy the wickedness surrounding his life.

Dolla then interrupted Prince's vision. "Prince I hope that shit with the cops not gone cause you to become some black revolutionary that hate crooked cops and drug dealers…because we hustling for life Brother Man."

The word cops irked Prince and sent a shock bolting through him. Prince jumped up and shouted, "Shut the fuck up Dolla you always joking like this shit a game…this shit is real out here…and that shit I went thru with them pigs made me see my life flash right in front of me…it only takes a second for yo life to be over…and I wouldn't want none of yall to experience what I experienced with them fucking cops…I almost lost my life and I almost lost my mind…this shit is real."

"Damn my bad bro I ain't mean it like that," Dolla sincerely apologized and gave Prince a brotherly hug, "I was just joking."

"I swear I wanna change my life before it's over," Prince focused his eyes up to the blue sky while they all stood on the avenue. "This the only life we ever knew and this shit gone rush us to the grave…I know it's more to life than this…this can't be the only life for us…I know it can't be…I don't know how…but I'm gone change my life for the better because this shit don't make me happy no more…word up…the murder, hustling, police beef…this not happiness…it's not."

"Nigga I know what will make you happy," Terror cut in brushing his wave cut while scoping his reflection on the shiny frame of his car, "Lets hit the town and snatch some hoes…we gone get our boy Prince laid by two hoes…a threesome gone make my boy happy."

"I'm down…word up." Cream and Killa agreed

"Count me in…hell yeah." Zulu and Dolla added. Zulu then pulled out his ringing cell phone and answered it. It was NyJewel requesting a late lunch for her and the ladies at the hair salon. It was a change of plans. Instead of hitting the town searching for some ladies, they were going to hit the hair salon where the ladies were at. The crew hit Ike's Steakhouse and copped almost a dozen steak hoagies and French fries then hit the salon ready to mingle with the ladies.

"Got damn some of these broads ugly as fuck without they hair done," Terror quietly told Cream as they slid inside the salon.

"It's between they legs' I'm focused on and how they mouth work...not they face," Cream responded.

With Dolla in the lead carrying several bags of food the crew stepped into the salon catching the ladies with their hair half done and exposing their true looks. "Hello ladies," Dolla greeted the ladies while sitting the bags of food on the table. "Ruff Buff's Chocolate Boy Wonder here to harmonize yall insides with this grubbing."

"Awww you so sweet Dolla," Lashelle rushed over helping Dolla sort out the food on the table cluttered with women's magazines.

As soon as Zulu stepped inside the salon Chocolate dipped into the bathroom and before she entered she peeped back and stole the sight of Zulu and NyJewel hugging and kissing. Chocolate quietly shut the bathroom door then dialed Destiny while checking out her new hair du in the mirror. Destiny didn't answer so Chocolate called again and still no answer. Chocolate knew Destiny didn't like her but if only Destiny knew Chocolate was only trying to open Destiny's eyes. Chocolate tried calling again and to her surprise Destiny answered in a nasty way.

"Bitch why you blowing me up like you want me to fuck you up?" Destiny screamed into the phone. "Bitch we not friends don't be calling my phone like that."

"I'm sorry I was just trying to tell you something important."

"What the fuck do you want you trifling whore?"

"Whoa calm down Destiny...what I'm about to put you up on girl gone have you thanking me for the true friend I really am...I'm at Creative Expressions and you need to get here now...I'm gone send you a picture of yo so-called man and that bitch NyJewel...hurry up girl and get here so you can catch them right in the act," Chocolate cracked the bathroom door open and peeked out into the shop and told Destiny, "They sitting up on the couch sharing a sub Destiny…you better---."

"Click." Destiny hung up in a rage.

Chocolate continued scoping herself out in the mirror, took a deep breath, twirled the braids dangling down her face then stepped out the bathroom. It seemed like all the fellas paired up with a lady and had lunch with them. Killa was the only one who sat dolo until Trick Daddy peeped Chocolate creeping his way, Trick Daddy did what he did best.

"Chocolate…bring yo sexy ass over here," Killa was busting his steak hoagie down like he wanted to munch on Chocolate's thick and succulent thighs swinging his way.

"What's up pretty boy?" Chocolate fell onto the sofa beside Killa observing everyone munching and mingling, everyone's focus was occupied.

"Damn I'm feeling yo braids…you just got em done?" Killa softly tugged at her braids.

"Yeah…you really like em?"

"Hell yeah…you look like *Regina King from Poetic Justice.*"

"I look better than her."

"Sure you right," Killa took a bite of his sub then cleansed his face and hands with a paper towel. He then threw his arm around Chocolate and moved the braids from blocking her ear and whispered, "I'm loving yo sexy chocolate ass right now…I wanna pull on yo braids in a gentle way while you moan my name."

"Ok so take a picture of me since I'm so sexy," Chocolate handed Killa her cell phone then swiveled around in her seat with her back facing Zulu and NyJewel. If Killa hadn't let his eyes get hypnotized by Chocolate's juicy titties bursting out her blouse he would've peeped Zulu and NyJewel all up in Chocolate's flick.

Killa captured the image, catching a smiling Chocolate blowing a kiss and, in the background, NyJewel sat on Zulu's lap while they shared a sub. Killa took the pics then handed Chocolate her phone paying no mind to the direct and incriminating evidence he just put together on Zulu. All he was focused on was dipping into the creamy chocolate pudding sitting in his face.

"Come on Chocolate let's break out," Killa stated observing Chocolate glue her eyes to her phone and checking out the flicks he just took of her.

"What you got for me Killa?" Chocolate was smiling while still scoping out the picture. "You talking bout you wanna pull on my braids…you bet not pull em out."

"I pay for yo braids sexy." Killa whispered in her ear while rubbing on her thighs.

"Ok then pay Tisha for my hair because I aint pay her yet…its 125…you get a discount price pretty boy," Chocolate told Killa as he guided his hand up and down her thighs. All Chocolate could think of was how the picture Killa just took was worth more than the sexual loving she was gonna put on him. The picture was worth Chocolate being Killa's hoe if Chocolate could pull off her scheme. And as Chocolate sent the picture to Destiny, all Chocolate could even think of was Destiny thanking her and crying on her shoulder.

Killa paid the hairstylist for Chocolate's braided hair du, and before the two dipped out the salon to handle their business, Chocolate shot Zulu a sly smirk and waved at him. When Destiny received the picture text from Chocolate, Destiny was at home jumping into her sneakers. Upon seeing the picture which told it all, Destiny stormed into her and Zulu's bedroom and without thinking, Destiny lifted and threw the king sized mattress off the bed with the strength of a body builder she had so much anger. She was on fire and ready to spit flames when she snatched Zulu's 38 snub nose which was under the mattress.

"I'm gone kill him…that bitch NyJewel…and that nasty bitch Chocolate…eww…I hate them," Destiny raged throwing the gun in her purse and storming out of the house in tears.

Back up in Creative Expressions.

NyJewel sat with her luscious butt planted in Zulu's lap getting intimate, so intimate they felt the piercing eyes of what seemed like everyone watching them. They then slid outside and jumped inside of NyJewel's ride for a little more privacy. If only Zulu had an inkling of intuition about Chocolate's misery loving company scheme, Zulu would've left the hood immediately and took NyJewel somewhere far far away from the danger Destiny was about to bring to the hood.

"Why you staring at me like that Ny?" Zulu asked as he lay back in the passenger seat. NyJewel's stare penetrated Zulu and ventured deeper than the physical shell she was looking at. She was in love with Zulu and entwined with his soul, but she wondered was his soul on the same plane.

"Because I love you so much Zulu." NyJewel leaned over and kissed him on his lips. "But Zulu," NyJewel cuffed Zulu's hand and lowered her gaze to their locked hands. "I hope you understand that I can't share you and I can't be second to no woman Zulu...it's not right."

"Here we go with the bullshit." Zulu sighed tensely hearing his inner voice ring out, *"I should've known this shit was coming."* Zulu told himself remaining silent.

"Zulu answer me."

"Damn Ny," Zulu inched closer to her still holding her hand. "You not second to no one...I love you with all my heart...you said you understood my situation and you would give me time...I'm just...damn what the fuck." Zulu was living the crazy life of loving two women. He didn't know what to do.

"Zulu I'm serious...you gonna have to choose who it's gonna be...me or Destiny...you can't have yo cake and eat it too."

"Why can't I...the cake supposed to be ate."

"This not a game Zulu...people feelings involved...you gotta make a decision if you wanna be with me," NyJewel stated igniting the engine. "I'm going downtown to run some errands...make up yo mind love...I'm not going anywhere...I'm here waiting on you Zulu," NyJewel gently touched Zulu's chin and looked deeply into his eyes before kissing him, "I love you Zulu but I'm not gonna let you crush my heart."

"Alright alright...I get with you later Ny," Zulu quickly responded jumping out of the car. He dragged his feet over to the salon and sat on the steps letting his thoughts get absorbed by his world of confusion. He was stuck between two gardens of paradise and didn't know which garden to choose. All the money and power couldn't solve this problem. And spitting game didn't make it no better when feelings were at play. In a millisecond Zulu's emotions and thoughts teeter tottered making his heart feel like a ton of bricks. His thought waves were scrambled all over the place and racing like the cars zooming up and down the avenue. His soul felt a cloud of confusion that weighed him down like the force of gravity. He couldn't think or move. Even when the purple Dodge Stratus recklessly swerved into the curb in front of the salon Zulu didn't budge. He wasn't on point at all and his life could be snatched easier than a pocket book on a mid-town Manhattan Street.

"What the hell is this you dirty cheating ass bastard?" Destiny jumped out of the passenger seat of the Dodge Stratus and charged Zulu holding her phone in her hand for him to peep himself in action.

"Huh—what." Zulu jumped up and cluelessly stepped to Destiny getting a view of what was on her phone. *"Whoa—what the fuck."* Zulu couldn't believe his eyes. He wondered how in the world could it be. Then it hit him mentally like Destiny hit him in the face physically. "How you gone believe Chocolate?" Zulu yelled holding his face which was stinging from Destiny hitting him with the phone.

"It's right here you dirty bastard," Destiny rocked Zulu again in the face. She then turned to her three friends who were jumping out of the car ready to send someone or some people to the ER. Destiny yelled to her friends, "Go see if that bitch NyJewel up in there and get Chocolate too…all y'all dirty bastards gone die today."

"Yo she was just--," Zulu tried explaining before catching more punches and scratches to his face by Destiny as her friends rushed into the salon.

"I can't believe you—why—how could you do this to me." Destiny let the pain of heartache and rage throw her hands pummeling into Zulu's face and upper body. Zulu raised his arms in defense before grabbing her and trying to restrain her.

"I love you Destiny it's not what you thinking…I—."

"Get off me you liar…I knew it…I hate you…you played me."
Destiny's lungs opened wide and her vocal chords blasted like a screaming rock
concert. Her three friends stormed back out of the salon furiously yelling and
being followed by everyone else who was in the salon. The scene became chaotic
like a mini riot. There was so much screaming and yelling combined with the
sounds of car horns of spectators cruising by it was total havoc.

Zulu struggled to hold the uncontrollable Destiny while the ruckus
ensued. One of Destiny's razor slashing friends then crept up on Zulu with a
razor in her hand yelling, "Get off my girl you dirty snake ass nigga." The girl
wanted to slash Zulu but Destiny was in the way.

Zulu hurried and released Destiny from his hold because he felt so
vulnerable not knowing if the other girls were behind him ready to surround him
and slash him.

"You cheating ass disloyal nigga…we gone rip yo ass up you dirty
scumbag…you always got my girl crying." Destiny's friend threatened charging
at Zulu swinging a razor.

"Bitch I wish you would," Terror stepped in front of Zulu and raised his
shirt revealing the gun on his waist. "Bitch back the fuck up."

"Word up yall need to mind yall fucking business," Zulu eased back to
the salon steps where the crew stood blocking Lashelle and the ladies of the
salon from hitting the sidewalk and clashing with Destiny and her friends. Curses
and every file name in the book was exchanged between the two groups of
females as the fellas stood in between.

"Yo we gotta get Destiny and them outta here before the boys pull up,"
Cream alerted observing the strip walkers forming crowds while people rushed
out of stores and cars held up traffic spectating the ruckus. "If the boys come
niggas going to jail."

"Hell yeah let's get these hoes outta here," Terror added nudging the
chrome on his waist. "Yo I'm gone hit the cut and bust a couple shots so
muthafuckas break outta here."

"Hell no you bugging," Prince cut in before he turned to Lashelle and
the other ladies on the steps of the salon, "Go on inside Shelle we got this."

"We gone fuck yall up and this tang a lang ass shop," Destiny and her friends ranted as Lashelle and the ladies began stepping back into the shop.

"What." Lashelle and her crew then spun around and attempted to charge off the steps. "I wish you bitches would." Lashelle shouted clutching a pair of hot curlers in her hand.

"Shelle go back inside." Dolla snatched her and motioned the ladies back inside while assuring them they would handle the situation.

"Come on Zulu let's bounce," Prince snatched Zulu and began stepping away to his car. "If you leave Destiny and her girls gone leave."

Destiny peeped Zulu skating away with Prince and ready to break out. She dashed to her girlfriend's car, yanked the door open and leaned inside. Everyone thought she was deciding to leave so everyone began heading to their cars. Destiny then leaned from out of the car with her hand in her purse.

"Zuluuuuu." Destiny's scream was like thunder causing everyone to fearfully stop in their tracks. Zulu was about four cars ahead on the sidewalk and Prince was behind him pushing him forward and telling him not to look back. Zulu was nearing Prince's car and went to reach for the door handle. It happened so quick no one had time to realize why Destiny screamed Zulu's name so loud. It was too late as everyone watched in shock as Destiny aimed the 38 Revolver in Zulu's direction.

"Boooom." The blast rocked the block. The deafening gunshot popped ear drums and the heavy smell of gun powder reeked in the air.

"Oh shit," Zulu couldn't believe his eyes when Destiny let off the shot as he jumped behind Prince's car. Destiny gripped the pistol firmly in a stance like a true gun clapper. As everyone realized what just had happened, they rushed Destiny and wrestled the gun from out of her hand.

"I got it I got it." Dolla shouted pushing one of Destiny's friends away as he took the gun out of Destiny's trembling hand. Destiny and her friends then jumped in their ride and peeled out. Prince and Terror's cars then murked off seconds later.

Terror followed Prince to a side street several blocks down the avenue. They pulled over on a side street and Dolla jumped out and hustled into the backyard of an abandoned house where he stashed the gun. Dolla jumped back in the wheel and they all headed over to Trinidad Park.

"Yo I'm staying back in the car." Prince told Zulu before Zulu got out the car to join the others who were heading over to the park. "That shit just took my breath away Zulu…this shit getting crazier and crazier yo…I never seen Destiny that mad…who would even expect she would do some shit like that."

"*Mannn.*" Zulu unbelievably blew threw his teeth.

"This shit just got me all fucked up Zulu…I'm tired Zulu…I feel sick…this shit is draining my energy bro for real."

"Nigga you act like it was you she was shooting at." Zulu shot back halfway out the car.

"Whatever Zulu…you act like you love this drama shit…we been having this drama for the longest…you don't get tired of this shit yo?"

"Nigga it's life what the fuck you expect."

"Whatever yo I'm gone sit here and take a nap…I'm literally tired."

"Stop stressing bro," Zulu stated jumping out the car and shutting the door. He headed over to the park where everyone was seated on the benches between the playground and basketball court.

"Zulu yo pimping weak as hell bro." Dolla threw in the air dribbling a basketball he snatched from off the ground.

"Man its simple Zulu," Terror stated sitting on a bench rolling up a blunt. "If you want both of them you gotta make em believe if they want you it's the only way they can have you…they can either accept it or reject it."

"Zulu a gangster not a pimp," Cream added tossing Terror a lighter.

"That's understood yo," Terror lit the blunt and inhaled deeply then blew O's out of his mouth. "But he a man…and in a relationship the man call the shots…right or wrong?"

"That's true but pimping aint for everyone Terror…we G's nigga…we get money and bust our guns…we aint playing with these hoes," Cream responded.

"Nigga I aint a pimp but that shit is real and one of the first jobs man had," Terror remarked.

Dolla was busy dribbling the ball but listening. Zulu sat on the benches stuck not knowing what to think about the situation. Zulu knew one thing about Terror. If Terror hadn't learned anything in life, he learned he had a thirst for blood and he knew a lot about the manipulative game of pimping from watching his grimy aunt and her pimp boyfriend. Terror's aunt always told him that a man who knew his power as a man and had the gift of charm could have a woman crawling on her knees and eating out of his hands. It was a man's world even though women made the world worth living in, but the man who had the influential skill of manipulation could enjoy the world through the submission of women.

"See check it Zulu," Terror continued after passing the blunt to Cream. "It's yo world and you the reason these broads going crazy...you the cause of it...and that show you the mental power you got over them...you got so much power over them you can make them happy or crazy...you make em crazy like you did Destiny and they will try to kill you...but if you make em happy they will submit to you to keep being happy...you feel me."

"Got damn boy I taught you well." Dolla stopped dribbling the ball in acknowledgement to Terror's philosophy. Dolla then snatched the blunt from Cream and asked Terror, "Why that trick ass brother of yours aint strong on his pimping like you Terror?"

"Ask yo self that Dolla...both of yall niggas is cold tricks and always giving yall money away to these broads...money don't make women happy it only make them comfortable and make em feel a little powerful...but it's the man who make the woman feel happy."

"Yo I feel you on that Terror," Cream raised his brow in agreement with Terror. "I give these broads dick and that's it...no strings attached and none of that shit...I work too hard in these streets to give my money away...my dick enough for these broads and they happy with that."

"Man all yall niggas is crazy." Zulu shook his head in confusion. "All this shit easier said than done."

"It's easier said than done because you never done it." Terror responded. "Nothing is impossible Zulu...it's all about how determined you is to make it happen…but like they say…pimping aint easy for everyone."

"Damn," Cream spit out. "I know one thing…I'm a G…I aint with the pimping shit."

"Word up."

They finished the blunt then decided to leave the park. Cream was the first to approach Prince's car which was parked next to Terror's. Cream jumped in the passenger seat to Prince's car and noticed Prince was reclined back in his seat knocked out sleep. He tapped Prince on his shoulder to wake him up and noticed Prince's Emory green Polo shirt was soaked in blood around his torso. Cream panicked.

"Yo Prince shot yall," Cream yelled out the car then started tapping Prince and shaking him. "Bro wake up…wake up bro."

Everyone rushed into the car and pulled Prince into the backseat. Cream jumped behind the wheel and pushed it to the hospital blowing red lights and swerving around corners in a rush. When they swerved in front of the emergency room entrance to the Erie County Medical Center, a few paramedics were standing by the automatic sliding doors conversing.

"Our friend was shot…he got hit by a stray bullet at a basketball court," Cream jumped out the wheel and motioned towards the backseat where the others were pulling Prince out. The medics snatched a stretcher and swung by the car where Prince was lifted and placed on it. Terror snatched everything from out of Prince's pocket except his license while the medics stuffed an oxygen mask on his face and used scissors to tear off his clothes before rushing Prince inside. Prince was still breathing and it was a 50/50 chance he would survive. It all depended on the internal damage the slug done to his gut and it was too early to know.

"*Damn,*" Zulu thought to himself as they all slowly climbed back into Prince's blood soaked car, "*He caught a fucking slug for me and my crazy world of women…I know my boy wanted a change…just please don't let him die…please.*"

CHAPTER 10

Under a full moon and a few hours after taking Prince to the hospital, Zulu found himself slumped back on the steps to a building next to Hakeem's deli on the avenue. He drowned his lungs with the smooth taste of the fiery Hennessy trying to wash away the pain eating his soul. His world seemed to be sucked into a black hole of depression, guilt, and sorrow. He never intended on crushing Destiny's heart in his pursuit of instant gratification which he believed was happiness. He wasn't trying to play with NyJewel's feelings. And to make matters worse, he hated the fact that Prince had to suffer for his actions. Regardless to Zulu's good intentions, he turned his world upside down into hell and dragged Prince into hell with him unknowingly.

Zulu guzzled his Hennessy and let the scorching liquor burn his thoughts of anguish into the ashes of his black soul. He wasn't a cigarette smoker, but since earlier after they took Prince to the hospital Zulu smoked almost half a pack of cigarettes and he was on his third pint of Hennessy.

The smooth gangster flow of *Bad Boy artist Shyne* could be felt and heard thumping down the avenue as the lyrics to *"Diamonds and Mac 10's"* echoed off the buildings on the block. It was Killa rolling the chrome spree-wheel rims of his Grand Cherokee in front of Hakeem's deli.

"Keep yo head up Zulu...don't let these broads have you out here sleeping and get caught slipping." Killa jumped out the truck shining like the gold Gucci link with the AK-47 medallion swinging around his neck with the matching bracelets and gold watch on his wrists. His butterscotch skin tone glossed equally with his jewels giving him an illustrious glow. "It's not the end of the world playboy...Prince just came out of surgery and they said he should be alright...yo world aint over Zulu."

"Yo I jive wish it was." Zulu sighed relieving his body of the tension before swinging the bottle of Henny to Killa who stood on side of the stoop. "Destiny hate me...Prince gone wanna kill me when he come out...and NyJewel don't even wanna deal with me and my drama anymore."

"It was a mistake Zulu and everyone know that…Prince ain't gonna hold that against you…everyone knows when women hurt and scorned they can cause earthquakes and fuck shit up for everybody…and its all because of us…see hear me out Zulu," Killa wiped the steps before sitting down next to Zulu.

"See when me and my brother was kids in Nigeria and we used to play rough with the girls, my Nana used to always tell us that the female is not to be treated rough in no way, shape, form, or fashion…she's precious and resembles the earth…in my people's culture back home it's called Yoruba…and they say the earth is Yemaya…she the earth goddess and that's the representation of the Black woman…look at how beautiful and lovely the earth is…the earth provides for us and nurture us just like our mothers do…that's why we gotta treat women right because they precious and sacred like the earth." Killa observed Zulu nodding attentively. *"See Zulu a lot of these dudes out here think women only here to be our servants and sex toys…them niggas is male chauvinistic and think women is only for our satisfaction…yo we all came into life through the womb of the woman…so they deserve more than the way we treat them…why you think they get crazy when they get mad…they go thru hell for nine months creating us…and they deserve so much honor for that alone…see my Baba (Father) taught us that over here in America, the Black Man follow the ways of the Wazungu (White People) and we treat our women the way they treat they women…the Black Woman was always highly respected and honored in Africa but over here the Wazungu don't honor women and we follow him so we don't honor our women like we should, but one thing about the Wazungu, he place the white women above all other women, we gotta place the black woman on top because we all come from a black woman…since we don't acknowledge our women's worth, that's why they get evil when we don't cherish them…they get to setting niggas up…getting niggas locked up…stealing from us…they even get to shooting and killing niggas--,"* Killa paused tucking his lips in trying not to laugh at the reality of Destiny trying to kill Zulu.

"Yo the shit aint funny nigga," Zulu shook his head angrily at Killa clowning on him, "Prince could've died yo." Zulu barked snatching his bottle from Killa.

"He aint dead though Zulu…he gone be good. I'm just saying yo, if you want everything smooth in life with yo women…you gotta treasure them…my Baba (Father) had a crew of wives back in Nigeria…he had like five wives and my mother was number one…but he treasured all of them and gave them all whatever they wanted so they let him be the Man."

"Man that shit may go down in Africa or wherever…but this the hood right here…and these women aint going for that shit…aint no way I can make that happen…aint no money or nothing gone make that shit happen."

"Yeah in yo situation you jive right," Killa raised his brow in agreement, *"All I know Zulu is that women just wanna be happy like we do…that's all yo…its simple…that's why every woman I deal with I make happy so they wont have a reason to put me on they shit list."*

"You call spending money on them making them happy…money don't make a thorough broad happy Killa…only them gold digging bitches satisfied with the money."

"See yall be tryna clown da kid like I'm a trick or some john or some shit…yall niggas got me twisted," Killa closed his eyes and said a prayer in his Yoruba tongue, *"Olodumare, Olodumare, Mojuba Gbogbo iku tiembelese (Supreme God I salute you and all the dead who sit at your feet always and forever),* Killa opened his eyes and forcefully let Zulu know, *"I'm Abadou Obatala Kadari son…I'm a young rich Prince and my ancestors are royal…my bloodline descend from the Orisas (Gods and Goddesses),"* Killa now jumped off the stoop and turned up. He began caressing his face feeling himself. "I'm a fly nigga yo…a gorgeous gangster…I'm the Pretty Boy Assassin," Killa let it be known observing cars speeding thru the intersection at the corner and banging their tires on the potholes covering the street. "When the ladies see me they get wet yo word up…I ain't gotta spend a dime or spit game for the ladies to love me…I do it because that make a lot of women feel happy…and that's why they love the Pretty Boy Assassin because I give them what yall niggas don't…I give women a material wonder that compliments their beauty…and it make women feel a little powerful when you share the wealth."

"Yeah whatever yo…you still a fucking trick you *Prince Akeem* ass nigga from *Coming to America*," Zulu smiled while glancing at the corner where a car with squeaky brakes stopped at the light.

"Fuck you Zulu…I'm telling you you gotta understand me playboy…I got this shit down to a science…you gotta get--." The sound of screeching car tires murking thru the intersection alerted Zulu and Killa who jumped on point observing a Buick Regal swerve in front of the building they were at.

"I told you niggas!" With the smile of revenge, Keyshawn Sparks was leaning out the passenger window of the Buick aiming a S.K. Automatic at Zulu and Killa. In that instant where they thought they were on point, they weren't. Keyshawn Sparks caught em slipping.

"Oh shit." Zulu mumbled under his breath seeing his life flash. It happened so quick they never expected it to go down like this. Killa wasn't ready to meet his Old Earth yet, so to save his life, Killa pulled his hammer out while eyeing the black hole of death Keyshawn Sparks aimed in their direction.

"Run Zulu," Killa shouted snatching the 9mm Glock from off his waist as Keyshawn Sparks opened fire. Killa felt the bullets whisking pass his frame so he dashed behind Zulu who flew towards the store. Killa sprinted backwards returning shots but the S.K. fired rapidly spitting slugs all over the stoop and the façade of the building. A slug banged Zulu in the hip then his lower back as he neared the front of the store next door. Killa was blasting back until a slug smacked him in the shoulder. Killa dropped his arm then raised it up to keep firing only to be hit by another slug in his abdomen which knocked him back onto the trashcans in front of the store. Zulu was running on all fours up into the store as the hot slugs in him sent a burning twinge jolting thru his body.

Keyshawn Sparks peeped the damage he was doing but he wasn't satisfied. He jumped out the Buick and ran up onto the sidewalk to finish his enemies. He peeped Killa spring up from off the knocked over trashcans and squeezed his trigger determined to lay Killa down and keep him down. A slug smacked Killa dead in his face. Killa's face felt like it was struck by lightning even though he was only grazed. His head felt dizzy and the pain in his shoulder and stomach had his balance off as he wobbled to the store entrance where Zulu was crawling inside.

"Hakeem get my gun." Zulu yelled halfway in the store on his hands and knees. The middle aged Palestinian store owner had already grabbed Zulu's gun when he heard the first shots ring out.

"Here you take my *brudda,*" Hakeem shouted in his middle-eastern accent as he tossed Zulu his 40 Caliber pistol. Zulu swiftly spun around and dropped onto his butt, stuck his head out the door and observed Killa a few feet away zooming at him while holding his face and stomach. Keyshawn Sparks was now standing by the stoop and aiming the crosshairs of the S.K. at Killa's back.

"Killa watch out," Zulu painfully sprung up off his butt and leaped out of the store doorway blasting and ready to die. With the tragic situation of earlier, Zulu felt so lifeless he felt he had nothing to lose. He was ready to die in this gunfight. Zulu shoved Killa into the doorway and blasted his pistol against the big gun of Keyshawn Sparks.

Zulu got off a few shots making Keyshawn Sparks dip behind a parked car, but Keyshawn Sparks then dashed back onto the sidewalk with the S.K. at his waistline and let the S.K. unleash its full force. He swayed the gun from left to right spraying up the whole corner and the front of the store. Zulu desired to face death and blast back but the slugs from the S.K. felt like hellfire. Keyshawn Sparks brought hell to the block and Zulu felt himself dying in the fire as hot slugs hit him in the chest and stomach knocking him down on the steps of the store.

Hakeem rushed to the shaking Zulu who lay at the doorway bleeding profusely. Hakeem used all the strength he could muster to pull Zulu inside as slugs banged the door and knocked out the store lights above the door. When Hakeem pulled Zulu inside then slammed the door shut, the gunfire ceased then the sound of screeching car tires was heard.

Not realizing how bad he was shot, Zulu tried standing up only to slip and fall in a puddle of him and Killa's blood. Killa lay face down inside the store not too far from the door with blood seeping from a wound in his back. Zulu squirmed on the blood soaked floor struggling to get up. The pain he felt moments ago was now combined with excruciating chest pain which got worse every time he breathed.

Zulu and Killa's hormones had flooded their bloodstream with so much adrenaline when the shooting erupted, the high output blocked their sense of pain. They were totally unaware of the numerous slugs punctured into their bodies. Zulu and Killa both lay on the floor squirming, feeling more and more pain stab at their life force every time they tried moving their muscles. This was it their minds quietly whispered as it felt like the Angels of Death were slowly pulling their life force from their bodies.

"*Z-z-zulu…the…the guns…the cops--,*" Killa stuttered painfully feeling like a mountain lay on top of his back as his face hugged the bloody and dirty store floor.

"*K-ki-killa…I think-I-I'm-b-b-bout to die—I-can't breathe.*" Zulu felt himself becoming breathless. Zulu's mind was bombarded with thoughts of life, death, Destiny, NyJewel, and Prince. He wondered would he ever see them again to tell them he was sorry.

"*Ha-ha-keem…o-our…guns…get em.*"

"*We-we-we bout to die…fuck them gu--.*" Zulu's eyelids felt heavier than the force that seemed to snatch his life force away, causing his consciousness to fade to black.

"No no you no die my *bruddas,*" Hakeem covered both of them with towels then ran outside to find their guns before the police arrived on the scene.

....

Zulu's eyes shot open for the first time in what seemed like years. He wondered how long he been in the hospital as the beeping sounds of the machine caught his attention. An IV rack with tubes and chords attached to his body sat between him and the machine.

"Fuck." Zulu groggily moaned arching himself up. His body was aching with so much pain it felt like he was stabbed with a thousand needles. His mind was cloudy and woozy from the medicines inserted into his system. All he could do was lay stiff, the less movement the less pain. He then tuned his ears to the hallway outside his room where the sounds of feet scuffling along the waxed floors mingled with the voices of nurses and doctors. His room door was slightly ajar then swung open. It was NyJewel being followed by Sun-Z and his wife Iyana.

"Oh my God baby you awoke!" NyJewel ran over to Zulu's bed and hugged him tightly, smothering his face in her chest. Zulu was in enough pain and NyJewel squeezing him made it no better. "Baby look at you oh my God," the tears began pouring from NyJewel's eyes. Her heart was numb looking at Zulu's famished and injured body being fed liquids thru the IV machines. "Oh my god Zulu."

"It's gone be okay Ny," Iyana held NyJewel who began to lose her composure. "Come on let's go outside Ny," Iyana kissed Zulu on the forehead then lead the distraught NyJewel out of the room.

"NyJewel acting like she got shot," Zulu groaned arching himself up once the ladies stepped out of the room.

"She loves you that's all," Sun-Z dropped into the chair next to Zulu's bed. "Love is pain and pain is love...sometimes we bring joy and pain to the people we love...it's life...but anyway...how you feel?"

"Fucked up...what up with Killa?"

"Fucked up like you...he took a few slugs...and he lucky too because he got hit in the back and luckily the slug didn't touch his spinal cord...but other than that he good...but yo boy Prince--," Sun-Z sighed deeply showing creases in his forehead while swinging his head from left to right depressingly.

"*Nooo.*" Zulu could feel his heart ready to explode and he became weak, causing dehydration to suck up the last fluids in his throat. Prince was gone and Zulu could feel it in his soul. Zulu could even see the look of loss and mourning in Sun-Z's eyes. "Please Sun...don't tell me Prince aint make it...please don't tell me he---hell knaw."

"He gone Zulu," Sun-Z cracked a slight smile. "He dead...but not the dead you thinking about."

"What the fuck is you talking bout?"

"Let's just say the Prince you know is dead and it's a whole new Prince with a new life..."

Zulu scrunched his face in confusion and would be in for a rude awakening when he was released from the hospital.

....

Dolla had just rolled the armor-all and crispy white wall tires to his sparkling money green Cadillac out of *Big Son's* car wash on Bailey Avenue. Terror rode shotgun with Dolla and they cruised down Bailey Avenue passing the many urban apparel stores and retail shops. When Dolla rolled passed a clothing store called Hip Hop Legacy, him and Terror felt like the Angels of God who caught the Devil without his pitchfork. They peeped an individual named RK from the GFL click walking into the clothing store like everything was sweet on the streets.

Dolla and Terror was excited, angered, and just basically ready to put that work in. They wasted no time in riding on their enemy. Dolla swerved onto a side street and parked on side of the clothing store. Terror snatched the pistol off his hip and laid back in the passenger seat waiting for RK to bounce out the store. Right in broad daylight Terror was going to empty his clip in RK and let everyone in the streets know that if they had beef with the Young Assassins, it didn't matter where at or what time of day, enemies would be blasted on sight.

"Yo Terror," Dolla observed the surroundings and his common sense kicked in, "You can't clap that nigga out here on this block…look at all the people." Terror and Dolla both glanced at the traffic jam on the avenue and the walkers window shopping.

"What if I just wrap my face up with the shirt ain't nobody gone see my face."

"You a damn fool…someone gone see you get out my car and they gone have a APB on my car and we won't make it back to the hood…check it…I'm gone pull down the block, just go in there and clap the nigga while he inside the store."

"Why you gotta pull up the block…you scared nigga?"

"Nigga I'm smart, it's not what you do but how you do it…oh hell knaw…now look at this shit," Dolla was looking in his rearview mirror when he tapped Terror to look at what he just peeped. Terror spun around in his seat and peered across the street observing a security guard enter a bank across the street not to mention a conservative dressed lady entering the clothing store with several Youth.

"Ok check it out, I got a better idea," Terror opened Dolla's glove box and retrieved an 8 inch lock blade Dolla kept in the stash. "Don't even go up the block just stay right here…I'm bout to go up in there and open that nigga up like a can green beans."

"Huh…what?" Dolla looked at Terror like he was suicidal. "A knife Terror."

"Nigga listen I'm gone be quick and do what I do," Terror handed Dolla his 45 caliber, then pulled off his IceBerg T-Shirt and covered his face up with it like he was using it as a sun blocker. "Stay right here Dolla I'm gone be in and out…nice and silent."

"Alright hurry up," Dolla stated clutching the pistol while watching a tank top wearing Terror with tattoos all over his yellow arms jump out the wheel and slide into the store. *"Fucking Kadari Twins is bugged out."* Dolla thought to himself. *"They really love this beef shit."*

Terror entered the clothing store where the music of Bad Boy Artist *Black Rob* was playing at a low volume. The two Arabs standing at the counter greeted Terror as he stepped inside looking exhausted from the heat with his shirt covering his head. Terror scanned the store and peeped several shoppers eyeing different items. He paid no mind to the women scattered throughout the store scoping out the different garments. His eyes then hit the back wall and that's where he peeped RK checking out a fresh pair of Bo Jackson's. Terror crept right up on RK as RK inspected the sneaker closely and held it close to his face.

"This for my brother and Zulu." Terror slid behind RK and threw him in the chokehold with one arm while thrusting the 8-inch blade into RK's back. Forcefully, Terror rammed the blade deep into RK's back while shoving RK up against the wall of the sneaker rack. RK never had time to react or respond the way Terror caught him from behind. As Terror lunged the blade deep inside RK, RK painfully grunted which alerted everyone in the store of the attack. Terror then tried covering RK's mouth while stabbing him but everyone in the store heard the grunting and peeped Terror in action. Terror yanked the knife out of

RK's back and watched RK slide down the wall knocking several sneakers off the rack.

"You bitch ass nigga." Terror kicked RK in the face as he lay on the floor curled up moaning. Terror then spun around and got to dipping out the store pointing his knife at the people watching and quietly shouting in fear. *"Shut the fuck up crying and yall bet not say shit."*

Terror was a few feet from the door when a loud boom erupted inside the store. All hell now broke loose like an atomic bomb hit the store. Women started screaming their lungs out and men began diving behind clothes racks and running in the back as Keyshawn Sparks opened fire. The whole time Keyshawn Sparks was in the dressing room trying on a pair of Evisu jeans. He stepped out the dressing room just as the women began screaming when Terror was stabbing RK. Keyshawn Sparks observed RK on the floor squirming and then his instinct directed his vision to the front of the store where he peeped Terror nearing the exit.

"Boom boom boom." Followed the first shot. Slugs flew pass Terror's dome piece missing him by inches. Terror felt the slugs whisk pass his covered up face then bang the mannequin standing in the window by the door. Terror ran so fast out of the store his feet escaped gravity and he flew outside where Dolla was wobbling out the car gripping the pistol with his 59/50 fitted cap pulled low over his face. Dolla shuffled onto the sidewalk as Terror ran pass him to the car. While standing on the sidewalk Dolla peered into the store and him Keyshawn Sparks locked eyes. Keyshawn's gun was already in fire mode and he had it aimed right in Dolla's direction.

A slug blasting from Keyshawn's gun shattered the store window between him and Dolla. Dolla then returned fire easing backwards to the car. Terror jumped behind the steering wheel shouting for Dolla to jump in. All Dolla could hear, see and feel was the power of the gun as him and KeyShawn Sparks exchanged slugs. A slug caught Keyshawn Spark's right below his collar bone. A second slug then splashed Keyshawn in the chest. Dolla peeped Keyshawn stumble backwards then jumped in the wheel and Terror peeled out.

When Black Bull and Gonzalez arrived on the scene which was blocked off by yellow tape and flooded with cops and paramedics, they figured the shooting was involving one of the crews from Bailey Avenue. This wasn't Black Bull and Gonzalez' problem. But when they observed Mrs. Vickey Simpson, a prominent African American council woman on the scene crying and shook up, they knew this was going to mean that every cop on the force would have to expend their time and energy in taking down the perpetrators of this violent incident. A violent incident which not only took place in a business establishment where Mrs. Simpson was purchasing sneakers for a few high school students, but one of the students who was a marvelous basketball player and soon to receive a scholarship was injured by a stray bullet during the shootout. No good.

What really put the icing on the cake is when a young lady who witnessed the incident told law enforcement how she grew up in the area all her life and never seen the individuals involved in the incident. It didn't take much intel for the authorities to run Keyshawn Spark's and RK's info to know who their number one enemies were. Keyshawn Sparks and RK kept their mouths shut about their attackers and there was no detailed witness testimony about the attackers, so it was only speculation pointing at the Young Assassins.

Right on the scene where local news crews interviewed distraught shoppers on the Avenue the Mayor announced live on TV that the city would crack down on all violent drug gangs and the city was going to usher in the support of numerous law enforcement agencies to help smash all the drug gangs responsible for the violence terrorizing the city of Buffalo. For the next few weeks there would be dozens of drug raids, arrests, and heavy police presence throughout the city and still, violence would plague the hood like an unstoppable virus. This would end the war with the Young Assassins and the Gangster for Life crew. Keyshawn Sparks would end up facing a weapons charge from the shootout with Dolla and the Federal Authorities snatched up the GFL crew for the drug activity and violence they were responsible for in their own neighborhood.

....

Destiny was absorbed in her own world of guilt and grief day and night. The physical pain of her not eating and being unable to sleep was by no means in comparison to the spiritual, mental, and emotional pain of guilt harassing her soul. When she snatched the gun to shoot Zulu, her intellect and rationale was clouded by heartache. She never meant to shoot anyone. That wasn't her and she couldn't find an inch of reasoning to justify what she had done. No matter how angry Zulu made her feel she knew deep in her soul she had no right to do such a thing. And poor Prince. He had nothing to do with her and Zulu's drama, but he was the one to suffer the painful consequences of their actions.

On most days Destiny found herself visiting church and praying to God for forgiveness. She would even visit Prince at the hospital and ask for his forgiveness. She also took on the burden of feeling responsible for Zulu and Killa's tragedy. She spent a lot of time visiting them as well and wishing she had the power to change all of their lives for the better. On one occasion Destiny stopped by Zulu's room and found NyJewel sitting by Zulu's bedside and Destiny treated NyJewel like a friend and apologized for all the drama.

Destiny and NyJewel put their differences to the side and squashed the beef. Destiny accepted the fact that Zulu and his doggish ways just wasn't what she wanted to deal with. She would always love Zulu but she couldn't accept him being unfaithful. Destiny wished NyJewel the best and hoped Zulu would be faithful to NyJewel.

And as Zulu, Killa, and Prince made their recoveries and their bodies healed up, Destiny's soul began to get bathed in the light of the lord and her sins were washed away. She felt like a new woman when she visited Prince on the day of his discharge from the hospital.

"Destiny." Prince happily shouted as he sat on the edge of his bed while a nurse helped him slide into his button up shirt. "Peace Black woman."

"*Heyyy Prince,*" Destiny slowly stepped into the room and seated herself. "I see you happy to be leaving this place."

"It's more than that Black woman," Prince stood up and began buttoning his shirt while watching the nurse leave the room. "I'm happy because you saved my life Destiny."

"Huh?" Destiny was confused as she helped Prince button his shirt. "What is you talking about Prince?" Destiny quietly asked making sure the nurse wasn't around ear hustling. "You almost lost yo life because of me trying to shoot Zulu…I'm so sorry Prince and please forgive me."

"You just don't understand how you saved me Black Woman…If I hadn't come to this hospital room," Prince snatched a book from off his bed. "I wouldn't have done the knowledge (read) to this Supreme Wisdom if I hadn't been up in this hospital room."

Destiny took the book and studied the cover, ***"From Niggaz to Gods, by Akil."***

"Yes Black woman…that book opened my third eye to reality and allowed me to see the ignorance and darkness I was living in…I'm not living like a nigga no more…that's not the Blackman's true nature to be living like savages, thugs, gangsters, niggas and bitches, and fools that thrive off ignorance…the Whiteman made us niggas and taught us to be slaves so he can use us as tools…that's why they want us being illiterate…dropping out of school and playing the streets…I'm thru with that life of ignorance and destruction…I found myself and I know what motivate me to be the greatest and be what the Creator created me to be…I wasn't created to be a nigga…I was created to be God-The Supreme Being Black Man with Divine Knowledge…I want to be the greatest and I know my position and role in the universe as a Blackman…that Thug Life, the sex, money, drugs, and violence is tools the Whiteman promote and give to us so we can kill each other and ourselves…the white man want to keep us mentally dead so we can't use our creative genius and supreme intelligence that lies within our black minds…it's in us to be builders of civilization…not no slaves, prisoners, and the savages we been acting like…we are the greatest and we just don't know it, " Prince manifested this wisdom with so much life, conviction, and rhythm.

Destiny was amazed. Prince sounded so vibrant and full of life. He was different and experienced a transformation.

"So what are you gonna do with yourself Prince?" Destiny asked helping Prince bag up his possessions.

"I'm going to get up with the Gods and the righteous brothers in the Nation…I'm gonna help them clean up the minds and bodies of our people," Prince then paused and stopped Destiny from bagging his clothes. He gently placed both his hands on her shoulders and peered into her chinky black eyes with such sincerity. *"I wanna thank you Black woman from the bottom of my heart…and I need you to know that…if it's anything I can do for you I'm here for you…I owe you my life Black Woman because you saved me from the destruction I was headed to,"* Prince embraced Destiny feeling blessed by her warmth.

"Many will be called but only a few shall be chosen." Prince was one of the fortunate ones chosen to allow his mind to absorb the Supreme Knowledge of Self which would save him from destruction and keep him from falling into the trap of the Devil's wicked civilization of spiritual darkness. Prince was like the *biblical Lazarus* in the valley of the dry bones being brought back to life. He was one of the lost and found who was once mentally dead, but now his mind was activated with the realization of life on a whole new mental plane. Throughout his whole life of suffering and living in the wilderness of the streets with savages, he experienced hell; a state of confusion and ignorance where he lived an uncivilized life. But thru the natural process of transformation and elevation he was put thru the fiery furnace of hell and he came out mentally pure and refined with the power to change, and his past actions of devilment was overcome by the Supreme Power and Force of the indwelling God who was in the soul.

....

The atmosphere inside Allah's Temple was fiery and mentally stimulating as Supreme Minister Dahvi delivered a spiritually uplifting and motivational speech. His speeches always carried a force that activated the third eye of the brothers and sisters and elevated their minds onto a plane of greatness. He encouraged them with the wisdom to go into the community and wake up the mentally dead who were in the streets living like savages.

Prince sat in the front row feeling a mind activation he never felt in his whole life. Prince's vision beheld the righteous aura surrounding Supreme Minister Dahvi. His physical shell radiated a divine glow and his dark raisin colored skin possessed a clear gloss free from the intoxicants and impurities clogging the pores of the average people. He was refined with a neatly faded haircut. His well-built physique was adorned in a well fitted royal blue tailored made suit. He spoke so eloquently and his wisdom ignited a spark in Prince's mind and soul he never felt.

Prince went to church as a kid a few times, he even went a few times as an adult but only to satisfy a female he was trying to get to love him like she loved Jesus. Out of all the sermons Prince ever heard in church, the Preacher never manifested a wisdom that woke up the sleeping giant inside. The Preacher never made Prince feel a connection with the Creator of the universe. Supreme Minister Dahvi on the other hand spoke about a knowledge of self which meant the knowledge of the Creator, the universe, and all life.

Supreme Minister Dahvi held a Bible in one hand and a Koran in the other hand. He said both books were the same in context. They were just written in different languages but spoke of the same prophets, the same trials and tribulations of man, and how man must acquire knowledge of his true self in order to overcome the wickedness of life and find true peace.

"Peace my dear beloved brothers and sisters," Supreme Minister Dahvi opened the Koran and read from Surah 2 (Chapter 2), "It says right here in the Holy Koran that Allah created the first Man from black mud and it also says how Allah put his soul and spirit into this Blackman and that all things in existence, including the Angels must bow down to the Blackman...Allah created the Blackman to be a Khalifah (Ruler or Vicegerent) over all things in existence. ...it's here in Surah 2 written in black and white...it's not me making this up." Supreme Minister Dahvi now sat the Koran down on the podium then opened the King James Version of the Bible.

"Now even here in the bible it states that the God of the Universe is the Black Man with wooly hair and skin like burnt copper...it's in Revelations and the book of Daniel and many other places...and here in 1 Corinthians chapter 3 verses 16-17 it tells you that you are the temple of God and that the spirit of God dwells in you Black Man...and it also says to keep your temple clean because your temple is holy which is the Temple of God...you are the Temple of the

Creator Black Man…Therefore my brothers and sisters, according to these two books, the Holy Koran and Bible, you Blackman and Black woman, you are the highest form of creation and you must connect with the Creator dwelling inside of you, you must allow the God within to rule your life…you are not to let the drugs, sex, liquor or any of the poisons the white man have giving us to rule our life…not the money he created nor the material possessions he give us which we allow to lead us into wickedness…no my brothers and sisters…we must cleanse ourselves of the white devils poison and strengthen our minds and bodies with knowledge and discipline--," Supreme Minister Dahvi took a gulp of his lemon water sitting on the podium. He then let his eyes scan the beautiful and radiant faces of the people seated in the temple.

"We must come to realize that the 500 plus years of slavery we endured under the Europeans have destroyed us mentally and spiritually as a people. They destroyed us mentally by stripping us of our self-esteem and the way we view ourselves as a people. They stripped us of our African languages, our holy names, our culture, religion, and the knowledge of the Creator which influenced us to reach our full potential. They used Christianity to destroy us spiritually since it was in the name of Christianity and Jesus they enslaved us…they hung us from trees in the name of Jesus and Christianity…they raped our beautiful black woman in the name of Jesus and Christianity, and they lynched us in the name of Jesus and Christianity…after they took our religion from us they gave us Christianity because Christianity doesn't teach us how to be true Black Men with the Power that the Creator created us with like these holy books teach us…Christianity taught us to be other than ourselves…Christianity taught us to be slaves who feared the white man…they forced Christianity on us because Christianity doesn't teach us of our true power to destroy the oppression this society inflict on us…Christianity teaches us to worship the white man as God…it teaches us to serve him faithfully and hate ourselves…talk to me I aint lying."

"That's right," one of the men in the audience shouted, "Teach Black Man teach."

"They got us believing in a white Jesus...subconsciously got us believing that the white man is some holy being that we should fear...how is the white man holy when he committed atrocities against us and the Native Americans ...he committed so much violence and wrong during slavery and after slavery you know he the devil...look at the terror the Ku Klux Klan committed against us after slavery all the way up into the 1970's and even now with the police brutality...members of the Klan are devout Christians and leaders of this society...I don't want no religion that teach me to fear a man who wicked like the devil...I don't want no religion that teach me to love my enemies...I want the knowledge of my true self...I want the knowledge of my creator and the knowledge of the Supreme power and potential that lies within me as a Black Man...I want the knowledge of my divine role in this world and universe...I want that Supreme Knowledge the Black Man in Ancient Egypt had that he used to build Pyramids and engineered some of the greatest civilizations ever known to man...the Black Man is the Father of Civilization and he the one who developed mathematics and science...that's the knowledge of self we all should desire as Black people...we shouldn't feel intimidated by education when our African Ancestors was masters of knowledge...we should all want the knowledge that will motivate us to be the best that we can be...we were created in God's image...therefore we look like God and we should act like God...we wasn't created to be drug dealers, killers, hoes, drug addicts, and bums...that's why we must desire the knowledge of self that will influence us to be Gods and Goddess' who have the intelligence to build and engineer civilization and master the arts and sciences of education."

Supreme Minister Dahvi took Prince's mind from the depths of hell up into the light of the sun. Prince never felt so powerful and motivated to do right in life. He never knew he wasn't in control of his life and he was living a lifestyle someone else wanted him to live. The Thug Life he once lived was a pre-planned lifestyle the government created for the disenfranchised blacks by depriving them access to a high quality education and a proper knowledge of self and spirituality. Without a good education the unfortunate was giving low paying jobs which kept them poor and miserable. And that's where crime and drug use played a role in survival and destruction. With the lack of a good education and living in poverty, most Thugs like Prince got into crime because that was the only promising economic tool available in the ghetto. The thugs sold drugs because the drugs were there. The thugs didn't put the drugs there. The government put the drugs in the ghetto as a plan of genocide. Even with the black on black violence. The thugs didn't make the guns or place them in the hood, but the thugs were killing each other with guns and knives they didn't make. All the thugs were playing a game someone else created.

Prince looked back on his life and realized that he, like many others were mentally blind, deaf, and dumb and couldn't see the life of death and destruction they were living. Prince was thankful and felt blessed to be receiving the true knowledge of self which was saving him from the ignorance destroying his people. Prince just wished his friends and many of his lost peers could wake up and learn their true knowledge of self before it was too late.

....

Hawk and Desiree watched Zulu angrily toss his bags of clothes into the backseat of his car. Destiny got rid of Zulu like he was a disease. She checked up on him daily while he was in the hospital recovering, but she terminated the lease to their apartment and sent all his clothes to Hawk and Desiree. Destiny moved on and wasn't looking back.

Zulu wanted to see Destiny so he kept begging and persisting until Hawk and Desiree finally gave in and decided to take Zulu to go see her. They pulled up in front of a community center on Genesee Street. The red, black, and green building was designed in classical style architecture with two small gardens on both sides of the double doors. The building's African colors was blessed on its front and side exterior walls with a vivid artistic mural of beautiful black children sitting at the feet of a Black Pharaoh and Nubian Queen who were teaching the children. There were also perfect portrait paintings on the wall of the great black leaders *Marcus Garvey, Noble Drew Ali, and Harriet Tubman.*

In front of the building sat two long tables where free lunches were being served by a group of ladies. Zulu couldn't believe his eyes as he watched Destiny feed the babies. She was beautiful and angelic. She looked like she was strait outta heaven and not the gutters of E. North. Her body was clothed in 3/4ths and she was sacredly covered in black and gold Kente cloth. Her smile was that of peace and paradise and knew no stress. Zulu froze up upon seeing Destiny in this state of peace. She looked pure, tranquil and out of this world and Zulu's corrupted soul seemed to have no place in her presence. Zulu could see happiness written all over her and it was a happiness that was off limits to savages like Zulu.

"Come on Zulu what you waiting on?" Desiree parked the car across the street from the center. "You did all that whining now look at you...you look scared."

"What's wrong the cat got yo tongue?" Hawk asked flicking his cigarette out the window before exiting the car.

Zulu was stuck and in his own world of silence. He observed the joy in Destiny's demeanor and he didn't want to disturb it. Destiny seemed to have transformed into a new beautiful person Zulu was a stranger to. Zulu couldn't believe it.

"Come on Zulu just say hello and apologize like you said...be a Man baby boy and get it off yo chest." Hawk encouraged opening the car door for Zulu to get out. Zulu slid out the car and the three dashed across the street and onto the clean sidewalk crowded with the young seeds getting their free lunches.

"Welcome to the *Universal African Cultural Center*," an older lady greeted the trio.

"Oh my God Zulu," Destiny lifted her eyes from the box of food she was in. She was so excited seeing Zulu she dropped the tray of food she held on the table and ran to Zulu with open arms. "I can't believe it...look at you Zulu," Destiny caressed his face while they hugged. She stepped back and looked Zulu up and down. The last time she seen Zulu in the hospital he lost at least 20 pounds and was wired up with tubes and cords everywhere like a computer. Now he had his weight back and looked like he was never shot four times. "Oh my God I'm so happy to see you looking so healthy Zulu."

"No I'm happy to see you Destiny...you look *soooo* beautiful, damn...I don't even know what to say--," Zulu was truly at a loss for words inhaling the sweet fragrance of the African Myrrh emanating off Destiny's skin. "What's this you wearing?" Zulu waved his hand up and down her soft Kente cloth. "So you into yo African Culture now huh?"

"She the Queen-Goddess now," Desiree announced jokingly before her and Hawk dipped inside the center.

"Don't pay them no mind Zulu," Destiny playfully smacked Desiree on the shoulder before her and Hawk went inside the center. Destiny then motioned for Zulu to sit beside her at the table outside. "Well Zulu as you can see I'm into my Afro-Centric consciousness…it's knowing who I am as a Black woman and knowing that I am a Queen who deserves to be honored and respected by all…it's knowledge of self Zulu…the black man and black woman lost self-respect and respect for each other during slavery and this is why we don't cherish and appreciate each other now…But knowledge of self teaches us to appreciate each other because we all we got."

"I understand and I just want you to know that I apologize for all the wrong I ever done…the lies…cheating…I apologize and I know you didn't deserve any of the drama I caused you."

"I know your sorry Zulu," Destiny softly held Zulu's hands, "You know right from wrong…but I won't punish you for your ignorance…your just like many other men who follow the lusts of your animal nature…you don't know any better so I forgive you Zulu."

Zulu took a deep breath and braced himself knowing he already knew the answer to the question he was about to ask Destiny. "Well since you forgive me do that mean you will give me another chance to make you happy?"

"I'm happy with myself Zulu…and you must find happiness within yourself before you can make anyone happy…see Zulu…you have to realize that the pleasure you seek in chasing women, running these streets, and living the life you live is not true happiness…if that was happiness you wouldn't have to keep doing those things because you would be satisfied…true happiness is when you are content within yourself Zulu, it's not on the outside, it's all within you and all you need is the God that exist within you…God is inside of you and God is the happiness we all seek."

"Now she on some other shit and kicking me to the curb," Zulu thought to himself.

"That's right my brother, happiness come from the inner self." Prince stepped outside the center being followed by Hawk and Desiree. *"We must save ourselves before we can save others...and you save yourself by acquiring the knowledge of yourself which will give you the ability to master life and not fall into wickedness Black Man."*

"Yo Prince," Zulu jumped out of his seat excited to Prince. It's been a minute since they last seen each other and Zulu never thought he would experience this moment again in life. "Prince what up bro," Zulu asked as him and Prince embraced for the first time in weeks.

"Knowledge of self is what's up Black Man." Prince placed both his hands on Zulu's shoulders and peered into the blackness of Zulu's eyes. *"We must get knowledge of self to elevate our minds to the highest level of perfection...word life Zulu."*

"Hold hold hold--." Zulu took a step back in confusion. He glanced at Destiny then at Prince with a twisted look on his face. "Prince...I know you and Destiny not fucking yo?" Zulu asked feeling his adrenaline flare up while his heart skipped beats. "You got my girl on this African shit like she yo Queen and you her King? What the fuck going on?" Zulu clenched his fist and began biting his lip.

"Zulu come on now," Prince shrieked at Zulu's ignorance. Everyone peered at each other smiling hilariously but Zulu. "Come on bra that's non-cipher (no)...in the streets we don't establish sexual relations with our partner's women...and when you got knowledge of self you don't look at women lustfully and only for sexual pleasure...I will never look at yo ex girl or any of yo women sexually Black Man."

Destiny then stepped in between them with her fierce and dignified attitude, "Zulu you know I ain't no nasty woman to be sleeping with any of yo friends...cut it out boy...knowledge of self is what turn me on...I don't need a man."

Zulu was confused and needed answers. "What the hell going on...how the hell yall get on this back to Africa shit?"

"Check it out Zulu," Prince explained folding his arms across his chest. "I told you I was gonna change my life…I didn't know how but I did…and Destiny felt guilty about what happened and I told her if she felt she owed me anything she should come and hear the brothers and sisters of the nation build on the sciences of life so she can get knowledge of self…that's all I asked her to do and this is the result of that."

"So yall not fucking or nothing?" Zulu asked unbelievably.

"Oh my God would you get yo mind out of the gutter Zulu," Destiny blurted straitening up the table.

"Damn my brother," Prince threw his arm around Zulu's shoulder, *"Listen my G…when you got knowledge of self you learn about the Creator of the universe who exist inside of you…you learn about the creative power and discipline you have to control the animal or what some people call the lower nature…see when we lack knowledge of self we think it's normal to be controlled by our emotions, passions, and negative thoughts…we live our whole life for physical pleasure, sexual pleasure, and mental pleasure through drugs and liquor…and emotional pleasure through material things…but knowledge of self teaches us how to utilize our discipline and divine will power to control that negative part of our self and then we began to look at life from a higher perspective…we no longer look at women just for sexual pleasure…we look at the Black Woman as a Queen who sit beside us to help us get thru the struggles of life…and we come to understand that sex is a tool for pro-creation to carry our existence on for infinity…you feel me Black Man."*

Prince had everyone's attention and Zulu was lost in the sauce. Zulu couldn't believe Prince and Destiny's transformation. This was real.

"Zulu I would love for you and the crew to come down and hear the Gods drop the science…it's time for change Blackman…when I lay on that hospital bed I told myself that if I die then let it be…but if I survived I gotta do something different with my life because the path I was on only lead to death…we did everything wicked in these streets since we was kids and it's a blessing most of us still here…I'm telling you Zulu we gotta change before it's too late."

It took a moment for Zulu's consciousness to come back down to earth. It was the vrooming of cars zooming pass the community center that snapped Zulu out of his deep thought. Zulu nodded his head at Prince understandingly, "I feel you bro."

"Please Zulu bring the crew to the center to do the knowledge to the science of self."

"Yeah Zulu," Destiny embraced Zulu. *"Our people could change the madness we living in if all you strong brothers in the streets got knowledge of self and used yall intelligence and power to make a change for the better instead of selling drugs and killing each other."*

Zulu smiled while thinking to himself, *"Fuck them and this black pride shit...the only thing I'm tryna change is my muthafucking bankroll...the only niggas I give a fuck about is my niggas and we gone get rich...fuck everybody but my niggas...it's time to get rich and take over the city."*

CHAPTER 11

The Pine Harbor Housing Projects was located on the Westside of the city at the foot of downtown. The projects were a row of four and five story buildings which sat not far from the waterfront harbor where Canada sat across the river. The occupants of the projects were a mixed boiling pot of blacks and Hispanics. This crowding of the two different cultures often times caused a clash between the two groups when it came to the drug flow in the projects. For years' blacks and Hispanics either competed with each other or went to war for control of the projects.

Old School Al found himself in the heart of the Pine Harbor. There was no war going on and no competition these days. Old School Al had an open pass to capitalize on the mega thousand-dollar a day flow in the projects. And this was because of an individual known as Mel-Cash. Mel-Cash was born on the eastside of the city but raised in the Pine Harbor Projects on the west side, and he never forgot his roots because he was like a distant cousin of the A-Squad.

At the height of the last war in the projects a few years ago, Mel-Cash wreaked havoc on the legendary *Puerto Rican 12th street Mob*. The only competition that ever existed for Mel-Cash was the 12th Street Mob. The 12th street Mob had heroin blocks outside the projects and all through the lower west side that was producing so much cash they stopped beefing with the crazy and wild Mel-Cash and left the projects all to him. The Pine Harbor now belonged to Mel-Cash, the God of the Hood who was a force to be reckoned with. Being that the projects was his realm, Mel-Cash wanted to see his people eating and partaking of the hood riches his business was producing. That's where Sun-Z and the crew came in at. With Mel-Cash and Sun-Z now forming like Voltron, in no time they would have a monopoly on the major drug flow from the east side to the west side of Buffalo.

In his cream Salvatore Ferragamo spring jacket with the matching *Christian Louboutin* tennis shoes on his feet, Mel-Cash posted up on his *Alfa Romeo Milano* looking the part of a businessman/college grad. From appearance he looked nothing like the getting money gun slinger he was because his attire was certified designer, every now and then would you catch Mel-Cash in hip-hop apparel. He stood in the parking lot of *El Taino Sabor*, a local Hispanic restaurant in his neighborhood. And thru the tinted lens of his Versace frames he observed Hawk's ice blue Denali truck and Sun-Z's black Benz roll into the parking lot.

"Family what it do?" Mel-Cash greeted them as everyone exited the two vehicles. They embraced like long lost family and engaged in brief conversation outside the restaurant before the smell of delicious food pulled everyone inside.

"*Que Pasa Bichote*? (What's up Gangster?)." A sultry Latina waitress greeted Mel-Cash as he stepped inside with the crew.

"*Dimelo mami.*" Mel-Cash respectfully kissed the mami on her rosy cheeks before she led the group to a large round table near the back wall of the restaurant. The petite waitress was then assisted by another waitress who helped her pull out chairs for everyone to be seated while she conversed with the bilingual Mel-Cash.

"*Como esta papi que no te avista*? (How are you Poppi. Where have you been?)."

"*Ya tu sabe estoy chillin ma bregando ne negosio.* (You know just chillin ma handling my business.). Mel-Cash explained still standing and gazing down into the mami's eyes. He then gestured towards the Family. "*Este es mi familia...tratemelos bien.* (This my family treat em good.)"

"*Si papi.*" The mami held the seat for Mel-Cash as he plopped his lanky frame into the seat.

"So what's been good with you my G?" I hear it's been quiet over here with yo wild Spanish speaking ass," Sun-Z stated with a smirk on his face as the waitress sat glasses of cold water in front of everyone.

"Come on Sun you know me," Mel-Cash uttered at a fast pace. "You know I been a lot of places, seen a lot of faces, and verbalize the lango of many different races, but I'm chilling."

Hawk downed his glass of water then let out a rude belch before excusing himself then hitting Mel-Cash with, "Yo gift of gab fast talking ass ain't changed a bit."

"*Yo how Biggie said it,*" Mel-Cash browsed the faces of Cream and Killa who he sat between, "Aint shit changed but the numbers on the range…word life Sun."

"No question," everyone responded at Mel-Cash's quit witted response while eyeing the menu. Everyone then placed orders while engaging in chit-chat before Sun-Z got down to business.

"So let's build Mel-Cash…we at the round table…whatever manifested in this cipher stay within this cipher."

"Yeah yeah no question Sun…but check it right…Old School Al been making crazy progress on this side with that flavor yall got so yall already know what I'm trying to do…I'm definitely throwing my gold in the pot with y'all…just like back in the days…going straight for the mass appeal."

"What's the math you calculating?"

"I got a duce and some change on hand right now…to be exact I got a hundred geez for 1500 grams of boy (Heroin), and I got like a hundred and fifteen geez for six bricks of that snowflake."

"Ok ok let's eat," the business discussion ceased when the waitresses brought out everyone's' food. Mel-Cash was a good asset to have on the team. He was loyal, thorough, and been around since day one. He was all about the money that's why he was called Mel-Cash. Mel-Cash was slim and lanky like a basketball player but he carried a force with him that intimidated people like he was a heavyweight champion. He was the center of attention. Handsome, well dressed, outspoken and he spoke fast and swift like a *Harlem World* hustler. Mel-Cash was sharp as steel. His only downfall was his love for attention. The crew needed an asset like Mel-Cash on the team because Mel-Cash had the key to the city with his west side flow.

"So yall ready to get this cipher spinning so we can get this mass appeal?" Mel-Cash muttered with a mouth full of chicken before washing his food down with some Parcha juice.

"Nigga what type of question is that?" Hawk replied splashing his yellow rice with red bean sauce. "*Can I fuck two bitches at the same time…while*

I'm eating the third broad pussy and the fourth hottie slobbing my balls...come on hell yeah...I'm the Hawkster...and we do this baby."

"You still a damn whore Hawk," Mel Cash blurted over everyone's laughter. After their meals everyone then drove out to Mel-Cash's 16 acre-estate 45 minutes outside the city near *Darien Lake's Six Flags Amusement Park*. Mel-Cash made his street dreams become reality and he was living the life of luxury. He made hustling look easy and very fruitful. From his shoes to the garments he wore, from the cars he drove to the mattress he slept on, Mel-Cash lived in Thug Paradise and he was living every hustler's dream.

His estate sat about three miles off the New York State Thruway in the middle of nowhere but trees, fields, and more trees and fields. A back road winded thru a cluster of trees and the spacious three-story house sat off the back road. About fifty yards behind the house sat three small cottages. And further behind the cottages was an in-ground swimming pool enclosed by a ten-foot fence. Everyone rolled their cars down the long driveway extending off the backroad. They drove around the three-story house and parked on a huge lot on side of the house.

"So this what that west side money get you huh man?" Everyone was amazed at Mel-Cash's trophy of success as they exited the cars and let their eyes peer to where there was a picnic area under a gazebo, a basketball court, the cottages and the swimming pool.

"Yo yall won't believe how I came up on this country estate." Mel-Cash stated leading everyone behind the house to the picnic tables. Mel-Cash made a quick phone call then continued explaining how he came up on the big estate.

About two years ago after the war with 12th street, Mel-Cash was providing heaven for the poor depressed soul of a woman with the powerful blast of the crack rock. The woman was married to an abusive alcoholic husband and she was smoking up all the proceeds from the cattle raising her family lived off for decades. The woman would escape the abuse of her husband and the boring country life and flee to the city of Buffalo. For days she would find herself floating on the clouds of crack heaven while she smoked out in one of Mel-Cash's crack spots in the Pine Harbor projects. Mel-Cash loved the hundreds she was spending, but when she found one of his stashes and she smoked up two ounces of his crack, Mel-Cash became furious. He took her up to the roof of his building and threatened to throw her off unless she paid double for being *"a filthy disloyal white crackhead."*

The woman begged and pleaded for her life and promised to withdraw the last $ 8, 300 out of her joint bank account. The drugs were more powerful than her life because the money in her bank account was the money to pay the county taxes for her and her husband's 16-acre estate. She gave Mel-Cash the money, and when her and her husband were unable to pay off the taxes, her husband went on a war path and began to beat her senseless. The husband was so heated, to cool himself off he picked up a joint of weed his wife had laying around. Little did he know the joint of weed was laced with the soul snatching crack rock. He wondered what kind of weed could produce such pleasure and he wanted more. The wife confessed that it was weed mixed with crack. So instead of finding a way to pay off the taxes on the estate, the Husband and Wife went to Mel-Cash feigning for more crack. They explained their situation to Mel-Cash and how their estate would be foreclosed on if they didn't pay the taxes and Mel-Cash took advantage of the situation.

"Yo I had them peckerwoods sign everything over to me and I paid off the muthafucking taxes...this shit mines...and y'all family so make y'all selves at home...this the kingdom," Mel-Cash announced. He then escorted everyone from the picnic area and over through the brush. They trekked along a trail and the shrilling sounds of a saw could be heard cutting away in a huge two-story garage. On one side of the garage about a dozen dirt bikes and snowmobiles were lined up. On the wall ahead of the bikes was a large canoe. In the middle of the garage sat a small speed boat. Further to the left of the garage sat a race car hoisted up on a lift. A greasy and oiled covered Caucasian man wearing a pair of oiled stained overalls with nothing under popped out from under the race car with a cigarette in his mouth and a saw in his other hand.

"Look at this devil...this one of my slaves," Mel-Cash chuckled as they neared the garage. "This whole plantation used to belong to him and his stanking ass wife...now it's mine and they ass my slaves...how the saying go, what goes around comes around…you enslaved mines I enslave yours."

"Mel-Cash you one sick dude yo." Sun-Z and everyone laughed at Mel-Cash's retribution.

"Hey guys how youurrrr doing?" The oily mechanic drawled in a heavy country accent. "The bikes are all gassed up and ready to roll out Shamel."

Mel-Cash twisted his lips then blasted "What the fuck I tell you to call me you damn devil."

"Sorry Great God Mel." The man responded.

"Alright come on everybody grab a bike," Mel-Cash stated observing the look on everyone's face. *Mel-Cash had a super ego because of the God-Body Philosophy he acquired in the county jail and he moved around like he was the Original Man-God of the Universe and everyone else was beneath him.*

"Yessir Great God Mel," Dolla started clowning as everyone began jumping on the dirt bikes.

"The Black Man is God and the White man is Devil," Mel-Cash stated, "But check this out right…that Black and Gold bike mine." Mel-Cash slid over to a wall decked with mechanic and carpenter's tools and a few hunting rifles. He grabbed a Carbine 15 Rifle from off the wall and threw its strap around his shoulders, "Whenever yall want we can have target practice." Mel-Cash informed jumping on his dirt bike. "Let's hit these trails now."

Everyone was on their bike and zoomed out the garage with Mel-Cash in the lead. They flew thru a trail which traversed thru a forest with man-made trails and dirt roads. Some of the trails were smooth enough for vehicles and others were rugged and bumpy but perfect for the dirt bikes. They zipped thru the trails like professional motor cross drivers flying up the dirt hills and doing wheelies while racing each other. They zig-zagged hitting sharp turns and busted 360 spins letting their back tires throw dirt at each other. They were like young boys having fun. The scene was like an old western flick and Mel-Cash looked like the Chief Indian on a horse shooting his rifle in the air and at the animals as he led the crew thru the trails. After an hour or so of riding thru the wilderness they jumped off the bikes and hit the crib to freshen up and have a few drinks.

While everyone lounged in the large living room kicking it, Mel-Cash snatched Sun-Z and took him upstairs where he gave Sun-Z a leather Brooks Brothers bag stuffed with over two hundred thousand dollars' straight cash. Sun-Z then slid back downstairs and yelled out for Zulu to meet him by the circular stairwell in the hallway. Zulu slouched over to Sun-Z with his head low like he lost the world. Everyone was lively and having fun being entertained by Mel-Cash, and Sun-Z wondered what could be bothering Zulu at a time like this.

"What the hell wrong with you Zulu?"

Zulu slowly lifted his eyes and caught Sun-Z's stare. "Destiny, Prince, I don't know yo."

"Listen baby boy, as far as Destiny I'm gone be honest...you lost her to gain NyJewel...that's what you wanted...and sometimes in life you gotta settle for the blessings you got...you can't be greedy and overindulge yourself by wanting everything or wanting too much...this what you wanted and this the choice you made...if you wanna be a player...you gonna win some and lose some...it's a part of the game...you understand me," Sun-Z nudged Zulu on the shoulder and seemed to uplift Zulu's spirit with the wisdom he bestowed upon Zulu. "You may have lost Destiny but the wisdom you could gain from this is realizing that everything that glitters ain't gold...when you satisfied with something you need to appreciate it...don't trade in something with a precious value for something you not sure of...just be thankful you got what you got...and now you got NyJewel so be happy because that's what yo hot and horny ass wanted," Sun-Z busted out laughing watching Zulu light up.

"And as far as Prince Zulu...he where he need to be...I'm happy for Prince and you should be too...we don't need everybody in this Thug Life and throwing bricks at the penitentiary...we need some of our people doing the right thing in life...Prince is one less brother we don't gotta worry about getting killed in the streets or going to prison," Sun-Z observed Zulu nodding in agreement. Sun-Z then threw the bag on Zulu's chest, "Now get yo head out yo ass and go make it happen."

"No question big bro." Zulu smiled carrying the bag back down the hall then downing a glass of freshly squeezed lemonade before he saluted everyone and hit the road.

With his seatbelt strapped on, Zulu hit the New York State Thruway and drove west back towards Buffalo. Cautiously, he drove the 65 mph speed limit on cruise control and was being extra cautious eyeing the state troopers who hugged the thruway hoping to catch speeding vehicles coming from nearby *Six Flags amusement park.* Zulu slid into the right lane carefully and drove the 45-mile drive back to the city at ease. When he hit the city, he drove into Williamsville and pulled into a parking garage where he met NyJewel. She was seated behind the wheel of the black Nissan Pathfinder on the third level of the parking garage nervously scanning the surroundings as cars rolled in and out of the parking ramp.

"Oh my God baby I was worried," NyJewel hugged Zulu when he jumped inside the truck with the bag of money.

"Stop worrying all the damn time," Zulu stated leaning into the backseat and throwing the bag under the suitcases and bags in the back of the truck. "Relax sweetheart."

"I am it was just too many cars pulling in here."

"I had you meet me here because I ain't wanna come to the hood with all this money I got."

"You right baby," NyJewel pulled out of the parking ramp and headed to the 290 west expressway heading to Niagara Falls. With over two hundred thousand in the Brooks Brothers bag and over four hundred thousand stashed in a drop box stashed by the gas tank of the Pathfinder, they crossed the Queenston-Lewiston bridge into Canada and hit the Fallsview Casino. They pulled into a designated parking space in the parking ramp where Marcel Francois' son sat in an Oldsmobile Alero waiting to switch rides with Zulu. Zulu jumped out of the truck and the two men greeted each other before NyJewel instructed them on what luggage and bags to remove from the truck and place into the Alero. Once all luggage was placed in the Alero, NyJewel tried slamming the trunk of the over packed Alero but was unable to. Zulu and Marcel Jr. then shot a pesky look at each other men do when women overdo things. They then removed a few bags from the trunk of the Alero and threw them in the backseat. Zulu and Marcel Jr.

then shook hands and said a farewell knowing business was halfway taking care of. Marcel Jr. jumped in the truck and Zulu jumped in the Alero where NyJewel was already sitting in the passenger seat. NyJewel then guided Zulu onto the Queen Elizabeth Expressway heading to Toronto, Canada which was about 70 miles north of Niagara Falls Ontario.

They reached Toronto International Airport an hour later. And after tossing the heavy luggage on the check in machine and checking in, they received their flight itinerary and Zulu discovered where his destination was.

"*The Bahamas.*" Zulu was caught by surprise as they headed to the boarding gate, "Sweetheart...damn."

"Yes love," NyJewel was snatched by Zulu who was feeling good. "It's just me and you baby and I'm getting you away from the streets...I love you."

"I love you too," Zulu responded before they swapped tongues in the crowded boarding area.

Several hours later

"*Welcome to Nassau my brutha and sista!*" Was the Caribbean greeting Zulu and NyJewel received from the Bahamian man with locks in his hair and his skin was onyx Black.

NyJewel owned a time share and the Bahamas was like her second home. The place she called home on the island was a beachfront condo sitting amidst a cluster of coconut trees along the crystal white sand beach where the warm turquoise waters of the Caribbean Sea softly splashed on the shore.

After stepping into the beachfront dwelling and unpacking, Zulu slipped into some Lacoste Beach shoes and swim trunks then stepped back outside into the sun. The environment was so natural and tranquil like the warm breeze soothing the skin. Lime green Iguanas and Lizards crept thru the flora freely as colorful parrots and macaws chirped with the peaceful sounds of the currents of the water washing on the beach. Zulu's mind was massaged by the island atmosphere and all his stress and tension was stripped away like NyJewel, who stepped outside stripped down to her teeny bikini and designer Louis Vuitton shades.

"Come on love," NyJewel took Zulu by the hand and led him to the beach where couples and families lounged enjoying the atmosphere. Zulu and NyJewel then kicked up the soft white sand and scurried over to a 36-foot cabin cruiser floating near the shore. They hit the warm water and waddled over to a young Bahamian man who was leading tourist up onto the boat.

"Na na na," Zulu waved the man's hand away from NyJewel when the man attempted to lift NyJewel onto the boat. "I got her boss man...you can look at her all you want but she mines and mines only to touch my brother." Zulu was seriously joking while jumping onto the boat then extending his hands for NyJewel. The man understood Zulu's overprotection very well and returned a courteous smile to Zulu.

"Boy stop it," NyJewel smiled as Zulu pulled her onto the boat while Zulu and the man were laughing. Once everyone was on board the man hit the engine and whirled the boat a few kilometers into the sea near a huge sparkling florescent coral reef which glimmered under the turquoise waters.

Zulu became frightened when he observed everyone on board including NyJewel throwing on snorkeling gear. Zulu then freaked out when people began jumping overboard.

"Hell naw Ny what we doing here...I can't swim...get me the fuck up outta here."

"Baby relax you just slip these on," NyJewel was so amused while handing Zulu some fins, "All you do is flap...the water not even deep...trust me love." NyJewel kissed him then sashayed her jiggly bubble butt to the deck of the boat. She stopped at the edge then turned around and peered into Zulu's shiny fudge colored face. Zulu looked like a scared child holding the fins. NyJewel then swirled her tongue around her glossy lips before rolling her index finger motioning for Zulu to follow her as she jumped feet first into the water.

"*Hell yeah,*" Zulu threw the fins and snorkel on and was temptingly lured into the water by NyJewel's exotic sex appeal. The Caribbean sun blessed NyJewel's caramel flavored skin tone and flossed its light on all the curves of her well-proportioned body. If Zulu was a shark NyJewel looked like a healthy fish dipping into the water and Zulu dived in right after her ready to feast.

"See its easy love," NyJewel floated in place as Zulu swam to her. She then hugged him and slid her tongue in his saltwater tasting mouth. "Let's go under and see the fish my love."

They swam under water and explored the multitudes of different fish striped with all the bright colors of the rainbow spectrum. The colors of the fish and the underwater environment was beautiful. Fish swam peacefully around the people who floated around the long rocky colorful coral reef glittering in the streaks of sunlight beaming on its rocky surface.

"*It's beeeaaauutifuul.*" NyJewel blew bubbles in Zulu's ear. Zulu shook his head yes squeezing NyJewel tightly under the water. With their big black eyes, the fish became the audience watching the two lovers kiss as they swam in schools thru the endless sea.

On one particular night under a bright white crescent moon amidst hundreds of glimmering stars, Zulu and NyJewel lay wrapped in each other's embrace on a deserted beach. A warm breeze rolled swiftly with the smooth swishing sounds of the sea swelling on shore, while the humming and buzzes of insects buried in the flora along the beach vibrated the night air.

"This is unbelievable being here with you Zulu," NyJewel planted her face softly onto Zulu's bare chest as they cuddled in a beach chair, "This is like heaven baby."

"Hell yeah...I never felt so good and at peace in my life," Zulu inhaled deeply on the exotic island weed wrapped in a Bahamian leaf. "Since we been here I ain't had to carry no guns...I aint heard no gunshots...we been sleeping with the doors unlocked and windows open not worrying about anything but lizards...I never been this comfortable in life," Zulu softly touched NyJewel's chin and looked into her sparkling eyes. "I love you Ny and I thank you for showing me the beauty of life."

NyJewel pulled Zulu's face close to hers and tenderly kissed his lips, "Anything for you love...I want us to make this our home so you can always have this peace...we got enough money...what you think baby?" NyJewel searched Zulu's blank face as he held the spliff in his hand.

"I don't know." Zulu loved the peace but he really desired the action of the street life, "Maybe…we will see about moving here Ny."

"Baby just think me and you here alone living our life…I don't have to worry about losing you to the streets…come on Zulu…if you really love yourself and you love me you would do this…and it's not just for me but it's for you as well baby…I don't want you in the streets forever…you know the streets wasn't made to be played forever…this right here…the peace we have on this island…this is a hustler's dream and goal baby…to get out the game and live in paradise…I want us to enjoy this forever baby."

Sensations tender as NyJewel's soft skin surged thru Zulu's system as he held her in his arms. Thug Paradise is what the street life was supposed to deliver. And right now Zulu felt the streets blessed him with Thug's Paradise for real.

Zulu smiled peering down into NyJewel's eyes, "We gone enjoy this alright." Zulu whispered before sliding his tongue deep into NyJewel's mouth. Zulu then lifted himself up and laid NyJewel on her back. He then climbed on top of her and blew softly in her ear, "We gone enjoy this paradise forever…just lay back beautiful."

The energy of sensual pleasure guided Zulu's tongue from NyJewel's ear lobe down to the curves of her succulent breast. He untied her bikini top then began to suck on her thick nipples like he was thirsting for her sweet breast milk. He then softly kissed her smooth stomach and headed down to her sexual paradise between her legs. NyJewel could feel shocks of pleasure pulsating along her sensory body as Zulu's tongue caressed her inner thighs. She could feel her secretions unleashing inside her as Zulu glided his tongue around the bikini covering her crotch. He then pulled her bikini loose at the waistline with his hands then used his teeth to remove her moist and creamy bikini from her dripping wet paradise. He tossed her bikini onto the sand and dived face first into her squishy loving between her thick thighs. He let his mouth savor the watery tasting cream gushing from her loving while nibbling at her clean shaven clit.

"*Oooo Zulu*," NyJewel moaned wrapping her legs around Zulu's neck as his tongue twirled round and round her clit. "*Yessss…ooooo…just like that baby yessss."*

Zulu now dipped his tongue between her fat and creamy soaked pussy lips before swiping and swirling his tongue inside her tight and wet pussy. The tingling joy shooting thru NyJewel had her bumping and grinding uncontrollably as she lay back in the beach chair. She took her hands and stuffed Zulu's face deep into her and buried his face in her crotch. She then rolled over on top of his face and sat on top of him humping slowly while suffocating his face.

"You trying to kill me," Zulu wiggled his face from under her squirting pussy while gasping for air. NyJewel then scooted from off of his face and slid down to his chest and kissed his cum drenched face.

"I kill you softly with my love." NyJewel then scooted further down and used her hands to grip his hard pipe. She slowly eased herself on top of it massaging her pussy lips with it. Slowly she inserted it inside her while gazing up at the beaming stars while moaning her soul out as his pipe massaged her tight wet walls.

"Sssssss," Zulu slithered in ecstasy feeling the warmth of NyJewel's womb swallowing his pipe. Her womb had all the pleasures of paradise. Her insides were warm, tender, sweet, and lovely. And for NyJewel, Zulu's manhood had the power and glory of God which had the keys to open her gates of paradise as he hit her spots causing her inner sex glands to open up and splash the milk and honey of paradise on his manhood. Under the stellar sky they sexually engaged each other with such a force their climaxing orgasms took their minds higher than the stars watching from above.

CHAPTER 12

The terrorist attacks that wreaked havoc on America on September 11, 2001 had devastating effects on the government all the way down to the ordinary citizen. The economic catastrophe it caused had ripple effects from Wall Street corporations down to the street corner hustlers. Gasoline prices skyrocketed as well as the price of drugs being consumed on Wall Street and in the ghetto. From city to city and hood to hood there were droughts on the supply of drugs and the prices were sky high. Fortunately for those who had mother loads of drugs in their clutches before the 911 Terrorists attacks, the prices went up to the hustlers' benefit. One group of hustlers who would benefit from the rising prices of the 911 drought was Sun-Z and the crew since they reed-up a few days before 911.

When word hit the streets how the prices were doubling, Sun-Z and the crew took full advantage of the situation and turned a negative reality into a positive one. This meant larger profits and more clientele since many hustlers throughout the city no longer had consistent connects. With Marcel Francois and the French Connection as the plug, Sun-Z and the crew would always stay flooded with work.

For Mel-Cash and his super ego of Power, this situation meant more control and power for him to expand and to make any and all rivals starve. Mel-Cash wouldn't sell to certain hustlers just because. When certain hustlers who he wasn't feeling didn't have work, Mel-Cash wouldn't supply them even if they begged to pay triple. Instead, Mel-Cash took their customers and set up shop in their hood. Mel-Cash was like a *Tim Hortons or Dunkin Donuts* coffee shop and began setting up spots all over the west side. Wherever street corner hustlers faced a drought, he flooded their blocks like hurricane Katrina. Now that Mel-Cash was biting more than he could chew, he shared a big piece of the cake with his family from the east side and brought them over to the west side. Mel-Cash's west side flow was faster and more lucrative than the east side flow. Mel-Cash's westside neighborhood was a hop, skip, and a jump from downtown and right across the river from Canada. He had the best of both worlds. On a daily it wasn't unusual during lunch hour to witness a high standing member of society creeping into the Pine Harbor to intoxicate their exhausted minds, then rush back to their offices a few blocks away downtown.

The west side was Buffalo's melting pot where people of all different races mingled and the green dollar came from people of all shades. Even for the hundreds of Canadians who ventured into Buffalo on a daily to take advantage of the lower taxes on shopping, many Canadians found themselves on the west side taking advantage of the euphoric journey the drugs would take their minds. The appetite for drugs on the west side was off the chain and Sun-Z and the crew had the substances to appease the whole city's hungry appetite.

Around this time of 911, there wasn't many who had mother loads of work on deck so competition was almost non-existent for anyone who had work. Sun-Z and the crew along with Mel-Cash seemed to be taking over the city from east to west. They became known as the Get Rich Crime Family because they seemed to be getting rich while others were starving due to the drought. There was so much money to be made competition didn't matter as long as no one stepped on anyone else's toes, and the only big toes that could get stepped on was the 12 Street Mob.

Since everyone was eating and no one trespassed on each other's livelihood, there were no problems. The year of 2001 ended terribly for most but not everyone. America was rebuilding and bouncing back on its feet from the devastation of the terrorist attacks, and on the streets hustlers were doing the same and waiting for prices to drop so they could get back to bubbling.

....

The summer of 2002 jumped off with Kenyatta's beach party at Angola Beach, located less than an hour south of Buffalo. Hustlers from hoods all over Buffalo showed off the hood riches they amassed over the winter of 2001 and the spring of 2002 at the beach party. New whips with shiny rims and earthquake thumping bass rolled thru Evansgola state park where crowds of people spectated the procession of the flashy dope boy rides. Sexy ladies with smooth skin tones and some with a little cellulite glossed their bodies with oil and swarmed the beach in thongs and G-string bikinis. Games of bat mitten, volleyball and dodge ball was played on the sand while others stood knee deep in the chilled waters of Lake Erie splashing each other. And up in Mickey Rats beach bar the party was stimulating as people downed liquor and stimulated themselves while grooving to the music.

The Get Rich Crime Family hit the beach party but not like all the other hustlers. The Get Rich Crime Family came splashing thru the waters on their 2001 LS Yamaha Jet Skis being followed by a 50-foot Yacht. They zoomed their jet skis close to the shore and scooped up several sexy ladies before zooming back out to the yacht where they mingled and partied with the ladies while cruising Lake Erie along the Buffalo shoreline. This was a helluva way to start the summer of 2002 off for the Get Rich Crime Family.

....

Zulu found himself sitting in the parking lot of suspected Mob affiliated *La Nova's Pizzeria* on W. Ferry street on the upper west side. He nervously lounged behind the wheel with thirteen and a half ounces of raw powder in a McDonald's bag sitting right in his lap as Dolla wobbled out of the pizzeria stuffing his face with a Taco pizza.

"Damn Zulu the dude Floss ain't come yet," Dolla dropped into the passenger seat noticing the McDonald's bag still in Zulu's lap.

"Hell no." Zulu barked scanning the cars pulling into the parking lot. "I'm about to hit Mel-Cash now and see where Floss at."

Mel-Cash had his hands tied up on the West Side with all the licks available so he had the Get Rich Crime Family hitting half of his licks so he wouldn't lose them to other crews like the 12th Street Mob who had a lock on the west side as well. Right now Mel-Cash sent Zulu and Dolla on a mission to see a hustler named Floss.

Zulu hit Mel-Cash up complaining how Floss hadn't showed up at La Nova's. Mel-Cash then made a call and told Zulu he had to meet Floss on 7th street.

"This some bullshit yo," Zulu complained pulling out of the parking lot and heading to 7th street which was on the lower west side by Mel-Cash's hood.

"Why you complaining when we about to go get this money?" Dolla asked placing his half eaten box of pizza in the back seat.

"Because I got a hammer (gun) on me and damn near a half of brick in the wheel you fucking clown."

"Yo relax and stop being noid, we got license'dick just do the speed limit."

"Whatever yo." Zulu shot back. Once on the lower west side Zulu hit Porter Ave where dozens of marathon runners were pacing to Busti Park which sat at the foot of the Peace Bridge and along the west side's I-90 expressway. Zulu blew it down Porter Ave and passed a Burger King next to a gas station before turning onto 7th street where an ice cream parlor and abandoned restaurant sat on the corner.

Zulu hit 7th street and between two light poles a group of Africans and Hispanics challenged each other at a game of soccer in the middle of the street. They were so much into their game they didn't notice the cars moving thru the block so they continued playing instead of letting the cars thru. Zulu and the other cars then pounded on their horns before the footballers decided to move out the way.

"Next time we gone run yall monkey and goat face fucks over," Dolla yelled out the window as they eased thru the crowd. The footballers paid Dolla no mind and went back to kicking the soccer ball around on the asphalt.

Zulu headed down the block to where Floss and two of his homeboys stood in the street by a parked car. Zulu pulled in front of a mechanic shop which was directly across the street from where Floss and his two mans stood.

"Yo what's good cousin?" Floss jumped in the backseat of Zulu's car pulling stacks from out of his Rocawear jeans.

"First off my cousin not gone have me driving all around with almost a half of brick…you know we don't even know our way around here like that…why you aint come to La Novas?"

"My bad cuzzo I had to meet up with my man to pick up the rest of the bread, so I figured I just have you come on the block."

"Yo fuck all that let's get this shit done," Dolla received the three rubber band knots from Floss. Each knot was $ 4,000. Zulu then tossed Floss the McDonalds bag as Dolla counted the money. Zulu then scanned the environment as cars rolled up and down the block.

"Count correct," Dolla stated before a purple Acura Integra coupe with deep dish rims then bent the corner banging loud reggae tone. The Acura then stopped in front of Floss's two homeboys who still stood in the street by the parked car. The Acura was about two cars behind Zulu's car.

"Who the fuck is that yo?" Zulu yanked out his pistol as the driver in the Acura spoke to Floss's homeboys.

"Chill chill I got this cuzzo that's my rican nigga." Floss stuffed the McDonald's bag in his drawers, jumped out the wheel and dashed over to the passenger window of the Acura. Zulu had his window down so he could hear the conversation.

The driver of the Acura was a Spanish hustler from 12th street named Snakey. And Snakey barked on Floss for calling him and having him bring work to the block and Floss had also called someone else.

"Listen *Papa*," Snakey told Floss, "Make up yo mind either you copping from us or Mel-Cash and them...no playing both sides *Pa*." Snakey let Floss know before slowly pulling off and easing by Zulu's car. Snakey then locked eyes with Zulu and Dolla.

"*Yo what up yo?*" Zulu shouted out the window seeing where Poppi wanted to take the face fighting. Snakey stepped on his gas pedal and peeled off the block giving Zulu and Dolla the fumes from his dual exhaust. Floss then handed one of his man's the package who ran it inside the house. Floss then stepped back over to Zulu's car and stood at the driver window explaining the situation with Snakey. Floss said the only reason he called Snakey is because he thought Zulu and Dolla wasn't coming.

"That's some bullshit yo," Dolla responded. "You shouldn't be fucking with them niggas anyway...you supposed to keep the money in our circle...fuck them *oyes*."

"Word you gone get one of them niggas clapped coming thru with the face fighting shit." Zulu added massaging the chrome sitting in his lap.

"Na it aint even like that…they don't want no problems…but that's why I'm gone start meeting y'all somewhere else so niggas don't bump heads." Floss advised.

"Nigga fuck that we gone get money wherever it's money to be got…just stop fucking with them niggas because you outta pocket…you fucking with the enemy…you know Mel-Cash and them niggas don't get along…you can't be two faced yo…keep the gold in the pot with the family you heard…just holla at us," Zulu peeled off.

It was only business and Floss was a neutral hustler playing both sides. He was gonna cop from whoever had the fire and whoever got to him first. In the streets this was dangerous because when egos got involved, gangsters became territorial and felt they was king over everyone else. Everyone had to eat, and when someone felt their appetite wasn't being fully satisfied because someone was taking off their plate, here comes the drama.

....

Musitanos' auto dealer on Transit Rd stood out like a sparkling diamond amongst gold. Musitanos huge dealership was one of many car lots on Transit Rd amongst the many strip malls and restaurants in Clarence, NY. This was one of the many suburban shopping centers of Buffalo which was a magnet for the wealth of the affluent and the hard-earned cash of the middle class and low income people. This was a big bankroll mecca that attracted many hustlers desiring to spend that fast money on new whips, jewelry, and the other trophies of the drug game and American Dream.

The Get Rich Crime Family was on Transit Rd at Musitanos car shopping. Money was good and piling high, and now it was time to be treated and flaunt the gold the street kings was being blessed with. In B.M.W 's, Infiniti's, and Benz', the crew flew off the lot after dropping off a leather Burberry bag filled with a couple hundred thousand of fresh new bank money. The wise and intelligent investments of real estate and businesses was already on the crew's asset list, but the purchasing of flashy cars was the sweetest joy hustlers desired like children loved toys. The crew spoiled themselves with high end vehicles of luxury. Dolla and Mel-Cash really treated themselves and styled on a level of Supreme Balling by copping two Porsche GT Carerras. The Get Rich Crime Family was riding foreign in an all-American city.

Old School Al was the only one who hadn't copped his prized possession yet and everyone wondered what he was waiting on. He was celebrating his second year of recovery and abstaining from frying his brains with the sizzling crack rock. Old School Al's bankroll was on a supreme hustler level. He made it happen like he said he would do. No one knew it, but Old School Al was going to treat himself to one of the most extravagant prizes anyone could deserve. Old School Al was about to show the crew, the city, and the country that street dreams came true when hard work and dedication is a hustler's ambition.

It was a sunny afternoon and the sun's solar radiance emanated an illustrious glow on Zulu's Pepsi Blue 750 LI B.M.W. sitting on Pirelli rims. Zulu smoothly slid his wheels up into the Maryland Towers apartments to snatch Old School Al. Old School Al had woken Zulu up earlier in the morning sounding happier than someone who hit the mega millions.

When Zulu answered in the morning Old School Al yelled into the phone, *"Yo Zulu zulu...come get me...come get me...it's here it's here yo aww man it's here."*

Zulu thought to himself Old School Al must've copped a space shuttle that would take the whole crew on a journey through the universe as he pulled in front of Old School Al's building. Old School Al was in front of his building pacing in circles and talking to himself. His energy was turned up like *LL Cool J* in the *"I'm Bad,"* video. Old School Al was dressed in a powder blue Adidas track suit with his jacket open exposing his bare chest which revealed a tattoo of a lady smoking a blunt on his torso.

"Homeboy," Old School Al greeted Zulu while opening the passenger door to the Beemer. Old School Al then yelled up to his girlfriend who lounged on the second-floor terrace smoking a cigarette while reading a Don Diva magazine. Old School jumped in the Beemer and told Zulu to hold on for his

lady.

Luana was her name. She was full blooded Puerto Rican but looked like a sister with her honey bun skin tone. She stepped outside looking like an innocent tenderoni in her late teens who thought she was the Diva Goddess. She was far from innocent and she was nowhere pure in heart and soul like a teenage tenderoni. She was in her thirties but looked like a young hottie. On the material plane she dressed and had the class of a hood diva who had a baller as her King.

Shirley Temple curls dangled down to her shoulders behind her big gleaming Platinum XO earrings. Authentic Dolce and Gabanna shades covered her hazelnut colored eyes and her neck was draped with several XO and link chains. She opened the back door to the Beemer fanning her cigarette which was drenched with rosy red lipstick on the butt. As she fanned the smoke her hand revealed fingers full of rings. She leaned into the car while pulling a long drag on her cigarette.

"Hi Zulu can I smoke in yo ride?" Lulu asked in her squeaky voice.

"Hell no that shit stink what the fuck yo." Zulu screwed his face turning the AC on high and retrieving some air freshener from the arm console. "You outta yo damn mind coming near my whip with that shit."

"It ain't nothing but a lil flake (coke) in it Zulu," Lulu responded swiping her Kooli (Coke cigarette) on the ground then ashing it out.

"I don't give a fuck what that shit is that shit stink throw that shit out if you wanna get in my ride."

"It's not lit Zulu."

"Lulu." Old School Al shouted while spinning around in his seat and demanding, "Throw it out Lulu and show some fucking respect."

"I'm sorry Zulu," Lulu stated throwing her Kooli on the ground and destroying it with her Coach tennis shoes.

"Damn yo what the fuck?" Zulu shot an intense glare at Old School Al as Lulu jumped in the backseat. "How you letting yo girl do that shit...I thought you stopped...don't that shit tempt you?"

"Na homeboy I made a conscious decision to use my will power to overcome that urge...plus Lulu wouldn't want to see me go back down that route…she loves this glamour life we living…she don't want me rocking the bells no more…aint that right ma?"

"You know it poppi." Lulu leaned forward from the backseat and kissed Old School Al on the cheek.

"Yeah whatever," Zulu asserted focusing his eyes on the road as he pulled out. Zulu then played *Big Punisher and Noreaga's* hit song *"You came up,"* thinking about Old School Al and Lulu's history.

Since back in the days as far as Zulu could remember, Lulu had Old School Al wrapped around her finger like the crack she wrapped in her weed filled blunts and cigarettes. She was the evil angel who tempted Old School Al to flirt with the demon of crack. Old School Al wasn't the only victim she seduced with her alluring beauty but he was the one to fall in love with her. Since the 80's when Lulu first started getting high all the way up into the New Millennium Lulu used her cunning charm to entice and seduce hustlers to dance with the devil. Lulu was a pretty woo-head who never sucked the glass dick. She preferred cracks and weed. And even though that physical appearance devouring drug was her slave master, she was just as gorgeous physically as she was since a teenager and she was Old School Al's first and only love.

"Yo we gotta kick it when we get back yo," Zulu yelled under the music. "You bugging Old School…I hope you not gone fall off again yo." Zulu declared in a scolding tone.

"We can talk now homeboy," Old School Al lowered the volume of the music.

"We don't talk business in front of our women and you know that," Zulu sharply replied whipping his wheel onto the expressway.

"Come on Zulu…Lulu my woman and she down like NyJewel is…we can talk in front of my woman."

"Her and my woman two different people and my lady don't know everything."

Lulu felt offended and the guilt of her actions of the past began gnawing at her conscience. Lulu and NyJewel were the same age but they took different paths in life even though they both grew up on the same streets. The way Lulu felt, NyJewel was a stuck-up bitch who wasn't thorough enough for the streets. NyJewel was a woman who rather sit back and be pampered by a hustler whereas Lulu was gonna be out on the field with her hustler. Truth be manifested, Lulu was the one who let the weakness of her lower self become enslaved by the streets. NyJewel utilized the divine power of her mind to stay above the weaknesses of the streets. NyJewel used her intellect to help hustlers make legitimate power moves with their drug money. But still in all and regardless to her flaws, Lulu had a high self-esteem and she wasn't gonna let no one clown her, because no one can judge another since everyone has error.

"Zulu if you feel some type of way speak yo mind nigga," Lulu blasted the words with her squeaky voice. "I know I'm not NyJewel...I'm Lulu Quinones and I'm a solid bitch...You can't say nothing about me ain't nobody else already said."

"What." Zulu heatedly glared back at Lulu. "Ok fuck it then...you right because everyone know how you got my man Old School hooked on that shit in the first place. I'm just happy he got his shit together and he getting his chips up like he supposed to...but Old School," Zulu gripped the wheel but turned his gaze upon Old School Al, "I ain't tryna son you...but yo you don't need to be around that getting high shit...you getting bread and you focused and if you let that shit come into yo world it's gone tempt you and have you slipping."

"Man Zulu my will power is stronger than the temptation of getting high...I make money selling to those who get high homeboy," Old School Al reached inside the pocket of his Adidas jacket and whipped out a folded one-hundred-dollar bill. He unfolded it and it was chunks of soft pearly white cocaine inside the bill. He took out his drivers' license and dipped the corner of it in the powder, scooped up some and took a vacuum sniff with each nostril before passing the bill to Lulu. "You see Zulu...I'm not gone ever smoke that rock again," Old School Al explained looking in the mirror on the passenger visor and wiping his nose clean. "Just a lil flake to celebrate my success...trust me homeboy...this just for celebration...I got this."

"Alright no question...I just don't wanna see you fall off again that's it."

"When you been down for so long you can only come up homeboy…and when you up at the Most-Highest level you can be…you can only go down into the ground six feet under where the show gone be over…and right now," Old School Al lowered the passenger window and sparked a cigarette, "Let's go get this show started and pick up my prize so I can show these rabbit ass fools how it's supposed to be done."

Zulu pushed his V-8 engine to the max flying down the expressway and only slowing down when approaching the toll booths heading into Grand Island which sat between Buffalo and Niagara Falls. Once on the island Zulu hit Ron Catalino's foreign and domestic auto sales. Zulu rode thru the spacious car lot filled with its new and used high end and exotic vehicles before heading to the customer service center. Posted up in front of the service center was a hot Smurf blue *Ferrari Enzo* gracing the asphalt and sitting so pretty.

"Yo this it Zulu," Old School Al shouted jumping out the Beemer before Zulu even stopped. "I did it…I did it." Old School Al jumped in the air like he was reaching for the sun.

"*Ooo shit*," Zulu was awestruck beholding the perfection of one of the world's most exotic cars. "Yo this nigga really done it…this shit look like some transformer shit…this shit brawlic as hell yo."

"It's showtime Zulu," Old School Al bragged heading into the service center to see a sales attendant. About 45 minutes later Old School Al was shooting out of Catalino's in his new trophy. The Ferrari ripped the expressway with its powerful output of horsepower and was so fast everything looked like a blur. It looked like Zulu's high performing Beemer was moving in slow motion compared to the lightning speed Ferrari. Zulu mashed his pedal to the floor trying to stay within distance of Old School Al but it was impossible. The Ferrari lunged forward over the Grand Island Bridge then vanished into thin air as it took off at atomic speed.

They hit the city and pulled up into the E. North section where Zulu parked his Beemer on the ave then jumped in the Ferrari. Old School Al then pushed the Ferrari Uptown to Bailey Avenue where the crew awaited to see Old School Al's long awaited trophy.

The Ferrari veered its gripping tires onto Bailey Avenue's congested strip where the traffic slowly eased forward amidst the swarms of people pacing the strip. While waiting for traffic to move, Old School Al hit neutral while mashing his foot on the gas pedal forcing the high-powered engine to growl with thunder. He kept the car in neutral for a minute or so letting the engine roar. He now held up traffic as his lane of travel cleared. Women bouncing in and out of the shopping stores felt their insides shiver as the Ferrari roared. The young hustlers posted in front of the corner stores felt their adrenaline pumping and their ambitions of hustling was testifying right in their face. Old School Al knew all eyes was on him. After several car horns screamed in acknowledgement and honked for him to move, he shifted the gear into drive and flooded the gas pedal unleashing the torque of the Ferrari's power as it screeched from 0 to 60 in 3.0 seconds. He had all the busy shoppers and store owners on the avenue startled as he blasted down Bailey Avenue headed to a Jamaican Bar and Grill.

The Ferrari swerved into a mini-plaza which served a mini mart, clothing and hair store, and a Jamaican bar and grill. Amongst the few hoopties and common American made cars filling the parking lot, Dolla's money green GT Carrera and Killa's white Q 45 Infiniti illuminated the parking lot with their gleaming exterior frames. The several Kawasaki motorcycles lined up between the GT and Infiniti added more gleam to the scene with their multi-colored frames. The parking lot was a display of Street Dreams.

"Yo what the fuck this damn fool done did?" Sun-Z couldn't believe his eyes observing the Ferrari swerve into the parking lot. "I can't believe this damn fool."

"I told yall I was gone do it," Old School Al jumped out the Ferrari clutching his Molsen Ice beer. He then started rapping like *Kool Moe Dee* with his arms extended in front of the Ferrari, *"How ya like me now."*

"How the fucking Feds gone like you?" Hawk responded.

"Yo Sun I clearly told everyone nothing to exotic, flashy, and too bright," Sun-Z furiously shook his head disappointedly. "I congratulate you but why you cop a rari yo? You bugging."

"Yeah you really gotta be saluted…you over did it," Killa jokingly stated stepping around the Ferrari with everyone else and eyeing it with desire.

"You had to spend yo whole stash on this joint." Cream blurted out. "This a fucking dream car yo for real…you wasn't playing huh man."

"This shit a dream car alright," Hawk threw in the air stepping back and posting up on the trunk of Killa's Infiniti, "But this shit also a federal nightmare for niggas in the game like us."

"Whatttt." Old School Al spit out unbelievably. "How yall not gone--," Old School Al almost lost his breath and felt like he was hit in the gut. "Everybody got new whips…what the fuck wrong with mines."

"Nigga look," Mel-Cash motioned towards all the people coming out the stores and the cars slowing down to peep the Ferrari. "Wasn't nobody paying us any attention until you came…now all eyes on us because you got yo fast and furious car out here."

"Yall niggas is crazy," Old School Al screwed his face up, "Mel-Cash you and Dolla copped Porsches…the Kadari Twins got Infinities…Zulu and Hawk got Beemer's…and Sun-Z you and Cream got Benz'…what the fuck wrong with my car."

"If you don't know go figure it out," Sun-Z barked, "Don't ride around the hood in that flashy ass wheel because you gone draw way too much attention…please stay away from me in that joint…you gone have all of us going to a fed jail flashing like that."

"Word up Sun," Mel-Cash added while sitting on his motorcycle, "Nigga we in ghetto ass Buffalo…you drive Raris in Miami, LA, Vegas or even in Manhattan…but not in this raggedy ass town."

"Damn why yall coming at the man like that," Zulu stood up for Old School Al while rolling up a blunt, "The man treated himself…he deserves it…we all got new whips and niggas do this every day."

"And niggas who do this everyday end up in the feds every day," Sun-Z blurted out.

"Word Old School you need to go treat yo self in Miami with that hot ass wheel, you really did it yo I can't even lie," Hawk stated throwing his bike helmet on and jumping on his bike, "But as long as we in the hood homie…don't come near me in that rari yo…and you should know better Zulu…that shit a ticking time bomb."

"Word up Zulu," Mel-Cash cranked his bike up, "You shouldn't be riding with that fool around here…shit like that bring the feds out."

Dolla finally spoke up ready to clown, "Old School Al what they basically saying is you not that fly nigga like me to ride boss status…just give me the keys to the rari and let a real G do him…because it's not the car…it's the man behind the wheel that got the drive for these hoes."

"Man that's fucked up yall hating on me," Old School Al replied as everyone began jumping on their bikes and into their cars. "Everyone can cop new whips but when I cop my shit it's a problem…that's some bullshit."

"Poppi I love your car," Lulu yelled out the passenger window of the Ferrari.

"No you got it wrong Old School," Sun-Z wheeled his bike over to Old School Al, "I'm happy and proud of you…you accomplished yo goal…but you gotta be sharper…we on the low and gotta stay low…it's alright to flash but we aint trying to be the flashiest…you see Benz' and Beemer's all day everyday..but a Rari…you only see them sports stars driving them shit's around here and they legit…we not legit because we still throwing bricks at the penitentiary…you gotta think Sun and don't be foolish…just go and enjoy yo self where you can fit in with yo nice prize you feel me." Sun-Z stated.

"Old School you gone put the feds on niggas," Hawk stated before blasting off on his bike, "I hope you enjoyed yo ride in the rari Zulu because that car gone have you riding to a jail…trust me lil bro."

"Damn Old School," Zulu muttered watching Sun-Z, Hawk, and Mel-Cash zoom off on their bikes and flee from the scene like it was contaminated with Ebola. "I ain't mad at you Old School you my boy."

"Old School just give me yo keys and you can take my Carrera," Dolla stepped close to Old School Al while Cream and the Twins were standing around laughing. "And I'm telling you…if you start back smoking again I give you a brick for the Rari...what you say Old School."

"Get the fuck out of my face you fucking clown."

"Come on Lulu talk to yo man," Dolla shouted to Lulu as he headed to his Carrera, "You would love that wouldn't you Lulu…I give yall a whole brick for the rari…yall be the real Wu-Tang masters then." Dolla had Cream and the Kadari Twins laughing their souls out as they headed to their cars.

Lulu rolled her eyes at Dolla not paying him any mind, even though Dolla was a crack god she could never seduce and take off his hustling square like she done most hustlers. Dolla would let Lulu slob on his lollipop for an eight-ball and that was it.

"Yo yall stop clowning my boy and stop hating," Zulu shouted as they jumped in the wheels and peeled out. "Respect my boy hustle."

"I know you my boy Zulu it's just fucked up yo…everybody got expensive wheels that cost bank rolls…Mel-Cash and Dolla spent over a hundred on them GT's…Sun-Z ain't get on shit with them…but here it is I copped something I wanted and niggas mad because I treated myself…if that's the case we all should be driving fucking hoopties…what's the purpose of getting money if we can't buy the things money can buy."

"Man fuck them niggas yo you a grown ass man," Zulu cheered Old School Al up and led him over to the bar, "Let's go and have a toast for yo success and yo new trophy."

"No doubt homeboy."

CHAPTER 13

Floss from 7th street on the west side found himself being squeezed between a rock and a hard place. He was determined to get money but he wasn't feeling being in the middle of Mel-Cash and the 12th Street Mob's beef. He had to choose sides because loyalty and trust not only ensured survival, but it would guarantee the opportunity for success. It was a no brainer for Floss to decide where he was wanted and who he would get rich with, and that was with Mel-Cash and the Get Rich Crime Family. That's when some Puerto Ricans from 12th street shot up one of Floss' crack spots because he wasn't copping work from them anymore. Floss now chose to roll strapped up and ready to splash a Rican on sight.

It wasn't long before Floss caught a 12th street member slipping. Floss banged shots at the Rican but missed, and to make matters worse, someone who knew Floss peeped his face. A witness statement to police about a shooting caused a warrant to be issued on Floss. If Floss knew he had a warrant on him he would have stayed off the streets because he was wanted by the cops and Parole.

While riding thru his hood, Parole and Police swarmed on Floss and caught him in the possession of $ 6, 300 in cash, a half ounce of strawberry Kush and a loaded firearm. Floss would be up north for the next three years rocking state greens and being told what to do by the redneck hillbillies. The hustle didn't stop, and even though Floss was up north, 7th street would keep booming.

12th Street figured since Floss was snatched off the scene 7th Street was open for the taking. 12th street should have known better. Floss' crew was rolling with Mel-Cash and the Get Rich Crime Family. 7th Street had the opportunity of a lifetime being on the Family's side. Mel-Cash and the Family fronted 7th street enough heroin to attract feins from all over the lower west side. This was a strategic move because the feins could just go to 7th street instead of trekking all the way over to 12th street which was across Niagara Avenue. The feins around 7th street was thanking Jesus for the high-powered boogie they now had in the neighborhood. 7th Street was thankful to the God of the Hood-Mel-Cash for the blessings of the hood riches they were making. And Mel-Cash was paying his honor, respect, and gratitude for being linked up with the Get Rich Crime Family. The 12th Street Mob on the other hand was getting fed up due to the way Mel-Cash and his east side partners was moving thru the west side taking over.

....

"Yo mama cita kaypaso…what's good?" Terror let the words roll softly off his tongue as he gently touched the mami's hand when she slid pass him.

The mami repulsively yanked her hand away from Terror since he was a stranger. Her fiery brown eyes glared at him with disgust as she kept swirling her medium size hips into the corner bodega on Jersey street.

"Damn ma you think you all that. I was just tryna tell you you had a bugger in yo nose with yo ugly ass." Terror was joking knowing she was gorgeous like model Ayisha Diaz with the cute little mole on her cheek.

"Cabron." The mami muttered loudly checking herself in the reflection on the glass door of the bodega hoping she didn't have a bugger in her nose. She then spun around in Terror's direction and snapped for letting Terror play her. She should've known she didn't have a bugger in her nose because she wiped her nose extra clean after she sniffed a line of that coco before hopping out of her wheel. "No me togue Pendejo (Don't touch me asshole). You punk you not worthy of a woman like me." The mami stated drifting into the store to grab her wine cooler and cigarettes.

"Whooooa." Mel-Cash fluted his lips at the mami's feistiness while lounging on the trunk of Terror's misty grey Infiniti. "Damn she strait curved you and kicked you strait to the curb like a sewer hole…yikes." Mel-Cash shouted.

"What the fuck was that Spanish shit she said?" Terror asked stepping away from the payphone.

"Yo you don't even wanna know and it don't even matter."

"Yo I wanna know when them pastelito's gone be done," Dolla spit sitting in the passenger seat with the car door open. His stomach was growling and his mouth was watering as his nostrils sucked in the spicy aroma of the Spanish cuisines seeping into the air from inside the bodega. "Yo, where them 7th street niggas at with that bread...we been out here for like twenty minutes."

"I think this them right here," Mel-Cash responded observing a Tan Chevy Tahoe coming thru the block.

"Dolla yo fat ass ordered 10 pastelitos you really think them shits gone be done in twenty minutes?" Terror stated as him and Mel-Cash observed the Tahoe parking across the street from the bodega.

Mel-Cash then ran across the street and stood at the driver window of the Tahoe. Mel-Cash suspiciously looked up and down the block, then grabbed a brown paper bag full of money from the driver then stuffed the bag in his pockets. Mel-Cash gave the driver dap then jettted back across the street with his pockets bulging.

"Yo them boys damn near finish and they gone be ready to re-up," Mel-Cash stated stepping to Dolla who was now standing on the sidewalk next to Terror. Mel Cash then sat in the passenger seat and stashed the brown paper bag under the passenger seat. "Yo Dolla go check on yo food because we need to hit the spot and get they package together because them boys gone be hitting us in bout an hour or two."

Dolla spun around to hit the bodega and the mami was striding out the store with her head high in the air like the cigarette smoke she blew thru her thin lips. Her intense eyes shot bullets thru Terror.

"Yo what this bitch said in Spanish yo?" Terror asked Mel-Cash once again.

"Oh," Mel-Cash began laughing, "You still trying to get over being curved Sun? Alright she called you an asshole in a nasty Puerto Rican way...ugly yo."

"What...bitch fuck you."

"Fuck you *Cabron*," The mami stopped in her tracks as she headed to her car parked on side of the store. She turned red and started spitting fire the way she roasted Terror in half Spanish and English before saying, "Stay right here I be back you *monicone*."

"Bitch I be right here waiting."

"Come on Terror," Mel-Cash was laughing, "Why you gotta come on my side of town and start trouble...we like peace over here Sun...y'all east side niggas always wylin," Mel-Cash jokingly stated.

"Come on both yall niggas bugging," Dolla stated before bouncing into the bodega, "I'm tryna eat and you gassing Action Jackson up to start some bullshit with Pablo Escobar's niece or whoever the fuck she is."

"Man I ain't got shit to do with Terror and Ms. Spicy beef...I'm just a translator...don't kill the messenger," Mel-Cash was still joking.

While Dolla was inside the bodega munching on a large bag of Funyuns and waiting on his pastelito's which were coming out of the deep fryer, Mel-Cash and Terror stood outside on the corner eyeing a Honda Accord stopped at the light. The Honda had about 5 wild Hispanics crowded in the car blasting loud reggaeton. The light turned green and the Honda bent the corner and disappeared down the block where the blasting music could still be heard. A few moments later, a golden yellow Silverado pick-up truck with shiny chrome and black wheels pulled up on the corner being followed by the mami in her Mitsubishi Galant.

"Aw shit," Mel-Cash mumbled to himself before asking Terrror, "You got yo toast on you right?"

"I wouldn't be caught six feet under without my shit," Terror alerted as him and Mel-Cash watched the passenger window of the Silverado roll down.

"*She-male*...I mean *Sha-Mel*," a deep raspy voice shouted from the passenger seat of the Silverado. "What the fuck pa...you just can't stay where you belong like a fucking animal in yo cage." The short heavyset man climbed out the passenger side of the Silverado. This was Megalito, the King of the Infamous 12th Street Mob.

"Who the fuck this nigga talking to?" Terror snapped.

"Chill I got this just hold me down," Mel-Cash told Terror before he edged closer to the curb, "*Gortho Pendejo (Fat greedy muthafucka). Yo soy dios y hago lo que quiera (I'm God in these parts and I do what the fuck I want), take yo fat ass back across Niagara Street...this my side nigga.*" Mel-Cash manifested standing firm on the curb with Terror at his side. Dolla just happened to step out the bodega stuffing a pastelito in his mouth. He peeped the situation and swiftly tossed his food in the car, clenched his fist and was ready to rumble as he stormed over to Mel-Cash and Terror's side.

"Yeah whatever pa...you might be God on this side of Niagara street...but you in my world and you been violating...for one you disrespecting one of the queens," Megalito glanced back at the mami as she stood halfway out her car. "And then you got these monkeys from 7th street pumping boogie (Heroin) all up in my shit and stepping on my toes."

"Nigga I step on yo toes right now you fucking chump," Dolla blasted storming towards Megalito before Mel-Cash stopped him.

"You wanna get it on Pa?" Megalito braced himself to knuckle up before Mel-Cash stopped Dolla. Megalito then whistled and them same rowdy Hispanics that was in the Honda Accord flew from behind the building across from the bodega and rushed the three outsiders.

"Step the fuck back or I blast all you muthafuckas," Terror snatched the gun from off his waist but kept it at his side. The brawlers stopped in the middle of the street still yelling and cursing in Spanish eyeing the big 44 Desert Eagle Terror gripped. They all then dipped and covered themselves on the other side of the Silverado truck. The mami jumped back in her car and sped off. Mel-Cash, Terror, and Dolla continued standing their ground on the corner and was fearless.

"*Paraqueate ahi y saca la pistol pullo* (Pull over and grab the gun.)," Megalito ordered his driver who swerved up onto the curb and jumped out clutching an AK-47 with a 100-round drum. "We a leave yall lifeless on this corner pa...that's what yall want?" Megalito asked stepping closer to Mel-Cash but keeping his distance several feet away.

Megalito's driver shielded himself behind the truck and aimed the chopper right at Terror's dome piece. Terror peered into the barrel of the chopper ready to squeeze as he aimed his Desert Eagle at Megalito's shooter. They all knew that one little inch of movement or the wrong sound would be the end of life. And knowing this, Dolla wanted to leap forward and pound on Megalito before getting chopped down by the chopper. Terror wanted to let his one shot off and kill his killer because he was ready to die and at least take someone with him. And Mel-Cash, for the first time in his life he utilized his intelligence to see that they had no wins and they would have to fight another day. As much as Mel-Cash wanted to risk everyone's life by telling Terror to shoot, they couldn't do it.

"*Arggh,*" Mel-Cash bit his lip in anger before letting his intellect say, "You got that fat ass."

"I know I got it *She-male*...I mean *Sha-Mel*...don't be disrespecting no Latin queens ever again...and stop stepping on my toes...I was the first one to be hitting dudes from 7th street and the Lakeview Projects with that boogie...them was my licks...you trespassing and got them niggas hitting all my feigns...stay over in the Pine Harbor where I let you stay and eat."

"I'm God Fat Boy and I'm gone eat wherever the money is...I see you around though." Mel-Cash shot back before they jumped in the ride and sped off heading to the east side.

....

"*Pop pop pop pop Boom,*" was the blasting sounds of the fireworks being lit by a group of kids in the middle of Courtland street. Zulu, Cream, and Killa posted up on Cream's black on black 500 SEL Benz on the corner of E. Delavan and Courtland sipping some Incredible Hulk (Hypnotiq and Hennessy). Fourth of July was right around the corner and they were loaded with so many fireworks they were riding thru the city giving out fireworks to the kids. When they swung thru the jam-packed parking lot of the *Tradefair* plaza on E. Delavan and Courtland, they decided to post up and mingle with the flocks of ladies dancing to the live D.J. rocking the party in the plaza.

Everything was going smooth watching kids lite the fireworks while the trio hollered at the ladies. As the sounds of hip-hop artist *Nelly* romped thru the speakers, the intoxicating liquor stimulated the animal instincts of the trio and their lustful eyes began preying on the succulent flesh of the booty shaking ladies who was *dropping down and getting their eagle on*. One phone call changed the whole mood and made the trio cut their conversations with the ladies short. It was an emergency so they jumped in the Benz and flew to the hood in a hurry.

....

Right after the face off with Megalito, Terror hit E. North and pushed his Infiniti onto a smoke-filled street cluttered with wrappers and fragments of fireworks. The smell of fireworks flooded the steam blowing nostrils of Terror, Mel-Cash, and Dolla who jumped out the car and stormed over to the porch Zulu, Cream, and Killa sat on.

"What the fuck is so important that we had to leave the fucking party we was at?" Cream vexed from the porch as the three pranced over to the steps. "It was some sexy ass ladies over there…yall boys sure know how to fuck the mood up."

"Them fucking Rican niggas was gone bust my melon open." Terror had death in his green eyes as he stood at the bottom step angrily pacing in circles.

"Yo that's my word I wanted to rock that Super Mario looking ass Rican in the mouth," Dolla was punching his hands before he sat his fat self on the steps breathing deeply. His adrenaline had him ready to explode out of his body.

"Yo fuck all that," Mel-Cash ran up onto the porch and stepped to Zulu, Cream and Killa who sat at a small table rolling up blunts. "Yall still got them half sticks of dynamites?"

"Yo fuck dynamites lets go kill these fucking oyes," Killa jumped out his seat on the porch. "How the fuck they almost split yo cranium and yall was strapped. They should've killed yall because it's on"

"Hold hold hold," Cream interjected, "What the fuck happened?"

"Man fuck what happened let's make it happen," Terror shouted.

Mel-Cash took a deep breath while visually telling Dolla and Terror to shut up with that look in his eye. He had to come up with a good excuse to do what he planned on doing because Sun-Z wasn't gonna tolerate any non-sense and any move that would stop the cash flow. Mel-Cash would tell the truth but not the whole truth.

"Yo we went to a bodega near 7th street and we seen the nigga Megalito. Nigga run up on us talking bout we stealing his licks and stepping on his toes," Mel-Cash pulled out a cigarette and sparked it. "I told his fat ass fuck him, words was exchanged and then the heat was pulled out on both sides."

"How the fuck guns get drawn and nobody got hit?"

"I don't know," Dolla exclaimed.

"And now you wanna start a war because words was exchanged and yall pulled out on each other?" Cream asked.

"Nigga is you deaf or what?" Terror vengefully asked Cream while flailing his hands as he talked, "Them niggas ran up on us and pulled a K out...if I wouldn't have pulled out yall be watching the news hearing about 3 niggas killed on the west side while yall was up in some pussy like some fucking dickheads."

"Word," Dolla stated catching his breath. "Terror saved us for real...if it wasn't for Terror we would've been lunchmeat for that K-Cutter."

"Mannn," Cream stated unbelievably. "We gotta call Sun-Z a.s.a.p." Cream pulled out his cell phone.

"No no no," Mel-Cash stopped Cream, "I got a plan we aint gotta start a war."

"Fuck that I wanna take them niggas to war," Killa barked.

"Hell yeah I'm ready," Zulu sparked up a blunt still seated. "We can call Sun-Z later after we show them *oyes* how it feel to play with death."

"Oh boy," Cream shook his head in confusion. "I don't know what the fuck going on now Mel because as crazy as you is you don't want a war but you tryna get busy with dynamites...I think you just don't like them people."

"Na na Sun you got it all wrong yo...all I'm saying is I got a plan to hit these niggas where they not gone know it was us and it's not gone be a war...trust me...Megalito and 12th street got mad beef...I just need the dynamites...we aint gotta call Sun-Z because nobody gone get hurt...trust me it's not that serious to start a war."

"I'm not feeling how niggas gone pull a chopper out on yall and it's not gone be a war," Killa stated letting his grey eyes peer into space.

It's more than one way to strategize war tactics Killa," Mel-Cash threw his arm around Killa. "I just need them dynamites...4th of July weekend gone be here real soon and I'm gone put on a show...watch me."

"*Ooooh hell yeah*," everyone's eyes lit up except Cream's. "Let's have a toast to this shit." They all toasted before Cream snatched Zulu and took him for a ride.

Zulu and Cream was cut from the same cloth but they were opposite sides of the same coin. Zulu was an intelligent young thug who loved to act savage. Cream was intelligent and more reserved; he knew when to act savagely. While they went for a ride, Cream let it be known to Zulu that he wasn't feeling the situation one bit. And to make matters worse, they were gonna make a move without consulting Sun-Z.

Ever since Zulu's first of the month massacre, Sun-Z let it be known that no moves should be made carelessly if it affected the whole team, but according to the circumstance of life and death, it was self-preservation and self-preservation comes from knowing one's ability to swiftly adapt and respond automatically in any situation for survival, at a time when it's no time to think. This is where the intellect that guides animal instinct makes the law of the concrete jungle kill or be killed.

"Sometimes you don't think do you Zulu?" Cream asked while whipping his Benz through the blocks. "We getting a lot of money right now and we don't need to act the way we did when we was teenagers banging and shit…I'm loving this life yo…this what we been dreaming of since we was on the corner…it been hell getting here and I'm not tryna lose this for some bullshit that could be prevented…word life Zulu."

"You talking bout you aint tryna lose this bankroll we getting?" Zulu shot a sarcastic look at Cream. "Well you better act like you don't wanna lose this bankroll because these Rican niggas got shit fucked up thinking they control everything and we can't eat on the west side…if you wanna keep eating on that west side we gotta get busy and show these niggas they not stopping shit…niggas respect violence Cream and that's one of the reasons we can eat like we eating...you know it…ever since we was young we had to get busy so niggas wouldn't try taking our shit…and it's the same thing now but on a higher level…don't let this big money turn you soft and make you forget yo dog fighting skills."

Cream thought for a moment. Zulu was right. Whenever it was money involved there was always an opposition to stop it, whether it was competition, stick-up kids, or the law. There was no moving forward without friction.

"You right hell yeah," Cream smiled with a look of greed and a lust for riches in his eyes. "We gotta show these niggas we gone get rich or die trying."

CHAPTER 16

"New York, New York. The Big City of Dreams.
It's so nice they named it twice. The city with bright lights
that make you feel like a star. NY is the city that never sleeps. The
city where hustlers and stars materialize their dreams.
New York, New York."

In a world of blaring lights high in the sky with multitudes of people moving in any and every direction, while swarms of yellow cabs and cars stuck in traffic the screaming ruckus of car horns, Old School Al posted up on his Ferrari on the corner of 44th street and Broadway in bustling mid-town Manhattan. His eyes took in the glaring lights of Times Square down the strip, but his mind's eye took his visual consciousness to a virtual place deep in the depths of his mind where he watched and listened to his thoughts while his two physical eyes blindly watched the action of Times Square.

For the past month Old School Al not only stayed away from the Get Rich Crime Family, but he stayed away from the city of Buffalo. For the past month Old School Al and Lulu journeyed all across the country in his prized possession.

From gambling at Casinos and hitting the boardwalk in Atlantic City, to cruising the strips of Virginia Beach and Myrtle Beach, all the way to indulging in the nights of pleasure in the hottest bars in Miami Beach and experiencing wild fantasies with Lulu in New Orleans, Old School Al had an experience many couldn't even dream of. His travels were priceless and he was living like a superstar with a super bankroll.

While driving in the Ferrari in some of America's hottest cities and hot tourist spots many people thought Old School Al was the one and only *Ladies Love Cool J (LL Cool J), Mr. Todd James* himself. Old School Al ran with the make-believe impersonation of L.L. living the life of a superstar and being treated like royalty.

While Old School Al sat zoning out in Manhattan, a city where the poor lived amongst the rich, he had to face the reality that his rich and extravagant excursion had to come to an end. The fleeing happiness he experienced would always be carved on the stones of his memory banks like the *Medu Neter* (Hieroglyphics) were in Kemet (Egypt). Now he had to end his journey and go back to Buffalo which was the 3rd poorest city in the northeast and get back on his grind.

New York City had the Supreme motivation to spark a hustlers' ambition. Old School Al was going to get back to the gritty streets of Ruff-Buff and build his bankroll back up, because he was now *broke* and just a nigga with a Ferrari and a story to tell that many people would love to experience.

"*Money making Manhattan,*" Old School Al journeyed from the womb of his mental galaxy and returned his consciousness back to Times Square. "I'm bout to go back to that small pond and be the big fish I am…If I made it happen once I can make it happen again."

Old School Al returned home, parked his Ferrari in a storage place, jumped in Lulu's Honda Accord and hit E. North with his hand out crying for help. He went straight to the big boss Sun-Z to get a front on the arm so he could get back to rolling. Sun-Z was the Head Nigga in Charge because his caliber of thinking was on a high plane of Power and Intelligence. Power because he used his ability to stay mentally sharp and focused. He knew to be the best he had to think on a high level to prevent negative and limited thinking from filtering the bounds of his intelligence. "***The mind of greatness is only known to the man of greatness.***" And Sun-Z was on a level of Supreme Intelligence because he allowed his experience to give him Supreme Knowledge and Wisdom to make the right judgements and decisions. One wise judgement Sun-Z made that was right and exact was the intolerance of ignorance.

Old School Al was celebrating his recovery from smoking crack which was beautiful. He deserved the rewards of success but he celebrated in a foolish way. It was just like the wise scribe of the Bible manifested, "*A fool and his money shall soon part.*" The memories of his travels in the Ferrari, the places he visited, the people he met, and the insatiable joy and happiness his soul experienced was equivalent to the riches of the earth, but in reality it was a foolish way to celebrate since he threw away all his hard-earned success through celebrating. This was the ignorance Sun-Z didn't tolerate.

"So let me get this straight Old School," Sun-Z thoughtfully cued after Old School Al bragged about his trip then sobbed about his financial situation. "You spent damn near yo whole bankroll on that Rari…then you took the rest of yo gold and went on a partying trip all across the country stunting…and now you back home broke and you need a lookout?" Sun-Z asked wrinkling his forehead while eyeing Hawk for his input.

"Yeah homeboy you told me to enjoy myself…I did and now I'm just saying look out with something light to a giant…you know…like a half of brick so I can get back on my feet." Old School Al responded.

"Nigga you need to get hit in the head with a brick," Hawk snickered. "You act like a damn fool with money Old School."

"Yeah nobody told you to go spend yo whole bankroll… I don't understand you," Sun-Z spoke stiffly in his bossy tone of voice, "You played the cards you were dealt with no respect for the game…you was very careless and reckless with spending yo money…that's straight foolish to do what you did…and now you expect us to give you another chance to act foolish again and blow our money…hell no…you need to learn a lesson…and you need to sell that Rari and get yo money back."

"I'm saying just give me--,"

"Nigga what the hell Sun just say." Hawk cut Old School Al off. "Go take that Rari back and come see us when you get that bread…ain't nobody putting shit in yo hands you damn fool."

Old School Al couldn't believe it. He felt he did nothing wrong. He did what most hustlers attempted to do but didn't even get close to accomplishing. There was no way he was trading in his trophy just yet. There were other helping hands he could reach out to. He slid over to the west side to go see Mel-Cash.

"First off Old School," Mel-Cash shot a bawled expression as him and Dolla parlayed on his GT Carrera in front of the Pine Harbor. "Nobody told yo dumb ass to spend all yo gold on a car and a fucking adventure…who do that and where they do that at? Tell me please because I need to know Sun."

"I tell you who do that," Dolla chimed in joking, "Crackheads who try to be hustlers do that…that's them crackhead ways you got…you spend all yours on satisfaction and now you want us to satisfy yo needs…I got a brick for that Rari right now if you that desperately in need."

"Chill out with the disrespect homeboy…all that even called for." Old School Al twisted his face at Dolla then turned back to Mel-Cash. "Come on homeboy I been making bankrolls in these projects for you and with you and now you treating me like you don't know my worth and how I do…come on homeboy…back in the days you risked yo life for me and almost lost yo freedom."

Mel-Cash peered into space thinking how Old School Al always got himself into a jam and needed to be rescued. "That was a different situation back then and I still do that if someone violated you…but when it come to this cash…I'm just saying Sun…how you expect me to put a half of brick in yo hand and you running around with Lulu on that Wu-Tang shit…don't think the streets don't talk…you can't be serious Sun."

"Word up," Dolla added on. "You only a couple of laced blunts away from the pipe…I wouldn't put no work in yo possession unless it's an even exchange…you can get 36 ounces of fish scale for the Rari…speak now forever hold your peace."

"Dolla you a fucking fat clown you fucking bozo," Old School Al rambled after making his last plea. "Yeah Mel I blew a couple of woos but only on some party shit…I ain't fucking around and that's my word…I just need some help to get back…come on homeboy and help me out."

"Sun you got a quarter million-dollar car…aint no way you should be begging niggas…you better take that bitch back to the dealer and downgrade and get some of yo money back…Sun-Z spoiled yo ass but you gone learn now." Mel-Cash declared.

"The nigga high off them woos and can't think straight."

"Fuck you Dolla," Old School Al stepped away feeling so disappointed. He made a mistake and was being crucified for it. Where was the forgiveness? Life was supposed to be a school where Man lived, committed errors, learned from his mistakes and imperfections, then got a second chance to do better and move on. Where was Old School Al's second chance?

Lulu had a cousin named Kato who was Big Boy status on the upper west side of town. Old School Al went to him for a lookout but the only front Kato could give Old School Al at the time on a business level was front Old School Al whatever he copped. It was a shame because Old School Al had a Ferrari but couldn't even buy 125 grams.

So back to E. North Old School Al found himself looking to be saved by his favorite homeboy/little brother from another mother. Old School Al stepped to Zulu explaining the situation but Zulu cut him short because he already knew what was going on.

"Listen bro you aint gotta explain shit to me…I'm just glad you accomplished yo goal and you not rocking the bells no more…prices been sky high since that 911 shit…I can't afford to take no losses…not a ounce loss…a big eighth (125 grams) loss…and especially a whole half of cake…*yooo*," Zulu sighed deeply. "Man if I front you a half of cake I need 16 stacks back," Zulu observed the creases on Old School Al's forehead. "Yo don't even look like that I'm fronting you out of my work so that would be a loss I'm taking if you fuck up."

"I'm not gone fuck up Zulu."

"You damn right you bet not fuck my money up…and I'm charging you interest…on a front for 500 grams you best believe I want interest and it's only right because you about to profit 10 times more than what I'm gone profit by fronting you."

"You right Zulu," Old School Al happily flashed a mouth full of platinum grills. "You always was my little man Zulu."

"Nigga I'm a grown ass muthafucking Man I don't wanna hear that little bro shit…this business nigga and I want mines…don't start that getting high shit either…you know how I feel about my money," Zulu shot that murderous look at Old School Al.

"Yo homeboy I swear to God you can trust me," Old School Al sensed the destruction that could befall him if he fucked up Zulu's money, "As a matter of fact," Old School Al reached inside his pocket and pulled out the keys to his Ferrari. "Homeboy it aint gone happen but if I was to start getting high the Ferrari all yours…but I swear on the homies Big Love and Tone A that I'm not gone fuck up…trust me Zulu."

"Hmmm." Zulu hesitated for a while then snatched the keys, "Since you letting me hold the keys…I wanna push that bitch for the 4th of July…fuck what Sun-Z say I'm pushing yo Rari and stunting, hell yeah it's gone be show off time."

"No question baby boy."

. . . .

The electrifying sounds of Reggaeton King *Daddy Yankee* blasting out of speakers rocked the brick buildings, storefronts, and houses on 10th and Virginia streets. Dominoes were slammed on shabby wooden tables as men guzzled Puerto Rican Rum and Bacardi while choking on spliffs of sticky lime green weed. Kids lit fireworks on the block under streetlights while mami's grooved their sultry bodies like snakes and danced for the hustlers of the 12th street Mob. The 4th of July weekend was here and about to pop off.

Lil Flip and Crumbs pulled onto Maryland and West Street a few blocks from the party on 10th street. They dipped into a small and narrow backyard next to a trap house operated by the 12th street mob. The trap was a long two story house that stretched from the street all the way to the small concrete backyard, where a small patch of thirsty grass lay being ate up by dirt and weeds.

Lil Flip and Crumbs climbed the six-foot fence to the trap house then jumped onto a tool shed and scared a family of kittens beneath the shed. The back of the two-story trap house stretched right along the tool shed. They stood on top of the tool shed and faced a bedroom window on the second floor. Lil Flip snatched his pistol from off his waist and peered into the dark bedroom window. Crumbs slid out the bookbag on his back, unzipped it, and pulled out a crowbar and what appeared to be a six pack of beer. It was two Molotov cocktails in a six-pack case. Crumbs took the crowbar and silently jammed it into the base of the wooden window and began prying it open. He lightly tapped the bottom seal of the windowpane while Lil Flip held the window in place. After several taps

Crumbs was able to slide the wooden seal off and take the window out. Lil Flip then climbed thru the window and entered the bedroom. The bedroom was empty besides a mattress on the floor and there was no door for the room. With his gun extended in front of him, Lil Flip crept to the threshold and peeked down the dark hallway where he could see flickering T.V. light in the dark living room up front. Lil Flip tip toed back to the window and shook his head yes.

"I got you," Crumbs whispered lighting the Molotov cocktails while Lil Flip kept his eyes on the threshold of the room just in case someone popped up.

Lil Flip grabbed one of the lit cocktails and crept to the threshold, stepped into the hallway and took a few steps towards the living room then launched the lit cocktail at the T.V. The glass shattered and a muffled explosion sounded before the flames engulfed the living room. No one was there luckily. Lil Flip sprinted back to the room and climbed out the window before Crumbs sent the second cocktail smashing into the bedroom wall causing flames to torch the bedroom.

"We out," Lil Flip muttered in a hushed tone as they both jumped off the toolshed. They hit the yard and left the way they came as the second-floor apartment went up in flames.

They jumped into the wheel where their friend was waiting and then they drove a few blocks over to 10th Street. This would be the show Mel-Cash and the Get Rich Crime Family was desiring to see.

With the head lights off, they pulled onto 10th street at the far end away from the crowd down at the other end. They pulled behind a car a few houses from the corner and scanned their surroundings before jumping out and creeping up the block with their guns cocked and ready to fire.

Megalito's Silverado pick-up truck wasn't parked on the block amidst the fleet of 12th street members souped up rides lining the block. The purple Acura coupe sitting pretty on them deep dish rims belonging to Snakey was right there in the middle of the block, about 8 houses from the crowd on the corner of 10th street.

"It's on you," Lil Flip whispered crouching low as they approached the Acura.

"I got this," Crumbs handed Lil Flip his pistol then pulled out a half stick of dynamite, hit the ground and crawled under the Acura while Lil Flip stood on guard clutching two pistols.

Crumbs gripped the dynamite with his teeth while using his hands to tear duct tape and tape the dynamite onto the gas tank. "Oh yeah," Crumbs taped it perfectly onto the gas tank then hit his pockets for a lighter. He flicked, flicked, and flicked but there was no flame because a piece of lint from his pocket was inside the lighter. "Yo this some bullshit Flip." Crumbs kept flicking.

"What nigga?" Lil Flip dropped low and looked under the car. He peeped Crumbs flicking away. "Fuck." Lil Flip scanned the area then laid one of the pistols on the ground before going into his pocket and pulling out a lighter. "Hurry up nigga." Lil Flip jumped up while Crumbs lit the dynamite.

Lil Flip never peeped the car parked in the driveway across the street from the Acura. A shooter from 12th Street was reclined back in the driver seat of his Impala while a mami was slobbing his Johnson. She was sucking him so good he had his eyes closed with his head tilted back. He didn't have a clue of what was going on right in front of him across the street.

"Come on we out move nigga," Crumbs slid from under the car as the long wick of the dynamite lit up wisping.

"What the fuck ma?" The shooter just happened to open his eyes and looked up when the mami gagged on his wood. Just as he opened his dreary eyes he peeped Crumbs pop up from under the car. "*Pare pare* (Stop stop)," he shoved the slobbing mami from off his lap and grabbed his pistol as Crumbs and Lil Flip jetted down the block. He jumped out of his Impala clutching the pistol in one hand and buckling his pants with the other hand while dashing into the middle of the street. He stood in the middle of the street watching Lil Flip and Crumbs jump in the car down the block. He figured they were beat jackers trying to steal Snakey's sound system. That's when he heard the sizzling wick under the Acura.

"*Oh no Dejesus*," he sprinted back over to his Impala before the explosion violently burst with such force the Acura blew up in flames. The force of the explosion shattered car windows and house windows close by and knocked out streetlights. The once candy painted and kitted up Acura was now a roasted vehicle frame up in flames.

Mel-Cash and the crew was posted up outside the Rendezvous lounge several blocks away when the booming earthquake explosion erupted. Everyone in the area heard the explosion and felt the force. The blast even caught people at the lounge off guard and while sipping their drinks some people fearfully dropped their glasses out of sudden shock.

"*Happy 4th of July to 12th Street fellas.*" Mel-Cash held up his glass grinning.

....

"Take care of my pride and joy Zulu". Old School Al fondled the roof of his Ferrari like it desired to be caressed. "You gotta stroke her with love and affection, you can't go manhandling her because she will rock your world and give you a ride you not ready for."

"Nigga I'm gone have a cold sexy dime piece riding me while I push this Rari Old School...watch me...the town bout to witness a real nigga strait balling."

"Alright baby boy." Old School Al was amused at Zulu's excitement as Zulu sat in the driver seat inspecting the controls on the lit-up interior. "It's the holiday and it's gone be mad live Zulu...be careful...drive safe and please don't get too drunk...please don't."

"Yo I aint new to this...I do this." Zulu took a swig of the smooth Remy XO sitting between his legs and blew the scorching heat in his throat into the air, "Nigga I been outside as soon as I came out the womb. Peace out Old School and *Picture me rolling.*" Zulu zoomed out the storage garage blasting *2Pac "Picture Me Rolling."*

It was party time and Buffalo's party scene was about to explode until 4 a.m. when bars and clubs shut down to let the after-hour spots carry the parties into the early morning rising sun. The night was jumping off at the First Niagara Center's 20, 000 seat auditorium in downtown Buffalo. *Jay-Z and R. Kelly's Best of Both Worlds tour* was in full effect and Buffalo was one of their first destinations. The First Niagara Center was filled to capacity.

Zulu pushed the Ferrari with Terror riding shotgun into the Cobblestone district in downtown Buffalo. The Ferrari wheels gripped the old brick paved streets with ease as they cruised thru the crowded streets flooded with party goers heading to the concert. People became electrified and began screaming and shouting with excitement like the exotic car was driven by superstars.

"Yeah boy I'm gone get you laid tonight," Terror yelled over the music observing females jumping up and down as the Ferrari crept by the crowds on the street.

"You gone get who laid?" Zulu asked sarcastically, "This rari getting us laid nigga…fuck you talking bout."

"Nigga whatever…let's just hope Old School Al start rocking the bells again because if you keep this rari nigga…we gone fuck bitches from Buffalo to Cleveland back up to Toronto in two weeks my dude…trust me."

"Let's make it happen," Zulu shouted getting hyper and aroused scoping sexy ladies flashing their titties and throwing their asses in the air. "Let's get this shit popping yo."

Zulu swerved the Ferrari into an All Pro parking lot a few blocks from the auditorium. Zulu and Terror jumped out the Ferrari feeling like Superstars as all eyes focused on the riches they travelled in and adorning their bodies. They're visually stunning and glistening jewels rested on top of their expensive garments not to mention the aura of supremacy they stepped with. They were shining something illustrious like fallen angels. They approached the center where new whips of all kinds and a fleet of limousines hugged the strip outside the center as hundreds of people stood in line.

"Yo yo Zulu and Terror," Mel-Cash and Cream yelled over the boisterous crowd as they stood up out the sun-roof of one of the stretch limousines.

"Yooo," Zulu and Terror stepped over to the limo Mel-Cash and Cream was in, "What's the *dealy* playboys?"

"Come on yall already know," Cream turned a bottle of Crystal up to his face, gulped some, then spit the suds out before pouring some of the champagne out onto the street. "Popping champagne and living the life."

"Come on and jump in we going around to the back where the stars at...you know we don't do the lines…this our town," Mel-Cash shouted dropping into the limo.

"Hell yeah," Zulu and Terror climbed into the plush limo lit up with the glow of about 8 sexy wine fine ladies in short designer skirts lounging with Dolla, Killa, Cream, and Mel-Cash.

"This the life of a King my G," Dolla sat between two ladies smoking on a blunt one of the ladies held to his lips.

"Ok we see how yall doing it," Zulu and Terror squeezed themselves in between a few ladies before the limo pulled from in front of the center and swung around to the back. The limo found a parking spot amongst several tour buses, news trucks, limousines, and many other exotic luxurious vehicles.

After Mel-Cash rapped with a few security guards and slid them a few bills, the crew and their entourage of wine fine ladies slid thru the back doors of the auditorium and strolled down the long corridor where the loud echoes of thousands of shouting fans could be heard while *Memphis Bleek and The Yung Guns* was performing. They strolled thru the corridor and the clamor became louder as they approached another group of security guards guarding the dressing rooms of the celebrities. They passed the dressing rooms and hit the backstage where it was a moment of hood celebrities mingling with Hollywood celebrities. From journalists to news reporters to groupies the backstage had its own party. Lights of cameras flashed as people flicked it up with the stars. Clouds of weed smoke flooded the air and bottles was popped. Females in love with the music of the stars exposed what their skimpy skirts and blouses couldn't cover.

After hanging backstage with the stars, a few backstage groupies joined the crew and their entourage of wine fine ladies and hit the floor and spectated the concert from front and center. As the crew strolled through the crowd and posted up amongst the live and interactive fans, it seemed people made room for the Get Rich Crime Family and gave them space. Most fans in the front focused on stage, but many eyes laid their vision on the crew like they were stars of the show. The electrifying vibrations of the live performance aroused everyone's energy and had their focus on the performers, but the crew felt a piercing energy radiating from the eyes of numerous people watching them instead of the show.

"I know you feel all these eyes on us," Cream yelled to Mel-Cash over the loud music while eyeing females whispering to each other while dancing to the music. Even the fellas were enviously eyeing the crew while bopping their heads. "Is it the jewels and garments we got on because these muthafuckas scoping us out for real."

"Of course it's the way we shine but they know who running the city Sun," Mel-Cash responded with his braggadocios God of the Hood demeanor with his arms around two sexy ladies while winking his eye at other ladies who were focused on him and the crew.

Jay-Z nonchalantly stepped on stage like the King he was and performed "*Jigga,*" making the crowd jump to the thumping anthem. He brought his female artist *A.M.I.L* out and their dual performance of "*Can I Get A,*" turned the crowd upside down as fellas rapped with Jay-Z taunting the ladies while flashing money, "*Can I get a Fuck you to these bitches from all of my niggaz who don't love hoes...they get no dough.*"

Then the females returned the teasing and began rapping with A.M.I.L when she spit, "*Can I get a Fuck you to these niggaz from all of my bitches who don't got love...for niggaz without dubs.*"

Jay-Z then fired up the mood for R. Kelly and when Kells came out on stage, the live mood became sexual and females began grooving their bodies with that serpentine fire when R. Kelly performed "*Grind for Me.*"

As Zulu and Terror stood amongst the crowd casually bopping their heads, Zulu caught eyes with two sexy stallions who had fire and desire in their eyes peeping him and Terror. The two stallions swayed their bodies with such sex appeal Zulu became instantly aroused. When he tapped Terror to peep game, Terror lifted his gaze from the bubble butt mami grinding on him and said "*Damn*" when he did acknowledge to the two stallions Zulu was nodding to.

"Them bitches 360 for real," Terror's lustful greed was no longer satisfied with the mami grinding on him. The lust of his mind's eye began undressing the two sexy stallions in their strapless dresses exposing their juicy cleavages, with their curvaceous forms tightly fitted underneath as they danced with each other like two sexy lesbians. "Yo them the baddest bitches I seen all night Zulu."

"And they want us yo," Zulu stated watching the two stallions now smiling at him and Terror.

"Yeah they done chose us yo."

"Come on let's go holla at em," Zulu stated observing the two stallions whispering to each other and nodding their heads at Zulu and Terror.

"Na nigga we don't sweat these hoes," Terror spit while rubbing the mami's ass who was dancing in front of him. "I keep telling you this pimping I got is real...nigga we got like 15 cold broads with us that's bout it bout it...if them two hoes want us they gotta come to us and show and prove that they got more excitement to offer than these hoes we got right here...you feel me," Terror now slapped the mami's ass dancing in front of him, "Them hoes gotta do more than look and smile...just follow my lead and I'm gone show you some pimping like *Pimp C*."

Terror palmed the soft ass of the mami dancing on him then spun her around to face him. He whispered in her ear while keeping his gaze on the two stallions. The mami then glanced at the two stallions and winked her eye and blew a kiss to them before whispering back in Terror's ear. She kept her eyes on the two stallions the whole time as she slow grinded on Terror. After a few seconds, her ecstatic gaze lured the two stallions over.

"Nigga we Thugs but we play like pimps when it come to these hoes," Terror told Zulu as the two stallions sashayed over to them. "Pimping the only way to play when it come to these hoes...you see it."

The two sexy stallions waltzed over to Zulu grooving with their arms outstretched to him while twirling their hips. They approached Zulu and sandwiched him and started freaking him something sexual as R. Kelly was on stage performing.

"My name Fantasy and her name Holiday," Fantasy pressed her plush lips softly on Zulu's ear.

"My name Zulu."

"Oooo…like the warriors," Holiday blew in Zulu's other ear.

"Yeah…why they call yall Fantasy and Holiday?"

"Because we a fulfill yo fantasy and make yo day happy like a holiday," They both squeezed Zulu between their luscious breast and rubbed their thick thighs on him. "What's up with yo fine ass friend…he gone let you have all the fun."

"Oh shit," with his arms around Fantasy and Holiday's slim waistlines, Zulu raised his eyes in excitement at Terror. "Yo we bout to get it popping yo," Zulu yelled to Terror. Then like a pimp not amazed, Terror whispered something to the mami dancing on him, then nonchalantly stepped over to Zulu and joined.

In the midst of the live crowd and with no care in the world, with their insatiable freakiness of kissing like two lesbians while rubbing each other's breast, Fantasy and Holiday gave Zulu and Terror a brief demonstration of the sexual paradise they would experience behind closed doors. That's all it took for Zulu and Terror to snatch Fantasy and Holiday and breakout.

"Yo what up with yall dudes yo," Cream asked rolling a blunt while a rump shaking red bone stood in front of him bent over dancing.

"We out."

"Is yall niggas dumb or what?" Dolla shouted throwing a double stacker ecstasy pill in a freak mama's mouth, "All this pussy we got yall niggas acting scared."

"Nigga you lost yo fucking mind ever thinking I was scared of anything," Terror responded. "We ain't got time for yall champagne drinking groupies…yall need to give these bitches some Henny so they can loosen up and get freaky like our bitches," Terror slid his hand up Holiday's skirt and massaged her moist loving, "Yall bitches gone have to drink 10 more bottles of Crist before they ready like ours…ours ready now and we out."

"Word up look at this nigga," Zulu pointed at Killa who was hugged up with a gorgeous diva whispering in her ear. They looked like a happy couple enjoying the concert.

"What…yall…yall niggas *cr-cr-crazy* sun," using two females to hold him up while he clutched a bottle, Mel-Cash staggered over to Zulu and Terror.

"B-br-bring yall tw- two sexy bitches," Mel-Cash slurred his words like his intoxicated spinning mind, *"The Adams Mark Hotel...bring yall b-b-bitches...it's orgy time."*

One of the sexy ladies with Mel-Cash then said, "Presidential Suite on the 9th floor at the Adams Mark where our after party gone be at...make sure yall come," the sexy lady then licked her lips.

"We gone be there sexy," Fantasy blew smooches at the sexy thang before their party left the concert. When the four hit the parking lot and approached the Ferrari, Fantasy and Holiday felt their insides screaming with uncontrolled passion. They were ready to slide out of their skirts right in the parking lot and let Zulu and Terror fulfill their fantasies on this happy holiday weekend.

"You driving Terror," Zulu quickly tossed Terror the keys indicating he was going to get it popping immediately while Terror drove.

"You slick muthafucka," Terror rambled zapping the keypad and lifting the doors up.

They entered the car and Zulu let the taste of his sexual appetite pick and choose which tender flavor he wanted. Would it be Fantasy or Holiday? Fantasy had that light hazel wood complexion with the lively personality to match her sexiness. And Holiday seemed sweet, soft, and pleasant like her smooth Hershey colored skin tone. Both of their bodies was stacked and more than enough to satisfy the biggest sexual appetite.

Zulu lustfully watched Holiday's heart shaped butt climb into the back seat and he followed suit. Terror pulled out and swerved into the bumper to bumper traffic and hit the town. The town was live and everyone was out partying. In front of night clubs and bars lines of people wrapped around buildings waiting to get in. When Terror swerved the Ferrari in front of club Sensations which was one of the livest in town, all eyes beheld the luxurious Ferrari as Terror slowly crept thru the jam-packed traffic. Everyone was in awe and when Zulu stood up out the sun-roof and Terror lifted the doors up, females outside screamed, *"That's Zulu and Terror from E. North...the Get Rich Crime Family getting money."*

That street fame made Fantasy and Holiday's spirit vibrate with passion being with two supreme respected and powerful thugs who was street king rich. While Zulu stood out the sun-roof yelling to the crowds in front of club Sensations, Holiday unbuckled his pants, reached inside and whipped out his chocolate bar and began savoring his hard pole as it massaged her wet and warm mouth.

"*Yooooo,*" Zulu shouted into the air of the live night as the warm sensation of Holiday slobbing on his chocolate bar made his insides tingle. "The life of a young rich nigga...yeah."

"No doubt my nigga...we Boss style," Terror let the doors come down and blew it thru traffic as Holiday let Zulu's chocolate bar melt in her mouth. Fantasy observed Holiday's saliva glistening on the snake like veins pulsing thru Zulu's dick making it look like a King Sized Snickers bar.

"*Ummm...damn,*" Fantasy sat up on her knees in the front passenger seat, threw her right hand onto Terror's lap and began unzipping his pants. While Fantasy whipped out Terror's genital steel and began stroking it with her hand, she helped Holiday slobber on Zulu's Snickers bar.

"What the fuck...oh shit...yooo," Zulu yelled up to the moon as the two sexy stallions swallowed on his hard chocolate like he was their Valentine's day gift. Fantasy and Holiday were like two sexy angelic freaks of pleasure who took Zulu's mind up to sexual paradise.

Holiday then pulled Zulu down into the car and laid him on his back. She pulled out a condom, slid it on his chocolate, then jumped on it and dipped his chocolate bar into her dripping wet pudding.

Fantasy removed her hand from Terror's genital steel and let her mouth do the stroking while he gripped the wheel to the Ferrari while driving thru the town. Fantasy let Terror's steel massage her throat as she slurped up and down savoring his flesh of steel.

"Like whoa...got damn," Terror hit Church Street where it was less traffic, and from the tingles racing thru his system from Fantasy's super head, Terror mashed the gas pedal to 120 mph while smoking a blunt and getting head. He dipped around the few cars rolling down the strip before he swerved into the

Adam's Mark hotel parking lot. He found a parking spot near the back by a huge mega bus. After Fantasy and Holiday made Zulu and Terror yell with the sweetest pain and joy from squirting the cream of life, Fantasy and Holiday kissed each other after gurgling with some Listerine they pulled from their purses.

They slid into the Adam's Mark hotel and hit the 9th floor. When they stepped out the elevator into the hallway, it was a world of natural but unrestrained sexual desires at its peak. It was girls gone wild. Several butt naked females with breasts swinging and asses jiggling ran thru the hallway as Mel-Cash chased after them spraying champagne on them like he was a fireman.

"Yall came," Mel-Cash stopped in his tracks stripped down to his boxers and greeted Zulu and Terror while lusting at Fantasy and Holiday. "Come on and join the party…yall two sexy ladies gotta get butt ass naked," Mel-Cash demanded before he guzzled some champagne, then shook it up and sprayed Fantasy and Holiday. "Let me see you get naked…*come onnn*." Mel-Cash yelled running into the Presidential Suite after the flock of ladies he was chasing.

"Oh my God what is his problem," Fantasy and Holiday was shocked, heated, embarrassed, and turned on at the same time as they wiped champagne off themselves.

"This nigga off the fucking chain…outta this world," Zulu and Terror glanced at each other laughing before leading Fantasy and Holiday into the suite. It was everything a strait and natural man desired in his sexual fantasies with a woman taking place in the suite.

Cream got loose on the living room sofa with three women. He had a big booty female bent over doggy style ramming his pole into her squishy sounding vagina squirting clear secretions all over the sofa. Her banana cream colored ass cheeks was red from Cream smacking fire out of her big booty. Cream's midnight black body was a striking contrast to the red bones banana cream body as he pounded her insides from behind. The red bone had her face buried in another red bone's vagina who was twirling her mouth on the rosy pink vagina of a chocolate sweetheart who sat on her face.

"That's a real fucking train yo on some *Big Pun* shit for real, *Trisnathaniel* style," Zulu and Terror stepped into the suite peering straight ahead in the living room at Cream's foursome. Cream was in his own world sweating like the liquids gushing from the vaginas of the ladies a part of his train.

Fantasy and Holiday then peeped into the kitchen by the entrance and spotted a pile of ecstasy pills on the kitchen table where several thong wearing females stood feeding each other pills and sniffing white lines of coco. Fantasy and Holiday helped themselves to some pills then hit the bathroom to freshen up.

Between the kitchen and the living room Killa lay up in a bedroom passionately making love to a beautiful sweetheart. They lay under the covers slowly indulging each other in pure sex that was righteous.

"This nigga making love to a whore...he probably going raw dog too...wow," Zulu and Terror stepped thru the living room now cheering Cream on before they hit the circular stairwell winding downstairs to the lower level of the suite.

This is where Crumbs and Lil Flip were lounging in their boxers with several ladies smoking blunts and drinking. Mel-Cash was in the master bedroom on the king sized bed wrestling with the ladies he was chasing thru the hallway. And then there was Dolla, who popped from out of nowhere in a shower robe holding a camcorder.

"Check this shit out yall," Dolla gestured towards the other bedroom. It was Old School Al's girlfriend Lulu and another girl butt naked in the bed smoking cigarettes dipped in cocaine.

"Yo you buggin Dolla," Zulu stated as Dolla closed the bedroom door then locked it.

"No them woo head bitches bugging," Dolla sat the camcorder on the counter in the kitchen then poured shots of Hennessy for Zulu and Terror. "Them bitches smoked up 5 grams of my shit so now them bitches my sex slaves and they on lock down until I say so."

"You terrible Dolla," Zulu and Terror had a few shots with Dolla then went back upstairs, snatched Fantasy and Holiday, then broke out with Zulu jumping behind the wheel. It was switch-a-roo time and Holiday jumped in the backseat with Terror. They wasted no time in gratifying their sexual desires which was still stimulated and increasing with that erotic intensity like the speed of the Ferrari as Zulu blew it thru the city streets dipping around cars and running through streetlights. Zulu hit the expressway and flooded the gas pedal letting the Ferrari show off its high performance of turbulent speed as it accelerated and flew down the expressway like a shooting star. The engine growled with a forceful vibration that sent heated chills racing through Fantasy and Holiday's temperate insides.

Holiday was in the backseat slobbing and slurping ferociously on Terror's flesh of steel before she slid her skirt up and jumped on top of Terror and began riding his pole like the Ferrari rode the expressway, fast and furious. The joyful sounds of Holiday's moaning shrieked under the blasting sounds of N.O.R.E. yelling *"Getting Head in the Whip and noth Crashing it."*

Fantasy's arousal then caused her to lean from the passenger seat over into Zulu's lap and unbuckle his pants. She pulled him out and placed it in her mouth. Her breath was warm and soothing on Zulu's rod. Her moist and wet lips felt extremely good. She sat in the passenger seat on her knees blessing Zulu with her Fantasy head while Zulu dipped his finger in her dripping wet vagina.

"Fuccck…I'm cumming…I'm cumming," Terror yelled from the backseat thrusting his body up into Holiday forcefully making her moan even louder.

"O-o-o-me too…don't stop," Holiday threw her arms in the air out the sunroof shaking uncontrollably before laying on top of Terror and kissing him on the lips.

"Bitch don't be kissing on me," Terror shoved Holiday up off him then snatched some napkins from the backseat to wipe himself. Terror then sat up and peeped out the window wondering where in the hell they were at. Everything was blurry and the Ferrari moved so fast under the street signs on the expressway Terror couldn't even read them. It was like they were flying and Terror wondered was he dizzy from the nut he just busted because his eyes were straining trying to focus on the blurry outside. He looked up front and felt his heart flutter. "Zulu slow down you doing almost a duce (200), don't crash getting dome yo…slow the fuck down."

"I got this I got this," Zulu blurted feeling extremely pleasured by Fantasy's fellatio. Zulu was so caught up in the rapture he didn't even realize he was doing almost 200 mph because he was in paradise. The expressway began to curve and Zulu began pressing the brakes as he gripped the wheel. There was a car ahead who switched lanes to let the speeding Zulu pass. The Ferrari banged a pothole on the expressway and Zulu blacked out, losing control as the car slid into a guardrail before hitting another bump then spinning out of control. The speed of the spinning Ferrari was so forceful the car flipped over several times before smashing into a wall under a street overpass.

When the paramedics arrived on the scene, they found three people scattered all over the expressway and far from the scene of the accident. One of the passengers of the Ferrari was stuck in the front windshield. This was a fatal accident that turned the paramedics' stomachs upside down. This fatal accident would make local headlines about young people living too fast and dying young in fast cars.

CHAPTER 15

"Good morning Mr. Johnson!" the young blonde nurse' aide spoke to Zulu when he opened his eyes.

"What the hell?" Zulu groggily spat attempting to raise both his hands to wipe the cold out his eyes but his hands were wrapped in bandages and hurt like hell. His left arm was in a cast. He then focused his blurry vision upon the aide wondering how did he end up in the hospital room. "How the hell did I get here?" Zulu asked painfully easing himself up in the bed.

"Let's just say you better thank God this is where you ended up and not the morgue." The aide informed checking Zulu's pulse. Zulu glared at the aide in confusion while she scribbled notes on a clipboard before telling him he was suffering from short term memory loss but once he fully awoke he would remember. She then left the room and said she would return shortly as Prince stepped inside.

"All praise due to the Most-High you still in the physical form Blackman...Praise Be." Prince stood unbelievably eyeing Zulu like it was a miracle. Prince stood in a daze holding a cup of coffee in one hand and a shopping bag in his other hand.

"Why you just standing there like that...come sit down yo." Zulu achingly swung his swollen legs to the edge of the bed so he could sit up on the edge.

"I'm just happy at least you alright," Prince stated placing Zulu's bag of clothes on the bed beside Zulu. "It's not so good for everyone else," Prince stood beside Zulu peering into Zulu's scraped and bruised up face. Zulu looked like a sculptor tried carving him a new face with a Ginsu knife.

"Everybody else?" Zulu opened the bag of clothes still in a state of confusion and suffering from the blackout spell of the liquor. "What the fuck happened?"

"Brother," Prince seated himself in the chair next to the bed while sipping his hazelnut coffee. "Terror in a coma...it's been three days and he still haven't woke up and his vitals is crazy."

"What?" The mystery of three nights ago was nowhere near the surface of Zulu's consciousness.

"Blackman that's not the worst…but the Sista's that was with yall--," Prince grievingly shook his head staring into space. "Man the Blackwoman carried us thru the torture of slavery—she been a dedicated nurturer of love for us no matter what…and we just don't appreciate her…all we do is make her suffer…we killing them softly and we don't even know it."

"Yo stop this black history shit Prince and tell me what the fuck happened?" Zulu sharply replied jumping off the edge of the bed and standing up. He felt disoriented and the pain bombarding his body made him feel like he was between two brick walls squeezing him tightly. His whole body twinged with pain when he took one step forward before falling back onto the bed for support. Prince quickly jumped out of his chair and held Zulu as Zulu crouched over the bed.

"Relax bro…yo body took a serious beating in that car accident a few nights ago. I don't know what actually happened but I heard yall was drunk as hell, pulling up in front of clubs stunting and acting like fools in that Ferrari. A lot of women was wishing they was in that ride with yall until everyone watched the news and seen what happened.

Zulu couldn't remember a thing about the car accident. Fantasy who was in the front seat with Zulu was undergoing her second surgery for her arm and face due to severe nerve damage. She flew into the front windshield and received over one hundred and fifty stitches from her torso to her beautiful face. She would be partially paralyzed in her right arm and if she desired to happily look herself in the mirror she would need reconstructive surgery to her face. Poor Holiday was paralyzed from the waist down due to severe spinal injury from when she was ejected from the car along with Terror. Terror's knee hit the pavement so hard it busted open and shattered. His leg was so destroyed it had to be amputated. When and if he was to awake from his coma he would never be the same.

"What the fuck—how—what?" Zulu asked himself looking over his body and wondering why wasn't he suffering from severe injuries like the others. He searched his mind but couldn't remember much after the concert. Prince then began unpacking Zulu's clothes and left the room so Zulu could get dressed. As Zulu struggled to get dressed he forced his consciousness to search his memory banks for the events leading up to the car accident. Nothing sparked his memory banks and the only thing to flash across his mental screen was glimpses of that tragic night.

Zulu spotted a pair of crutches by the bed and used them to hop into the bathroom after getting dressed. He peered into the mirror and almost didn't recognize himself from the scrapes, bruises, and swollenness of his face. Even though he was in excruciating pain, he wondered why his suffering was not as injurious and serious as everyone else's. He gazed into his crystal-clear reflection in the mirror but his mind was blurred and foggy struggling to remember.

"Zulu the nurse and doctor here." Prince yelled into the room snapping Zulu out of his blank mind zone.

"Ok here I come," Zulu used his numb fingers to gently splash warm water on his face then gargled with the mouth wash on the sink before leaving out the bathroom.

The nurse and doctor checked Zulu's vitals and upon seeing he was recovering, he was discharged. They gave him a long list of instructions on what to do and not to do. He was advised to take his medicines and make his follow up visits so they could check his healing and re-development. Zulu snatched his discharge papers and was released from the hospital.

When Zulu and Prince stepped out of the hospital into the fresh air, the intake of fresh oxygen began to revitalize Zulu's nervous system. The spark of oxygen began to activate his memory banks and flashes of stopping by the hotel before the accident began to play on his mental screen.

"Well my brother," Prince helped Zulu into the passenger seat of his CTS Cadillac. "You got a lot of time to sit and think…no running the streets."

"How the fuck you figure?" Zulu shot back carefully falling into the plush leather seat while Prince ran around to the driver side and jumped in.

"Look at you Blackman...you can barely walk...you need to heal...stay out the damn streets because it's the streets and this fast life that got you like this."

"You done got knowledge of self and now you a changed man...and everything about the streets is bad...I see you driving this nice ass Cadillac because of the street life...what you gotta say about that?"

"I'm a poor righteous teacher being that I'm here to teach and uplift my poor people...but that don't mean I gotta suffer and deny myself the riches the earth has to offer...riches come from the earth and the earth belongs to the Original Black Man and the 12 Jewels of life is the rewards we get blessed with when we do our duty as civilizers and live righteously."

"Nigga black people poor as fuck and white people rule the earth."

"Blackman, black people only poor right now because the white man made us ignorant and he using us as tools to build everything for him...Africa has the richest soil on earth and the white man robbing Africa for all its mineral wealth...you can't name one African civilization that existed before slavery that was poor." Prince shot an inquiring look at Zulu as he ignited his engine.

"Whatever Prince," Zulu reclined back in his seat as Prince pulled out and headed to take Zulu home. Zulu closed his eyes letting the fatigue of his mind and body slip away as he relaxed himself in the reclined passenger seat. Zulu was rushing to go to sleep and trying to tune his mind to think of something besides the music Prince was playing.

> *"Original Man is first...I wanna say Peace to the Gods*
> *and the Earths...My Universal Fam living out the universal*
> *Plan...ay yo tell em who I am...G.O.D."*
> Lord Jamar-The 5% Album.

On the way home Zulu dozed off momentarily only to get a glimpse of the moments leading up to the car accident. He jumped out of his trance like sleep when he dreamt of the car sliding along the guardrail then flipping over. Prince slid over a pothole causing Zulu to jump out of his skin thinking him and Prince were about to crash.

"Zulu you alright bro?" Prince placed his hand on Zulu's shoulder as Zulu sprung forward in the passenger seat breathing deeply.

"Yo I was dreaming about the night of the car accident...Terror was yelling like slow down...I don't know what happened next but fuck yo...I was the one driving...damn...I almost killed us," Zulu felt his soul being strangled by guilt and self-pity.

"Listen black man what happened happened...and you can't press rewind to change it...only thing you can do is move forward...and you can't move forward feeling miserable and letting the guilt eat you up...just take responsibility for your actions and strive to change this cycle so it won't happen again."

"What cycle Prince?"

"Black man...this cycle of destruction we been putting our people thru...especially the Black Woman...enough of blaming the white man...we putting our own selves thru hell now. Especially the Black woman...we been failing to respect her strength and her tenacity to struggle with us and stay by our side throughout the struggle...she hasn't given up on us yet...we let her get violated by them devilish slave masters and we didn't protect her at all...and she never left us...here it is we constantly go to prison and we leave her out here to struggle alone with our children and she still don't leave our side...see you gotta understand Black man...we The Creators-The Suns of Light-and we create the situations of our lives...we control our destiny and we responsible for the hardship we put ourselves thru...once we realize this we will start using our creative ability to make things better in life...you understand."

"Kinda Prince...but what that gotta do with my situation and how I almost killed us in that car accident? What the fuck black history got to do with this shit?

"It's simple brother you just can't see it...but them sistas yall had rolling with yall is like a lot of the sistas out here...they just love the Blackman regardless to the dangerous lifestyle he living...they faithful and will risk their lives for us...we are their leaders and they follow us...and if we keep running to destruction they gone follow us to destruction...now if we start walking the path of righteousness they gone be right there by our side shining brightly...we gotta change our lives because we dragging them into the hell of this street life with us…you feel me Black man."

Zulu lowered his gaze to his legs feeling kind of bad. Fantasy and Holiday were just two young women trying to have fun with two fast and fun young men and they almost lost their lives, not to mention the physical damage they would live with for the rest of their lives.

Prince pulled up at Zulu and NyJewel's heavenly abode. Prince helped Zulu inside where NyJewel was hugged over the stove making breakfast.

"Baby oh my God," NyJewel dropped the frying pan of scrambled eggs on the flaming eye and rushed Zulu with tears in her eyes. "Ooh I'm so happy you home baby…they thought you wouldn't wake up like Sahku (Terror). I been there with you day and night baby."

"It's ok calm down," Zulu calmed NyJewel.

"Ok yall sit down so I can make yall plates," NyJewel was moving like lightning around the kitchen. "Baby you sit here…I'm gone run you a hot bath and get you comfortable just relax and eat first," NyJewel blessed them with their plates of breakfast then went to run Zulu's bath.

"And oh yeah black man…thank me later for lying to NyJewel and telling her that you and Terror crashed into some girls on the e-way."

"That's what I'm talking bout my boy…you can take a nigga out the streets but you can't take the streets out a real nigga."

"I'm not a nigga black man…I'm God…a nigga is an ignorant slave the white man created…and lying is devilment just like the white man lied and said that God was white and the black man was a nigga…the black man is God."

"Whatever little Farrakhan…good looking for coming thru for ya boy."

"Anything for you Blackman…I'm gone be coming thru for you while you here at the kingdom healing up physically…and I'm gonna bring some knowledge thru to heal yo mental."

"I don't want none of that God Body back to Africa shit…bring me some G-Shit by my man *Al-Sadiq Banks like Block Party.*"

"No no no…I bring you a book of Truth by the *Great Mind Supreme Understanding Allah called The Science of Self.*"

"Yeah whatever little Farrakhan."

"Peace Black man." Prince left Zulu in his realm of peace with NyJewel and made it his duty to check up on Zulu on a daily like a true brother should. For the next few weeks Zulu lounged around the crib getting nurtured by NyJewel's love and affection as he slowly healed.

Terror was still in a coma and from the looks of it there was no telling when and if he would awake. As for Fantasy and Holiday, they were physically healing but the physical scars on their beautiful faces and bodies created emotional scars of having a young life destroyed.

On one particular night during Zulu's recovery, Zulu's subconscious mind spit out the accident vividly during his dream state and he awoke yelling, causing NyJewel to fearfully jump out of her sleep.

"Baby are you alright?" NyJewel asked tapping Zulu as he sat up staring into space soaked in sweat. NyJewel waved her hand in front on a non-responsive Zulu trying to get his attention.

"Damn bay," Zulu slowly turned his gaze to NyJewel who sat beside him now rubbing his back. "Sun-Z was right…that fucking Ferrari just caused problems…I should've listened…now Terror all fucked up…got my dude in a fucking coma…it's all my fault fucking with that damn Old School Al."

....

Zulu was finally healed up and his energy was restored. He was ready to hit the streets and get back to moving down that lane of the fast life. Only problem was his fear of being in a fast-moving vehicle, like Old School Al's new burgundy metallic Jaguar.

"Yo you gotta slow the fuck down yo," Zulu braced himself while hugging his seat as Old School Al blew it down Fuhrman Blvd heading towards downtown. "You and yo fast cars the reason why we got fucked up…slow the hell down yo."

"Ok my bad Zulu," Old School Al slowed down as they pulled onto the congested route 5 Expressway heading into downtown. "But it wasn't the car Zulu it was the liquor…you gotta have all yo senses to control her." Old School Al explained caressing his steering wheel. While Zulu laid up recovering and healing, Old School Al received a beefy check for the total damage of the

Ferrari. He then used the little bit of intellect he had to downgrade and cop the Jaguar. "It was my fault for letting yo wild ass drive that monster Zulu."

"Man my bad for tearing yo shit up…I can't believe Terror in a coma yo…this shit crazy."

"Yeah the material shit don't mean nothing because it can always get replaced…you can't replace the damage the shit caused yall…I hope Terror come out that coma…word up…but yo," Old School Al sparked a cigarette as the traffic entering downtown came to a halt, "That night yall got into that accident Lulu overdosed up in a telly."

Zulu shot a surprising glance at Old School Al. Zulu could clearly remember the last time he seen Lulu butt naked on the bed with her friend tweeking. Zulu remained silent as Old School Al carried on.

"Word homeboy…she was up at some after party our so-called Fam had and a room maid found Lulu on the bathroom floor unconscious," Old School Al angrily bit down on his lip. "My so-called homeboys' man…they gave her a fatal blast…they gave her that shit and her heart almost busted open."

"Who?" Zulu asked playing dumb.

"I don't know but I bet it was Dolla…everyone acting like they don't know and don't care…I just know that you, Terror, Sun-Z, and Hawk wasn't there and I can't get mad at yall."

"What you thinking about getting back at niggas?" Zulu asked feeling the rage in Old School Al's voice.

"Na but niggas ain't right…we supposed to be peoples man…like family…how could they let that happen homeboy."

"Mannn," Zulu felt he had to cover up Dolla's wrongdoing despite the fact Old School Al knew Lulu always had a thing for the Chocolate Boy wonder. "Lulu liked getting high Old School…you can't blame nobody for her addiction…you give her drugs…and look at all the people who try blaming us drug dealers when they loved ones O.D…ain't no one forcing them to get high…people get themselves high and O.D. because of their greed…it's not the supplier fault…Lulu did that on her own."

"Yeah I hear you but that's not how shit should have went down being that she was with my so-called peoples."

"Yo is she alright now bro?"

"Yeah she good." Old School Al responded twisting his lips in anger.

"Cool...everything gone be good bro...so since you got reimbursed for the rari...what up with my gold?"

"You know I got you homeboy," Old School Al lifted his arm console and pulled out two thick envelopes. One envelope contained $ 16,000 and the other held $ 12,500 Zulu calculated after counting.

"So you want a half square or you giving me this twelve five for my pain and suffering?" Zulu jokingly asked wishing it was true.

"I wish I could homeboy...but listen I'm only copping light from you because I got some plans in the making...some real power moves...you know whatever I put my mind to I'm gone make happen...watch Zulu I'm gonna make a million if not more with this new plug."

"What? A new plug." Zulu looked at Old School Al like he was speaking Mongolian. "Is you stupid...why would you stray away from family to fuck with outsiders."

"Homeboooy." Old School Al shook his head with a great degree of reluctance. He didn't want to say what he had to say but he had to get it off his chest. "You my man Zulu, but shit ain't the same with the fam...it's like they don't respect my hustle...this town too small for too many giants...they think they the only ones who supposed to be king...I thought we was all supposed to be on top...but it's like since I made it to the top they not happy seeing me up there."

"Na it's not that they just want you to be smart...anybody can make money but it takes smarts to keep it...and we all gotta make decisions for the whole."

"Yo I'm a grown man Zulu. I stand on my own two feet...I'm gonna be smart for me because I don't feel a part of the fam no more...and you gone learn Zulu, just like *Nas* said in *The Message on It Was Written*, "*A thug changes...and love changes...and best friends become strangers...*" I love yall but I gotta leave the nest and spread my wings."

"Dammmmn."

"Man aint shit gone change with me and you homeboy…you was the only one to come thru for me in a clutch and I never forget that Zulu…and when I make this power move and come up on that mill ticket I'm getting out the game but I'm gone smash you with a bankroll to keep in the pot as an investment…I got you homeboy…trust me word is life."

Zulu couldn't relate to Old School Al's past of getting high, but he understood him. Old School Al pulled himself up from the bowels of crack addiction to shine like a supreme hustler but his own crime family didn't seem to acknowledge that giant leap he took in utilizing his divine will and supreme power to elevate beyond that low level of destruction.

When it came to Lulu, she was the closest soul to Old School Al's heart and the fam didn't honor that either. They treated her like the average chicken in the wilderness partying and having fun. Old School Al was a man regardless to his mistakes and past flaws and he demanded respect like any man. He was going to be respected one way or another. He would go out on his own to create his own universe where he would sit on a throne everyone would respect, even the heavens. He was going to make this materialize with Lulu's cousin Kato, a Puerto Rican plug who had more white than a Buffalo winter. Ever since Zulu fronted Old School Al the half of brick several weeks ago, Old School Al done tripled that half of brick profit with Kato plus he was working with the lump sum from his collision check. Old School Al was destined to do numbers and run it back up. At the moment Old School Al was just showing Zulu a little love by paying Zulu back and spending a little bread with him.

"Know what I'm saying be the truth Zulu…when Kato come thru I'm gone bless you something special…I'm only copping short from you right now because I'm waiting for him to get back from P.R…but dude got bricks for 13 geez."

"Get the fuck outta here Old School."

"Word life Zulu…while you was recovering he sold me a half of brick on two different occasions for 7 geez each and he gone give me the bricks for

13…I'm telling you Zulu if I got it you got it."

"Wow…that's a power move…everybody paying anywhere from 21 to 25 since that 911 shit...damn."

"You gone pay what I pay if you fuck with me…but everybody else paying top dollar," Old School Al stated pulling onto E. Parade Street where Zulu's stash house was located. Zulu slowly hopped out the wheel scanning the block as he skated onto the front porch then inside. About ten minutes later Zulu bounced out the house and jumped in the wheel.

"This all you Old School," Zulu retrieved the half of kilo from his waist and handed it to Old School Al as they headed over to E. North park. Old School Al pulled into the park passing a church group who were watching children play at the playground. Hawk and Dolla were on the ball court shoving each other around.

"Listen Zulu," Old School Al gave Zulu dap before Zulu jumped out the wheel, "Don't tell no one my business…not even Sun-Z…I'm gone show these dudes homeboy…but I got you…alright."

"Yeah no question." Zulu opened the door giving Old School Al a firm handshake. "I know dude might got it for cheap, but everything that glitters ain't gold…but you yo own man and you know what you doing...this conversation won't leave this car."

"My man."

"Yooo Old School," Hawk yelled from the ball court backing Dolla down while he dribbled the ball towards the hoop. "What up with you comrade?"

"You know me Hawk," Old School Al replied rolling the passenger window down as Zulu shut the car door and headed inside the basketball court, "I'm gone get with yall I gotta make moves homeboy…Peace."

Hawk and Zulu threw up the peace sign but Dolla threw up his middle finger while putting defense on Hawk who went up scoring a lay-up.

"Zulu you still associate with that dickhead," Dolla knelt to catch his breath after Hawk scored. "You ain't had enough of that nigga bad luck yet?"

"First off he our peoples, second he get money and snatch heavy weight," Zulu stepped onto the court. "But don't worry about me and his business."

"Word up Dolla," Hawk stood at half court tossing the ball at Dolla yelling check before saying, "You need to worry about this business me and you got on this court…score 8-2 and I'm up."

"Hawk you ain't doing shit," Dolla tossed the ball back at Hawk. Hawk caught the ball and dribbled his way into the short brick wall Dolla. Hawk was taller than Dolla but Dolla's physical frame seemed to suffocate Hawk's middleweight physique as Dolla blocked him from charging forward as Hawk struggled bouncing down the court.

Hawk was shirtless and his cappuccino skin was slippery with sweat as he shoved his shoulder into Dolla's blubbery chest covered under a sweatshirt. Hawk dribbled jerking left to right unable to skate around Dolla. Hawk then busted a move on Dolla, faded away and faked a jump shot. Dolla raised his heavy arm and leaped towards Hawk to block the shot but Hawk spun around out of Dolla's way then zoomed forward down the court to shoot a lay-up. Dolla hustled his 325LB frame like a lightweight point guard and zoomed after Hawk. Hawk neared the hoop and went up to shoot but Dolla came from Hawk's blindside and jumped with his 2-inch vertical into the air and snatched the ball out of Hawk's hand like it was a butterball turkey.

"Give me mines little nigga," Dolla dribbled the ball back up to the file line. "I'm tired Hawk so I'm just gone jay on you." Dolla shot jumper after jumper swishing every time he jumped two inches off the ground. The score was now 13-8 and Dolla was up. Game was 16 and the prize was $2,000.

"Hell knaw Dolla you been carrying, travelling, and filing all game…fuck that," Hawk blasted feeling like the game was over.

"Nigga I ain't even been moving like that …I been right here on this file line jaying you…Zulu even peeped game."

"Yeah Hawk," Zulu shot in the air standing at the sideline. Zulu couldn't lie. Dolla was not only the best fat boy baller, but he styled on some of the nicest ballers in the whole New York State Junior League Basketball with his two-inch jump shot. Not too many could beat Dolla on the court.

"Yo Hawk Dolla been swishing on you the whole time I been here...give it up big bra."

"Hawk I'm just gone end it with this three-piece shot right here," Dolla stated dribbling back to the three-point line. "You know the score Hawk and you know what the prize is." Dolla rambled while showing off his fat boy handle smacking the ball thru his legs and behind his back.

"Come on its 13-8 but when I take the ball from you it's gone be 13-16 and them two stacks gone be mine," Hawk flew to the three-point line to check Dolla.

"Stop embarrassing yo self," Dolla styled on Hawk tremendously. Hawk couldn't keep up with Dolla because Hawk smoked too many cigarettes which had his lungs screaming. Hawk gave up and knelt to catch his breath.

"This game right here Hawk," Dolla stopped dribbling and held the ball up in front of his dripping wet black face and focused his eyes on the hoop.

"If you miss I win." Hawk was still kneeling and sucking in oxygen.

"Bet."

"Aw shit...this nigga Hawk stupid," Zulu mumbled to himself. Dolla glanced at Zulu then at Hawk, then he closed his eyes and threw the ball up to the hoop. Dolla grew up playing on this ball court all his life and he could shoot from any angle blindfolded and with precise aim and make his shot. And he proved it when the ball went inside the hoop only touching the net.

"Swiss." Dolla opened his eyes as the ball was swallowed by the net. "That's all mine right there." Dolla let his eyes roll over to the stack of money sitting between a gallon of water and two Gatorades on the sideline. "Come on Hawk let's play 21 now...two more stacks I give you a chance to win yo money back."

"Fuck you Dolla," Hawk sounded defeated watching Desiree pull into the park. "I'm too tired." Hawk sluggishly hit the sideline and guzzled some Gatorade before snatching his shirt from off the fence and wiping his face.

"Zuluuu." Desiree shouted happy to see Zulu as she pulled up into the parking lot, "Come here love."

"Sis what up?" Zulu skated thru the fence into the parking lot and hugged Desiree when she jumped out the wheel. "How you been sis?"

"Question is how you bra?"

"You see me I'm back from the dead with new life."

"Oh my God Zulu we was praying for yall and we still praying for Terror…I hope he come out of that coma and be the same person…I'm so scared for him…I really am Jesus."

"Let's just pray because that's all we can do and hope them doctors on they job."

"I know Zulu but listen," Desiree pulled Zulu closer to her and began whispering even though Hawk and Dolla were on the other side of the fence on the ball court. "Zulu I'm pregnant and Hawk don't know."

"Hold on," Zulu glanced back at the court where Hawk and Dolla were counting the prize money Dolla just won from Hawk. "You been fucking around on Hawk and got knocked up?"

"No boy," Desiree shot at Zulu reaching into the car and grabbing her pack of Newports. "Hawk the only man I been with for the past two years since he been home…this his seed in me…it's just I'm scared to have this baby Zulu."

"How many months is you?"

"I'm two months and I'm scared because I'm not ready to be a mother Zulu…I'm only 26 and I'm having the time of my life…I'm not ready to have no baby spoil my fun and tear up this flawless body I got…what should I do Zulu?"

Zulu took a deep breath and raised his brow with an expression of inexperience. "I don't know Desi…why don't you talk to Destiny?"

"Come on Zulu you know she gone want me to have the baby…I don't wanna kill my baby I just don't think I'm ready to be a mother."

Desiree was two years older than Destiny but Destiny was like the big sister because she was the more responsible and mature one. Destiny was intelligent and had street smarts with the wisdom of God to follow the right path. Desiree on the other hand had a Doctorate degree in street knowledge but she grew up fast in the streets and never had the chance to learn of her virtuous womanly qualities like maintaining a home, raising children, cooking, and how to live a civilized life. Everything was about being sexy and living the fast life with Desiree.

"I don't know what to say Desi...I do know you shouldn't be smoking."

"I'm only two months so it ain't harming the baby...its people out here doing worst shit under the sun with babies in they womb."

"Yeah ok," Zulu shot back observing Hawk and Dolla step out the park into the parking lot. "Go see Prince and them Gods...they should give you some good advice...you know I don't know shit about having babies or being no father."

"Umm...I don't know why I ain't think of going to see Prince," Desiree thoughtfully chimed. "Come with me Zulu...please."

"Come on Desi I don't wanna be around them righteous dudes," Zulu sighed deeply as Desiree grabbed his hand begging. "Alright...I take you to go see little Farrakhan."

"That's why you gone always be my brother Zulu." Desiree squeezed Zulu tightly then whispered in his ear, "Remember don't let no one know."

"I got you sis," Zulu stated pulling away from Desiree to give Hawk a pound and hug before Desiree and Hawk jumped in the Beemer and broke out.

"Let me find out you got Desiree tryna get you back with Destiny?" Dolla asked stepping over to his GT Carrera and popping the trunk. Zulu replied no while Dolla reached inside the trunk and pulled out a Sauna suit. Dolla threw the sauna suit on top of the sweatshirt he had on. It was over 82 degrees outside and Dolla was trying to sweat his insides out.

"You tryna lose weight fat boy?" Zulu asked watching Dolla maneuver himself inside the heavy clothing he had on.

"Yeah I ain't gone even lie Zulu," Dolla began cheesing while slamming his trunk shut. "I bagged this cold ass chick...ma special...aww man Zulu...I'm really feeling this chick."

"Word." Zulu blurted with wonder seeing a light gleam in Dolla's eyes. Dolla was never one to be head over hills for love. But he looked like he was happy about this new chick.

"I think I found a winner Zulu."

"Yo that's what's up playboy," Zulu slapped Dolla's hand before they began strolling the perimeter of the park. "She gotta be something special if she got the Pillsbury doughboy tryna lose weight."

"Yeah I gotta have my stamina right for shorty…she like going out dancing and shit…she like taking walks in the park…shit like that you know…and then she a superfreak and can fuck her sexy ass off…so I gotta have my shit right to keep up with her you feel me."

"I feel you," Zulu added as they spun the park. Zulu then questioned Dolla about the incident with Lulu at the hotel and how Old School Al emotionally felt.

"Listen Zulu…Old School Al just jealous and envious because the same bitch he fell in love with got him sucking on the glass dick and that same bitch is my sex slave and she will never get me to fall off my square…he just mad because he not strong enough to not let a bitch pull him down…fuck that nigga."

"Well all I know is he feel like he can't trust niggas."

"He shouldn't trust that bitch...that bitch gone suck and fuck whoever got that bread and whoever got the fire…he a dickhead…fuck is we even having a conversation about that dickhead for…change the subject Zulu because if he feels any type of way he know to come see me."

"I feel you yo…let's go hit the ave and see what's shaking…it feels like I did a bid I ain't been outside so long," Zulu changed the subject as they exited the park still on foot and hit the avenue.

They stepped on the avenue and walked into the orchestra of the blasting music of cars and the growling engines of buses and cars stuck in the late afternoon traffic jam. Summer school had just let out so the streets were flooded with teeny boppers posted up at bus stops and in front of the stores and shops. As Zulu and Dolla approached Al-Hamza's Market, Lil Flip and Crumbs was posted up on a sparkling Ice Blue Grand Prix with 20 inch rims blasting *Camron* out of its 15-inch bass tubes.

"Yo look at the phat ass elephant man," Crumbs began clowning when he spotted Dolla bouncing towards them in his sauna suit. "Yo the nigga look like a elephant wrapped in plastic…look like he broke out the circus."

Dolla knew Crumbs was clowning on him under the loud music of

Camron because everyone with Crumbs began laughing after Crumbs opened his mouth. Since time immemorial Crumbs was Dolla's comedy student. They battled all the time.

"Yo French Frie wally what the fuck you got everybody laughing at?" Dolla shouted over *Camron spitting Come Home with Me*.

"Candy bar wrapper looking ass nigga got jokes," Crumbs retorted exchanging handshakes and hugs with Zulu and Dolla. "You look like a fucking sea lion Dolla."

"I know yo lizard face ass ain't trying to get embarrassed," Dolla eyed the females standing with Crumbs and Lil Flip. "You skinny ass ostrich neck looking nigga."

"These niggas crazy," Lil Flip posted up with Zulu. "What's good with yall boys though."

"Shit cooling…yall tryna hit the Taste of Buffalo with me and Dolla."

"Hell yeah." Lil Flip and Crumbs both responded. Dolla then dipped into the market to quench his lungs with some H2O while Zulu stood outside shooting the breeze with Lil Flip and Crumbs. They posted up on the car letting their ears take in *Killa Cam's* verbal gymnastics before a lady walking with a young boy about 9 years old approached the market. The lady waved Lil Flip over to her after she gave the little boy some money and sent him into the market.

"I got 70 Flip look out for me before my bad ass son come back out the store," The lady was fidgety as she stood on side of the market in the parking lot. The little boy was inside the store but he stood by the door observing his mother give Lil Flip the money. The little boy then stormed out the store with tears in his eyes shouting.

"Get away from my mother you drug dealer…I hate yall." The young boy ran up to his mother then pushed Lil Flip away.

Lil Flip froze up in shock, "Yo what the fuck." Lil Flip backed away from the lady as the young boy hugged his mother crying.

"Take yo bad ass back in the store got damn it," The lady smacked the little boy in the head then forcefully shoved him back into the store.

"I hate yall...yall all savages and yall gone die...leave my mother alone," tears poured from the young boy's soul as he fussed his way back into the store.

Zulu and the females looked on feeling sorry for the young boy's pain. He was young, but his soul knew about his mother's chemical dependency and how the drug dealers were feeding her the poison. Instead of the young boy's mind being focused on enjoying his life as a child, his young mind was forced to stress about the spiritual destruction the crack had over his mother.

"Yo you gone have to go on Stevens Street and cop...you ain't getting served over here with the drama that little nigga bringing," Lil Flip barked on the lady ready to give her her money back.

"Flip get the fuck outta here you damn fool," Crumbs snatched the money from Lil Flip. "She keeping that money in our hood with us...nigga you a fool sending her to some other niggas block...I want it all nigga we ain't rich."

That's why Crumbs was called Crumbs. He grew up with nothing and he was told he would be nothing. Crumbs said if he had the power he would never let that happen. He would get every crumb he could get until he had a full plate. One hundred pennies equaled a dollar, and every dollar was a digit closer to 100 and the math keep adding on. Crumbs served the lady in the parking lot and then she went into the market to get her God-Child. When the lady walked away with her God-Child, everyone cringed at the powerful glare of the young boy's red tearful eyes.

"Yall better hope that little nigga don't come back and slump yall," Zulu stated seeing a force in the young boy's eyes that was more powerful than the eyes of one who played with death. There was a force inside the little boy that was bigger than a mountain which made him a God-Child.

"I ain't worried bout him or no one else because when my mother was smoking nobody worried about me and my siblings...that lil nigga gone be alright," Crumbs let it be known watching Dolla bounce out the market eating a chicken finger sub.

"How the fuck you tryna lose weight and you eating that shit...you should be eating a salad," Zulu spit at Dolla.

"Elephants don't eat salad Zulu," Crumbs joked.

"Fuck both of yall niggas…this my breakfast…I'm ready to get fresh and hit the Taste of Buffalo for the real festivities…yum yum."

....

The Taste of Buffalo was a local festival hosting the many international tastes of the city's diverse population. Mediterranean dishes, Asian Cuisines, Caribbean and Soul Food dinners, and the traditional meals of America filled the atmosphere of the festival as chefs and cooks stood in their booths and portable kitchens harmonizing the foods of their culture. Thousands of people from all over Western New York and Ontario Canada bombarded the festival located in the heart of downtown Buffalo.

Zulu, Dolla, Lil Flip, and Crumbs found themselves filtering thru the jampacked crowd feeling the sweltering heat of the sunshine on them. Zulu was happy to be healed up and out the house. Lil Flip and Crumbs had craving appetites not for the food but for the swarms of young tenderonis blossoming in their mini-skirts and coochie cutter shorts. And Dolla, even though he was trying to lose weight, he was in Fat Man's heaven. They ventured from booth to booth watching Dolla experiment on different dishes of food. Dolla devoured everything in his path. And whenever his nostrils sucked in a delicious smell that was delightful to his senses, he walked right up to the counter skipping everyone in line and whipping out his bankroll.

Dolla would skip the line and say, "Don't worry about me skipping because I'm buying everybody food…thanks for letting me skip yall," Dolla would butter up the hungry and frustrated people who he skipped in line.

Lil Flip and Crumbs was busy rapping with every young lady they bumped into. Zulu just observed everything while snacking on his fried dough and sipping his ice-cold Loganberry. It was a long two hours of being fired on by the sun, bumping into sweaty people, walking in circles, and watching Dolla go from booth to booth. It was time to go but Dolla had to make one last stop at *Gabriella's Cosina Caliente*. Dolla ordered a dish of yellow rice and chickpeas, red beans and sauce, Goat meat, chicken, and Plantains. This would appease his super appetite and seal his stomach's gluttony.

After being served his food, Dolla told the lady serving, "Yes mami *gracias gracias*." Dolla spoke with a twist in his lango with a yellow Lacoste towel covering his sweaty head. He paid for his food then spun from the booth digging his fork into his rice and beans scooping up mouthfuls. He then tore the juicy drumstick piece off his chicken and slurped the tender meat off the bone and followed with a few more scoops of rice.

"*Ugh,*" Dolla spit up his food distastefully pulling a long string of hair from out of his mouth, "What the fuck…oh hell knaw."

"Yo fat ass shouldn't be eating so much," Crumbs shot at Dolla as he spit the food out of his mouth. "Elephants is vegetarians on some real shit…they eat peanuts and leaves…not the shit you eat."

"You fucking little baboon," Dolla flipped while still plucking rice out of his mouth. "I almost swallowed some nasty ass hair you fucking monkey and you joking."

"Dolla you ain't had enough you been pigging out since we been here," Lil Flip cut in.

"Word I don't know why you keep stuffing yo face…that's a sign for you to stop eating." Zulu added. "Talking about you tryna lose weight."

"Fuck that I'm gone curse these muthafuckas out," Dolla stormed thru the crowd and headed back to the booth and stepped right up to the counter rudely stepping in front of the customers placing orders. "Yo mommy, how you serving food at this festival with hair in this shit?" Dolla dropped his tray on the counter. "This real unprofessional and nasty." Dolla then turned to the patrons in line and said, "Don't eat this nasty shit they got hair in the food."

"Excuse me sir but no need to get loud," The mami respectfully told Dolla, "I can give you your money back and another plate of food…I'm sorry sir."

"Fuck yo food and I don't need money from you…yall shouldn't be selling food at this festival with hair in yall shit."

"Hey you no talk bad to her like that," an older Hispanic man inside the booth leaned over the counter and shouted at Dolla.

"Man fuck you who the fuck you think you is."

"Dolla come on you bugging yo," Zulu tried pulling Dolla away as him and the man continued arguing. People waiting in line looked on annoyingly while others stepped out of line and went to other booths. As Zulu pulled Dolla from the booth, Megalito and a few goons from the 12th Street Mob rushed thru the crowd and approached the booth.

"It's fucking you again huh pa?" Megalito recognized Dolla from the last encounter. "You got a fucking problem what up."

"Muthafucka what." Dolla yanked his heavy platinum Franco chain off his neck and tossed it to Zulu before stepping to Megalito. Megalito rubbed his hands and began storming towards Dolla. With hundreds of people around, it was about to go down.

"No no poppi no no," two women stepped in and grabbed Megalito while Zulu stopped Dolla in his tracks seeing there was too many women and children on the scene not to mention the dozens of police at the festival. Women and children became fearful of the violence that could erupt as Dolla and Megalito was held at bay while cursing at each other.

"Yo Lito Lito check it," a 12th street goon began tapping Megalito as he closely examined Lil Flip and Crumbs. They looked so familiar he knew he seen them around before. His instinct then stroked his gut with that intuition of where he remembered them from. He would never forget Crumb's high yellow complexion and the dreads hanging out of the black hoodie Lil Flip had on that 4th of July weekend they blew up Snakey's Acura and burnt up the trap spot.
"That's them Lito," The man spit in Megalito's ear but Megalito was too occupied with the verbal fight him and Dolla was having.

"You lucky it's too many cops around here you fucking punk," Dolla shouted as Zulu led him away.

"Yo I swear to God if them niggas would have jumped in we was gone air they ass out...they was too deep for us to fight." Lil Flip and Crumbs barked as they raced thru the crowd and left the festival.

"Yo I swear I'm gone whip that fat nigga ass," Dolla thundered as they strolled down Washington Street headed to the vehicle.

"Yo if yall two fat niggas fight," Crumbs began joking as him and Lil Flip kept swiveling their heads behind them looking back and being on point. "Yo that shit gone look like two Sumo wrestlers getting--."

"Yo watch out," Lil Flip shouted peeping two Puerto Ricans gripping pistols spin the corner at Huron and Washington streets behind them and start blasting.

"*Blong blong—blam blam blam*," The Puerto Ricans busted off when Lil Flip turned around and shouted. The crew dipped between two parked cars on the street as Lil Flip and Crumbs pulled their bangers out and began exchanging slugs with the Puerto Ricans. The two Ricans then dipped into a shoe store doorway on the corner and continued blasting.

"*Boom boom boom-blap blap blap*," rang out as slugs banged the glass windows of the shoe store and slugs hitting cars parked on the street triggered car alarms screaming off. People leaving the festival several blocks away screamed while snatching children and running for cover hearing the loud gunfire echoing off the buildings. Bullets were flying everywhere.

Then out of nowhere loud shotgun blasts exploded and the cars shielding the crew shook as deer slugs rattled the cars. It was Megalito at the corner ahead of the crew. The crew was now surrounded and sandwiched in between the two parked cars as slugs rained on them from both sides.

"Fuck yo, we trapped," Lil Flip and Crumbs blasted at both corners realizing they were boxed in. Zulu and Dolla was shook up as they covered their heads from the raining glass of the cars while sitting on their butts curled up shaking every time deer slugs rocked the cars shielding them.

"*Whoop whoop.*" A cop car a few blocks away flashed its lights while hitting its horn. The cop refused to drive into the shootout ahead. From the cop's view down the block it appeared from a distance that Megalito was having a shootout with the two shooters in the shoe store doorway as Megalito stood on the corner ahead of them blasting the shotgun in their direction.

"Yo the cops here we fucked." Lil Flip observed the cop car several blocks down slowly creeping towards them flashing the lights and screaming the horn.

"Hell no I'm blasting they not taking me," Crumbs responded.

"You fucking fool you bet not shoot at them cops," Dolla peeked from behind the car and seen Megalito dip off and the shooters broke out as well.

"Throw yall hammers in the sewer hole right here," Zulu shouted peeping the sewer drain on the curb.

"Get low don't let the cops see yall," Dolla cautioned while watching the cop car speed down the block then turn the corner chasing after the two shooters. The crew hid behind the bullet riddled cars for a few more seconds hearing sirens blasting all around them. They then heard gunshots ring out about two blocks away. The sirens then faded. The crew jumped to their feet brushing glass off while skating across the street where a cop car swerved around the corner.

"Keep running." They all kept it moving like track stars refusing to get caught. The cops paid the four African-Americans no mind. The cops were on the hunt for the three Hispanics who were having a shootout with each other and for the two Hispanics who just shot at a Police Car on Huron street. Fate saved Zulu and the crew from bullets and handcuffs.
Later that night.

"Yo no disrespect Dolla," Mel-Cash stated as him and the crew stood around a pool table loading up weapons. "But I want Megalito fat ass on a rotisserie…I want him roasted like them fat ass pigs that be having the apples in they mouth…but instead of an apple I want a slug in that fat pigs mouth."

"Ain't no disrespect taking," Dolla shot back sitting in a chair throwing slugs into a riot pump shotgun.

"Let's just hit these niggas quick fast and from every angle," was shouted on top of the click clacking sounds of bullets being inserted into the chambers of the assortment of weapons being loaded.

It was war on the lower west side. From the Pine Harbor Projects across Niagara Street, down Carolina Street over to 12th Street, up to Massachusetts avenue, over to Jersey street and 7th street back up to the Shoreline Projects bullets were fired day after day night after night. The streets on the lower west side weren't safe for innocent citizens or hustlers the way bullets were flying on the daily. With the Labor Day and Puerto Rican day parades fast approaching, the sponsors of these events cried out to the mayor and Police Commissioner to shut down the operations of the warring drug crews that was not only threatening the safety of the citizens, but threatening the safety of the thousands of participants who would participate at the upcoming parades which took place on the lower west side.

The mayor and police commissioner answered the city's cry to crack down on the drug dealers on the lower west side. The lower west side became like a military garrison with police stationed on nearly every corner and block where drug activity was known to thrive. The Pine Harbor Projects became headquarters for police. With police heavily patrolling the hood, it was hard to get money in the projects and around 12th street. In the projects business had to be moved inside to the hallways but that was like a trap when the cops rushed into the hallways. The young hustlers who were fast on their feet began getting tired of being chased by police every time they hit licks or served customers. Even the feigns got tired and began trekking to the upper west side across Porter Street to get served, this was bad for business.

On one particular evening a hustler from the Pine Harbor said there would be no more running because he was just too tired. The hustler just hit a lick in the parking lot by his building and a cop observed the whole transaction from a far. The cop shouted for the hustler to stop and put his hands up, but the hustler said hell no and kept it moving to his building since he had in his possession a loaded firearm and a mega-load of bundles of heroin and cracks. The hustler dipped inside his building and began strolling towards the elevator. The elevator was broke so trying to catch the elevator wasn't an option. He hit the stairwell and out of nowhere he felt the hands of the police officer snatch him by the shoulder as he entered the pissy smelling stairwell.

The hustler's heart exploded with so much fear he never knew the power of his knuckles could keep him out of jail. The hustler spun around as the police officer grabbed his shoulder and he rocked the cop right in the face, on the cop's brow between his eyes the knuckles forcefully connected. The cop fell straight back into the stairwell door with his eyes closed and his head feeling like a thumping bass tube of pain. He was knocked out cold.

The hustler then ran onto the fourth floor to an apartment where Zulu, Mel-Cash, and Killa were lounging at. Up inside the apartment was enough drugs and guns to get everyone at least 20 years in prison. When the officer awoke, he couldn't recall who or what had hit him, but he had the whole building locked down with police stationed on every floor and he was going to make sure every hustler in the projects paid for the two black eyes he received. For a whole day and a half, Zulu and the others were trapped in the apartment unable to leave until there was a shift change the next day. The cops turned the Pine Harbor projects into a zero-tolerance drug free and gun free zone and began monitoring all movement coming into the projects and going out. Mel-Cash had to relocate his flow to the upper west side while he cooled down in E. North where Sun-Z called a sit down.

"Yo yall was supposed to shut that nigga Megalito down from the jump," Sun-Z barked in his baritone voice as they all lounged inside Pristine Kutz Barbershop. "Ever since that 4th of July incident yall should have been put the pressure on them niggas instead of that partying shit…you know better Mel-Cash…all that shooting back and forth shit got yo hood hot as fuck…you already know when it's beef we handle it immediately so we can get back to the money."

"Sun we on it…we all thru there trying to find the nigga," Mel-Cash explained.

"Yall niggas been wasting slugs…I don't wanna hear that shit…you, Zulu, and Killa having fun being some trigger happy fools…all yall been doing is shooting each other blocks up and making it hot…Mel-Cash you supposed to find out where that nigga Megalito laying his head and get it over with," Sun-Z flared up telling Mel-Cash who took the criticism like a man. "Look at this shit Mel…you got two bricks of soft (Cocaine) and a whole brick of boy (Heroin) being held hostage in yo projects…plus you got three spots that aint clicking and making the money they usually make…you happy about that shit…what's more important, war or making money?"

"I'm saying Sun we got mad gold in the stash we ain't pressed for bread…we all holding."

"Do you hear this dickhead Hawk," Sun-Z shook his head in frustration at Mel-Cash's ignorance. "You acting like a fucking amateur in this game Mel...you act like you don't know this fucking game and the level we playing on...and this for all yall...we not on no corner level of hustling and we not no petty crew worrying about 1 to 3's and 2 to 4 years upstate...this weak ass war costing us money and it could cost us our freedom...if this shit keep up our bank definitely gone get low because you can't hustle hard when you at war...that's when you end up spending yo stash...quarter millions get blown in months...you could blow hundreds in weeks...and then look at the work just sitting right under the cop's nose in them projects...if they rush them spots people going to jail and that's more money being spent on bail and lawyers...that's why this shit should've been handled...and since yall can't seem to end this shit by knocking this King Poppi nigga off...I'm going to get up with Old School Al... Old School think I don't know but he fucking with some Ricans on the upper west side that might know this Megalito nigga...I'm going to see if we can have a sit down first then I got a plan for King Poppi ass...because he gots to die."

So until the sit down was to take place and the heavy police presence faded on the lower west side, Mel-Cash took his lucrative hustle to the upper west side where he faced even more competition.

....

When the Get Rich Crime Family turned their back on Old School Al and taught him a lesson by not lending a helping hand, Old School Al set up shop on the upper west side on Hampshire street with the half of brick Zulu had fronted him. Since he been on Hampshire Street, Old School Al wished he would've came to the upper west side sooner and hooked up with Lulu's cousin Kato. Kato was all about money. He didn't care about no one's personal issues or what beefs they had, his only concern was business.

Being that the war on the lower west side had all the feins from the lower running to the upper west side to chase that high, all the hustlers followed the feins and set up shop on the upper west side. This was disrupting the flow and starting to cause friction. A sit down was definitely needed because Kato's business interest was being jeopardized on the upper west side.

The interdependence of living organisms in the universe is inevitable and everything and everyone plays a role in this universe of life. All life forms need each other to survive, just like everyone on both sides needed Old School Al. Finally, Old School Al was acknowledged and his worth was sought after. Old School Al wasn't rocking the bells so he was doing his natural and calculating figures like a mathematician. And while everyone else was complaining about the slow grind money making on the west side because of the war, Old School Al wanted to make the Get Rich Crime Family sweat. As far as the 12th Street Mob, Old School Al didn't give a damn if they had to start selling pastelito's to eat. Being that 12th Street and other hustlers like Mel-Cash from the lower west side were setting up spots on the upper west side, this was interfering with Kato's monopoly on the drug market. Kato was Old School Al's supplier and the key to his million-dollar goal. So there it was, Old School Al had to hurry up and make the sit down happen and stop playing tit for tat. There was no time for grudges and emotions when food was being taking out of peoples' mouths.

Kato had 12th street willing to sit down and call a truce, and Old School Al was under the impression that Sun-Z and the Get Rich Crime Family wanted the same. The meeting was set and soon to come, but with everyone having ulterior motives and hidden agendas, a disaster was set to come.

CHAPTER 16

"I send Universal Peace to the Black Man, Black Woman, and Black Child and to all the human families of the Planet Earth." The wise orator named *Great Master Mind Messiah* shouted into the microphone as he stood on stage in front of a large audience at the African Cultural Center on Masten Avenue. It was an enlightening of the minds meeting and the Gods was in the building to drop the science on the people and open their eyes to the True Knowledge of Self. Zulu and Desiree was in attendance to see Prince and seek the advice Desiree needed in regard to her pregnancy.

"See listen people," Great Master Mind Messiah verbalized as he rhythmically flailed his hands while building on stage. "The Black Family is the vital building block of the black nation...And its unity that keep us together and strong...we establish our unity as a family by knowing our roles and duties we owe to our family...See do the knowledge family...the Blackman is incomplete without the Blackwoman and vice versa...and how can the Blackman and Blackwoman be complete and carry on the legacy of perpetual life without the beautiful black child...how?"

"Drop the science God and elevate the minds of the people Lord. Build," a God yelled from the audience.

"See I need yall to do the knowledge to this wisdom with yall full mental ability...I want yall to use that same mental ability, energy, and focus we use to learn about ignorance...but we gone reverse it and learn about ourselves on a positive and righteous level...and I'm gone start with the Blackman and his role...the Blackman is symbolic to the most dominant force in this universe, and that's the sun...The sun is a star and the star is a sun...but it's the sun that provides the life giving force to the planets in our solar system...the sun gives the planets the energy to keep spinning and the sun keeps everything in order. The sun provides us with heat to protect us from the cold...and the sun is everything of power to us, just like the Blackman is to his family...the Blackman has the life force in the seed of the sperm cell...he is the source of life...and all

races of people come from the black nation…the Blackman blesses the
womb of the black woman with life just as the sun bless the womb of the earth
with life…The Blackman must provide for his family and keep his family in the
motion of life experiencing love, peace and happiness just like the sun keep the
planets in harmonious motion…and the Blackman must also protect his family
from the cruelties of life just like the sun bless us with the warmth that protect us
from harsh weather. Wake up Blackman, we can't fulfill our duties and
obligations to our families in a jail cell or being hooked on drugs and alcohol, let
alone in the grave…wake up…man up Blackman."

"Word is Bond to the Father Allah," Two Gods seated in the front row
stood up shouting. "Manifest the truth of the Original Man…teach Allah teach."

"That's your nature Blackman and those are the duties you owe to this
beautiful Queen Goddess and mother of the Black Seed," Great Master Mind
Messiah peered into the audience where many beautiful sisters sat. "See the
Blackwoman is like the moon. And just how the moon reflect the light of the sun,
the Black Woman reflects the light (knowledge) of the Blackman…if we
ignorant the Black Woman gone manifest ignorance and that reflects on the
seed…the Black Woman is also like the earth…see do the math…people talk
about aliens and life on other planets and all that other non-sense…well I ain't
ever been nowhere but on earth and the earth is so beautiful and heavenly just
like the Black Woman…see the earth has all the essential and necessary
conditions and supportive environments to produce and nurture life as we know
it in the highest form of existence that we call Man…and Blackman," Great
Master Mind Messiah inhaled deeply the sweet scented air of the perfume the
sisters wore as he looked in awe at the beautiful sisters. "The Black Woman is
our earth…she is our paradise and heaven…she bring forth the life of our
seeds…she possess the divine soul and heavenly spirit to love, nurture, and care
for our seeds just like the earth do all life…the Black Woman has the power to
stand strong and keep her divine beauty no matter how rough it get and no matter
the conditions…just like the earth remains beautiful regardless to the disasters
and catastrophes that happen on earth…that's why we must appreciate

and cherish the Black Woman my brothers…we must learn to love and respect her because if we don't how will we survive as a people…she is the producer of the child and she is the child's first teacher…if she isn't respected by us then the children won't respect her…and if she was to give up on life we would become extinct…the reason we still here is because of her…we endured over 400 years of slavery, torture, rape, and murder, but the Black Woman kept the family together throughout the whole struggle even when the Black Man gave up or was too weak to be a true man…she carried us on her back when we as Men wouldn't stand up against that devilish slave master who broke our families apart and did everything to destroy our souls…it was the Black woman who did her best to raise our seeds while the devilish slave master murdered the Black Man…just remember Harriet Tubman, a Black Woman who had the courage to rescue our people and lead them up out of slavery…we owe our Black Woman…we owe her more than a shopping spree…we owe her our God duties to get knowledge of self and become the Gods who are the Suns of the Most High so we can treat her like the Goddess she is…this is why the men of all races honor and respect their women…and don't get mad at the Arabs for lusting our women…we don't respect and protect our women and that's the only reason these Arabs can do that…you see they honor and protect they women so we don't get a chance with they women…the Black woman is our holy land that's sacred and she must be cherished…and Black Woman you must demand your honor and respect because you are the Blackman's motivation…without you the Blackman has no desire to live because you make life exciting to live with yo lovely and beautiful self sista."

"Add on Lord…manifest the truth…the Blackman is God and the Black Woman is his Queen," people applauded."

"See these things reflect on our seeds who are our future…and the fruit doesn't fall too far from the tree…and you know a tree by the fruit it bears…you know the growth and development of a tree by the seeds planted…that's why we must plant the proper seeds of knowledge of self, education, self-empowerment, self-worth, and divine guidance because these are the forces that will shape and mold the minds of the seeds planted in the Black Woman. The black child is our seed and a seed can only grow to be that which it is...if you plant an apple seed that's what you will get. If a man and woman's mind is rooted in ignorance, then they will plant a seed of ignorance and produce that which reflects them; ignorance. See we look at our youth and wonder why they are so wild and ignorant, but people, these are our seeds and they learnt from us...we are responsible for them...we blame t.v., music, and society, but in reality we must blame ourselves because we allow the minds of our seeds to be influenced by this devil's civilization...and the only reason why we allow this devil's civilization to influence our children's minds is because we don't have the knowledge of self to destroy the trick-knowledge of the devil...if we don't want our kids to learn wickedness then we have to elevate our minds righteously then teach them righteousness and the proper knowledge of self...if we ignorant and following the wickedness of these white devil's society then that's what we gone teach our children or allow them to learn. We must get knowledge of self of our true blackness and teach our seeds culture-refinement...teach them the sciences of life which will activate their minds to be creative geniuses...the supreme knowledge of the ancient master builders of Kemet (Egypt) who built pyramids and mastered mathematics and science is the same knowledge that lies deep in our genetic core. It is our ancestral intelligence and that's why we must teach our seeds their Black history...their true black history of greatness that will spark their minds to be great and master the knowledge of today...this is how we will produce a new mind state in our people and stop the ignorance that is destroying us...it starts with us and the seeds are our future that will take us further," Great Master Mind Messiah continued with his mind elevating build before putting on a film titled *"How to Give Birth to a God"* by *the Honorable Minister Louis Farrakhan.*

The lights dimmed in the packed auditorium and the live build of Minister Farrakhan flashed on the large screen projector. Prince then slid to the back of the auditorium where Zulu and Desiree were seated. Prince gestured for them to follow him and they stepped out into the hallway graced with pictures of Great African-American thinkers and leaders on the wall. The three then strolled down the hallway and passed the library before entering a small office near the end of the hallway where the restrooms were located. Once inside the small office, Prince seated himself behind the office desk cloaked with a red, black, and green cloth as Zulu and Desiree seated themselves in front of the desk.

"So you pregnant huh Desi?"

"Yes and I don't think I'm ready for this Prince."

"It's about sacrifice Desi…you been living that negative lifestyle for so long you don't wanna give it up to be a mother," Prince observed the guilt trigger the muscles in Desiree's face as she listened to the truth. "We can't live a certain way our whole life Desi…it comes a time for change…everything in the universe goes thru change and transformation and it's a change for the better…nothing stays the same because life evolves in this evolutionary cycle…babies learn to talk and walk to become young children who grow to become adults…it's all about growth and development…it's like the wise man said in the Bible, when I was a child I did childish things but now as a man I put the childish things away and do the things men do. We all gotta grow up and take on responsibility…we can't remain like children forever Desi…don't you wanna stop being a selfish young lady and become the mother the creator is calling you to be?" Prince asked Desiree whose mind was shaky like dice.

"Oh my God Zulu." Desiree squeezed Zulu's hand as the light of the fiery truth began to burn her insides causing the baby to make movement inside her womb.

"I want both of yall to knowledge this wisdom," Prince stood up out of his chair and slid halfway around the desk then leaned against the desk. "We all grew up in broken homes…some of us didn't know our fathers, and our mothers seemed to not pay us much attention…we had to take care of ourselves at a very young age and it was hard…a lot of us didn't have childhoods because we was forced to grow up…we didn't ask to be in this hell we call life and we damn sure don't wanna bring children into this life so they can suffer like we did. I don't want yall to ever think I forgot where I came from or forgot the struggle…never that…but one thing I came to learn since I got Knowledge of Self is that life is truly beautiful and life is what we make it…we responsible for our happiness and our suffering…and being that we are made in the image and likeness of God that mean we have that creative ability to make our life the best we can possibly make it and enjoy the happiness of life…so when life is called into existence thru the womb of the black woman that's a testament showing and proving that the creator of the universe is manifesting its creative power to bring life into the world. We gotta realize this is something special Desi…don't think your pregnancy is something to take lightly Black woman…this is the creator of the universe expressing itself…and it's a young god or goddess in your womb right now…so think deeply on it…it's your choice to create life or destroy life, which will you choose Black woman?"

With the Supreme Knowledge and Wisdom penetrated in the womb of Desiree's mind, she felt like she was mentally impregnated with a new life force to bring a new life into existence mentally as well as physically. She was ready and she felt it in her divine soul just like she felt the new life in her womb floating in her divine waters of life.

Desiree knew it was time for her to change. Everything in life happens for a reason and she knew it was time for her to slow down. She lived her life in the fast lane since she was a young flower and with the revelation of having a baby, she knew she had to do the right thing in life to raise her baby righteously so the seed wouldn't grow to suffer in the wilderness of the streets.

A baby meant life. A baby was a beautiful life with the potential to reach the stars if it was nurtured and educated right. That was one of the main goals of life. That was reincarnation and how the God of the Universe manifested in the physical form. It was through pro-creation how man and woman extended themselves and perpetuated their existence to last forever. So with Prince and Destiny serving as spiritual god parents and mental providers for Hawk and Desiree's unborn child, they would have the support of the village to raise a God-Child.

....

The meeting was set and the Get Rich Crime Family would meet the 12th Street Mob at a neutral location in North Buffalo. The Northside was another realm with its affluent and safe atmosphere away from the drug infested war zones of the east and west side. Business owners and residents made sure heavy police presence in their Northside business districts kept danger at a minimum. Konos restaurant was an upscale dining place sitting on Hertel Avenue amongst the dozens of Italian and Greek eateries, middle-eastern Kebab shops and traditional Ice Cream parlors. During the busiest hours of the day the strip would be crammed with middle aged couples walking their toy dogs amongst the wealthy businesspeople dining on the patios of the restaurants.

Zulu and Cream sat tucked away in the back of a parking lot to a tavern across from Konos. They had an open view of the strip outside Konos and they were peeping for any 12th street goons who might try ambushing Sun-Z and Hawk who sat inside Konos waiting for Old School Al and the Poppis to arrive. In front of a fitness gym a block away Killa and Mel-Cash sat parked eagle eyeing the strip and ready to spray if need be. They were just sitting patiently waiting for the meeting to start and finish. When the meeting was finished, the plan was to follow Megalito back to the west side and finish him, Sun-Z's order.

"Yo you ever think about us losing everything we accomplished out here Zulu?" Cream asked as he glued his eyes on the people easing in and out of Konos.

"Man," Zulu pushed his words deep from the solar plexus in his stomach thinking about the extravagant lifestyle they were living. They were young men in their mid-twenties but they seen just as much money as bank managers if not more and they lived exquisite lifestyles like middle-aged millionaires. They were successfully living the fast life at high speed and this was the life any man of adventure desired. But how long would it last since nothing lasts forever.

"Yo Cream…it aint gone be over till the fat lady sing and that bitch aint even ready to go up on stage yet."

Yeah no question," Cream eyed Zulu with a thoughtful gaze as Zulu gripped the 45 caliber handgun sitting on his lap. "I just want this war shit to be over with so we can get back to stacking up on that west side flow…ever since Mel-Cash gave us a line over there my shit been multiplying like crazy…yo I'm telling you Zulu…by next year," Cream closed his eyes, smiled, and clenched his fist with an emotional joy that spoke of supreme success. "I ain't told no one yet…but I'm only a few hundred geez short of a million…I'm pass a half a mill

Zulu…word up."

"What?" Zulu was amazed with his eyes opened wide. "You at almost a million?"

"Man Zulu I'm stacking and I'm on it…and if this move go right and the heat die down on that west side I'm gone be there by next year Zulu…a whole million…that west side flow been doing a nigga justice."

"Hell yeah you aint lying…I mean I'm just passing that quarter mill mark but yo that's what's up."

"Zulu that's why I always tell you…money over everything…fuck that war shit…I just want Sun-Z plan to work and let's get back to the money." Cream stated eyeing the ringing cell phone mounted on the dashboard. It was Sun-Z and Hawk calling.

"Yo Old School and them oyes a half hour late…I called Old School two times already and his phone going to voicemail…we gone give em twenty more minutes and if they don't show up we gone go find these niggas…because this shit gone be over today."

"Alright," Zulu and Cream gazed at each other wondering what lie ahead. Whether the Poppis showed up or not it was going to be murder. And as they all waited the next twenty minutes which seemed like eternity, everyone thought of the cash flow they were missing out on. One thing for sure, only murder would end the beef which was interrupting the cash flow.

Twenty minutes passed and then another twenty minutes passed. There was still no communication from Old School Al and a reason for why the meeting didn't take place. Megalito wasn't stupid at all. And just how Sun-Z had a trick up his sleeve to finish off Megalito, Megalito had a trick up his own sleeve and it wasn't meeting up with his enemies on their terms. Megalito was sharp as Sun-Z and he wasn't King of the infamous 12th Street Mob for being weak in the jungle.

Old School Al couldn't show up to the meeting and there was no way he would. When Megalito was first contacted by Lulu's cousin Kato about a meeting for a truce, Megalito played it like he was all game for it. Around this same time Old School Al had finished a major package he copped from Kato and he was in need for another re-up. Kato was waiting on a package from Puerto Rico so he couldn't hit Old School Al with that Fuego. Kato was all about the money and just because he didn't have work didn't mean he couldn't make a dollar. Kato and Megalito was copping work from the same plug in Puerto Rico so they had the same Fuego. Megalito was sitting on a motherload since it was slow due to the war and he was giving it up for cheap. This was perfect for Kato because he could tax Old School Al like the IRS.

When Kato told Megalito about the meeting and how Old School Al also wanted to cop some heavy weight, Megalito took advantage of a situation that was beautiful. Megalito was a schemer down to his bone marrow and at the glance of any free meal, he was gonna eat. Megalito told Kato it would be perfect for him and Old School Al to meet face to face and conduct business because that would solidify a tight business relationship on top of a truce.

This was sweet Old School Al thought. If only Old School Al would have stayed in his lane and played with the players he always played the game with. At first and on the surface Old School Al thought he was making a good move by linking up with Kato because that was a bridge to success he couldn't achieve with the Get Rich Crime Family. Kato had no devilish and grimy ways in his heart besides always wanting to make a profit which is the honest spirit of a hustler. Hooking up with Kato was a power move but hooking up with Megalito was the wrong move. Megalito and Kato were of two different breeds and the consequences of Old School Al's actions would prove that he should have never strayed from the nest and tried soaring with hungry vultures like Megalito. Kato was a good dude but his thirst for riches would prove fatal.

Kato introduced Old School Al to Megalito and they discussed business and also set up the date for the so-called truce meeting. The business between Old School Al and Megalito would take place first and then the truce meeting would follow a few hours later. Everything was set. Old School Al and Megalito would meet up without Kato even though Kato was going to receive his profit from the deal from Megalito. Kato would soon regret sending a good business customer like Old School Al to Megalito, let alone even hooking them up with each other.

About an hour before the truce meeting, Old School Al and Megalito met up to conduct their business at a pier on the upper west side known as the foot of Ferry. Megalito and one of his associates stood outside a MPV van when Old School Al pulled into the parking lot facing the river at the pier. Old School Al parked right on side of the MPV and hopped out observing the cars in the parking lot which were mostly empty. Most of the people at the pier were fishing, jogging, or just watching the fast and powerful currents of the river flow north to Niagara Falls.

"What's good poppi?" Old School Al and Megalito slapped hands like familiar comrades as they stood between Old School Al's Jaguar and the MPV.

"Just cooling Pa…you ready to butcher this cow and eat right?" Megalito asked with his chinky eyes flashing the flame of a serpent.

"Yeah I got my bread right here," Old School Al nodded towards his backseat as he stood at his passenger door. "You got them bricks right?"

"Of course Pa they right here," Megalito stated peeping the bag on the floor of Old School Al's backseat before he slid the side door open to the MPV van. A man sitting in the backseat of the MPV had a duffel bag on his lap. The man smiled at Old School Al and winked his eye, before unzipping the duffel bag, snatching a shotgun from out the bag then aiming it in Old School Al's face. Old School Al froze up not believing this was happening. Megalito then shoved Old School Al inside the van so swiftly, no one seen a thing it happened so quick. Megalito then opened Old School Al's back door and snatched the bag of money from off the floor, slammed the car door shut then jumped into the MPV.

They drove Old School Al over to a building not too far from the foot of Ferry and that's where they shoved him into a dark damp basement itching with spider webs and stale air. A light dangling from the ceiling was flicked on and Old School Al was hog tied to a rusted and cold metal chair. He sat there in fear feeling stupid while Megalito and two of his goons counted his money. After they finished counting the money one of the men left with the bag of money and that's when Old School Al was told there was never going to be a truce, and Megalito thanked Old School Al for being a stupid ass monkey.

"I may not be the smartest poppi...but I'm not that dumb enough to go and meet with them crazy ass peoples of yours from the east side...I'm a little crazy pa but I'm not suicidal...and going to meet with your peoples would have been suicidal...because they was gonna murder me poppi...you think I would go for that...fuck no...but I thank you for your heart poppi because you were very bold to come see me."

"Oh my fucking God," Old School Al thought to himself, *"What the fuck I got myself into."*

Megalito could see the fear flooding Old School Al's system. He told Old School Al to calm down and relax. Old School Al wasn't the one who Megalito wanted to kill, it was Mel-Cash. Megalito promised Old School Al as a man that if he gave up Mel-Cash's spot on the west side where he rested his dome piece, Old School Al would live to see another day and he might get a brick or two of Fuego. Old School Al may have made some stupid decisions and felt dumb, but there was no way he was gonna give up the whereabouts of any of his people. Regardless to the ridicule and criticism the Get Rich Crime Family put him through, none of that was worthy of death due to treachery and betrayal at the hands of Old School Al. Old School Al could be anything people wanted to label him, but one thing he wasn't was a rotten soul who would sell his people out.

Old School Al remained silent focusing his vengeful eyes on Megalito. Old School Al was standing tall under the pressure and even after ramming the shotgun barrel forcefully into Old School Al's face, breaking his nose and causing his jaw to swell, Old School Al withstood the pressure like a true G and kept his mouth closed only moaning the pain he felt.

Megalito then rambled how he would not only give Old School Al the five bricks he was supposed to get, but Old School Al would be protected by 12th Street, all he had to do was give up the location to Mel-Cash's spot.

"Fuck you you fat muthafucka." Old School Al yelled before spitting the salty tasting blood in his mouth at the man holding the shotgun. "Just kill me muthafucka."

"Cabron," The shotgun toting man wiped the bloody spit from off his face before smacking Old School Al in the head with the butt of the shotgun.

"Come on poppi think about it," Megalito pleaded with Old School Al who dropped his head feeling the weight of regret and plain stupidity flood his emotions. He was no longer scared, he just felt stupid for putting himself in this situation and he knew dying would be the only way he could feel better. "You might as well tell me where his spot at poppi because it's no way I can let you leave here alive unless I know you got my best interest and you on my side…come on pa I'm giving you a chance to choose life over death…and you gotta choose poppi…be smart and think for yourself…this yo life and you gotta choose who life it's gonna be…his or yours…I promise I won't kill you if you give up Mel-Cash…may *DeJesus* be my witness I won't kill you or none of my people will kill you…you wont die if you give up Mel-Cash."

"Fuck you," Old School Al's voice was now faltering with fear, "Fuck that…do what yall gone do to me because my people gone kill me anyway if I tell yall…and I aint telling yall so yall might as well kill me because I would rather yall kill me instead of my own people killing me…I'm gone die no matter what…*Fuccckk.*"

Old School Al couldn't believe it. This is the moment his whole life was lived for. He thought he was making a power move that would position him at the center of his own universe. He never thought he was ending his universe. He thought he was networking which would allow him to establish an enterprise where he would be boss and calling the shots. Who would have seen this coming Old School Al thought to himself? Zulu told him to keep it in the family. Why didn't he keep it in the family? Everything that glitters aint gold and the bricks Kato usually got for 13 thousand wasn't worth one moment of this situation Old School Al found himself in. Why couldn't he take the bitter with the sweet and follow the law and order Sun-Z had the family following for their own success and safety.

Sun-Z knew about Old School Al copping work from Kato, but if he would have known Old School Al was gonna do business with Megalito before the meeting, he would've seen this situation happening through the crystal lens of a microscope. Sun-Z didn't really like the idea of Old School Al dealing with Kato but Old School Al wanted to go on his own so Sun-Z let him be his own man.

"God why...why did you let me fuck up...why." Old School Al heard his conscience scream from the depths of his soul as Megalito hovered over him. *"Why...why didn't I keep copping with the crew...what the fuck was I thinking...why...why."* Old School Al felt sorry for himself and felt a tear drizzle from his eye.

"Listen poppi I understand yo loyalty and I like that...but I'm tryna be easy with you...I don't wanna be in this basement...and I don't wanna kill you...I don't even know you...poppi look at me bro," Megalito stood over the trembling Old School Al and gazed into his blank eyes. "I don't have problems with you or none of yo people from the east side...all you gotta do is give me that fucking she-male...don't get yo self killed for that asshole because I know for a fact he would kill you if his back was against the wall and he was hungry...he don't love no one but cash pa...and you know it...that's why yall call him Mel-Cash," Megalito stated thinking how Shamel's love for money and lust for violence severed their childhood friendship a long time ago.

Shamel was one of the few black kids in his hood who attended a Hispanic Catholic School. Shamel hated it being surrounded by a bunch of Hispanics who was always picking on him and saying his name was She-Male. Shamel was small for his age but he had the heart of a lion and he fought every day in school to earn his respect from the Hispanics.

Megalito whose real name was Miguel was the only cool Puerto Rican Shamel befriended. Shamel and Miguel became real good friends until they became of age and started dancing with the street life. There was an older Hispanic hustler named Roberto who was supplying the Puerto Ricans from 12th Street and the Blacks from the Pine Harbor. Roberto had everyone eating even though he showed favoritism to his fellow Hispanics. It really didn't matter because everyone was getting theirs and holding bankrolls.

One day Roberto was found shot dead in a stash apartment he had in the Pine Harbor. They found him with a bullet in his head and all his money and drugs were gone. He was even stripped of his jewelry. It was a strait massacre robbery. No one knew who did it, but everyone knew Shamel disappeared and fled to the east side. He came back to the west side several months later now known as Mel-Cash. Mel-Cash blew up big time and was now claiming to be King of the Pine Harbor, and the once lion hearted Shamel who was always quick to fight hung up his knuckle game for a deadly gun game that was putting slugs in anyone. The Puerto Ricans began blaming Mel-Cash for Roberto's homicide, but Mel-Cash and Megalito remained cool somehow. Megalito was then told by his people that he either stay away from Mel-Cash who was a walking dead man or he would have to set Mel-Cash up for Roberto's people who wanted Mel-Cash's head. Blood is thicker than water and the unity of a people's nation is stronger than friendships with outsiders. Megalito did what any soldier would do for his nation. He set up Mel-Cash to get killed but Mel-Cash survived the attempt on his life. All that did was bring the dragon out of Mel-Cash who started spitting fire on the Puerto Ricans. The war been going on ever since and Mel-Cash seemed to truly be the God of the Hood, unable to be touched by the mortals of 12th street.

"Poppi listen to me," Megalito persisted in trying to persuade Old School Al. "That dude don't care about no one or nothing…why would you lose yo life for him…I swear to Dejesus I will let you go if you just tell me where that dude be at pa…give me one of his girls' address or something…please pa."

"Mannn," Old School Al knew this was his last stand. He could look in Megalito's cloudy red eyes and see Megalito was a killer who was trying not to kill him. Megalito wanted to kill Mel-Cash. This was Old School Al's moment of truth and he would accept this last moment of his life like a true G. His heart melted and he felt tears streaming down his face as he told Megalito, "Just kill me because I deserve to die…and please…the least you can do for me is tell Lulu that I love her…and just so you know…when you kill me you killing a part of Lulu."

"No no poppi why you gotta be so fucking tough bro," Megalito pulled out his cell phone and began dialing Lulu's number. "I'm not gone kill you yet…I let you talk to Lulu first," Megalito then held the phone to Old School

Al's ear and mouth.

"Lulu," Old School Al's voice trembled upon hearing Lulu's sweet and soft squeaky voice answer the phone sounding like a little girl.

"Hey poppi everything ok?" Lulu sensed something wasn't right from the sound of Old School Al's voice.

"Na Lulu…just…just know I…I…I love you and tell Sun-Z…aw man…tell him I…I fucked up…but I stood up like a G."

Megalito snatched the phone from Old School Al, "Lulu listen it's Megalito."

"What the hell you doing to Al?" Lulu screamed into the phone

"Yo tranquilo (calm down) mommi," Megalito began speaking in Spanish to Lulu and after a brief conversation Megalito placed the phone back on Old School Al's ear.

"Poppi you have to do it…you have to do it for everyone…don't be stubborn…do it for me…please don't let the war continue Al…don't leave me poppi I need you…everyone need you to make the right decision poppi…please poppi do what they ask you…we all want peace."

"Lulu you don't understand…I can't…I love you more than I love myself but I can't…bye Lulu," Old School Al jerked his face from the phone feeling his heart spurt pain through his system causing more tears to pour uncontrollably as he began crying like a baby. It was heart aching hearing Lulu's sweet voice beg him to do the most unforgiveable act a man could do. He loved Lulu so much he would do anything for her just like he fucked his soul up by smoking crack for her. But what he finally came to realize at this moment of truth as he looked into the black holes of the double barrel shotgun aimed in his face, was that his soul wasn't fucked up at all because he was about to die like a man instead of sacrificing a true and loyal friend for an enemy. At least he would rest in peace while Mel-Cash lived, because Mel-Cash sacrificed his life for Old School Al once upon a time when Old School Al's life wasn't worth the crack he was feigning for.

When the Feds snatched the A-Squad back in the day, and while Sun-Z and Hawk was upstate serving state time, Old School Al fell off drastically when

Lulu introduced him to the seductive mystique of the crack. Since Old School Al fell from the status of a fly hustler to that of a crackhead, everyone was trying to rob him for his jewelry since he wouldn't sell it for the crack he was feigning for. He got tired of the stick-up kids on the east side so he journeyed over to the west side with Lulu and her crack dreams which was a safe-haven for him. The west side was Mel-Cash's realm where he was God of the hood and just being seen with Mel-Cash would make everyone respect and fear Old School Al. Old School Al hit the west side jeweled up like he was the God Mc Rakim. Old School Al had jewelry galore and even though he was rocking the bells hard, he would die before he gave up his sentimental and precious metals for crack. And just like he experienced the hungry wolves on the east side coming for his shines, he attracted the sharks on the west side when the hustlers couldn't get him to come up off his shines. Stick-up kids then came thru to tax Old School Al.

Mel-Cash wasn't having it. When the A-Squad was at their peak and Mel-Cash was at war with 12th street after Roberto's murder, the A-Squad gave Mel-Cash a spot to lay his head on the east side and they provided triggers for Mel-Cash against his enemies. It was Thug Love. There was no way Mel-Cash wasn't going to return the Thug Love to Old School Al, and Mel-Cash definitely wasn't going to let anyone disturb Old School Al's peace and tax him while he was in Mel-Cash's kingdom. Mel-Cash heard the rumors of the sharks plotting on Old School Al's shines and let it be known that Old School Al was off limits. Everyone heard Mel-Cash but didn't believe he would go hard for a jeweled-up crackhead. A notorious stick-up kid from Breckenridge Avenue came thru and stripped Old School Al for everything, even his gold fronts like a true savage.

"Fuck Mel-Cash I did it…he aint the only one with guns," The stick-up kid told Old School Al after pistol whipping him. The stick-up kid flossed Old School Al's jewelry for the next two days while cruising around the west side strapped up and ready to see Mel-Cash. It was at the *Naughty by Nature* concert at Lasalle Park by the waterfront where Mel-Cash crossed paths with the stick-up kid. Hundreds of people were in the park enjoying the concert and jamming when numerous shots rang out by the bathroom. The God of the Hood didn't care

about it being broad daylight and many witnesses around because he emptied his clip in the stick-up kid then snatched all of the jewelry off his bullet riddled body. That same night Old School Al had all his jewelry back.

A little while later Mel-Cash was arrested and charged with the murder. He spent 18 months in the county jail fighting the murder rap until one of the witnesses recanted their testimony after a Thug from the Pine Harbor put the fear of the Devil in them. Mel-Cash inflicted death on one who violated Old School Al and he almost threw his life away for Old School Al by risking a murder rap he could've got life in prison for. Old School Al would die for Mel-Cash before he sold him out.

"He killed for me just so niggas would respect me on the west side...he gave his life for me just so I could live...Mel-Cash is like Jesus Christ to me...I don't wanna die but how could I live with myself." Old School Al closed his eyes as the barrel of the double barrel shotgun was pressed on his forehead. *"Help me God please...help me,"* Old School Al heard his conscience utter as the gauge on the shotgun was cocked, aimed at his cranium and ready to fire. *"Help me God."*

CHAPTER 17

Zulu swerved the corner heading to meet up with the crew when he spotted Prince talking to an older lady who was dressed in conservative business attire. Zulu pulled over and waited for Prince to finish speaking with the lady before he jumped out to speak with Prince.

"Blackman…What's good bro?"

"Everything is good Blackman," Prince's round eyes gleamed like the black and gold sun, moon, star, and number 7 on his shirt. "That was Ms. Jackson right there and she the council member for the hood, she want me to help her launch a youth program to get kids off the street, she lost both her sons to violence and she wanna develop a program that will get kids from all over the city to come together and learn self-love, and respect life so they can learn to love and respect each other so we can stop this self-hatred which is the source of this black on black violence.

"Here this nigga go with this righteous Black Man shit." Zulu puckered his lips wishing that could happen. With Old School missing it was going to be nothing but violence and black, white, Hispanic, or Chinese could get a bullet as far as Zulu cared.

"What's the problem Zulu?" Prince asked as they posted up on Zulu's car.

"We at war with niggas from the west side and Old School Al missing."

"Damn Zulu...damn," Prince felt kinda sad but it was reality of the street life, "It's time for dudes to start wanting peace instead of war."

"You act like you don't know how the streets is…niggas ain't gone never have peace on these streets…it's gone always be violence…Niggas got too much murder beef and too corrupted and turnt the fuck out…you can't change niggas like me…you can't even change them young niggas like Crumbs and Lil Flip…You think niggas like me feel comfortable without my gun…Niggas like me can't change…how…it's impossible."

"See that's where you wrong Zulu…look at me, I left the streets and all

the drama I had in the streets I destroyed it...I don't wanna hear that

ignorance...you just don't wanna change because you scared to change...you too

emotionally attached to this lifestyle and you think this the only way for a Black

man to live...we wasn't born as killers and gangsters. We was born pure and

divine...it's just we born in this world ruled by this wicked white government and

they teach us evil and we don't even realize it...they created a civilization that

was based on murder and robbery of the Indians and they land...and then they

designed the social, educational, political, and economic system that wasn't for

no one but white people and now that we a part of their system they made sure it

doesn't motivate and inspire us to be the best we can be...look at the

environments we grow up in and the lifestyle that's forced upon us...we grow up

poor...the education we receive in school doesn't spark any interest in us as

black people because all this civilization of devils acknowledge is so-called

smart and intelligent white people...it's many intelligent black people but these

white devils don't tell or teach us about our greatness as black people...that's

why a lot of blacks drop out of school because this system strives to make us feel

like the academic world of intelligence and scholarship is not for blacks and we

only qualified to be entertainers, athletes, thugs, and whores...and what do we as

black people do? We still act like slaves who believe whatever they white masters

tell them and we turn to the streets...just look at the mentality of our people...in

our environment most of the people who doing good either hustling, robbing, or

committing some type of crime to get ahead...the few people who are doing the

right thing in life and got an education either struggling to pay bills or they sell

outs."

Two young boys then spun the corner and approached Prince while he built with Zulu. One of the young boys was the young God-Child who fussed and cussed at Lil Flip and Crumbs when they served his mother some drugs. Zulu would never forget the powerful young boy and he would never forget Zulu, let alone any drug dealer who served the white man's poison in the black community.

"Peace to the Young Gods." Prince greeted the young gods, "What's the science with yall. I want yall to meet my 85% (mentally blind, deaf, and dumb) brother Zulu." Prince threw his arm around Zulu then told Zulu, "This the young god *Mathematical Intelligence* and *Powerful Knowledge*."

"Oh shit...it makes sense why this little nigga don't like drug dealers...Prince and these Gods brainwashing these little niggas...wow." Zulu then extended his hand for a handshake, "What's good yall."

Mathematical Intelligence went to shake Zulu's hand but Powerful Knowledge stopped him and spit at Zulu's hand with that glare in his eye that spoke forces of destruction to all drug dealers.

"You little muthafucka," Zulu jerked his hand away just in time but wanted to smack Powerful Knowledge like an angry dad smack his disrespectful son.

"I hate you you drug dealer," Powerful Knowledge screamed at Zulu. "He sell death and he be with them savages Prince."

"Calm down Young God," Prince jumped in between and snatched Powerful Knowledge and led him away before he returned to Zulu.

"Yo what the fuck yall teaching these little niggas," Zulu seriously asked Prince. "What the fuck is that evil little nigga problem...I thought the Gods was about Peace."

"What you think his problem is Zulu? There will never be Peace if we stay divided as a people. And there will never be peace as long as we carrying out the plan of genocide against our own people. This government of devils target the black community with drugs, liquor, and guns to destroy us...they don't have to have the Ku Klux Klan terrorize and murder us anymore because we do it for them...and as long as we do this to ourselves the government gone stay on top and we gone stay at the bottom...we kill each other and then the white man come and lock us up...if you knew history you would know that white people didn't get convicted for killing and lynching black people...we destroying each other for them and we don't even realize it...See we want peace Black man, but how can we have peace with the image of destruction we showing the black child who naturally pure in heart... every time we sell drugs to their parents we hurting that child by contributing to the destruction of that black child's parent."

"I ain't sell that little nigga mother shit."

"It don't even matter Zulu...this whole drug epidemic is just creating a cycle of hate and destruction that's why we can't have peace...if our people had knowledge of who the True and Living God is we would overcome this destruction. I'm talking about the Creator of the Universe who is the spirit of Man...it's in 1 Corinthians Chapter 6 verses 19-20...and it clearly states that the holy spirit of God is in us...why you think these white scientist and chemists made these drugs and guns which is destroying our people. It's because they know that as long as we on drugs we will never have peace and be able to live happily...and that's another reason they got us blind to the knowledge of our true self which is God because once we know that God is our true self we will stop killing each other...when we kill each other we killing God...we killing our self...we destroying ourselves with everything...we must utilize the power of our will to stop violence...stop using drugs and liquor...that's how we will have happiness and stop this cycle of destruction that plague us my brother."

"Well I aint gone lie Prince," Zulu got hyped, "I'm not gone stop selling drugs until I get rich...so you can try saving Black people with yo knowledge of self...just don't save everybody because I need people to buy these drugs you feel me."

"That's some ignorant shit and that's fucked up Zulu," Prince thundered at Zulu's ignorance. "Yall boys just be safe and I wish yall could squash that war."

"That shit beyond squashing Prince."

"Damn...I know how it is Zulu, just take care, I love you bro," Prince embraced Zulu and held him tightly like a true brother with concern before they departed, "Be safe out here and please travel in harmony...be safe Zulu and send the crew my love."

"Don't worry bra...my eyes open and I'm on point ready for whatever." Zulu stated before him and Prince went their separate ways.

Prince slowly walked off watching Zulu speed off like he was a soldier headed to war. Prince then zoned out feeling his heart melt as he reminisced on him and his friends 'life. Who besides the Creator of the Universe knew their destiny? Prince felt the indwelling wisdom of his soul stroke his mind with visions of him and the others and their childhood. As innocent children happily playing in the sandbox, they never knew the life of destruction they were headed for.

Prince was happy to have knowledge of self, but he felt sad thinking how his friends were deep in the game of destruction and knew no other way of life. If only he had the power to open their minds to clearly see the destruction they thought was happiness.

When Zulu met up with the crew, Sun-Z was verbally blasting Mel-Cash and Dolla. They were at war but Mel-Cash and Dolla was riding thru the city and stopping banks at dice games and drinking Cristal like they didn't have serious business to attend to.

"Listen all this drinking, partying and gambling yall doing over with," Sun-Z barked while standing firm like a focused general amongst the crew as they stood in front of the barbershop. "Yall know what time it is and we hitting the west side to set up shop and get busy…what the fuck is yall doing…yall gotta be on point," Sun-Z barked with a tone of rage in his voice while punching his hand.

"Come on Sun why you stressing?" Mel-Cash sipped his Cristal. "I live for this shit whenever…wherever…and no matter how I'm feeling…I been taking them 12th street faggots to war all this time by myself so you know they aint ready for the whole squad…come on and loosen up Sun."

"Hell yeah you big face Lion," Dolla jokingly added stuck in a chair while sipping his Cristal and feeling like the winning King he was. Dolla and Mel-Cash just came from a big dice game on Adams street and Dolla and Mel-Cash stopped a seventy thousand-dollar bank. Dolla would no longer be known as a degenerate gambler. He stopped the bank of the Adams Street Crew who was known to have a big bankroll. Dolla would now be known as a heavy bank stopper. "I done won so much lucci I can pay them killers from Box street to handle this beef with them oyes…we can sit right here in the hood doing us while the beef get handled because we King Status and too big to be on the streets getting our hands dirty."

"Fuck that," Killa rambled leaning against the building on point with his war face on, "I put my own work in and I will never pay a nigga to handle anything for me...yo fat ass getting too much money and getting lazy."

"Exactly," Zulu agreed. "Yall niggas need to get off yall high horse and get on point like Sun-Z said...with Old School Al still missing we don't know how these niggas playing."

"Man relax them 12th street niggas is pussy." Mel-Cash blurted bopping his head to *50 Cent's Power of the Dollar.*

"And Old School Al ass probably hiding somewhere," Dolla added joking like always. "He probably locked in a room somewhere smoking his brains out."

"Yall niggas think it's a game," Sun-Z shot a probing gaze at Dolla and Mel-Cash whose focus just wasn't there. "And whether Old School hiding or missing this shit getting handled now...we hitting these streets hard...the party over and we gone hit these niggas...I'm not stopping until that 12th street block don't exist...word is bond."

With that Sun-Z laid the law. He sent Cream and Hawk on a mission to make sure Lil Flip and Crumbs was strapped up with guns and loaded with drugs to handle all the business in the hood. Sun-Z then had Zulu drive Dolla and Mel-Cash to a spot where they would stash the gambling winnings while Sun-Z and Killa journeyed to a spot where an arsenal of weapons was stashed. Everyone would meet up later on the west side where they would strategize the hits they were about to unleash on Megalito and 12th Street.

With the top down and the mesmerizing flow of 2 Pac flowing thru the acoustic sound system, Zulu gripped the wheel to Dolla's sporty GT Carrera and blew it to his destination with Dolla and Mel-Cash riding along. With an illegal firearm on his hip and over seventy thousand dollars of illegally obtained money in the trunk of the Carrera, Zulu flew through the streets like he wasn't concerned with getting pulled over by police who would love to confiscate the bag of money which had no legal source, not to mention a gun charge they would love to stick on Zulu if they were honest police officers.

Everyone's mind was racing like the Carrera as it flew thru the cool breezing night wind. They all thought of Old School Al's disappearance and how real it was about to get. Their minds were hypnotized by the words of 2 Pac as 2 Pac spoke of the Thug Life they all related to. 2 Pac put them all in a zone and it seemed like he was rapping to them as he rapped about dead homies, prison, and the Thug Life.

"Yo this shit jive crazy with Old School Al," Zulu lowered the music.

"Old School Al a grown ass man who don't need niggas to shed tears Zulu," Dolla threw in the air not truly giving a damn about Old School Al missing. "And in this life we live as Thugs Zulu, some of us gone die…I hope Old School aint dead though…because he is a cool dude with his hustling crackhead ass…I hope he alive and somewhere smoking…because that would be fucked up to get bodied by niggas and he wasn't even a gun-clapper."

"Yo Dolla chill and stop hating on my homie," Mel-Cash interjected, "Old School Al my nigga no matter what fat boy…watch yo mouth."

"Yeah ok…go and get high with him since he yo man so much." Dolla joked.

"Zulu turn Pac up because I don't wanna hear this dickhead Dolla."

Zulu turned the music up quoting the words of Pac to the song *Heavy in the Game.*

"Yo I lived damn near my whole life as a gangster," Mel-Cash shouted sitting on top of the backseat with the bottle of Cristal in his hand. "This the only life I ever known and I love it…I aint got no regrets."

"Yeah this Thug-Life treated ya boy real good," Dolla threw in the air. "The Game been good to me like Pac said…Thug Life till I die."

"The life of a G is the only way a nigga can really make it happen without being under these crackers ya heard."

"Nigga it's all about that Thug Life you hear Pac," Dolla shot back.

"I fucks with my boy Pac but I was a gangster before Pac started rapping…I grew up to *Kool G. Rap and Scarface* my nigga and we grew up as gangsters…yall on that 2 Pac Thug Life shit."

"Yo would yall niggas shut the fuck up," Zulu interjected, "Thug…Gangster…it's all the same…it's like *The Lox* said, *"We are the streets,"* simple as that."

"No question," Mel-Cash guzzled some Cristal before passing the bottle up front to Dolla. "I love the fucking streets…I seen it all and done it all in these streets…word life."

"No doubt," Zulu threw the music back on blast and whipped the wheel though the east side heading to the Summer-Best train station area. Zulu blew it across Main Street passing the Utica street train station where a Niagara Frontier Transit Cop *(NFTA)* sat outside the train station in his cop cruiser. Luckily the cop was busy checking his computer because Zulu was pushing the odometer pass 80 mph. Zulu blew it down Utica Street before swerving south onto Delaware Avenue where he cruised down to Summer Street. He slowly rolled down Summer Street with its Gregorian style homes and Imperial brick buildings where the wealthy called home. He whipped the wheel onto Mariner Street and parked on side of a huge modern style tenement building at the corner. Most of the businesses on the strip were closing except for the coffee shop where a few patrons sat inside sipping cappuccinos and reading magazines. The night was quiet and the area was relaxed as a couple strolled the strip with their small Shitzu dog. Three young women who were probably college students or nurses took a late-night jog down the strip. And besides the buzzing motor of the delivery guy on a Mopad zipping through the block, the sounds of 2 Pac shattered the silence of the serene atmosphere of this middle to high class neighborhood where medical professionals, wealthy college students, and retired professionals lived in these highly expensive apartments and homes of the Summer-Best area.

Zulu lowered the music a little for the respect of the high-class neighbors as he parked on side of the building near the corner. Dolla was stimulated by the energy of 2 Pac more than the champagne he drunk and Zulu was disturbing the groove.

"Yo don't turn this nigga Pac down," Dolla raised the volume higher. "Do you hear this nigga…listen to this dude yo," Dolla eyed Zulu with his hand on the volume as he played the track back *"If I Die Tonight."*

"…They say pussy and paper is poetry power and pistols

> Plottin on murdering muthafuckers fore they get you
> Picturing pitiful punk niggaz copping pleas
> Puffing weed as I position myself to clock G's…"
> 2 Pac- If I die tonight.

"This nigga talking to us yo," Dolla was hyped and enthralled by the late great 2 Pac as he fell back in his seat rapping along with Pac.

"Well let Pac keep rapping we gotta put this bread up," Zulu yelled over the music while peering at the flashing headlights of a car making a turn at the corner ahead. Zulu studied the few cars rolling through the block making sure it wasn't police before jumping out the car and standing on the sidewalk, scoping the surroundings and standing on guard.

"Zulu you might as well run the money up baby boy," Mel-Cash scooted himself back on top of the back seat before dipping his hand into his pocket and whipping out a set of keys. "You already out the car, go handle that Sun." Mel-Cash shook the keys in front of Zulu's face.

"How you volunteering me to run upstairs," Zulu eased back refusing the keys. "Hell no I aint running up to no 5th floor, the elevator was broke last time yall sent me on that dummy mission…hell knaw."

"Don't look at me…you know my fat ass aint running nowhere," Dolla yelled over the music leaning forward in his seat to guzzle his champagne. He swallowed damn near the whole bottle in one gulp then hurled it against the brick wall of the print shop across the street. *"Thug Life till I die,"* Dolla belched real loud.

"Come on Zulu run it up," Mel-Cash insisted still shaking the keys in Zulu's face. "If the elevator still broke you can take a stack out the bag…my blessings to you baby boy…and yo Dolla," Mel-Cash glanced at the shattered glass on the clean sidewalk across the street. "This a nice neighborhood yo…keep that Thug Life ruckus back on the east side…here you go Zulu."

"What the fuck yo," Zulu snatched the keys watching Dolla hit the trunk button for Zulu to snatch the bag of money. "I'm taking two stacks fuck yall niggas," Zulu lifted the trunk and snatched the bag before slamming it shut and heading to the double doors of the building.

"Stop whining baby boy," Mel-Cash swung from on top of the back seat, jumped onto the street and skated over to Zulu who was heading up the steps and about to open the doors to the building. "Stop stressing about shit…we good in life and living better than a lot of cats out here can imagine…we aint got nothing to worry about…I love you baby boy and I wanna see you smiling because it could be rougher you feel me," Mel-Cash rubbed Zulu's wave cut like a big brother than roughly embraced Zulu. "Nigga we bout to hit these streets like navy seals and take these oyes to war…we gone find my boy Old School Al and then we gone go back to living like kings you feel me."

"Go sit yo drunk ass down," Zulu held the door open and stood there as Dolla lowered the music to say something.

"It's nothing but Thug Love for you Zulu," Dolla yelled from the passenger seat. "Thug love my G…for all my G's, even that dickhead Old School Al."

"Yall niggas drunk as fuck and yall need to go upstairs to rest up," Zulu shouted back at Dolla as he brushed Mel-Cash away before sliding into the building. Zulu stepped inside and headed through the clean lobby where a lesbian couple stepped out of the working elevator.

"Perfect," Zulu sprinted to the elevator before the doors closed. Maintenance was on their job in this high rent building Zulu thought to himself riding the elevator up to the 5th floor. He just hoped the rumbling elevator didn't break down while he was in it. The elevator reached the 5th floor landing and a boom erupted down the elevator shaft from its abrupt halt.

"What the fuck?" Zulu jumped out the elevator thinking it would probably be safer to take the stairs back down. The elevator doors closed and Zulu could hear the ancient box car rattling down the shaft as it went to its destination. "I would be the monkey to go on the dummy mission for these fools." Zulu told himself strolling down the hallway to apartment 8 E. He unlocked the deadbolt locks and stepped inside the well-furnished bachelor pad/stash spot. The air was cool breezing in from the halfway opened windows and the blasting music of 2 Pac could be heard and felt outside the window, echoing off the buildings outside as Zulu hit the bedroom and dipped to the closet.

"Fuck." Zulu realized he didn't have the code to the safe sitting in the closet. He then whipped out his phone to call Mel-Cash but Mel-Cash's phone went straight to voicemail. Zulu then hit Dolla's jack. Dolla was so hypnotized by 2 Pac and had the music so loud he couldn't even hear his phone ringing. Zulu then stashed the bag of money in the back of the closet behind a stack of sneaker boxers and a suitcase. Zulu stepped out the closet glancing back at the closet like a thief would. The bag of money had to go in the safe because the closet would be the first place someone would look since it was boxes of sneakers stacked up like a shoe store.

"I'm gone take three stacks since I gotta run back down there to get the code to the safe and run back up here…hell yeah." Zulu was heated. "I'm gone make these niggas never ask me to do anything for them again watch." Zulu blasted skating through the apartment and heading to the door. He stepped into the hallway and while closing the door he heard screeching car tires and car horns blowing outside.

"Let me find out these niggas rushing me," Zulu thought to himself stepping down the hallway towards the elevator wondering should he chance another ride. He tapped the elevator button and the door immediately opened. Zulu stepped into the elevator and took the rumbling ride down to the lobby praying he travelled in Peace. He made it to the lobby as expected and rushed outside ready to chew Mel-Cash and Dolla up for not reminding him about the code to the safe.

Zulu stepped outside into the sounds of 2 Pac while smelling burnt rubber and fireworks. Dolla was laid back in the passenger seat in his euphoric state of mind up in Thug Heaven like he was possessed by the Holy Ghost of 2 Pac's Thug Gospel. It was like 2 Pac was a Thug Prophet/Poet who took the minds of Thugs to Thug Paradise. When thugs listened to 2 Pac it was a nostalgic trance they would find themselves in just like Dolla who gazed up at the stars while reclined back in his seat with the gangster lean.

"Yo fat boy I forgot the fucking code yo," Zulu stood at the driver door and leaned into the car to turn the volume down. "And yo where the fuck Mel-

Cash go?" Zulu asked scanning the environment expecting to peep Mel-Cash spin from behind one of the buildings where he was probably relieving his bladder of all the Crystal he drunk. Dolla was in a zone and unresponsive to Zulu, Dolla was feeling it and in his moment of Thug Paradise.

"Yo Dolla," Zulu shouted now opening the car door and dropping into the driver seat, "Yo what the fuck is this Dolla?" Zulu lowered himself into the driver seat hoping he didn't sit in throw up when he stuck his hand in the gushy liquid on the arm console. Zulu hadn't closed the door yet when he looked down then over at Dolla.

Dolla's face was fixated with a deep concentration that was timeless. His gaze was deep and his eyes peered into infinity. Zulu quickly jumped out of the car while snatching the gun from off his hip while scanning the environment one more time before running around to Dolla's side of the car and opening the car door.

"*Yo what the fuck*!!!" Zulu felt like his soul jumped out of his body when he noticed the blood splattered on the front seat interior on the passenger side. Zulu couldn't believe it. A hole the size of a quarter was pierced above Dolla's right eye and blood drizzled down his face. The back of Dolla's head was busted open where blood poured and drained down his neck, back, and the car seat. It was a bloody mess and Zulu didn't notice it because it was too dark outside, but it was Dolla's blood Zulu had stuck his hand in when he sat in the car.

"*What the fuck?*" Zulu stumbled backwards into the middle of the street feeling little objects crackling under his feet. He looked down and it was Mel-Cash's cell phone shattered. He then glanced around the street noticing skid marks and Mel-Cash's Platinum chain glistening on the ground and broken in pieces like it was snatched off his neck. "*Noooo.*" Zulu yelled feeling fear and anger colliding in his system realizing what just had happened.

While Zulu was upstairs someone split Dolla's melon open and snatched Mel-Cash. This was ugly. This was a blast to Zulu's soul with the force of an atomic bomb so strong Zulu felt his legs buckling as he stood in the street eyeing Dolla. Dolla was just alive moments ago talking to Zulu and soaking up the Thug

Wisdom of 2 Pac, and just like that, someone murdered Dolla and left him slumped in the posture Zulu last seen Dolla alive in. And how could Mel-Cash get snatched like that? Who the hell in the world had the power to abduct Mel-Cash and snatch him up like they were supernatural Aliens? How could the God of the Hood get snatched up? How?

Zulu's life force shook his soul and woke him up to get on point before he was next. This was real and the war was blazing before the Get Rich Crime Family even busted a shot. Zulu took one more soul crushing look at his childhood friend/brother before he broke out running like a scared soldier trapped behind enemy lines.

The next day

The glass stem was brand new and the chore boy was shiny and fresh. The chore boy was stuffed in the stem and pushed down to the bottom end of the pipe by the tip of a bent-up hanger. A boulder of peanut butter colored rock was shoved in the stem on top of the chore boy. The stem was placed on the man's lips and the flames of the lighter scorched the tan rock. A sizzling sound was heard as his breath of life inhaled the demon of death the crack flooded his soul with. The intoxicating high of the crack smoke activated the endorphins and pleasure cells in the man's brain. It felt like he was in heaven as he closed his eyes and ventured into the all-white realm of light. He relaxed in this realm of crack heaven for what seemed like eternity. The tension and pain eating his soul was erased and his mind was lifted out of this cruel world where it was death and destruction. It was really hell on earth. But thanks to whoever invented crack because he felt like he was in heaven for the couple minutes the crack high lasted.

"*Oh no oh my God,*" Lulu, who sat by Old School Al's side on the sofa placed her hand over her mouth as she zoomed into the news flash on the T.V. "Poppi poppi look," Lulu tapped Old School Al out of his crack heaven. "Nooo poppi," tears began swelling in Lulu's glossy red eyes.

Old School Al opened his eyes to witness a young brunette news reporter on the T.V. standing on the corner of Mariner and Allen Street. Dolla's sparkling money green GT Carrera was the center of the crime scene bordered off with yellow tape.

The news reporter spoke of the violent incident detailing how a witness who was closing their business on the corner witnessed a dark colored van pull up on the corner on side of the sports car. Three masked gunmen jumped out of the van and one of the gunmen shot the passenger of the sports car in the face. The passenger was identified as 25year old Latrell Billups (Dolla). The other two gun men engaged in a brief scuffle and fight with another man who was standing outside the car. They then shot the courageous fighting man before shoving him into the van and fleeing the scene.

The news woman then turned over the news cast to another news reporter who was at a different location. The African-American male news reporter was standing on a set of train tracks near an overpass by an expressway. He stood a few feet from a burned up and scorched van believed to be the vehicle driven by the gunmen who shot and killed Latrell Billups and abducted the man he was with. After speaking on the suspected relation of the two incidents, the black news reporter revealed the grim news of how a man they believed to be 32year old Shamel Phelps was the corpse found burned up inside the van, which was discovered by a homeless man early this morning.

"Poppi what did they do?" Lulu unbelievingly asked while sobbing in tears. She had no clue what Megalito had her convincing Old School Al to do.

"What the fuck Lulu." Old School Al responded in a rage as he jumped off the couch. "Bitch you the one who told me to do what they asked…what the fuck you thought was gonna happen…that's why I didn't wanna do it…you thought they was just gonna talk."

"But they killed them poppi…they killed them…they killed Dolla too."

"Bitch stop this you convinced me to get my people killed just so I could be with you," Old School Al snatched the pipe from off the table and began stuffing it with boulders of crack, "We gotta think now aint no time for crying," Old School Al flame torched his pipe and fell back onto the couch sitting next to the weeping Lulu.

Lulu really thought there was going to be a truce. The slick and sly Megalito had Lulu under the impression that the Get Rich Crime Family were the ones avoiding the truce. Megalito had Lulu believing that he was only pressuring Old School Al to get them to meet up so they could form a truce.

"Listen Lulu," a tear slowly trailed down Old School Al's face while he regretfully massaged Lulu's back. Lulu mournfully lay her head on his shoulder while Old School Al stated, "Megalito owe me some bricks…but I'm just gone tell him to give me some money so we can go to Puerto Rico with yo family because it's not gone be safe over here…Sun-Z and them about to bring the Devil over here on this west side…a lot of people gone die and we not safe."

A few hours later

> *"Can I live…hell yeah but you still gone die…come on nigga you a thug but I'm still gone cry…and you done learned off experience I'm still gone ride…they kill me you gone kill them? I still got pride."*

Can I Live by The L.O.X

Killa gripped the wheel heading to the west side with Sun-Z riding shotgun and Zulu sprawled out in the backseat letting the avenging rhymes of The L.O.X melt into his vengeful soul. Dolla's bullet pierced face was plastered on Zulu's brain surrounded by pools of blood. It was the blood of revenge and Zulu could still feel the blood he stuck his hand in. As the LOX spit rhymes of retaliation, it was like Zulu heard Dolla and Mel Cash's voice on the track.

"Yo where we at?" Zulu sprung up in the backseat peering out the window at the unfamiliar surroundings on the west side.

"We bout 10 minutes from 12th street bro," Killa calmly remarked with his mind on murder. The whole ride no one said a word but the fiery emotion of murder could be felt in the air inside the car.

"Yo Killa step on it we gotta murk these niggas a.s.a.p," Zulu gripped the 40 Caliber he held tightly, *"I keep seeing Dolla face and it's like he keep telling me to put that work in…and then Mel-Cash…yo…I just keep seeing him telling me it's gone be good baby boy…handle yo business…it's like they not gone stop fucking with me until these niggas is dead."*

"Relax Zulu," Sun-Z quietly replied still unable to believe it happened. "You was the last one seeing them alive so yo mind just keep replaying the memories of they last breath, it's all in yo mind Zulu."

"Damn…I still can't believe two of the realest and sharpest dudes I knew got caught slipping like that." Killa remarked.

"It was my fucking fault," Guilt began to eat at Zulu's conscience. "I left em naked and didn't leave em my strap…if I would've left em my strap they still be here."

"Shit real like that Zulu," Killa responded, "You can't blame yo self…we all gotta die somehow and some way."

"Word we at war and war definitely gone bring death…it's just we supposed to be the death dealers," Sun-Z stated. "Just hit that Bodega on 12th and Maryland where they be pumping that boogie at…push it let's get there."

It was still light outside and the evening sun was slowly being swallowed by the western horizon when Killa swerved onto Maryland Street and pulled over. He parked on side of a tenement building a few blocks away from 12th street where they peered down the block and observed the corner. Killa then pulled pass the tenement building since there was a tribe of Africans sitting outside in front of the building. Instead of the older and nosey Africans keeping their red eyes on the children playing on the sidewalk, they shot a disconcerting gaze upon the three men in the vehicle pulled over in front of their building.

Killa slowly pulled pass the building and parked in front of a three-story house next to the building. With their eyes zooming a few blocks down, the trio observed all the activity on the block which was good and bad. Good because members of 12th street was on the block pumping like they didn't just murder two members of the Get Rich Crime Family. And what was even better was that throughout all the activity on the block, all the people pacing up and down the block and sitting on porches were engaged in their own activities. With all the people outside was kind of bad because someone would more than likely identify if not one but all the shooters who were about to blow the block up with gunfire. It was no time to worry about witnesses, they had meat to butcher and no one was gonna stop it or delay it.

"Check it right," Sun-Z knew how to strategize and manipulate any situation to get the best and desired result. "Killa, me and you gone walk down there but on different sides of the street…aint nobody gone pay attention to us. Zulu you jump behind the wheel and spin the block, meet us down there."

"Fuck that I wanna go put work in."

"Nigga jump behind the fucking wheel and meet us down there…you too emotional as it is," Sun-Z barked back, "You gone meet us down there because we can't come back this way once we hit these niggas up…that way all the people on this side of the block can't get a good look at us while we down there…they not gone know who or what put that work in."

"Man whatever."

"Zulu get on point," Killa stated cocking his pistol before jumping out the wheel, "Lets go big bro," Killa yanked his black on black fitted cap over his head before creeping down the block.

"Alright we see you in less than a minute Zulu," Sun-Z nodded while concealing the mini AR-15 in his spring wear Nautica jacket. Sun-Z then threw on his shades and pulled his baseball cap down real low and jumped out the wheel.

With Killa on one side of the street and Sun-Z on the other side, they both strolled down the block like everyone else who had a destination or who were just outside lingering on the block. Dope feigns and crackheads, some on bikes and others speed walking burnt the block heading to the Bodega on 12th street to cop their poisonous paradise. After scoring their vices of pleasure, some vanished and others raced into the backyards of the tall Victorian houses on the block to indulge in their pleasure.

Killa and Sun-Z were several houses from the bodega and they had a crystal-clear view of the three individuals posted up at the bodega pumping. One man served feigns in the doorway of the bodega while another man stood by the ice box in front of the store swinging his head in all directions like the exorcist playing lookout. The third man posted up on a two-tone blue, white, and red Toyota Camry with gold rims on it parked in front of the bodega. Dangling out of his mouth was a Newport and he spit Spanish jargon into the cellphone he held to his ear.

Sun-Z was creeping on the bodega side of the street. He glanced across the street at Killa who was slowly walking behind two young baby mamas with tornado swinging hips pushing their baby strollers. Sun-Z and Killa caught eyes with each other and nodded as they neared the corner bodega.

The lookout observed Killa behind the two baby mamas and paid him no mind, but when the lookout peeped Sun-Z swiftly moving towards the bodega, he knew something wasn't right. It was 75 degrees outside and here it is this big incredible Hulk looking Moreno (Black) was wearing a jacket with his hands in his pocket. Oh yeah, they knew the Get Rich Crime Family was coming, but they didn't expect them to come like this in broad daylight. Sun-Z was like a dead man walking the way he zoomed at a steady pace towards the bodega. The lookout could feel the danger coming with Sun-Z so he quickly muttered a few words without moving his lips. The hustler in the doorway stuck his head out the doorway and peeked Sun-Z's way. The man on the phone removed the phone from his ear in mid-sentence knowing what time it was but it was too late.

"Runnnn," the man on the phone yelled sprinting from the car towards the store doorway as Sun-Z unzipped his jacket and pulled out the AR-15. Sun-Z was about two houses away when he opened fire and blitzed the corner at full speed on his feet. The hustler in the store doorway spun around to run in the store but bumped into an older lady stepping out the store with a cart. He forcefully shoved her out of his way as he rushed forward and knocked the older lady down. He then tripped over her hearing the shots ring out behind him. The lookout and the man who was on the cell phone both hit the cluttered doorway where the hustler and older lady were on the floor scrambling. The lookout went to jump over the hustler who was pulling himself up from off the older lady. The lookout collided into the hustler's back and they both fell back onto the older lady who was now screaming with terrifying fear as the piercing gun blast rocked the store doorway.

"*Move move move,*" The man who dropped his cell phone shouted trampling over the bodies in the doorway as Sun-Z ran up on the store blasting in the doorway. Killa sprinted from across the street adding more fire into the doorway as the three men trampled over each other in the doorway. A fusillade of slugs pummeled into the backs of the lookout and the last man to hit the doorway. The hustler who was first in the store shifted his weight and crawled forward. He reached his feet and took off sprinting thru the bodega knocking cans and bottles of soda pop on the floor before he disappeared in the back.

"*Muthafuckas,*" Sun-Z and Killa hit the store doorway spitting slugs into the backs of the two men who crawled on their hands and feet into the store. The two men painfully scrambled into a can good aisle when Sun-Z was jumping over the older lady and stepping foot inside the bodega. Sun-Z was determined to make sure they would die and Killa followed suit.

With bullets in his back, one man felt the life-giving strength to rise to his feet and limp down the aisle into the back of the store but Sun-Z was at the foot of the aisle and let loose. The slugs ripped into the man's back and knocked him into the shelf. The other man jumped to his feet and shoved his friend to the side to get pass but the shower of bullets rained on them both and sent them both falling into the shelf and on the floor.

Killa and Sun-Z then ran down the aisle where cans were scattered everywhere squirting vegetables like the blood leaking bodies of the two men who groaned with agonizing pain while muttering their last breaths in Spanish.

"Y'all fucked with the wrong ones you fucks," Killa and Sun-Z let the slugs do the rest of the talking before they dashed out the store peeping a man behind the counter at the cash register covering his head. They jumped over the older lady who was still lying in the doorway shaking uncontrollably.

"Sorry miss," Sun-Z shouted jumping over the lady before him and Killa hit the street where Zulu was waiting out front.

"We got em," Killa jumped in the front seat as Sun-Z hopped in the backseat.

"One of em got away but--," Sun-Z was closing the backdoor when Zulu cut him off.

"Watch out," Zulu shouted aiming his pistol at a man on side of the store ready to open fire on the car.

"*Boom boom blam blam*," Zulu and the man busted off shots simultaneously. Sun-Z dived over in the backseat for cover as bullets shattered the back window. Zulu shot back while stepping on the gas and speeding down the block with the back door open. Killa then leaned out the passenger window and busted a few shots back at the man on the corner firing at the car.

"What the fuck," Zulu zig zagged the wheel dodging slugs before enough distance came between them and the shooter.

"Everybody good," Sun-Z jumped up brushing glass off himself.

"Yeah yeah yeah."

"It's on and every last one of these niggas gone die."

CHAPTER 18

"Matilda Guzman. 62 years of age. She was a loving mother of 9 children. Grandmother of 21 Grandchildren, and Great Grandmother of 12 great grandchildren. Matilda was loved and would be missed by hundreds of people in her community. From Buffalo to Puerto Rico Matty had the heart of an angel and would be missed by all."

Those were the written words for Mrs. Guzman's memorial. Poor Mrs. Guzman returned to the essence (died) from the result of a heart attack during the deadly shooting which took place at Ernesto's Bodega on 12th and Maryland streets a few days ago. Even though Mrs. Guzman wasn't harmed by a single bullet, it was the fear and shock of the gun blasts along with being shoved to the floor and trampled on which caused the rupturing of her heart which led to her fatal heart attack. May the Creator bless her lovely soul.

This was it and the city's African-American mayor, the Police Commissioner, and the F.B.I held a press conference advising the citizens and warning the thugs and drug dealers on the streets that they were gonna pay at all costs. When law abiding citizens were at risk losing their lives while walking to and from the store because of merciless Thugs, that meant law enforcement had to unleash its full resources of manpower to take down the thugs and drug dealers making society a hell.

Black Bull and Gonzalez were summoned downtown to police headquarters to attend the briefing after the press conference. They entered the briefing room where dozens of uniformed officers and plain clothes detectives were seated at several long tables row after row. At the head of the room where the brass in charge stood there was a board with dozens of photos divided into two groups.

On the left side of the board were pictures of high ranking members of the 12th street Mob. There were photos of the locations of the properties and businesses they owned, the locations of their drug spots and blocks, along with photos of the high-end vehicles they were known to drive. On the right side of the board were pictures of the Get Rich Crime Family and the intel on them respectively.

All officers and detectives in attendance were each giving a memo and files on all targets of the investigation. They were also giving each targets rap sheet so the officers and detectives could be aware on how to investigate the targets who were known to be armed and dangerous. The officers assigned to this investigation would be known as the *Wild wild west task force* since the west side of the city was the center of the war. According to intel of confidential informants on the streets and those in jail, the authorities knew the two drug crews were warring over the drug turfs on the lower west side. The authorities also knew that Mel-Cash, who was one of the biggest drug dealers on the west side brought the violent east side gang over to the west side to help him take over 12th streets territory.

The authorities were well aware of the past shootings between the two crews but the authorities assumed they had put a cease to the war with the heavy police presence on the lower west side. Now with the double homicides on 12th street within 24 hours of Mel-Cash and Dolla's murder, the authorities now realized that this was a war with the scope and magnitude that would require the full force of Law Enforcement's power.

The officers and detectives were ordered to heavily patrol the areas of the lower west side to ensure the citizens of the area that they were safe, but not to make any meritless arrest that would alert the targets they were under investigation. The key to this investigation was to keep heavy police presence on patrol in the war zone to deter shootings and killings, but mainly to pin-point the key drug suppliers of both drug organizations.

The meeting was over, but the investigation just started. Black Bull and Gonzalez left the meeting with only one thing on their mind; how to keep their appetites and pockets fully fed by the streets. Every good show comes to an end, but there's always another show to keep the party going, and Black Bull and Gonzalez wondered who would be running the next show because they were going to enjoy whose ever show it was regardless to whom or what. If only they knew the show a veteran detective name Jakowicz, whom everyone called Jake was about to enjoy. Detective Jake was a veteran detective whose character was astounding and honorary since the beginning of his career. In the late 60's and early 70's when it seemed like Buffalo's police force was owned by the Italian mob, detective Jake was one of the few who stood firm in fulfilling his duty to society and putting his code of police ethics first, not the money he could've made in the streets being a corrupt cop.

When Black Bull and Gonazalez were leaving the briefing at headquarters, detective Jake sat in his unmarked police car reviewing the files, and by fate he happened to peep Black Bull and Gonzalez toss some of the intel from the briefing into a trashcan. He waited until they left the parking lot before he hit the trashcan to inspect what was trash to them.

"Dirty and corrupt cocksuckers," Detective Jake ranted snatching the files of the Get Rich Crime Family from the trash. He always knew Black Bull and Gonzalez were in bed with the drug dealers from the east side. There were several police officers filling their pockets with rolls of drug money but who had the proof to prove it let alone investigate it. The actions Detective Jake just observed was more than enough to arouse his suspicions and confirm the rumors about the immoral and corrupt acts of Black Bull and Gonzalez. Once detective Jake's suspicions were proven accurate, he would report to Internal Affairs and see to it that Black Bull, Gonzalez, and any other corrupt law enforcement official would go down with the criminals who were under investigation.

Black Bull and Gonzalez left headquarters and shot over to the east side to meet up with Cream and Hawk. They met up at the *Buffalo Central Train station* which was now an Abandoned and colossal train terminal which attracted *Discovery Channel's Ghost Hunters*. Besides adventurous youth and criminals, no one ventured in or around the so-called haunted train terminal.

They met up behind the train terminal on the tracks out of the view of traffic swinging through the circle out on Memorial Drive at the front of the train station. Black Bull and Gonzalez informed Cream and Hawk on the investigation and about the intel the authorities had on them. For a hefty pay, Black Bull and Gonzalez handed Cream and Hawk the intel they had on Megalito and the 12th street Mob.

"Listen…with this info we're giving you guys, you should be able to end this war quickly because if you don't end it quickly, the feds is gonna end it and all you guys are gonna be in deep shit," Gonzalez informed observing Cream and Hawk looking over the files.

"Yeah and just so you know the brass is being pressured by the F.B.I and the ATF to put a stop to this or they're gonna come in and take this investigation over, and we definitely don't want them assholes taking over the investigation because we all would be going down," Black Bull added.

The letters F.B.I and ATF aroused a fear in Cream and Hawk that made them shoot a probing glare at each like they better hurry up and end the war before the authorities ended them. It was real. It was real as the deaths of Dolla and Mel-Cash, and it was just as real as Detective Jake who sat parked on Paderiski Street snapping pictures of the meeting between the two drug dealers and two corrupt cops behind the terminal.

With the photos of Cream and Hawk receiving the files from Black Bull and Gonzalez, along with the money the corrupt cops received in exchanged was enough to throw Black Bull and Gonzalez into the investigation as targets. Black Bull and Gonzalez' greed would not only consume them, but their greed would dig a deep hole that would swallow everyone down into the belly of the greedy beast.

·························

Old School Al felt his walls closing in. He found himself falling down the glass of the crack pipe scorching his guilt-ridden soul in the flames that torched his crack pipe. He smoked day and night not knowing what to do but get high since that was his only escape from the harsh reality of the nightmare he was living. He wanted to escape to Puerto Rico with Lulu, but Megalito basically deaded Old School Al on the chips he promised to return to Old School Al for giving up Mel-Cash. It was manipulation to the 10th power. Instead of giving Old School Al the bricks or money he was promised, Megalito had Kato piecing Old School Al off with ounces of crack just so he could rock the bells. Old School Al was the sweetest chump Megalito ever got rewards from. Old School Al was sweet as sex and the joy Megalito came off with was plentiful. Megalito came off with a bankroll and a victory over the God of the Hood. Despite the havoc the Get Rich Crime Family was wrecking around the lower west side, Megalito came off good thanks to the sweet sucka Old School Al. Old School Al felt like a coward and he knew he was. There was no justification for the treachery he pulled. It was death before dishonor and he chose to live with dishonor. Dolla and Mel-Cash was gone forever and would never resurface physically. This was a soul crushing reality Old School Al had to live in misery with forever.

To make matters worse, Megalito didn't hold up his end of the deal. Even though Old School Al felt like a coward, he still wanted what was rightfully his, but Megalito was giving him scraps. Old School Al wished he only had one ounce of courage in him to destroy Megalito like the Get Rich Crime Family was trying to do.

Black Bull and Gonzalez came thru in a clutch for the Get Rich Crime Family with the valuable information they had in regard to members from 12th street. They now not only knew the locations of several businesses owned by 12th street, but they had a few addresses to the places of residence for members of 12th street as well.

The Get Rich Crime Family spent long days and nights operating like undercover agents laying on locations ready to strike members of 12th street at the residences they thought they were safe at. Of all the properties they had their eyes on, Megalito wasn't seen in or around any of them. There were three properties where they observed three members of 12th street leaving every morning around 8 in their luxurious vehicles and returning home around 9 in the evening. Their houses were tucked away in nice residential neighborhoods so the three members weren't expecting to be caught slipping at home.

Good homework produced outstanding rewards. Zulu, Sun-Z, and Killa each layed in the cut of the backyards to each house early in the morning and caught each member of 12th street by surprise with a hail of gunfire. One member survived after being slugged six times at close range and he kept it true like a soldier and told authorities he couldn't get a good look at his shooter because they caught him as he was entering his car. Everyone knew who was responsible and Megalito became furious.

Old School Al was still looking forward to receiving his bread from Megalito, but Megalito was enraged and couldn't believe Old School Al still had his hand out after the Get Rich Crime Family was knocking off 12th street left to right. Old School Al was more stupid than the ostrich who seen a hungry lion approaching then stuck his head inside a hole and thought the lion couldn't see him. Megalito had something for Old School Al alright.

Megalito told Kato his plans of forcefully pulling more info out of Old School Al so 12th street could finish off the Get Rich Crime Family. Kato wanted nothing else to do with this. This wasn't Kato's lane at all. Kato was a hustler and that was it. He wasn't even from the lower west which was the wild wild west. Kato had a good thing going on the upper west side and he refused to let Megalito disturb his peace any more than he already did. Kato already felt bad for introducing Old School Al to Megalito which caused much bloodshed. And now Megalito wanted Kato to deliver Old School Al on a plate so he could put the fear of the devil into Old School Al for info and then kill him. No way. Lulu and the rest of their family would never forgive Kato, let alone Kato wouldn't be able to forgive himself.

Kato did the only thing that would keep his conscience clean and free from resentment. He gave Old School Al a nice grip of money and told him to run because Megalito was gonna kill him. Old School Al happily took the money, but the scheming crack demon influenced Old School Al with other plans instead of running.

Old School Al could redeem himself once more and not only make things right within his wretched soul, but he could go back home to the foundation. He had to run back to the shelter of the Get Rich Crime Family once again. With the devilment of his soul, he would have to lie about his disappearance. If that worked, then Old School Al could craft a way to lead the Get Rich Crime Family to Megalito which would keep his standing with the crew strong being that he was responsible for Dolla and Mel-Cash's murder. If his plan worked and Megalito was eliminated, Old School Al could bounce back and get his life in order once again. This was devilish deception at its best all powered by ill intentions.

....

The west side of town is where the damages of war was being felt, but the notorious and violent east side had its own killing fields that claimed lives and injured people on a daily. It was always murder beef on the east side, and in E. North, the energy of beef was felt throughout the whole hood. The everyday people went about their lives and social business as usual outside in the streets. Young boys played sports on the streets while young girls spectated and played their own games. Older people lounged in the heat of the sun wishing they were somewhere not as depressing as the east side of Buffalo.

But on the corners where the young hustlers pumped narcotics, and on the basketball courts where the dice games were jumping, and on almost every side street where illegal activity thrived, individuals ice grilled strangers and unfamiliar faces with a mixed vibe of vengeance and paranoia. Even though the deadly trio of Sun-Z, Zulu, and Killa was over on the west side raining a firestorm on the 12th Street Mob, the thugs and hustlers in E. North was strapped up and ready for whatever while trapping in the hood.

Hawk and Cream centralized the flow in E. North to a few blocks around Planet Rock. Planet Rock was headquarters and provided the best defense while business was conducted. Hovering high above the houses on Planet Rock and forming a canopy on the block were tall sycamore trees that not only provided shade for the hustlers posted on the block, but up in the trees clutching automatic weapons were shooters watching the block below. Since back in the day shooters were known to hide up in the trees on the lookout for stick up kids or whoever was trying to interrupt the money flow on the block. With the crazy Puerto Ricans pulling up in vans and body snatching people, Cream and Hawk made sure there were eyes and trigger fingers all around.

When Old School Al rolled up into E. North he felt all eyes suspiciously eyeing his shiny Jaguar with the tinted windows. When he cruised the side streets, he fearfully mashed on his gas pedal observing Thugs posted up on curbs sticking their hands in their pants gripping steel.

"These dudes ready to blast anything coming thru here," Old School Al thought to himself rolling onto Planet Rock where he spotted Lil Flip and

Crumbs posted up on a Green Eddie Bauer truck. He rolled his window down and yelled out, "It's me yall don't shoot," Old School Al then swerved over to the curb and jumped out.

"What the fuck?" Lil Flip and Crumbs had a look of confusion on their face. They thought they were talking to the walking dead.

Old School Al walked up observing their puzzled expression. "It's me here in the flesh."

"Yooo...let us clap yo ass to make sure you real," Crumbs spit jokingly.

"Where the fuck you been at yo?" Lil Flip surprisingly asked scoping Old School Al before him and Crumbs went back to letting their eyes scan the environment where cars banging potholes cruised down the one-way street.

"Man I been," Old School Al sighed with a deceptive headshake. "I-I-was locked up."

"Woooord...where you was at in the county?"

"Um..yeah yeah."

"Where you was downtown or out in Alden?"

"I was I was um...downtown."

"Word...so you was in that east side vs. west side war...we heard that shit crazy downtown and niggas from the east beefing with niggas from the west because our war out here." Lil Flip and Crumbs looked amazed and wanted to hear some war stories from jail because the streets were hearing a bunch of rumors on how the war in the streets made it to the county jail. "So what cell block you was on."

"Yeah yeah I was on um B block." Old School Al felt this conversation going somewhere he had no vehicle to go. He had to change the subject quick. "But yo they saying shit crazy out here with yall...niggas getting killed left and right...where everybody at."

"You already know," Crumbs responded stepping out of the street onto the curb as a car came strolling thru the block. The sound of squeaky brakes sent Lil Flip and Crumbs reaching on their hips when the car slowed down in front of them. The car was a Chevy Malibu with tinted windows that slowly rolled down. Lil Flip and Crumbs had swiftly eased behind the Eddie Bauer truck gripping their pistols when the car completely stopped on side of the truck.

"Come on gangsters keep yall guns tucked," a man shouted from the driver seat of the Malibu. "This my baby moms wheel my shit in the shop…but yo I need an onion (ounce) of hard (Crack)."

"We got you but don't be creeping thru like that nigga, you get splashed coming thru like that," Lil Flip shouted from the sidewalk before looking up at the shooter in the tree. Lil Flip motioned it was all good then slid over to the Malibu and shook the hustler's hand while Crumbs ran up into a backyard to grab the ounce of crack. Lil Flip then took the money from the hustler and spun from the car before Crumbs sprinted from the yard looking up and down the block. Crumbs ran to the Malibu and tossed the driver his ounce and told him to be safe.

"Damn yall took it back to the A-Squad days ready for war while getting money," Old School Al stated standing on the sidewalk by the truck.

"Yeah we had to switch everything up…Sun-Z made us step up."

"Well that's why I'm here I gotta get back on my feet…I need to get up with them boys a.s.a.p…where they at?"

"Naaa," Lil Flip sounded like Old School Al's request was impossible. "That's not gone happen Old School…but whatever you need we gone hit you…the big boys doing other things and can't nobody see them…we handling everything out here…whatever you want we got it."

"Na I need to holla at them about some other shit…this shit deeper than that homeboys."

"Listen just give us yo number Old School and we gone hit you back from a payphone whenever we get with the peoples." Crumbs let it be known grabbing a pen and paper from the glove compartment of the truck.

"And yo…what you was locked up for Old School?" Lil Flip asked looking into Old School Al's miserable looking eyes.

"Oh some domestic shit with Lulu," Old School Al quickly responded scribbling his number down. "Yeah I had to whip Lulu ass."

"Yeah ok we gone have the peoples get with you…they definitely gone get with you a.s.a.p because niggas thought them oyes offed you bro…word."

"Na na homeboys I'm still here in the physical," Old School Al felt his heart flutter and he kind of wished Megalito killed him. Old School Al then gave Lil Flip and Crumbs a pound and a hug before sorrowfully stepping to his car and peeling out.

After handling some more business and smoking a blunt, Lil Flip snatched the walkie talkie from off his hip and hit Cream and Hawk.

"Talk to me what's good?" Cream responded to Lil Flip's radio signal.

"Yo we just had a visitor from the dead."

"What," Cream asked hearing a little fuzzy static and music in the background.

"Turn the music down yo," Lil Flip motioned to Crumbs. "You hear me now Cream?"

"Yeah what's good?"

"You won't believe who just left the block."

"Yo aint nobody got time for guessing and no time for surprises just come with it."

"Yo," Lil Flip and Crumbs peeped a raggedy car bumping its tires down the pothole filled street. "Hold on one second big bro," Lil Flip told Cream as him and Crumbs got on point as the car approached.

"Nephews," an older man wearing an auto mechanic uniform yelled from the passenger seat of the raggedy Oldsmobile. "I need two grams of that fire."

"Got you Unc go pull over," Crumbs then whistled and a baby face teenager jumped off a porch across the street and sprinted to the car. He served the man his two grams of fire then dashed back onto the porch and sat in the cut.

"Okay now you hear me bro," Lil Flip spoke into the radio once the man pulled off.

"Yeah," Cream responded.

"Old School Al alive and he just left the block.

There was silence and Cream didn't respond. Cream handed the walkie talkie to Hawk because he thought his ears was playing tricks on him.

"Yo what the hell yall just say?" Hawk asked holding the walkie talkie up so him and Cream could both hear the response.

"Old School Al alive and he just left the block."

"We be right there."

....

With the bomb shell Black Bull and Gonzalez dropped on the Get Rich Crime Family about the investigation, and now Old School Al popping up from out the wood work yapping about he was locked up, the crew had to contact Leonetti to see if he could dig up any skeletons Old School Al was hiding since he claimed to have been locked up. Leonetti being a lawyer, a savvy lawyer at that, could find out many dark secrets when it came to any legal matter and issue. With pressure from the law because of the war and Old School Al's accusation of being locked up meant one or the other to the crew.

The crew felt that if Old School Al was locked up he had to have been questioned by the Police about the crew, and if so what did he tell the people. No matter what the situation the crew wouldn't let Old School Al step foot in their circumference until they found out the truth of this so-called dead man's whereabouts for the past few weeks.

With the advancement of technology for the legal world in the new millennium, the access to court information and records were readily accessible to attorneys. Leonetti was able to access criminal records at Buffalo city court to inquire about any arrest Old School Al had over the past few months. To Leonetti's surprise, there were no arrest records for Old School Al throughout the whole Buffalo-Niagara Falls metropolitan area. Leonetti even accessed the Federal Public Access Court Electronic Records (Pacer) to see if Old School Al had a fed case. There was nothing.

The crew wondered why was Old School Al lying? Did he get arrested and become a confidential informant and the authorities sealed his arrest records. Everyone became frightened and wrecked their brains like they were figuring out a Chinese arithmetic equation. Old School Al told a bold face lie about being locked up. And lying on the level he was lying on was devilment; an untrustworthy act the weak and wicked used to their advantage to cause confusion. The crew wondered what his angle. Or was he truly scared and just hiding?

Considering the tragedy and the odds against the Get Rich Crime Family, they really didn't have much to lose. And since they had no other ways of finding out Old School Al's reason for lying, there was only one way left and that was the G-Style way. Gangsters don't run from their problems. Gangsters run barrel first ready to blaze when it's a problem that can't be solved the intelligent way.

Old School Al was contacted from a payphone and told to meet up with the crew at a traditional bar and grill called Raphael's Kitchen. Raphael's Kitchen was located in the heart of the cosmopolitan Allentown section of the city. Raphael, who was the owner of the bar, was a loyal middleweight hustler who purchased ounces of coco from the crew. And being that the crew suspected Old School Al might be leading the feds to them, this location was perfect. The narrow streets and congested traffic made it easy for the crew to observe law enforcement. Upstairs from Raphael's kitchen Raphael had a plush studio apartment that overlooked the strip on Allen Street below. Peeking thru the drapes of the huge bay window offered the view of the many cars cruising the strip and others rolling in and out of the parking lots between the storefront tenements hugging the block.

Old School Al rolled the wheels of his Jaguar onto Allen Street eyeing the different bars and luncheons before reaching Raphael's Kitchen. His immaculate ride blended radiantly with the assortment of foreign vehicles driven by society's affluent Allentown patrons. He peeped a parking spot on the narrow strip where he cautiously pulled his ride between two vehicles. He parked in front of a boutique sitting next to an antique artifact shop a few doors down from Raphael's kitchen.

With the afternoon lunch hour flow of patrons and residents strolling the strip and swarming in and out of the cafes and diners, it was hard for Old School Al to peep Zulu, Cream, and Killa each lounging in different diners on the block peeping for any law enforcement agents that might be trailing Old School Al.

Old School Al stepped into Raphael's and spotted Hawk sitting at the end of the bar away from the boisterous construction workers who were gobbling their sandwiches and downing beers before their lunch break was up. Hawk sat with an upright posture with his eyes glued to a college football game on the T.V. above the bar. His hands were folded on the bar near a plate holding a corned beef on rye sandwich surrounded by sliced pickles and ruffles potato chips. The sandwich was healthy looking and screaming to be eating because Hawk hadn't taking one bite of the sandwich. Hawk's appetite was thrown off by the situation with Old School Al and Hawk sat frozen letting the game watch him as he thought of the past, present, and future.

"Bartender can I have a Becks?" Old School Al slid up on Hawk and dropped onto the stool next to Hawk. "Homeboy what's--."

"*Shhh.*" Hawk waved his index finger for Old School Al to be quiet while letting his stone eyes study Old School Al's face. Hawk could tell from the few seconds of looking at Old School Al's face that he was back rocking the bells. His jaws were sunk in like Skeletor and he had the zombie bags pulling on his eyes from living the vampire life of being up late night geeking.

Hawk now glued his eyes on the front and back doors of the bar watching those who came thru the doors. For the past hour Hawk observed the usual workers from downtown in business attire and construction workers rush in the bar to grab lunch before they stormed back out to work. From what Hawk's intuition and experience told him, there had been no authoritative looking, clean crew cut wearing, all powerful trying to be cool with a hip demeanor undercover agents posing as common place people in the bar. Professionals came in all forms and fashions and there were no absolutes. One could never be sure and certain and one thing Hawk was sure and certain of, was the fact that Old School Al was back rocking the bells with his jittery movements twisting around on the bar stool.

After the bartender served Old School Al his Beck's, Hawk gestured for Old School Al to sit tight while he slid to the bathroom. Once inside, Hawk radioed everyone on their walkie talkie and inquired how was the scene looking on the strip.

"It look like normal people out here."

"Yo it's a bunch of office workers looking at me like I'm out of place."

"Yo I'm surrounded by a bunch of dikes in this restaurant, it's no fucking cops here I need to get away from these bull dagger looking broads," were the responses Hawk got from Zulu, Cream, and Killa.

"Alright come on up to the spot and make sure yall not followed…Old School Al not right and I can feel it," Hawk shot back before placing the radio back on his hip and leaving the bathroom. He stepped to Old School Al, tapped him on the shoulder and motioned for him to follow. They walked to the rear of the restaurant and hit the back-exit door which led to a small hallway. There were two doors in the hallway. One led outside to the back-parking lot and the other door had three intercoms and three mailboxes for the apartments upstairs.

Hawk stepped into the hallway first and held the door open for Old School Al to step in. Old School Al stepped inside and stood on the landing while Hawk shut the hallway door. Old School Al didn't know if they were going outside or through the other door which led upstairs. He began to ease down the steps towards the exit and that's when Hawk snatched him by the neck and slammed him against the wall. Hawk gripped one hand around Old School Al's neck while he pulled out a 45 automatic and shoved it in Old School Al's face.

"*Shhh*." Hawk whispered removing his hand from Old School Al's neck then searching his upper body for a wire.

"Homeboy I would—I would—n-n-never," Old School Al nervously pleaded while Hawk finished patting him down. Hawk remained silent shooting a look of mistrust at his childhood homeboy. Zulu, Cream, and Killa then slid into the hallway through the back door. The trio stepped into the hallway just as Hawk pulled the gun from out of Old School Al's face. They all peeped the fear of the Devil on Old School Al's exhausted looking face as Hawk nodded an unsure look at the trio before he hit the 3rd floor intercom and pulled out a set of keys.

"Yo." Sun-Z chimed through the intercom.

"We coming up Sun." Hawk responded into the intercom keying the door then shoving it open. They shoved Old School Al inside and made him walk up first. Old School Al climbed up the stairs on legs shaking like rubber bands. He wondered did they know of his treachery and how he deserved a thousand bullets to the face. He wondered would he come out of this building alive or was he walking to his death. He took a deep breath believing there was a chance they didn't know of his betrayal. Maybe they believed he was locked up and just thought he was an informant since Hawk searched him for a wire. Old School Al didn't know what to think. If they wanted to kill him they sure wouldn't have met him here he figured. Or would they? Old School Al could feel each breath entering his terrified soul as they walked him upstairs.

They reached the third-floor hallway and stepped across the threshold of the open door to the spacious studio apartment. Raphael was an American born Italian who loved America, but his patriotic passion for his native Italian art spoke highly like the vivid life depicting oil paintings hanging on the wall of the apartment. Hand sculpted statutes of Roman Gods sat frozen in time on top of a long bookcase peering into the center of the apartment where a u-shaped sofa sat with a huge Plasma T.V. at the outer center. Sun-Z sat motionless on the center sofa looking like a Buddha focused on enlightenment as he watched a *BBC special on the Great African Warrior-King Shaka Zulu.*

"Ay yo," Sun-Z calmly spoke keeping his eyes fixed on the T.V. without moving a muscle as everyone stepped into the apartment. "*They say King Shaka could call one hundred thousand warriors into battle with the snap of a finger. They said the Zulu Kingdom was extremely rich and they controlled a major part of the Ivory and metal trade which extended all the way to India and China. Yo they found Elephants and Ivory in China which proves Africans and Chinese were trading with each other for thousands of years. The Zulu Kingdom was rich and powerful and if you equated the value of the ivory and metal they produced it was equivalent to billions in todays money,*" Sun-Z was enthralled at the strength and wealth of the great Zulu Nation and the joy of Black Pride gleamed on the tight muscles on Sun-Z's angular face.

"Damn." Everyone blurted gluing their eyes to the T.V.

"But see this what people don't know because the Europeans don't want people to know." Sun-Z rose to his feet and placed his piercing gaze upon Old School Al. "They portray Shaka Zulu as some bloodthirsty and power hungry king who was murdering all those who wasn't loyal to the Zulu Nation... na...that's white man lies...King Shaka was striving to protect the Zulu Kingdom and wealth of the Zulu Nation from the Europeans who were slowly moving on Zulu territory...first the Arabs took over the trade ports on the rich coast of East Africa, and then the European Portuguese, Dutch, and British began taking over South Africa and were approaching Zulu territory...so Shaka being the Powerful King he was began to unite everyone so they could form a powerful force to stop the Whiteman from taking their wealth and land...it was either you with us or you with the white devils...straight like that...King Shaka was no tyrant or wicked ruler...he was a Real G...King Shaka was as real as they come...and what made the Zulu nation so powerful was the loyalty...straight loyalty...and because the Zulu nation was so dedicated and loyal to the unity of the Zulu nation, they defeated the British when no one else could defeat the British...it was loyalty of the Zulu's which gave them the strength to defeat the British, Loyalty...Loyalty." Sun-Z emphasized the word loyalty as he methodically stepped to Old School Al who sat on a kitchen stool next to Hawk. "Loyalty is the force that keep everything in order...it's disloyalty that bring disorder and that's worthy of death...disloyalty is the reason for all the chaos," Sun-Z's steady gaze upon Old School Al was so intense Old School Al felt like he was under a microscope.

All eyes were now focused on Old School Al as Sun-Z moved in on him. Old School Al felt like a tornado was fast approaching as Sun-Z slowly approached him. Old School Al tried letting his eyes connect with Sun-Z's but Sun-Z's eyes pierced Old School Al with such a powerful energy. Sun-Z had a stare which peered deep into Old School Al's weak and wretched soul. Sun-Z's eyes were like those of a timeless statue of a *Black Pharaoh*. The guilty conscience of Old School Al didn't have the power of truth to look at the light shining in Sun-Z's eyes as he stood face to face with Old School Al.

"Now I'm gone ask you this one time," Sun-Z spoke calmly but with authority while folding his muscular arms across his bulky chest. He stood above Old School Al who was still seated on the stool unable to raise his eyes to Sun-Z's head level. "And don't lie…it's no reason for you to lie any further…we aint got time for lies…we in a middle of a war and we done lost our brothers…this not a time for lies…we need each man to stand strong…we don't need weak links who can break us apart…so tell me…tell us where the fuck you been because you wasn't locked up…why the fuck did you lie about being locked up…where the fuck was you at?"

Old School Al let his nostrils suck in so much of the tensed air he exhaled enough hot air to push a hot air balloon up into the sky. Old School Al sure wished he had a hot air balloon to jump in and fly away as he nervously looked up at Sun-Z with sad puppy dog eyes and said, "C-c-can I ha-have a-a shot first…please?"

"What da fuck!!" everyone shot a can't be serious look at each other before following Old School Al's eyes to the mini-bar on the other side of the room by the stereo system.

"Get him a drink Killa. As a matter of fact grab the whole bottle of Tanqueray…I'm gone need a shot too," Hawk told Killa since Killa was closest to the mini-bar. Killa snatched the bottle and a few shot glasses and slid back over to the kitchen counter and let Hawk pour shots for everyone. A libation toast was saluted for Dolla and Mel-Cash, the shots were downed then everyone huddled around Old School Al waiting for his answer to his whereabouts. The room was so silent they probably heard Old School Al's fluttering heart thumping.

"I-I fucked up yall." Old School Al spun around on the stool, poured another shot and downed it. He now felt his spirit get a boost with a stroke of confidence as the liquor kicked in. He inhaled deeply then said, "Man, they…they…I started back rocking the bells because they man…they--."

"This nigga an informant I knew it," Killa snatched his pistol from off his hip and aimed it at Old School Al.

"Chill chill we can't kill him here," Cream held Killa back while Sun-Z and Hawk was now in Old School Al's face questioning him about who was they. Zulu was just waiting patiently standing beside Sun-Z.

"Who the fuck is they Old School?" Hawk yelled into his ear.

"They kidnapped me and made me--."

"Whoa whoa whoa," Sun-Z raised his hands in confusion then motioned for everyone to calm down and give Old School Al some space so he could breath and feel more comfortable. "Who the fuck kidnapped you bro?"

Old School Al closed his eyes wishing he was somewhere else. He then dropped his head and shook it shamefully. The devilment of lying made him feel so guilty his soul seemed to leave his body and he felt lifeless. But somehow and someway, he felt the need to tell the truth. No more trick-knowledge because it would get him killed at this present moment.

"12th Street kidnapped me."

"Muthafuckaaaaa," Zulu, Killa, and Cream shoved Sun-Z out of the way and swarmed Old School Al swiftly as Hawk threw Old School Al in the chokehold. Killa then grabbed Hawk's pistol which was on the counter and began bashing Old School Al in the head before Sun-Z stopped him and took the gun.

"Fuck that we gotta kill this nigga," Hawk yelled as Sun-Z pulled him off Old School Al and shoved him to the side. "Why the fuck they let you go?" Hawk yelled as Sun-Z now pulled Zulu and the others off Old School Al who was on the floor between the stools curled up.

"Yo stop," Sun-Z pushed everyone away then snatched Old School Al from off the floor. He raised him to his feet then sat him on the stool. Sun-Z then shot a convincing look at everyone that said breathe easy. The air was so hot and tense in the room you could fry an egg from the steam. Sun-Z made sure the temperature was cool before he politely asked Old School Al why did 12th street let him go.

"Yeah why the fuck they let you go nigga but they killed Dolla and Mel-Cash?" Hawk was uncompromising and wasn't being levelheaded like Sun-Z. Hawk bit his lip pacing the floor holding back the fury inside like everyone else.

"They snatched me when I went to re-up with Lulu cousin Kato…and they held me until Kato gave them my bread," The trick-knowledge found a way to manifest itself through Old School Al's trembling soul. "If it wasn't for Kato they would've deaded me."

Everyone knew Old School Al wasn't right and this was bullshit. For the lives lost during this war, no amount of money was worth nor could bring back the people loss on both sides. *There was no way Old School Al was in the hands of the enemy and they let him go. No way. Money was never equal to revenge. It was only blood for blood and eye for an eye.*

So with the wisdom of intuition and past experience of street war, they knew Old School Al had to be sleeping with the enemy. The crew was several steps ahead. Old School Al should have known better than to try fooling the crew with his deception. Sun-Z knew how to play the art of seductive deception way better than Old School Al.

Sun-Z snatched Zulu, Killa, and Cream and had them search the area to see if Old School Al brought 12th street to them. The way the death angels were wreaking havoc on the 12th street Mob, Sun-Z could see Megalito releasing Old School Al without killing him only if he led 12th street to the Get Rich Crime Family. Old School Al couldn't be trusted any longer and he would soon return to the essence of life once he was utilized for the only thing he was now worth. Old School Al's fate was sealed and the only thing he was needed for was to lead the Get Rich Crime Family to Kato who would lead them to Megalito.

....

The summer was coming to an end and local community organizations came together to host a youth summit to encourage teenagers to attend school when it started in a few weeks. The summit's goal was also to motivate the youth to strive to make their lives better by avoiding the streets and the other pitfalls of life. Hundreds of teenagers, community members, and politicians filled the seats of the Buffalo-Niagara Convention Center as key speakers addressed the numerous issues plaguing the Black and Hispanic communities. From gang violence, lack of education, teen pregnancy, Drug abuse to peer pressure key speakers spoke on the social ills affecting the community.

Many high-ranking community leaders were begging Prince to speak to the youth at the summit but Prince was reluctant since the summit was drawing a lot of media attention. Prince was no longer in the streets, but his close ties with the Get Rich Crime Family could be used against him by the power structure. It didn't help the situation being that Prince was once a member of the Get Rich Crime Family.

Despite Prince's fear of drawing attention to himself, no one else was better qualified to paint the picture of the grim street reality but Prince who really lived the street life. Since Prince's enlightenment to the knowledge of self, he was honored and respected by many in the community being that he raised himself up from ignorance and darkness and now walked in the light of righteousness.

Prince thought deep on it when the summit kicked off with speakers going up on stage talking to the youth. Prince knew he had a duty to civilize the youth who were living the lives of savages. Prince also knew that with the media attention the Get Rich Crime Family was stirring up with the war, his name could ring bells with law enforcement and he could easily be associated with his friends if he got up on stage and dropped the bomb of truth about this wicked society which worked hard to destroy Black People.

Prince sat backstage with other key speakers waiting their turns to go on stage and speak. He sat in deep thought in his own universe hearing his conscience speak, *"You know what the prescribed law is Prince. You can't be scared of these devils who run the power structure...so what if they try digging up yo past...they do that to all the Righteous people...you only striving to teach the youth and prevent them from ending up like Dolla and Mel-Cash...it's yo duty to teach the youth about being civilized...how to be righteous...teach them knowledge of self...the science of everything in life so they can have true love, peace, and happiness...you gotta teach them about culture-refinement and how to live like civilized people and not thugs...if you don't wanna save the wicked from their wicked ways then you might as well die in the streets like yo friends...you will die in yo own iniquity...you might as well go back to being a savage and let another brother or sister do it who ready, willing, and able to save these babies. It's either do or die."*

Prince had no choice. This was his calling and this was his universal duty. He had the knowledge and wisdom to share with the misguided youth and for Prince not to share his divine wisdom would only make him like those of the Power structure who blood sucked the poor by teaching and keeping the poor illiterate so the poor would stay in poverty.

Prince hit the stage ready. He stepped on stage gazing into the faces of the many youths in attendance. Some looked innocent. Others looked as if their youthfulness was slowly slipping away from playing the street life. Prince took a deep breath hoping that what he was about to say could at least touch one youth and save their life.

"I come to you with the universal greeting of Peace...because without love there could never be peace...and I know many of you young brothers don't wanna be here tonight...but I'm one to tell you, you rather be here learning something positive than to be out in the streets right now committing a crime that will get you locked up...you rather be here than to be in a small, dirty, old jail cell...and believe me when I tell you, you rather be here than in the streets risking yo life where dudes is getting killed and shot every day.

"It's real out there...I know because I was once a Thug out there...I spent years in several juvenile centers all over New York...I did 18 months in the county jail for using a firearm...don't get it twisted thinking I didn't live that life...I'm only 24yrs old and I can't even count or remember how many friends I lost because I lost so many...I just lost--," Prince felt his emotions flare up with pain and a tear formed in one of his eyes thinking of the last time he seen Dolla and Mel-Cash a few weeks ago. He would never see them again and it was painful. He had to let these youths know the streets were death row and Prince didn't care who wanted to associate him with the Get Rich Crime Family. He had to deliver the truth.

"Two of my best friends were just murdered recently and I still have friends who are losing their lives out there in them streets...that's not how yall wanna live...you don't wanna live yo life not being able to go anywhere unless you got a gun on you...or every time you see the police you live in fear, worrying

will you go to prison...that's a stressful life...see when we young we don't know no better and we think the fast money, flashy cars, sexy women, and street fame is what's up and that's all life about...all that come with a price and it cost yo life...you only get Prison or death in exchange for that," Prince felt the Supreme Power and Force of the Creator flowing through his body as he paced the stage with a rhythmic and melodic flow.

"See my young brothers...it's nothing wrong with a life of luxury and the physical comfort and happiness life bring when you a civilized person living righteously...but can't we all see that it's wrong for us to risk our lives and jeopardize our freedom for material wealth...our lives is worth more than material wealth and if we take advantage of the mental and spiritual powers the Creator gave us we can get all the riches and happiness that life has to offer...just look at the people of society who not in the street life...I'm talking about the doctors, lawyers, entrepreneurs, architects, bankers, scientists, and many other high standing members of society who use their intelligence to live lavishly...I'm not saying they righteous, but those people not risking their lives in the streets and they living with great wealth...they got the big houses and nice cars...you young brothers can have that too instead of death and prison...You don't have to sell drugs, use drugs, rob and kill each other to have nice things...if you get knowledge of self, go to school and utilize the supreme intelligence of your minds you will master the knowledge and skilled trades that will allow you to create a job for yourself or get a good paying job that will provide you with the rewards of happiness and material wealth...We gotta stop destroying our brains with the drugs, liquor, intoxicants, and negative thinking because that's what's leading us astray and killing us as well...the brain is the storehouse of creative power and supreme intelligence...and when we keep our minds pure and live right we develop the ability to manifest that creative genius within us...I want yall to know that we living in the devil's civilization so this society is designed to destroy and keep us from being the great builders that we are...this is why there is so much negativity around us and so many bad things are happening...we must realize that we are Gods—children of the Most High and the Kingdom of Heaven is within us as it states in the Bible...no matter how

wicked this society is we must strive for perfection to be great and do all we can
to avoid them so-called street dreams because in reality they are only
nightmares."

Prince wasn't one for the attention and praise but he was honored by the
Mayor of Buffalo and given awards by the *Stop the Violence Coalition and The*
Mad DAD's organizations for his time and commitment towards helping the
youth. For doing his duty in teaching the youth, Prince felt a Happiness in his
soul which made him feel cleansed of his past wrong doings. His soul felt light
as a feather and it seemed his past burdens were removed from his heart and
soul. For the first-time in life he felt extreme happiness and peace despite the
trauma afflicting his childhood friends.

CHAPTER 19

It's been a long 48 hours of agonizing anxiety nibbling at the nerves of the Get Rich Crime Family as they camped out at Old School Al's house. Ever since they met up with Old School Al the other day at Raphael's Kitchen, they made Old School Al a prisoner and wouldn't let him leave their sight. Old School Al and Lulu were basically prisoners in their own house. Every move they made was monitored; from going in the kitchen to snatch something to drink to using the bathroom they were under the microscope and it would be this way until Lulu's cousin Kato showed up.

Old School Al made it this way with his lying and conniving self. Even though the crew wasn't aware of his betrayal which lead to Dolla and Mel-Cash's murder, they sensed through the third eye Old School Al was rotten. Besides the smell of the crack they gave Old School Al and Lulu to smoke in their bedroom, something foul was reeking from Old School Al's soul.

Kato was on his way back in town and would be headed to Lulu's once he got situated. He figured Lulu and Old School Al had smoked up the work he last given them and they were feigning for more. Kato didn't mind blessing Lulu because since kids she cheffed up Kato's favorite meals. And as far as Old School Al, Kato felt indebted to Old School Al. Kato made a grave mistake introducing Old School Al to Megalito and felt bad for the outcome. *"Blessed are the Peacemakers."* Kato was only attempting to be a peacemaker and do a favor for everyone by putting opposing sides together to make a truce, but as fate would have it, Kato was thrown into the war and didn't even know it. Megalito then added insult to injury when he not only robbed Old School Al for his chips, but Megalito killed those he was supposed to form a truce with. Kato felt Megalito manipulated him from the jump.

Kato was a true hustler who wasn't about the drama and long ago he realized that he should stay away from hungry sharks like Megalito. On the other hand, Megalito and others of his breed seen those like Kato as being soft as momma's love and would manipulate them at any chance. Out of Kato's kindness and sincerity, to show faith to Old School Al that he wasn't like Megalito and didn't have anything to do with Megalito's madness, Kato made it his bond to always bless Old School Al with work.

The time arrived at destiny's calling. Kato rung Lulu and told her to open the door as he pulled onto the street. Kato parked then exited his Lincoln Navigator carrying a bottle of Puerto Rican Rum and a bag of groceries. He stepped through the gate in front of the house then skated up the stairs peeping the front door open. He stepped inside and slammed the door shut not knowing the turn his life was about to take.

"Yo Lulu. Al. Que Pasa." Kato stepped into the dimly lit living room where Old School Al and Lulu sat on the love seat looking like zombies with eyes wide as the 8 balls they were smoking. Kato noticed they were high as a kite as they sat in silence staring at Kato like he was an alien. Kato knew they was out of their mind and now realized why he didn't smell the sweet aroma of his favorite dish. *"Why yall sitting in the dark like this? Yall high as hell?"* Kato stated stepping through the living room and heading to the dining room to turn the lights up.

"Don't move muthafucka." Killa jumped out of the closet in the front hallway by the front door and whacked Kato in the back of the head with the butt of the 9mm he gripped. Kato stumbled forward and painfully grabbed the back of his head.

"Yo what the fuck," Kato yelled in shock. Kato lifted his head and several guns were being aimed at his mug. The stinging sensation of the pain burning in the back of his head and the shock threw his mind in a blur as his mind tried understanding what the hell was going on.

"Sit the fuck down and don't say shit just listen," Sun-Z shoved Kato on the couch across from Old School Al and Lulu who was still sitting on the love seat trembling.

Kato couldn't think straight as fear began clouding his brain circuits. Thoughts of betrayal then struck him and he began thinking that Old School Al and Lulu was setting him up. If this was the case this wasn't major to Kato. Kato been robbed plenty of times and he had the money and drugs to make any stick-up crew feel they came up and didn't have to rob anymore. Only pain that was unbearable to live with was the betrayal of those he always showed love to.

"Come on how could you guys set me up?" Kato peered across the room at Old School Al and Lulu who was so geeked up and so scared they were both shaking. *"Come on bro...you know I give you anything...what do you guys need now...this un-called for Pa."* Kato ranted applying pressure to the gash on the back of his head. Kato now scanned the faces of the Get Rich Crime Family since Old School Al and Lulu's mouths were numb from the crack smoke and they couldn't talk. *"I got money poppi I just have to make a call,"* Kato stated reaching into his pocket. Wrong move.

"Bam." Sun-Z punched Kato right in the nose. Kato leaned forward in his seat and began painfully rocking while holding his twisted nose which was split and broken at the bridge beneath his eyes.

"Noooo." Lulu snapped out of her crack high and began pleading as she observed her cousin writhing in pain.

"Come on chill Poppi," Kato curled up while Sun-Z and Hawk roughed him up and searched him. "I'm not holding bro...I was reaching for my phone...I can pay you guys whatever you want." Kato pleaded as Sun-Z took his phone.

"This not about no muthafucking money," With a devilish grin on his face, Sun-Z barked while scrolling through Kato's contacts. "I want this fat muthafucka right now." Sun-Z showed Kato the phone with Megalito's contact on display. "This shit personal and aint got shit to do with money...yall muthafuckas killed my people...I want this nigga now or I make Lulu give up yo whole family and I kill all you muthafuckas," Sun-Z threatened nodding at Killa who aimed his pistol on Lulu's face.

"No no no no Poppi," Kato shouted not believing what he gotten himself into. At first it was Megalito whom he realized he should have never dealt with. But now it was Old School Al as well. How could he get pulled into something he had nothing to do with. Truth be told, Old School Al was responsible just as much as Megalito. There was no way Kato was gonna have blood on his hands. *"Poppi I had nothing to do with your peoples getting killed it*

was Al who told Megalito where your peoples was at."

"Whattt." was all that could be heard as Old School Al froze up saying no while shaking his head.

"You rotten piece of shit how could you set yo--," was all that could be said before Killa let off one shot that splattered Old School Al's cranium. The blood from Old School Al's head splashed Lulu who began screaming before Killa let off another shot putting her to sleep as well.

"Yo what the fuck." No one could believe this as they all studied each other's face. The truth had a harsh way of coming to light, so harsh it was hard to believe. The soul never lies and their souls knew this moment of harsh reality was coming as they all looked at their childhood friend they just murdered. It was devastating, more devastating than the death of Dolla and Mel-Cash who died at the hands of the enemy. Betrayal over loyalty was so sour it made the soul compel the stomach to feel like throwing up. This is what took over the moment inside the living room while they all stood in silence holding their guns and looking at the blood splattered and disfigured heads of Old School Al and Lulu.

"Poppa please don't kill me I had nothing to do with this," In tears, Kato broke the silence. How did it come to this? Never in a lifetime would he fathom this. He not only just witnessed two murders, but it was his female cousin he just seen murdered. Besides getting high, Lulu had nothing to do with the wretched of the streets where murder and betrayal reigned supreme. This was horrible. Guilt was the killer. And guilty by association was responsible for this. Kato's business association with the 12th street Mob got Lulu killed and him surrounded by these heartless killers. Kato did business with Megalito at a distance here and there and that was it. Kato nor Lulu had anything to do with 12th street's *Mi Vida Loca* but they were paying the price for their association with 12th Street. All Kato was about was getting stacks and providing for his family. From the bloody reality of this situation, Kato knew he would never see his family again unless a miracle could save him.

"We want this nigga or yo ass is dead like these muthafuckas right here."

"Ok ok ok I do whatever yall need me to do...just please don't kill me...I never shot nobody or did anything violent just please," Kato fumbled with his phone waiting for Sun-Z's instructions. Kato would do whatever he had to with no resistance to keep living so he could be the super provider for his family and the hood he was feeding.

Megalito had a plushed out bachelor pad nestled on the waterfront overlooking Lake Erie. The three-story condos were high end and there were surveillance cameras eyeing the grounds of the well-kept properties. Bright flood lights lit up the parking lot and the neatly trimmed walkways with their mulberry bushes in front of the buildings. Inside the buildings there was no cameras since a key was needed to enter the building and visitors had to be buzzed in.

Megalito received the urgent call from Kato talking about some major business, Megalito immediately told Kato to swing thru. Megalito was more than happy that Kato called because Megalito needed Kato. Ever since the Get Rich Crime Family was knocking off members of 12th street Megalito couldn't move at all. 12th street and the whole lower west side became a ghost town and Megalito needed Kato to help him knock his work off because Megalito was going to flee to Puerto Rico. Megalito didn't have time to be going to war with the savages from the east side. He killed Mel-Cash and that was a victory for 12th street even though 12th street lost a few. So before Megalito got caught slipping and his demise be a victory for the Get Rich Crime family, he was gonna shoot to Puerto Rico and live like the King he was.

Zulu, Killa, and Sun-Z held Kato at gun-point as they drove over to the waterfront condominiums. They drove pass the front office where an older white man with thick eyeglasses sat behind a desk yawning. He surely wasn't paying attention to all the surveillance monitors as he struggled to keep his eyes open.

With the 357 Magnum in the pocket of his black denim Rocawear jacket, Sun-Z had it aimed at Kato as he walked behind him. Sun-Z let Kato approach the door to Megalito's building by himself where Kato hit the bell and was buzzed in. They both entered the building and Sun-Z spotted a telephone book lying by the door. He stuck it in the door keeping the door open for Zulu and Killa who crept in the building a few seconds later. With their fitted hats pulled real low and hands on their guns inside their jackets, they tip toed up to the third floor with Kato in the lead. Kato led them down the hallway with its earth tone colors before they approached the apartment with its door slightly ajar.

Sun-Z now pulled his gun from out of his jacket pocket and steadied it on the back of Kato's skull above his gash and told Kato to slowly open the door. After pushing the door open Kato hesitantly crossed the threshold and stepped into the apartment. There was an eerie stillness inside the apartment. A dull light in the back corner shone on the cream-colored walls while the beaming light of the full moon cast its glow through the glass ceiling. They all tip-toed into the quiet apartment and crept forward across the sunken living room wondering where was Megalito? It was so quiet and gloomy inside it was perfect for a set-up.

While moving forward they all glanced back at the door expecting to be ambushed before noticing a woman in sexy lingerie with covers halfway on her sleeping on the couch further ahead in the living room. The flushing sounds of a toilet then broke the silence and the woman on the couch turned over in her sleep yawning.

"Kato that's you Poppi?" Megalito was in the bathroom rinsing his hands feeling the soft thumping of footsteps out in the living room.

"Y-y-yeah." Kato responded after Sun-Z nudged him to do so as they quietly slid across the living room floor towards the kitchen.

"Kato I was trying to sleep but I can't…I'm glad you called pa…we got mucho business to discuss," Megalito yelled to Kato as he bounced out the bathroom and stepped through the hallway heading into the kitchen. Megalito stood in the kitchen watching himself dry his hands with a paper towel saying, "You see my young mommi in there? She keeping me young for real." Megalito shouted while tossing the paper towel in the trash can on side of the refrigerator. He turned from the refrigerator and began sliding into the living room with his eyes focused on his young mommi laying on the couch. He slowly stepped into the living room and he felt more than one person to his left. Before he even looked to his left his soul alerted him to danger. When he rolled his eyes from the mommi on the couch and turned to his left, his heart stopped beating like he seen several ghosts coming for him. It sure was ghost coming for him. It was the ghost of death in human bodies he seen standing behind Kato who was several feet from where Megalito stood motionless.

"*Me Jodi Dejesus* (Fuck me Jesus)," Megalito's inner voice uttered as his thoughts travelled 24 billion miles per second thinking about any and everything his mind could flash all at once. This present moment encompassed the past, present, and future of his life. It seemed like time had stopped. Megalito couldn't feel or hear anything but his thoughts as he wondered how the fuck could a King like himself get caught slipping with his pants down. It was simple. Simple as the Kings he caught slipping during his reign of terror. It was just like he caught Mel-Cash and Dolla slipping. Old School Al led Megalito to his enemies, and Kato reversed it and led the Get Rich Crime Family to Megalito. Betrayal was like a vacuum in the streets sucking everyone in. Damn. Megalito even thought about his comrades and how they fell on the battlefield. His mind then made him think of Mel-Cash. He erased Mel-Cash from existence but that fucking She-Male was dead and his homies was like ghosts hunting down everyone from 12th street. For the first time since him and Mel-Cash became enemies, Megalito finally felt Mel-Cash was God of the Hood. And like the saying of Karma goes, Megalito felt his past caught up with him. If this was his time to go, he wasn't going out without a fight. No way. Even if an elephant could fit in a mouse hole it wasn't happening. In this eternal moment of now, Megalito felt an eruption of adrenaline burst within his chest that motivated his 400lb body to spin around and take off running through the kitchen and back down the hallway towards the bathroom and bedrooms.

"*Boom*," ruptured the silence of the apartment when Sun-Z splattered Kato's cranium with a slug from the 357 as soon as Megalito took off running. The mommi sleeping on the couch sprung upward and opened her eyes thinking she was dreaming. When Kato's body dropped and thudded on the floor her senses told her this was real life and not a dream.

"*Ahhhhh*," The mommi screamed as Kato's splattered face gushed blood onto the carpeted floor.

"Shut up bitch," Killa stormed over to her aiming his gun at her and forcing her to shut up while Zulu and Sun-Z sprinted after Megalito.

The floor shook as Megalito stomped thru the carpeted hallway passing the bathroom. Sun-Z and Zulu hit the hallway and each ran into a bedroom instinctively knowing Megalito wouldn't run to the bathroom as an escape. The bedrooms had balconies which the big and crazy Megalito might jump off to save his life.

Zulu kicked the door open to the bedroom right after the bathroom. With his gun leveled in front of him and ready to fire, Zulu searched the room before checking the small closet Megalito couldn't fit in.

The door to the bedroom at the end of the hall was wide open. Sun-Z cautiously approached the room peeping the drapes moving at the balcony's sliding door. Sun-Z crept towards the balcony looking around the room with his gun extended in front of him aimed at the moving drapes.

"Whaaackkk." Megalito moved swiftly like a lightweight Ninja swinging a machete which ripped into Sun-Z's hand which held the gun. The blade sliced between Sun-Z's thumb and index finger cutting deep.

"Arrrgggh." Sun-Z painfully yelled when he finally realized he was slashed by the machete. Megalito came from out of nowhere swinging his machete like he was a Jamaican in a sugar cane field. Sun-Z dropped his gun from the pain and shock but quickly regained his composure and switched into gladiator mode and went to battle. Megalito was trying to hack Sun-Z to pieces the way he fiercely swung at Sun-Z's neck. Sun-Z pivoted out the way of the machete and raised his arm to block the blade from ripping into his shoulder. The machete ripped through his jacket slashing his beefy forearm. Sun-Z then courageously grabbed Megalito's hands and wrestled him for the machete.

"Yo what the fuck going on?" Zulu stormed into the dark bedroom observing the two tussling with the machete raised high in the air. Zulu aimed his gun at Megalito but him and Sun-Z were all over the place and Zulu couldn't get a clear shot.

Killa then flew into the bedroom dragging the mommi by her long hair. He peeped the struggle taking place and threw the mommi on the floor near Zulu. Killa then stood there shaking his head smiling. He waited for Sun-Z to spin

Megalito around in his direction and that's when Killa made his move. He jammed the barrel of his gun into Megalito's back and began squeezing the trigger.

"Blong blong blong blong," the four slugs penetrated Megalito's lower back forcing the King of 12th street to fall into Sun-Z. Sun-Z stumbled backwards then spun out of Megalito's way as Megalito fell face first onto the dresser then crashed to the floor moaning.

"*O-ah-o-o*," Megalito groaned in pain laying face flat and crawling forward.

"Poppi," the mommi jumped off the floor and ran over to Megalito crying. "*Nooooo...nooo*," she screamed holding Megalito's head in her lap.

"Move bitch," Sun-Z tossed the lady off of Megalito and began choking Megalito and ramming his head on the carpeted floor. "You muthafucka."

"Watch out move," Zulu and Killa pushed Sun-Z out of the way and squeezed their triggers filling Megalito's body with more lead. Megalito had one strong soul and the body of a giant because his body jerked with every slug pumped into his body and he tried speaking.

"Nooo." The mommi jumped up screaming again when the shooting stopped. She ran to Killa swinging at him and knocking his hat off. Killa slapped her with the pistol then shoved her onto the floor next to Megalito.

"This muthafucka mines." Sun-Z barked painfully snatching the machete from off the floor. He grabbed the machete feeling his arm and shoulder burning with pain as he gripped the machete then stood over Megalito and grabbed his head.

"Yo what the fuck is you doing yo," Zulu shouted before Sun-Z swung the machete at Megalito's neck. Sun-Z then began whacking and hacking at Megalito's neck like he was trying to chop his head off. Sun-Z lost it and blacked out. "Yo chill bro we gotta get the fuck outta here," Zulu pulled the bloodthirsty and possessed Sun-Z from off Megalito as Killa stood over the lady who was screaming uncontrollably.

"Kill that bitch we out." Sun-Z yelled with vengeance in his eyes.

As Killa gripped the mommi by her long hair, he closed his eyes, placed the gun on her chest and let off one shot. The slug punctured her chest knocking her back onto Megalito's stomach. Killa then broke out the bedroom behind Zulu and Sun-Z while taking one last look at the two dead lovers lying with each other. The three then left the building with their hats low and broke out before the cops arrived.

When the cops arrived minutes later they could not only believe the King of 12th Street was murdered in his plush bachelor pad, it was how he was murdered. According to the coroners, it appeared the killers were trying to behead Megalito but became frustrated from slicing through ligaments then decided to shoot him to death. It was a horrible scene in the King of 12th streets bachelor pad where another high-profile drug dealer was murdered, and a 22yr old young lady was also shot but lucky to survive a gunshot to the chest.

This night in Buffalo became known as *The Night of Terror on the Wild Wild West Side* to the authorities who connected Old School Al and Lulu's death to Megalito and Kato's. The war of the wild wild west was over, but not the authorities' war against the crooked cops and the notorious Get Rich Crime Family.

....

The summer of 2002 had its fruitful rewards of success but the price paid could never compensate for the loss of Dolla and Mel Cash. The treachery of Old School Al devastated everyone to the point of no return. And even though revenge was exacted, the spiritual pain of murder battled the joy of the soul which only brought spiritual suffering.

As fall rolled in and the leaves fell to the earth, Zulu felt like his soul was crumbling like the leaves he would rake up in him and NyJewel's yard. NyJewel noticed the death all in Zulu's eyes. For most part of the summer Zulu stayed away from home since he was handling his business. NyJewel didn't question his time and commitment to his job in the streets, but when the war with 12th street jumped off, she questioned her soul would Zulu make it home since Dolla, Mel-Cash, and others didn't make it home and died in the streets. The war was now over and Zulu made it home which made NyJewel thankful to the Most-High. With winter approaching, NyJewel wanted Zulu to stay home where the heart is. The weather turned cold, and NyJewel had Zulu in the house of her loving where it was warm.

The winter of 2002 was disastrous for the Buffalo metropolitan area. An avalanche of lake effect snow bombarded western New York like it was urban Alaska. Residents were snowed in and made to hibernate inside their homes while mother-nature blew her cold currents of snow with no remorse. The city was shut down and business was put on hold, but where there is a will there is a way.

Drug addicts of all kinds had the will to shovel their way through the 4 feet of snow to hit drug spots where hustlers bared down in front of space heaters while playing PlayStation, smoking blunts, and still serving feigns through windows and holes in the walls of drug spots. *The hustle didn't stop and a Buffalo snowstorm never stopped a Ruff-Buff hustler from getting busy.*

Zulu, who was literally laying on a mattress full of cash, had no need to be out in the cold. He took this time to warm his ice box spirit and cuddle up with NyJewel. If it wasn't lying inside the paradise of her warm sumptuous thighs, just receiving her love and affection was enough to melt his ice-cold soul with a desire to love and see the beauty of life.

NyJewel expressed to Zulu how the goal of happiness in life was enjoying the rewards life blessed one with. What good was it to have riches but to not enjoy them? It was time for Zulu and NyJewel to enjoy the fruits of their labor. Living in a city plagued by drugs, violence, and snowstorms wasn't enjoying life's rewards. It was in the land of paradise where life could truly be enjoyed; the Bahamas. The weather was warm and beautiful all year round with a few rainstorms here and there and possibly a hurricane. The true beauty would be the fact that Zulu would be away from the street life. It was either now or never and Zulu chose now.

NyJewel put the plans of relocating into action immediately. She opened an overseas account where she deposited a bulk of Zulu's illegally earned funds. Without NyJewel, Zulu didn't know what he would do with his life. Zulu was thankful he had her to help him escape the madness and see his dreams become reality. Zulu been through so much hell in life he felt he deserved paradise, and paradise deserved one who would appreciate her blessings

....

Dozens of city snowplow trucks hit the snow-covered streets and began clearing the avenues and streets so the business of the Queen City could resume its operations. The hustlers and drug addicts was loving the city shut down because law enforcement wasn't on the streets and illegal activity thrived. From store break-ins to robberies of drug spots everything went down during the snowstorm. Feigns kept the snow shoveled at drug spots and made sure there was clear paths to come and go. Now the city was back moving and it was just another Buffalo winter where everyone including police was back outside.

The wheels of NyJewel's Range Rover truck crumbled the sparkling snow as her and Zulu drove over to Sun-Z and Iyana's house for dinner and cocktails. NyJewel was in celebration mode and relieved. She accomplished the whole relocation process and now her and Zulu just had to sell their house. So before her and Zulu became official residents of Nassau, Bahamas, NyJewel was spending as much time possible with her bestie Iyana.

Zulu was excited about becoming a resident of the exotic island, but deep inside he knew it would be a struggle to adapt to the island life. Not having the excited thrill of the street life would be boring. No matter the case, Zulu could always bounce back to the states for a little excitement, just like the excitement Zulu and NyJewel were having at Sun-Z and Iyana's.

Over margueritas and cognac, the couples lounged in Sun-Z and Iyana's living room entertaining themselves with their eyes on *Mike Epps stand-up comedy*. The voice of *Mike Epps* blew his soul tickling jokes thru the surround sound system creating a live show feel in the living room. The couples were really having a good time and it was like pain never existed the way Mike Epps had everyone laughing. NyJewel's bladder was so full of margueritas and she laughed so hard she had to race to the bathroom before she unleashed on herself. It was a funny sight to see.

After the laughter of the comedy show, Zulu's blank stare into space aroused an emotion of worry and fear in NyJewel's intoxicated soul. During the summer when the war was blazing, NyJewel feared for Zulu's life and prayed day and night he didn't end up dead. She spent many lonely and sleepless nights crying to God for Zulu's safety while he was running the streets with the angels of death. From the stress, her soul was eaten to the point she lost almost 20lbs in a month's time. God answered her prayers because Zulu was alive and they were headed to paradise, so NyJewel's stress was over. But now, as the couples sat in the living room, NyJewel felt a sadness in Zulu and she felt it had to do with him leaving the streets. She knew Zulu loved her sincerely, but there seemed to be a battle between his love for her and the streets. NyJewel knew Sun-Z's role and influence on Zulu was very strong. Sun-Z's influence rubbed off on everyone and NyJewel felt if Sun-Z encouraged Zulu to leave the streets Zulu would take his advice with more passion since he looked up to Sun-Z.

As NyJewel tuned into her thoughts while observing a silent Zulu, Sun-Z grabbed the remote from off the table and turned on the stereo system. The melodic flow of *Nas' StillMatic* album spit through the speakers. It was the song *"Flyest Gangsters"* featuring *Legendary Rap God A.Z.*

Zulu transformed and jumped to his feet spitting the rhymes like it was his song. Naturally the magnetic attraction of being A-Alike struck Sun-Z to jump up and join Zulu as they both performed the *Nas and AZ* hit song together. They both looked happy and was energized by the words of the street glory. They looked like they didn't have a care in the world and they loved the dangerous lifestyle which involved the murder, prison, and life of stress.

Iyana looked on entertained as Zulu and Sun-Z drunk from their bottles of liquor while rapping and slapping each other's hands victoriously. But to NyJewel, she felt sad knowing that Zulu loved the streets and didn't really wanna leave the streets for paradise. All Zulu really loved was being a Fly Gangster, he wasn't worried about death or prison. It was sad to NyJewel because moving to paradise with his woman didn't excite Zulu as much as the glorified street reality of being a Fly Gangster excited him.

NyJewel's sight then caught a picture hanging on the wall above the stereo system. There were many pictures on the wall, but it was one that caught her immediate attention. She glared at the framed picture which was a prison photo of Sun-Z and Iyana hugging each other in front of a brick wall in a New

York Prison. A look of distress painted itself on Iyana's pretty face in the picture. She was wrapped in Sun-Z's strong and protective embrace but her mood in the photo revealed a feeling of loneliness and wishing her husband could hold her at home and not in a Prison. On Sun-Z's face there was the look of pain from being caged in. A picture is worth a thousand words but prison pictures spoke a thousand emotions and these were not the emotions NyJewel wanted to experience with Zulu. She desired for their relationship to be free in paradise.

"Ny what's wrong girl?" Iyana observed the look of sadness covering NyJewel's glow as she responded shaking her head depressingly in response to Iyana's curiosity. Iyana sat by NyJewel's side inquiring like a best friend.

"Its Zulu Yanni…he don't really wanna leave this life," NyJewel softly spoke under the music as Iyana massaged her back. "I don't wanna lose him to prison or the streets."

"Girl it's gone be okay relax…yall got plans…stop stressing."

"Zulu don't seem that happy about our plans…this is what makes him happy…just look," NyJewel and Iyana both observed their men amped up from the music and grooving like they had no stress in the world.

It was a harsh summer and the heat of beef was so intense, Zulu and Sun-Z almost forgot what it felt like to be relaxed and enjoy music until this moment of listening to Nas & AZ while lounging with their ladies. And while they both zoned out to the music, they felt the piercing gaze of their women focusing on them.

"What's wrong ladies?" Sun-Z yelled over the music while clutching his bottle of Hennessy. "Yall wanna hear some Mary J don't yall?" Sun-Z remarked snatching the remote to the stereo and changing the CD to Mary J. Blige.

"No." NyJewel responded blankly before raising her tone of voice, "I wanna hear you tell Zulu to leave these streets alone for good and to be happy with the life me and him gonna live away from here." NyJewel spoke firmly staring across the room at Sun-Z. "Zulu listen to you and you should tell him the truth that he should be through with this life and focus on our plans."

"I am happy Ny what you talking bout," Zulu stated feeling his energy go from 100 to 0 and his soul turned blue as the sounds of Mary J. Blige came on. "I'm a grown ass man who can think for myself I don't need no one to tell me how to live my life…I know what I gotta do…it's about me and you love…chill out."

"That's right he a grown man and know how to make his own decisions, he don't need me for that," Sun-Z stated turning the Mary off and playing Scarface instead.

"Yall men just don't have a clue of how much us women love yall do yall?" Iyana declared still seated next to NyJewel. "It's time for all of yall to get out them streets…what is yall doing waiting to die like yall friends…or yall waiting to go to jail…NyJewel right."

"Oh my fucking God," Zulu threw his hands up feeling defeated. "How the hell we get on this topic when we was having a good time. What the fuck."

"I don't even know how this shit came up…bitches always fucking a nice time up…you know bitches just want attention," Sun-Z barked guzzling his bottle of liquor.

"Whattt." NyJewel and Iyana both felt that disrespectful word quickly transformed the mood from sadness to a flame of vengeance. It was one thing to call a dignified and strong Black woman a bitch, but to call her a bitch while she was stimulated off the wine and spirits was a challenge to a fight, word to mama.

Like a stark raving mad Black woman who felt her womanhood violated, Iyana leaped out of her seat cursing her husband like he was a stranger on the street. NyJewel became enraged as well but remained seated since Iyana was checking her husband's disrespect. Zulu stormed over to NyJewel yelling about her disrupting the good mood while Iyana and Sun-Z were having their heated dispute like the average married couple.

It was just a heated argument until Sun-Z said, "Yall bitches get a little wine in yall and start tripping…chill the fuck out its other shit we gotta worry about."

"Smaccck." Reflexively, Iyana slapped Sun-Z so quick and fast across his face Sun-Z didn't even realize what knocked the liquor out of his mouth as he wiped his face.

"Bitch I know you aint just smack me," Sun-Z felt the flaming sting on his face. This was it and Iyana wasn't having it. She knocked the liquor bottle out of his hand and then punched him square in the face. Sun-Z stumbled back in his drunken state more shocked than anything. Sun-Z then flipped. He snatched Iyana by her hair and began pimp slapping her as she cursed at him. She swung her hands uncontrollably trying to pull away from his tight hold before NyJewel jumped off the couch and dashed to Iyana's aid. NyJewel snatched the bottle of liquor from off the floor and went to whack Sun-Z in the head with it but he blocked it. He then tossed Iyana into the stereo system then back handed NyJewel who fell back into the Lazy Boy recliner.

Zulu couldn't believe this. He rushed Sun-Z and tried throwing him in a bear hug but Sun-Z's wide frame was too burly for Zulu to wrap his arms around him. Sun-Z then broke out of Zulu's grip and spun around into Zulu's face. Zulu jabbed Sun-Z then pushed him back. Sun-Z now lost it completely. He lost it a few months ago when Dolla and Mel-Cash were murdered. It was easy to go into killer mode but hard to come out. Once blood clouded a killer's vision it was hard not to see blood. Zulu could see that Sun-Z was seeing red the way they locked eyes with each other. Sun-Z had the look in his eye, the same look he had the night they murdered Megalito and Sun-Z blacked out and tried chopping Megalito's head off. Zulu knew nothing or no one could stop the beast he observed in Sun-Z from inflicting pain on Iyana, NyJewel, or himself. Sun-Z blacked out and went crazy.

Sun-Z charged Zulu with the angel of death look in his eyes as he held his hands out to grab Zulu. Zulu only knew of one thing to do to avoid the destruction coming his way and that was to snatch his gun from off his waist, step back, aim the gun above Sun-Z's head hoping Sun-Z would stop. Nothing would or could stop Sun-Z from embracing death. Death seemed to be the only thing he hadn't experienced. Throughout all the pain and suffering, maybe death was the only relief Sun-Z could find in this harsh reality of life. He continued charging Zulu in his drunken beast mode state.

"Blam." The shot into the ceiling didn't even bring Sun-Z back to reality as he continued charging Zulu. Zulu stepped back yelling for Sun-Z to stop. And like a ride or die chick, NyJewel was right there. She banged Sun-Z in the head shattering the wine bottle on the back of his head. Sun-Z crumpled to the floor groaning painfully. He was drunk and unaware of what had just taking place. The knock on his head by the bottle shut him down and knocked some sense into his head. He lay on the floor in pain saying sorry while NyJewel helped Iyana to her feet. Zulu kneeled beside Sun-Z feeling like their life was out of control and a mess.

"Big bro what the fuck yo?" Zulu glanced at the weeping women as they held each other while cursing and screaming at Sun-Z who still lay on the floor. The women then stormed out of the living room while Zulu sat by Sun-Z's side. "Yo you gotta sober up this is no good…you lost it yo…you was gone try to kill us yo…what the fuck…you losing it…get it together big bro."

"I know…I lost my brothers Dolla and Shamel…I can't find em…help me find my brothers…I gotta find them…where they at? I need to find them because I miss them." Sun-Z was drunk as he ever been and slurred his words of truth before shutting his eyelids. A drunk person speaks a sober mind.

"Fuck." Zulu muttered sitting on the floor like a helpless soul. Zulu curled up and sat his chin on his knees thinking of it all. The Get Rich Crime Family gained the world but in exchange they not only lost their comrades, they lost their souls to the wicked streets. It was so much pain in their souls the stress spilled over into their relationships, and the anger they intentionally took out on their enemies in the streets they unconsciously and mistakenly took it out on their loved ones through frustration.

While Sun-Z lay on the floor feeling the liquor take over his body, Zulu sat in a daze realizing how damaged their souls were. Truth be told, there would probably never be happiness for Thugs like the Get Rich Crime Family. No matter how much money or escaping the ghetto, there was too much spiritual pain to overcome and it would take extreme spiritual cleansing to wash away the bloodstains on the soul.

Zulu pondered this painful reality as NyJewel and Iyana came through the living room carrying some belongings of Iyana's. Zulu rose to his feet and told the snoring Sun-Z, "Get it together big bro…we gone be alright."

Iyana was out the door and through with her husband. Sun-Z turned into something she never knew nor seen. As far as NyJewel, she gave Zulu an ultimatum that he would have to leave this life behind and move on with her. There would be no looking back to the streets or she would leave him stuck there.

About two days later when Sun-Z sobered up he was suffering from the mental blackout of his drunkenness. He didn't remember too much but glimpses of what happened. He called Iyana to learn that she was fish grease hot with him and fed up with his ill-tempered and disrespectful self. So until he decided to change his ways and actions, she was going to leave him in his crazy world by himself.

Sun-Z begged Iyana to come home but Iyana said their home could never be a home as long as Sun-Z kept the demons of his soul lingering around, and until Sun-Z got rid of his demons, she wouldn't step foot back into their house. And just for starters, she was going to get away and find some peace of mind in the Bahamas with NyJewel.

Sun-Z told her that that was unlawful because she was his wife and that would be considered abandonment.

Iyana responded, "Watch me…until you leave them streets and demons alone…I'm gonna have peace."

Sun-Z jumped up in his groggy state, rushed out the house without even throwing a jacket on, jumped in his wheel and flew over to Zulu and NyJewel's. When he arrived Zulu was outside shoveling snow. Sun-Z parked his car on the snow filled street, jumped out and hopped through the snow huffing and puffing. Zulu was surprised to see that Sun-Z wasn't hungover not to mention he had no jacket on.

Sun-Z approached Zulu apologizing about the other night before pleading his case to Zulu about Iyana. Zulu explained how Iyana was claiming she was terrified of him and that if Sun-Z ever expected her to feel safe around him he would have to control his anger, because it almost got him shot if not killed.

As Zulu and Sun-Z stood outside talking, NyJewel opened the front door to lock the screen door from the inside. She told Sun-Z that he was welcomed to stay outside talking to Zulu but inside was off limits. He was a ticking time bomb ready to explode and no one wanted to be around him.

"I'm really sorry Ny you know I am," Sun-Z stood in the driveway speaking calmly. "Tell Yanni I'm sorry and I didn't mean none of that the other night…please Ny I'm sorry."

"I don't wanna hear it." Iyana appeared from behind NyJewel. "You always sorry and that's the problem…you just a sorry mess and sorry not gone stop you from bringing that negative energy you got into our life…I'm through with you until you change your ways Sean and I mean it."

"Come on Yanni," Sun-Z ran to the door yanking on the handle. "I promise I love you, you could trust me you know me better than that."

"Actions speak louder than words Sean," Iyana responded slamming the door in his face.

"You fucking cunt," Sun-Z flipped and began banging on the locked screen door.

"Yo Sun come on chill out you bugging yo," Zulu stood with the shovel stuck in the snow. "What you always tell me big bro…give her a little space…right?"

"Right Sean," Iyana now yelled out the living room window. "Be a man and let me be…you need to listen to Zulu because he acting more like the mature man than you."

"You know what fuck you bitch." Sun-Z scurried through the snow towards the window Iyana was yelling through.

"Zulu you better get him because if he keep it up I will call the police," NyJewel stood at the window shouting. "Leave Iyana alone she don't wanna be bothered with your madness and neither do I…if you don't leave Sean I'm calling the cops and I will have your ass locked up now try me."

"What." Sun-Z couldn't believe NyJewel was flipping.

"Yo Ny shut yo fucking mouth," Zulu ran to the screen door with his key and tried unlocking it but was unable to since NyJewel locked it from the inside. "Open this fucking door now Ny I'm not playing."

"No Zulu we want Sean to leave…we was at peace until he came…he need to leave us alone." Iyana shouted.

Yeah Zulu you need to leave him alone too," NyJewel added, "He's no good for you Zulu…and I'm telling you Sean if you try to convince Zulu from leaving the states I will tell the cops everything…leave us alone…you not pulling Zulu down with you."

"Ny open this fucking door now or I'm gone beat yo fucking ass," Zulu flipped and pounded on the screen door not believing this. Sun-Z couldn't believe it either. It was like the world was falling apart.

"Ny open this fucking door now or I swear to God you won't make it to them islands," Zulu yelled once again yanking on the door.

"I will only if Sean leave."

"Listen Zulu I'm gone leave because you better handle that," Sun-Z stood face to face with Zulu. "This yo problem not mines…just don't let it become our problem…these bitches done lost they mind."

"I got this yo but you started this shit flipping out the other night."

"Fuck these bitches Zulu…I was married to the streets before I put a ring on that bitch finger…and if you know what's right don't ever let no bitch fuck yo head up…you can run to them fantasy islands all you want but you can't run from the streets because that's all you is and all you know…you the streets Zulu and that's all you gone ever be…I'm gone and I'm gone leave you with these bitches…and you better check yo bitch Zulu…for real…go handle that Sun, I'm gone."

Zulu couldn't even think straight and fathom what was going on with everyone. Sun-Z was in beast mode and ready to eat any and everyone. Then NyJewel lost her mind making threats about snitching and Iyana was just tired of the drama. Zulu and Sun-Z just couldn't understand what their women were going through. One thing for sure, Zulu was sending NyJewel away to the Bahamas until he sold their house. He couldn't have her around saying the deadly things she was saying. Those words alone warranted death. Zulu loved NyJewel faithfully but as a Thug what's right is to follow the code of the streets, not the heart of love.

For the first time in life Zulu felt he had no one to talk to who could understand his situation. It was money over bitches with the Thugs. And now Zulu felt stuck between the love of his street dreams and the life of love and paradise. Not too many Thugs spoke openly about love. There was too much pride and male chauvinism that prevented Thugs from opening up to each other and speaking on such issues. And most women whether they were street smart or not couldn't understand the life of a Thug and how the cruel streets turned a lot of Thugs cold on the inside. A lot of Thugs lost the innocence of their souls and became entangled with the forces of the wicked streets. The streets provided Thugs with an emotional upliftment of power that was like sex. The rush was unbelievable. It became a street glory that Thugs would live and die for. Nothing else mattered and it was something only Thugs understood. One person who understood the life of a Thug but matured and found a new life as a Divine Being was Prince. Zulu hooked up with his brother from another mother to seek some wisdom about the situation at hand because Zulu didn't know who to turn to.

The way Prince seen it was simple as a raindrop. What is the life of a man without his woman? All Thugs and men who spent time incarcerated learned the hard way that life sucked without women. And when it came to getting money in the streets, women were the main motivation for hustlers to be King and outshine all others. Therefore, Prince made Zulu realize the fact that Zulu achieved his glorious street dreams and what else was it for Zulu to gain in the streets? Zulu had amassed a supreme fortune. He had the power and respect. And to top it off with the greatest good life had to offer, Zulu had one of the most intelligent, sexy, and beautiful woman the forces of creation brought into existence. Zulu had it all going for himself and he survived the madness. It was only right for Zulu to show his gratitude to the game, count his blessings, and enjoy the rewards the game and life blessed him with thus far.

"My advice to you Blackman," Prince explained as they sat inside Zulu's B.M.W at the J.F.K park watching kids sleigh ride down a mountain of snow in the park. "Go with NyJewel to them islands for good bro...and don't look back or even come back because this the end and it's about to be over for

all this." Prince waved his hands at the surroundings outside. "This civilization
of the white devils is coming to an end Blackman. That shit that happened in
Manhattan on 911...the whole 911 incident is a sign that this wicked government
on it's knees and about to be over with...this wicked society we love so much is
about to be destroyed...the government destroyed its own citizens on 911...and
then mother nature destroying America day by day...look at these tornadoes,
hurricanes, floods, snowstorms, and all this global warming...get the fuck out of
Buffalo, because if the snowstorms don't kill us in this raggedy ass town, we
gone kill each other...this the end of time and you need to enjoy life as much as
you can with yo woman...She love you Blackman and she gone do anything for
you just to enjoy life with you...fuck this street shit Blackman. You know the
streets don't love us like we love the streets...no matter how loyal, faithful, and
real you keep it with the game, the streets will eat us alive...it's so crazy out here
Black Man...the cats who don't honor the code of the streets and don't have no
loyalty live longer than the sincere brothers in the streets....the streets don't love
no one...the Black woman is the only true love we got Blackman...and when a
Black woman love you sincerely you better appreciate it and cherish it because
there's no greater love than hers...think of Mama...that's it...and understand
when I say this," Prince looked deeply into Zulu's eyes reaching his soul. "I love
all yall Zulu...yall the only family I ever really had...I knew yall all my life...but
fuck living for the Get Rich Crime Family...live for yourself because look at
Dolla, Mel-Cash, and all our other friends who was murdered out here, they all
in them graves by their self...Terror still in that coma on that hospital bed by
himself...and everyone in the A-Squad in them prison cells by their self...so live
for you and that Black woman because that's who gone always be there with you
no matter what and she what really matter in the end...the Black Woman is the
most precious Jewel Allah ever created...you feel me."

If Zulu never took heed to Prince's Wisdom he did now. Zulu's mind
soaked up Prince's wisdom which made him realize that he needed to be thankful
for the way the game treated him. He was dealt a good hand and needed to play
his cards right and cash out before the game was over.

CHAPTER 20

Mother Nature allowed the blazing sun to melt the snow away so plant life could spring from the earth and bloom as spring came rolling in. As the life within the earth manifested its colorful existence from the Divine black soil, Desiree pushed out of her womb of Divine Blackness a healthy female seed. She gave birth to a beautiful baby girl weighing in at 9lbs and 2 ounces. The baby was heavenly and her peachy skin tone would be blessed with enough melanin to give her a reddish ochre complexion. She had a head full of curly black hair and chinky black eyes that were distinctive to Desiree and Destiny's genetics. Baby girl displayed Hawk's cute full-size lips and medium sized nose.

Prince blessed the baby's existence with the righteous attribute name of Divine Princess Satori. She was divine because she was a pure and refined seed thanks to Desiree's abstinence from all intoxicants during her pregnancy. All babies are pure in soul and spirit. She was a Princess by birthright. And the name Satori was an Asiatic principle which meant enlightenment. Divine Princess Satori was the Divine Light of Life in these times of death and darkness her people were facing.

The happiness of going half on a baby was the greatest joy Hawk and Desiree ever experienced in life. Their love was already united and when their love created a seed that reflected the creative power of love within them, their love skyrocketed to the stars. It was time to celebrate and everyone brought in the celebration at Hawk and Desiree's.

Zulu was back in the states from after spending several weeks at his new residence in Nassau, Bahamas. He was growing to love the relaxed life of island settlement and he fell in love with the warm atmosphere. It was caressing to a tensed soul and allowed him to appreciate the simple beauty of life and to be thankful to be able to breathe while living on this beautiful earth. Zulu had to return home to the wilderness of North America because he had some finishing business to attend to. Him and NyJewel's house was still on the market to be sold, plus Zulu still had some profit to be made since he still had a portion of his bankroll invested with the crew. Plus, it was mandatory for Zulu to come and honor the celebration of the new life of Hawk and Desiree.

When Zulu arrived at the celebration party, everyone was in attendance and came out to show their love for the new life. From friends to family the house was packed and full of gifts for Divine Princess Satori. Zulu thought he was at a baby shower it was so many women in attendance showering Desiree with gifts and arguing with each other over who was next to hold the baby.

Destiny then shut the demonstration of showing off the baby when the tipsy women began kissing all over the baby with their liquor reeking mouths. Destiny let it be known that the baby was pure and too sensitive to have everyone's lipstick and alcohol drenched lips all over her beautiful face. And since Desiree was ready to celebrate and party, Destiny was taking the baby away with her. Destiny and everyone was proud and happy Desiree did the right thing during her pregnancy and refrained from the impurities of partying. Desiree utilized her creative will power to birth a young Goddess and she deserved a celebration such as the one at hand.

After Zulu made his presence known throughout the party, Zulu helped Destiny gather the baby's possessions and then helped Destiny to the car with the baby. Zulu carried the baby in her cute pink and purple car seat and he was mesmerized by the holiness of the baby. Since Zulu was a child he had forgot what innocence and purity was. For the first time in a long time he felt a glimmer of hope for a bright future as he peered into the beautiful black eyes of Divine Princess Satori.

When Destiny opened the back door to her car for Zulu to put the baby inside, she observed Zulu standing several feet behind her in a trance like state like he was absorbed by the pure innocence of the baby. It was a memorable sight to Destiny and she hadn't seen a smile like that on Zulu's face since they were kids themselves. Zulu didn't even realize how happy he was smiling at the baby while he gazed into the baby's face. Destiny smiled feeling happy and didn't want to interrupt Zulu's moment of peace with Divine Princess Satori. Destiny bent down and reached into the back seat to move some bags over and that's when Zulu's moment of purity was erased by his natural lust for Destiny.

He took his eyes off the baby and looked up, catching the view of Destiny's round heart shaped backside as she bent over into the backseat.

"Umm umm damn," Zulu began stepping closer to Destiny with his eyes locked on her like she was meat for the animal inside of him. His lust was energized as he eyed Destiny's juicy rump sprouting in her fitted knee length dress.

Destiny pulled herself from out the car catching Zulu's hungry eyes lusting over her and said, "Boy you still a freak…stop it and give me the baby." Destiny then remarked smiling while reaching for the baby. Zulu handed her the baby but took one last look at the baby and smiled, knowing that if he never was to find that pure peace he once had in life, at least Divine Princess Satori gave him a moment of peace he would never forget and always be thankful for.

"She brings so much joy to you when you look at her right?" Destiny asked taking the baby from Zulu and strapping her into the backseat.

"Yeah." Zulu responded with an energetic tone. "I never really paid attention to the happiness that babies bring to life…I been so caught up with this shit out here I done forgot how a lot of natural shit give you peace," Zulu leaned against the car and thought deeply as he peered down at the grass.

While observing the change in Zulu's demeanor, Destiny touched his hand and asked if he wanted to talk. Zulu shrugged his shoulders uncomfortably while still in deep thought.

"I know it's been rough out here for you Zulu going thru the things yall been going through," Destiny now grabbed Zulu's hands and peered into his lifeless eyes. "And I know you may have grown apart from me since we broke up…but I still love you Zulu and I care about you and I want you to know that...I'm here for you in any way…I could never turn my back on you…and it would hurt me to see--," Destiny stopped in mid-sentence not wanting to entertain the thought that worried a lot of mothers, sisters, wives, and women who loved Thugs. Her heart became mushy as she found the breath to tell Zulu, "I don't know—what I would do if I was to lose you out here Zulu…you may be with another woman but at least I know you alive and you alright…I don't ever want anything bad to happen to you because I still love you and I know you a good person who didn't ask to grow up the way you did," Destiny told him with a tear gleaming in her eyes.

"Come here love," Zulu pulled her close to him and softly pressed her face against his. "You aint gotta worry about anything happening to me Destiny...I'm uh--," Zulu knew him and Destiny still shared a bond with each other and he didn't want to crush her heart by telling her about him and NyJewel's move. But then again telling Destiny the truth could ease her pain of worrying if she knew Zulu was escaping the wickedness of the streets. "Listen Destiny...I'm moving out of town...I'm um you know...I'm already re-located."

"Really." Destiny's eyes stretched happily. "Why no one told me...what made you wanna relocate?"

"I just want to get away you know."

"Are you and NyJewel still together."

Zulu then thought to himself, *"Fuck. Why she gotta ask so many damn questions."*

"Yeah we still together Destiny."

"So your both moving out of town together?"

"Y-yeah."

"Oh, that's nice," Destiny forced a slight smile as she pulled away from Zulu's hold. She was happy and sad. She found herself falling back into Zulu's arms and burying her face in his chest as the tears slowly began pouring. "I'm happy for you Zulu...at least she was able to get you to straighten up...I guess you finally found the love you willing to do the right thing for."

Zulu felt crushed inside like never before. He never understood the deep love Destiny had for him. She was happy he was making the right decision with his life to get away from the streets, but deep inside her soul she wished it was her whose sincere love could have got Zulu out of the streets a long time ago. Since kids, that's all Destiny ever wanted with Zulu. Destiny only wanted a life with Zulu free from the negativity which destroyed so many relationships and lives. All she ever desired was a life of true love and happiness with Zulu, but for the longest she battled the streets and the unfaithful lifestyle that came with it, not to mention the worrying of prison and death. After all the dedication and suffering Destiny endured loving Zulu, NyJewel was the winner and reaper of the rewards Destiny felt was rightfully hers. Why couldn't she be the one to receive what she worked so hard for since childhood. Why?

Why is a question asked by those seeking *inner-standing* (Understanding)? And as these thoughts flashed in Destiny's mind while she cried on Zulu's chest, her question of why was answered by the indwelling divinity of her spirit. Through her soul's intuition, she realized that she was a Divine and Powerful Black Woman who learned to love herself when she couldn't receive it from the man she loved. She was an independent woman who found the Power of the Creator in her soul to protect her from the heartache and pain that came with relationships. Everything happened for a reason. And the reason was always cause and effect. The pain and agony of the selfishness, mistrust, and unfaithfulness in relationships were the effects that human beings allowed to happen which were usually the causes of break-ups and divorces.

Most times the decisions people make are the fulfillment of life's destiny. Destiny's decision to break up with Zulu was a part of her destiny to find peace and happiness within herself since she couldn't find it with her help-mate. Destiny learned to make herself happy, but a man needs a woman and vice versa. Life is incomplete without the spiritual mate which completes the other half of the equation of life. And Destiny now realized how incomplete she was without Zulu. She may have broken up with him, but her heart remained connected to him on a spiritual level and the emotion of joy and pain was a testament of her heart since Zulu was fulfilling a goal with NyJewel instead of her.

"Destiny I love you and it's not what you thinking," Zulu softly touched her chin and lifted her head to gaze into her sad eyes. "I'm just getting away for a while but you know I'm here for you and I aint ever lose no love for you."

"No Zulu…be with NyJewel…I'm happy for you…I can't be mad at you or her…I allowed you to go with her when I broke up with you…and I guess it's in the Creator's plan for her to make you happy since I couldn't."

"Na you bugging the fuck out…who said I was happy…I'm getting away because I'm not happy…and I don't give a fuck what NyJewel or you say…you always got my heart and I love you…and as long as I live I'm gonna keep a smile on your face," Zulu then began clowning and rapping *G-Unit's song "My Buddy."*

Destiny smiled while Zulu held her hands dancing and singing before they both peeked in the back seat and caught eyes with Divine Princess Satori. The baby was smiling with her beautiful black eyes spectating the show.

"Zulu stop and let me take the baby home," Destiny began to swing around to the driver side of her car. "But I love you Zulu and don't be a stranger…stay in touch."

"Of course," Zulu skated after Destiny like the hungry dog chased the cat. "Let me come home with you and keep you company." Zulu asked snatching Destiny by her waist.

"No boy stop…you still a cheater and haven't learned how to be faithful I see."

"Me and you still love each other what you talking about."

"Goodbye Zulu and I love you till death." Destiny jumped in her car, slammed the door, locked it, ignited her engine, and blew Zulu a kiss before zooming off.

"I love you too." Zulu stood in the street watching Destiny drive off wishing he could run like a cheetah and chase her.

....

Martin Luther King Jr. Park was in the heart of Buffalo's east side and from June 16-18 MLK park hosted *The Juneteenth festival*. The city of Buffalo with its large black population was one of the few American cities where African-Americans celebrated Juneteenth. Juneteenth was an honorary celebration for the last slaves to be freed during President Abraham Lincoln's Emancipation Proclamation. The slave masters in Galveston, Texas were reluctant on freeing their slaves when all other slave masters freed their slaves at the order of President Lincoln. During the month of June in 1865, the black people in Galveston stormed off the plantation as free people. They were the last slaves to be freed.

For decades in Buffalo and a few other cities Juneteenth was celebrated. The Irish had St. Patrick's Day. The Italians had their Italian Festival. Puerto Ricans had the Puerto Rican Day Parade. People of the Caribbean had the Caribana and black people in North America had Juneteenth to not only celebrate freedom from slavery, but it was the recognition of African culture and heritage.

On the west side of MLK park basketball tournaments were held during the festival. Right by the ball court there was a brick building housing restrooms which displayed a life sized mural painting which kept the deceased Latrell Billups alive. The artistic mural was a painting of Latrell Billups dribbling a basketball under a hoop while several young children watched. In the background of the painting, there was a sparkling money green GT Carrera. The sun shone atop the mural and within the sun it read:

> "In memory of a gifted and godly talented young
> Black man whose energetic skills of motion could have
> made him an NBA superstar. Too many black
> youth and men are losing their gifted lives to a life of
> crime and violence when they can be living a productive
> life. My young men, shoot for the stars and not the streets."

R.I.P Latrell "Dolla" Billups 1976-2002

Ronnie Smith was the founder and organizer of Young Stars Inner City Youth Basketball League and Dolla was one of its superstars from the mid 80's to early 90's before he put the ball away to dribble rocks on the block. Even when Dolla chose street dreams instead of hoop dreams, he still dedicated himself to be a supporter of the Young Stars ball league. He would even help coach on his spare time and contribute funds for games and trips the teams would go on across the country.

Even though he was a memory, Dolla was now a legend like the stars in the sky and he became a legendary memorial who would be celebrated at all the Young Stars ball tournaments like today at Juneteenth.

The ball court had its players ready to ball and the bleachers were full of spectators young and old, male and female. And in honor of Dolla, there was a moment of silence as everyone bowed their heads while the ball players all held hands standing in a circle on the court. Ronnie Smith said a prayer and then the sounds of the *late great Notorious B.I.G.'s song "Sky is the Limit,"* played as a testament for the youth to keep their goals as high as the Sun and never look down.

Zulu and Killa were in attendance and sitting amongst the crowd front row on the bleachers. They were honored seeing the multitudes of people sporting the R.I.P Dolla T-shirts. After swarms of people gave Zulu and Killa their condolences and well wishes for them to be careful in the streets, Zulu and Killa felt it was time to break out. Seeing Dolla's live reflective image on the T-Shirts and in the mural painting assaulted their souls with the mourning pain of never seeing their brother again in the physical.

They dipped from the ball court area and headed thru the park where vendors sold food, books, clothes, African artifacts and many other items. They skated pass the fountain pool where children got wet. After swinging pass the parade marching through the park, they passed a huge stage where local music artists showed off their talents.

They reached Killa's Infiniti, jumped inside and just sat there in a daze for a moment before Killa ignited the engine.

"Yo," Killa threw the gear in drive, "Gotta hit the liquor store yo...that shit was stressing as fuck right there."

"Word up," Zulu replied leaning his seat back then gazing up at the ceiling, "It's like that shit make you think he still here but the reality is he not...him and Mel-Cash gone and we not gone ever see them again unless it's in our minds."

"Damn," Killa hissed pulling out into the traffic on Fillmore Avenue which was crowded with people who were either heading to the parade, just left the parade, or just hanging out amongst the businesses supporting the festival. Killa swerved the wheel over to *Feel More Tipsy* liquors and Zulu jumped out and dashed into the crowded liquor store. Zulu stepped straight to the counter skipping everyone in line and no one said a word as Zulu stood at the counter looking like he was ready to unleash his anger on anyone. Zulu was like a sick patient needing the medicine for his mourning soul.

Several minutes later Zulu bounced out the store noticing a sparkling Pearl white Cadillac Escalade Truck sitting on 22 inch rims. The Escalade was double parked right next to Killa's Infiniti and had Killa's car blocked in.

Killa stood between his car and the Escalade having a deep build with two individuals who not only had the shines of hood rich hustlers, but their young faces looked more stressed and lifeless than Iraqi war veterans. This was Munchie and G-Boy from the Hyena crew off Bailey Avenue.

"Zulu what's good my dude?" Munchie and G-Boy depressingly greeted Zulu and gave him a tight handshake and Thug Love hug. From the energy radiating from the four, depression was all in the air.

"What's good with yall boys yall don't look too good yo?" Zulu asked after they embraced.

"Man Zulu," Killa took the fifth of Grey Goose from Zulu while shaking his head in response to hearing about Munchie and G-Boy's situation. "We not the only ones going through the bullshit Zulu."

"Yeah shit is real Zulu," Munchie leaned back against his Escalade truck. "I don't know what to do right now yo."

"Nigga you know what the fuck we gotta do," G-Boy began punching his hands and turning up. "We can't let this pressure stop us we gotta keep dancing in this muthafucking fire just like the Get Rich Crime Family."

"Hold on what the fuck going on with yall boys?" Zulu asked receiving the bottle of liquor from Killa and taking a guzzle before passing the bottle to G-Boy.

"Man everything yo," G-Boy took the bottle and poured some liquor out, "This for Black Boy and yall peoples Dolla and Mel-Cash."

"Nigga what?" Zulu was shocked. "What the hell you mean Black Boy."

"It didn't even start there yo," Munchie explained gripping a bottle of Tanqueray. "Ra-King Allah got jammed up too…it's wicked out here."

"What…Ra-King…and Black-Boy…na," Zulu couldn't believe it like Killa.

The Hyenas and the Young Assassins went back like corn rows. From the E. Ferry street boys home to the Alternative Bad Boys school to getting money in the streets, they were tight as the vacuum sealed drug packages they sold. Any devastation affecting either crew was emotionally felt by both sides. And just how the Hyena crew slid through E. North showing their support to put in work for the Get Rich Crime Family's loss, Zulu and Killa was willing to roll with the Hyenas.

Ra-King Allah was an older Thug who was a conglomerate and a-alike of Sun-Z. Ra-King was the mind and plug behind the Hyena crew. And when Ra-King went to re-up with his connect, the DEA was there waiting for him. He was arrested with almost a half a million dollars in strait cash and charged with conspiracy to purchase and distribute 35 kilos of cocaine. Ra-King's plug set him up. That situation was devastating and life changing to the financial lives of the Hyenas like a stock market crash because Ra-King had all of their money. The Hyenas was left broke and dry, but with determination and persistence, the Hyenas bounced back quickly after pulling a few robberies. They slowly built their bankroll back up and was back in the game.

Black Boy was a young and gifted hustler and he made the numbers multiply when it came to flipping coke. Black Boy got the Hyenas back on top and enjoying success until a few days ago when he went to sell 375 grams of cocaine to the wrong dudes.

"Hating ass niggas gone kill my sun for 10 geez worth of coke yo," Munchie couldn't fathom the evil of player hating. "For three Big Eights they killed Black Boy yo...they could have just walked him...they aint have to slug him."

"Niggas know they can't walk us because we a stop they ass from walking literally," G-Boy added while looking around suspiciously then whispering, "But we knocked the one nigga brother off...strait downed the nigga...and we gone keep hitting everybody them niggas know until they come out from hiding...word to Black Boy." G-Boy thundered patting the chrome under his shirt. "Them niggas not gone be able to hustle here I'm telling you...yall know how I give it up."

"Damn yo." Zulu couldn't believe this. The Hyenas were victims of true player hating. The game was breeding different type of players, hating players who was out to destroy the real players who played the game with honor.

"Yo let me know who these niggas is and what hood they from," Killa placed his hand on Munchie's shoulder. "I fucked with Black Boy hard so I go put that work in tonight just give me some info."

"It's the nigga Eric and them from C Street but we got this."

"Word up we got this yall got yall own problems," G-Boy gripped Zulu's hand and held it tightly, "But we gone be needing a new plug for sure. That's how yall could help us."

"Word yo Black Boy had the plug in Detroit but fuck going out there we can just plug from yall I know yall gone hit us for the low," Munchie stated.

"Hell yeah yall already know." Zulu responded.

"Real niggas do real things but I wanna bust a shot for Black Boy," Killa shouted.

"He was one of the coolest and humblest dudes I ever met…he would give you the shirt off his back and them faggots downed him…I don't like that shit…I gotta come thru for Black Boy."

"Listen Killa I know how you fuck with us…but this shit personal and we gotta handle this," Munchie placed both his hands on Killa's shoulder, "Yall just come thru with that fire…that's what we need."

"No question we got yall," Zulu responded before they all embraced then broke out feeling the Thug Love and appreciating the sincere support of each other. No matter the trauma afflicting solid individuals, solid individuals are a foundation for each other to stand on when there's nowhere to stand. And in time, Munchie and G-Boy would show and prove they were as solid as steel when it came to loyalty and being a crutch for a fellow Thug in a life and death situation.

Zulu and Killa jumped back in the wheel and slid into the bottleneck traffic on Fillmore Avenue. It seemed like the whole Black community from all over the city and elsewhere came out to the festival and crowded MLK Park and Fillmore Ave.

Killa pushed his Infiniti at about 10 mph for several blocks before traffic cleared and he was able to blow his dual exhaust engine down the strip. Killa then got a phone call from his God-Mother Yemaria, the Afro Cuban Priestess.

"*Ashay Ashay Nana,*" Killa answered his phone while placing his phone on speaker.

"*Ashay Jahtu...whud you doing now bwoy?*" Yemaria asked in her heavy Afro-Caribbean accent.

"I'm with Zulu and we coming from Juneteenth."

"*Zulu...how hour you me yung child?*"

"Hello Ms. Yemaria...I'm ok how you?"

"*Oh me young lady getting younger each day...but me calls because you bwoys must come to de hospeedal...de Orisas (Forces of Nature) visited Sahku (Terror) and he opened his eyes...come now you both.*"

"Nana his eyes opened...he awoke?" Killa asked excitedly as him and Zulu gazed at each other happily.

"*Bwoy whud me say...you come now...both you...come now...Ashay.*" Yemaria hung up the phone.

"Yoooo," Killa mashed his foot on the gas pedal and blew it down the strip like he was on a racetrack.

"Hell yeah," Zulu shouted turning the bottle up to his face to guzzle but Killa was recklessly swerving around cars and people. Zulu spilled liquor on his face as he rocked around in his seat from Killa speed racing. "Slow down yo."

"Man fuck that my brother woke up...we gotta--," Killa peeped the flashing lights in his rear view mirror. "Fuck yo...the fucking cops...damn."

"Told yo dickhead ass to stop speeding," Zulu barked closing the liquor bottle then snatching the pistol and stashing it in the glovebox stash. Killa then pulled over in front of a bus stop by a corner store which was the only place to park as the cop cruiser pulled behind him.

A young police officer who looked a few years older than *Justin Bieber* hopped out the police car with his crispy black uniform and shiny badge on. He hadn't been on the force for a whole year yet. He strutted to Killa's car nervously eyeing the youths who stood at the bus stop coughing up lungs from the exotic weed they were smoking. People passing by in cars and others on the strip began making comments about racists cops harassing blacks during their parade and so on as the young cop stepped to Killa's window.

"What's the hurry why you speeding guy?" The young cop asked admiring the lavish Infiniti as he stood at the driver window. Killa already had his license and registration hanging out the window. "You shouldn't be doing over 100 on a city street in this bad boy...this is a hot car my friend." The young cop smiled while taking Killa's documents.

"Listen just give me my ticket dude," Killa barked looking into the cop's baby face. "I'm in a rush so hurry yo please."

"Hey man no need to be pushy and rude...if your license is legit I'll give you a pass just stay put."

"Man I don't need no pass I just need to get to where I'm going...come on man why you still standing here...either give me my paperwork back and let me go or go give me a ticket I aint got all day."

"Chill bro chill," Zulu cut in seeing the cop didn't really want to give Killa a ticket.

"Right you should listen to your buddy...no need to be an asshole." The young cop stated before strolling back to his car. He opened his door and began to sit in the driver seat when he felt a car zoom right up on side of him and stop. The car was double parked right on side of him and was so close the car's bumper was almost touching his open car door. It was two veteran detectives in a grey Crown Victoria.

"Hey you fucking rookie asshole," The veteran detective sitting in the passenger seat yelled leaning out the window. "Whaddya think you doing rookie."

"This guy was speeding so I'm doing my job."

"Fucking rookie," The detective jumped out of the Crown Victoria and stood face to face with the rookie cop. "Those are members of the Get Rich Crime Family and their targets of a joint investigation with my department and the Feds...they are not to be apprehended for anything you asshole," The detective then snatched the documents from out of the cop's hand and scanned them. The detective then leaned into the Crown Victoria and whispered something to his partner before turning back around to the cop. "You pulled over Jahtu Kadari better known as Killer, and he's a suspect in a homicide case…you gotta let him go because their building a case as we speak and we got agents tailing these guys."

Maybe it was because it was so much commotion and activity going on in the strip the detective thought he was whispering. Well sound travels and those ears on Killa heard his name and the words suspect and homicide. Killa's engine was still running with the gear in park. Without thinking Killa slammed the gear in drive and murked off blowing engine smoke in the cops' face.

"You fucking rookie you blew our cover," The detective now yelled as they watched Killa speed off into the traffic. The rookie cop wasn't sure what to do. Should he stay there getting chewed up by the senior detective or give chase.

"I'm gonna do my job as a police officer sir…I'm sorry," The young rookie jumped in his police car and gave chase.

Fillmore Avenue became a drag strip as the Infiniti raced down the strip being chased by the rookie cop. People scrambled out of the street and cars swerved to the side out of the way. The rookie cop couldn't keep up with Killa who swerved into the oncoming traffic lanes and blew it through red lights. Killa whipped the wheel onto a side street and the rookie cop began to have second thoughts about pursuing Killa on the violent and drug infested side streets. It was just five years ago two Buffalo police officers was murdered chasing a suspect. And in the last two years on three separate occasions police officers were seriously wounded by criminals on the run.

Killa hit Interpark Street and blew it to the parkway which led him to the expressway. The rookie cop said it was too early in his career to play hero and get killed. He turned onto Interpark Street and pumped his brakes, busted a U-turn and gave up the chase. There was really no sense in chasing suspects whom the Feds had under investigation the rookie cop then realized, because no one escapes the Feds.

Killa hit the 33 East Expressway at lightning speed and ripped through the lanes before sliding off at the Grider street exit noticing the cops wasn't behind him. Killa blew it across Grider Street and pulled onto Mapleridge street then smoothly pulled up into a driveway which led to a backyard. He zoomed all the way into the yard and stashed his car behind the house where it couldn't be seen from the street out front.

"Zulu tell me you heard what the fuck I heard," Killa breathed deeply resting his forehead on the steering wheel in disbelief.

"Yoooo." Zulu didn't wanna repeat what he heard feeling a knot of fear tighten in his stomach.

"I'm not doing life in prison Zulu hell knaw…I rather be with Dolla, Mel-Cash, Black-Boy and the rest of my niggas…fuck that."

"*Fucccck.*" Zulu banged the dashboard. "I'm bout to call Leonetti and find out what's going on." Zulu stated whipping out his cell phone. With trembling hands he dialed Leonetti's number and Leonetti answered on the first ring.

"Law office."

"Leonetti what the hell going on?" Zulu asked after he put the phone on speaker.

"Listen I'm gonna make this quick…tell Jahtu that wherever he is to stay tucked away because a warrant for a homicide is being issued for his arrest as we speak…the D.A. contacted me about an hour ago saying she got an indictment signed yesterday and Jahtu is formally charged for the murder of ah-," Leonetti tried thinking of the guy's name. "It's a cold case homicide but there's a witness pointing the finger at Jahtu…just sit tight while I work on getting a bail."

Zulu and Killa both froze up upon hearing this bad news. Killa then closed his eyes while shaking his head in disbelief. A cold case homicide? Killa had skeletons in his closet alright. He had a couple of bodies that he sometimes forgot about and now he wondered who was coming back to life to hunt him. It really didn't matter because he wasn't getting captured by the white man, not Abadou Obatala Kadari's son.

"Yo Leonetti you not gone be able to get me a bail…I wasn't born in this country so they gone consider me a flight risk…it's over I'm not going to sit in no cage."

"Damn it Jahtu," Leonetti knew that would be sufficient grounds for the DA to request no bail. "Just sit tight I'm gonna work something out because these cold cases--.'"

"Don't even waste yo time Leonetti," Killa opened his glove box and retrieved his pistol. "I'm not turning myself in to those people and expect you to do a miracle like you did when me and my brother was younger…hell no I refuse to rot in a cell," Killa cocked his pistol. "I'm staying out here on the street and if the cops want me they better come and find me…and if they find me they better be prepared to die because I am…I'm holding court out here in these streets," Killa hung up the phone then softly massaged his cheek with the barrel of his pistol thoughtfully.

"Damn what the fuck yo?"

Killa remained silent in deep thought thinking before he lowered his head. After a moment of contemplation, Killa lifted his head and locked eyes with Zulu.

"I gotta go back home to Nigeria Zulu…it's either go home or me and the cops kill each other because I'm not gone grow old and rot in a cell Zulu…I seen my mother grow old and rot in that mental institution…I refuse to go out like that…I rather die in the streets with my muthafucking gun than to live the rest of my life in prison."

Zulu placed his elbow on the car door and depressingly dropped his head into his hand. The ground beneath the Get Rich Crime Family's feet was literally opening its mouth and swallowing them. This couldn't be life. It seemed like tragedy upon tragedy was befalling them.

Later on that night.

Killa and Zulu quietly entered a house and crept through the back door. The house was dark and sent a creepy type of shiver up the spine. It was like they stepped into another realm as they tip toed down into the pitch-black basement. The energy created a chilling fear represented by the triple darkness. It was an unknown fear of not knowing what was in the darkness. Killa seemed to have the nocturnal vision of a cat because he led Zulu thru the dark basement knowing his every step.

"Shhhh." Killa held Zulu close to him before Killa quietly flicked on a light which hung from the center of the ceiling.

"What the fuck is this?" Zulu mumbled to himself when the light revealed what was in the darkness of the basement. It seemed like most of the basement was a Garden of the Gods. Beautiful plants of all colors and delightful smells created a tropical atmosphere in the center of the basement. Watching with timeless eyes that peered into infinity sat several statues of *Yoruba Gods and Goddesses* amidst the garden. The statues were inanimate objects but they generated the soulful energy of the divine hands of the Yoruba artists who sculpted the statues. Zulu was mesmerized as he stood frozen feeling himself become soaked up by the African Unconscious which was the origin of all. Zulu felt like he was back in the motherland of Africa and Zulu's ancestral memory banks slipped his mind into a nostalgic trance.

"Come on bro," Killa tapped Zulu out of his trance then led Zulu over to a cabinet mounted on the back wall of the basement. Killa snatched several items from off one of the shelves and placed them on a table in the corner. He then slid the back panel from out the cabinet and there was an electronic safe mounted on the basement wall. Killa began tapping in the electronic code and that's when him and Zulu both felt the swift force of someone and something creep up on them from behind.

Zulu was too scared to turn around and face whatever he felt behind and Killa froze stiff like water in a freezer.

"Whud me tell you bwoy bout entering me garden under moonlight," Yemaria aimed a double barrel shotgun at Zulu and Killa. "The Orisas need rest too."

"I'm sorry Ms. Yemaria I was following him," Zulu turned around to lock eyes with the little old lady. She favored Cicely Tyson but her skin was a lot darker, black and beautiful as the night sky.

"I'm sorry Nana...I really mean it," Killa spun around from the safe and caught the stare of Yemaria's eyes of wisdom. Her 94 years of physical existence was faithfully devoted to being a medium of the Orisas (Forces of Nature) and they seemed to keep blessing her with youthful vigor. She still moved swiftly like the black and golden brown striped cat kneeling beside her. Yemaria's lean vegetarian body could blast that double barrel shotgun with ease like a hillbilly. "May Oludamare (The Creator) forgive me for trespassing…but it's an emergency Nana," Killa went back to punching in the code to the safe.

"Me know you bwoys in trouble…that's why Orisas wake Sahku…dat bwoy like vegetable and his energy not good…he may not be here for long and want to see you bwoys before he go back to Orisas (Die)."

"Oh no." Zulu and Killa both felt their souls tremble from that shocking news. What good was it to be alive to be a vegetable. It was better to be dead. Killa paused for a moment then spun around and looked deeply in Yemaria's eyes.

"He gone go back to Orisas Nana?" Killa asked feeling like pain was melting his heart.

Yemaria remained silent with her gaze fixated upon Killa for what seemed like eternity before she turned around and slid into the center of her garden. The black and golden brown cat followed her before jumping on top of the windowsill and looking over the garden. Yemaria sat down in the lotus position amongst her statues and began quietly chanting in her soft voice.

"Come on we gotta hurry yo." Killa whispered to Zulu while pulling stacks of money from out of the safe. Killa grabbed him and Terror's money. He took several stacks and placed them in his pockets then he put the rest of the money in a bag and gave Zulu the bag. They both quietly crept pass the garden observing Yemaria meditate. Killa quietly dimmed the basement lights in the basement before him and Zulu then tip toed upstairs and waited for Yemaria to finish her meditation and oracle consultation.

About a half hour later the cat pranced upstairs being followed by Yemaria. She found Zulu and Killa waiting in her bright tropical colored living room wishing their mood could be like the cream sofa and soft turquoise carpet.

"Both you come now." Yemaria stepped into the dining room then waltzed into the back room. There was no door for the room but black, green, yellow, and red beads hung from the door frame as a cover. Light from the candles in the room flickered on the wall casting swaying shadows of the statues and figurines on the sanctuary in the room.

The sanctuary sat on the eastern wall in the center. And gracing the sanctuary was lit candles, fresh fruit, expensive jewelry and ornaments, beautifully colorful metallic stones, and at the top of the sanctuary sat a picture of a man who was black as the universe. The old Blackman had a bald head which reflected the sun's light as he sat meditating on a crystal white beach in Cuba. Yemaria called this man *Babalau*.

"No no Nana," Killa stopped at the threshold of the room. Zulu stood further behind Killa and wanted no parts of Yemaria's Ancient African spirit readings which could reveal one's destiny. "Nana please no...I don't wanna know...I don't nana...I just you need to--."

"Bwoy you shut you mouth and come now...come and sit...Zulu...you too," Yemaria ordered sitting in front of the sanctuary. "Both you come now I say."

"Aw please God why you doing this to me." Zulu was scared and didn't know what to do as he hesitantly eased forward outside the room. Yemaria was like a demanding grandmother you couldn't disobey. She had that spiritual charm of love that pulled you close to her.

"Nana please listen I gotta leave I'm in trouble with the Wazungu (White people)," Killa slid through the beads across the threshold. "You gotta call Abuja for me. I can't stay here the Wazunga looking for me."

"You can't run Jahtu," Yemaria spoke calmly with her gaze focused on Babalau's reflective picture while she kindled a beaded necklace in her hand. "Trouble will chase you...you must face it with Ogun-Lano's courage."

"Nana look at me," Killa stormed over to her and touched her shoulder as he knelt beside her. Yemaria zoned out and journeyed deep into the higher realms of consciousness where she was consulting with the spiritual forces which directed the course of human life. Killa gently tapped her a few more times and Yemaria was still unresponsive as she sat there in a daze. Killa then grabbed her shoulders and shook her yelling, "Nana listen damn it...I need you to call Abuja for me so I can leave, forgot these fucking Orisas I gotta-."

"Smack." Yemaria quickly ventured from the spirit realm back to physical reality and smacked saliva out of Killa's mouth for not only yelling and cursing at her, but he disrespected the Ancestral Culture of his genetics. Just as angels were messengers of God in Christianity, Islam, and Judaism, the Orisas were spiritual messengers of the Creator as well in Yoruba.

For that violation Yemaria smacked Killa so hard it sounded like thunder and Zulu felt it. Zulu stood at the threshold between the beads watching Killa drop to his knees feeling so weak in his soul he became overpowered by the guilt and began crying like a little boy who stole from the priest.

"Nana I'm sorry…I'm sorry…Oludamare (The Creator) please forgive me." Killa hugged Yemaria tightly and planted his face on her soft face as he shed tears. He felt sick to his stomach and the wickedness of the streets caused him to forget not only respect for the elders, but he became so entrenched in the wickedness of the streets he forgot about the Creative Power of the Universe which was God. He became so attached to the material world he lost his connection to the spiritual realm of the Orisas which were the forces of God which directed our lives and shaped and molded our destiny. In Jahtu Kadari's African culture, this was an extreme violation against nature itself.

"I'm scared Nana…I don't know what to do…please Oludamare please help me…please forgive me…please…I'm sorry Nana."

"You young men have deep trouble ahead and you cannot run…it will follow you…you have to face it to stop it…it's the destiny of Orunmila…this is you bwoy's Ori (Destiny) and the life chosen for you and the only way to stop this is to follow the divine guidance of the Orisas who are the only forces that can protect you from Eshu."

"Oh my God yo what is this shit she talking about." Zulu mumbled to himself feeling his intuition stroke his soul with the truth of Yemaria's words and spiritual gift of insight.

"Please Nana," Killa's voice was trembling with fear as he held Yemaria tightly like a scared child held their mother. "I just wanna go back home to Abuja please…please nana I'm scared to stay here…I done some bad things here Nana and the Orisas gone punish me if I stay…please make the call for me please nana."

Yemaria did what she knew wouldn't help Killa in any way. It was his life and decision. And being that our destiny is a universal phenomenon, it doesn't matter where one runs to on the face of the earth. Neither Zulu, Killa, or anyone else in the Get Rich Crime Family could escape the destiny designed for them. Everyone's whole life story was written by the hands of time before they entered the physical realm. Time was just a force of nature that walked man into his destiny.

Yemaria made the long-distance call to Toronto where she got in touch with a group of East Africans who were responsible for smuggling people into the U.S. through Canada. For the right price these East Africans could give a person a new life with fake passports, I.D., and new names. Everything besides plastic surgery they could make happen for a new identity.

After Yemaria contacted her source and made arrangements for Killa's departure, she blessed him and Zulu with palm oil and frankincense to shield them from the harm hunting them. She hugged them both tightly not wanting to let them go. Her embrace was lovely and warm. She was a very spiritual woman and her soul could be felt with so much loving she could bring peace and love to the mind of the most-evil person. She gave off a feeling of grace and Zulu and Killa both felt a sense of safety in her embrace. The three held their embrace so tight no one wanted to let go of the divine magnetism holding them together.

Zulu and Killa left Yemaria and it was sad for all of them. It was soul crushing seeing Killa leave Yemaria. It was like watching a mother send her only son off to war. And for Killa, he felt he was leaving his heart. When they left the house and pulled out the driveway, Yemaria stood at the front door watching them leave like a young child watch their parents depart. It was heartbreaking. So heartbreaking that the cold blooded Killer that Jahtu Kadari became in the streets didn't exist in the presence of Yemaria. Zulu drove away and Killa broke down in tears uncontrollably. He couldn't keep up the cold-blooded barrier he did in the streets. Yemaria was his heart and soul. The only love him and Terror ever had since the death of their mother. Yemaria wasn't their blood, but spiritually she was their mother. Yemaria was the only one who could bring the sweet tingle of joy to the Kadari Twins and now Killa was causing a tremendous pain within Yemaria's soul.

"Zulu please take care of her for me…please bro."

"You know I got you bro," Zulu observed Killa peering out the passenger window. Killa was avoiding eye contact with Zulu as his tears poured. "We been brothers since day one bro…I know Yemaria like yo mom's and I will always be there for her."

"Zulu," Killa now turned to Zulu wiping his eyes and said, "These tears for all of us bro…I may never see my brother again…I know I'm never gonna see Dolla and Mel-Cash unless it's in my dreams…and then I gotta leave yall…this shit is ugly and fucked up…it's never gonna be the same for us ever again Zulu…I feel it…I feel it."

Zulu knew it was the truth because he felt it too. That gut feeling of danger ahead was bubbling in both their stomachs. Even though Killa was the only one in trouble as of now, a cloud of bad fortune was forecasted to be swinging above the Get Rich Crime Family. The omen had already struck and was claiming its victims.

Zulu drove Killa up to Lockport, N.Y. which was a few miles east of Niagara Falls and the source of New York's Erie Canal. Zulu drove Killa to a Motel 6 where they were to check in a room and wait for the East Africans who would come and pick Killa up in two days, take him to the Canal and get him into Canada. Zulu sat with his brother from another mother cherishing their last moments they would probably ever spend together. It was a moment Thugs shared when they reminisced about their lives before the streets came into play. They reminisced about a time before the drama and pain, a time they could remember laughter and innocence. A time when they only knew the good side of life and not the evil side of murder, betrayal, greed and the many other evils of the human soul which plagues the world and make life a living hell. A hell of misery and tormenting pain like Zulu and Killa were experiencing now.

"Bro I love you and not for nothing," Killa sat in a chair while Zulu sat at the table by the window, "We can't be sad or cry because this what Oludamare (The Creator) chose for us…we only going through this because Oludamare made us strong enough to get through this…don't look sad Zulu…we made these decisions and knew our life was coming to this…just be happy we able to be in each other presence and tell each other the love we got for each other before we depart…come on bro…you was with Dolla and Mel-Cash before they left but you aint get a chance to tell them you love them…so no matter what happens next…I thank Oludamare for this time with you bro because it may be our last time."

"Damn bro…you right."

"But you know what my dude," Killa jumped up and got hype after feeling a glimpse of hope that no matter how hard it was, life do get better until it's over. "It aint over yet we still here…and when I hit the other side and you have NyJewel wire me the rest of my bread we gone link up in the Bahamas my dude…it aint over till its over…we gone link up again soon Zulu I feel it…I know it…word to Oludamare."

"Hell yeah," Zulu and Killa slapped hands and hugged, "The Bahamas yo…we gone link up there…word."

"I love you my G."

"No question love you too…Thug Love forever."

CHAPTER 21

Black Bull and Gonzalez were like two leeches under the microscope of Internal Affairs. They violated their oaths to protect and serve the citizens of the community and instead they protected and served the dope boys. This double dealing was about to soon end because detective Jake was on his job and building a strong case against two of the most crooked cops on the east side of Buffalo. Federal authorities along with the city's special narcotics and homicide units were about to dismantle the underworld of Buffalo's crime scene, and Black Bull and Gonzalez along with the Get Rich Crime Family was number one on the list of crews to be taking down.

As of the summer of 2003 the investigation was still under way. And a few days after Zulu slid Killa up to Lockport, NY to skate away with the East Africans, Black Bull and Gonzalez along with their fellow officers who were on the payrolls of other drug dealers threw themselves a wild extravaganza party. The party was a live gathering of top notch escort strippers from all over Western NY and Canada. At the party the indulgence of sex and cocaine would be the bon appetite of the party. And the raw cocaine would come from none other than the Get Rich Crime Family.

The night before the party, Black Bull and Gonzalez met up with Cream and Hawk for their payoff and for expense money to cover the escorts, as well as the three ounces of coco for the party. The crew was making sure they paid their dues to the law, but Black Bull and Gonzalez wasn't doing their job for the crew. This was a big issue and the crew was vexed at the fact there was a warrant for Killa's arrest for a homicide. Black Bull and Gonzalez had access to files and records and could easily eradicate any evidence. As far as witnesses, they were police who could persuasively make a witness change their mind about testifying on a suspect for fear of getting the wrong person convicted. Witnesses felt extremely bad if police made them believe they were getting an innocent person to spend the rest of their life behind bars.

When Cream and Hawk met up with Black Bull and Gonzalez, they put the cops on blasts for not utilizing their power which the crew was paying for. The crooked cops let it be known that some issues within the department were out of their control and the only way to avoid any murder beef with the law was to leave no witnesses, something Killa knew.

If only Black Bull and Gonzalez knew that a lot of information pertaining to the investigation was being withheld from them due to them now being targets of the investigation as well, they would realize they wouldn't be able to help themselves even if they had Jesus on their side when the law came down on everyone. It was the greed and arrogance of Black Bull and Gonzalez which blinded them and made them think their corrupt acts was going unnoticed.

They gave the Get Rich Crime Family the impression that all was under control at headquarters besides the situation with Killa. And to add injury to insult, Black Bull told Cream they should feel victorious because they terrorized the 12th Street Mob and destroyed their organization. Even though Killa was wanted for a body, he was still alive. Everyone else had their freedom and was still in the streets to make more money. They should count their blessings and keep counting the money. If only Cream, Hawk, Black Bull, and Gonzalez knew how many pictures of their illegal meetings detective Jake would be counting in a courtroom, they would know no amount of money was going to stop the Federal Government from putting them all under the jail.

The day after meeting with Cream and Hawk, detective Jake followed Black Bull and Gonzalez to a private social club on the Northside of Buffalo. The owner of the social club was none other than Marty Nitoro, an old and retired made man in Buffalo's decaying La Cosa Nostra. Detective Jake snapped photos of several crooked cops from different police districts in the city as well as a dozen and more high-class escorts entering Mr. Nitoro's club where they all would be indulging in a world unacceptable for officers of the law.

With the photos of the party added to the dozens of photos detective Jake already had, this was more than enough evidence to get a federal grand jury to indict the crooked cops and their drug dealing cohorts. If this wasn't enough, detective Jake felt the city was about to be taken over by inner city drug lords and crooked cops because that meant they were above the law if they continued with these transgressions against society.

....

Zulu sat in the middle of his living room floor feeling a storm of mixed emotions as he sat surrounded by stacks upon stacks of money neatly organized all over the living room floor. Exhaustion and fatigue rattled his mind from counting over six hundred thousand dollars of re-up money. It was three in the morning and he been counting since 1 o'clock in the afternoon.

Zulu rose to his feet yawning while stretching his aching muscles and unbelievably eyeing all the money. He then stepped out of the money filled living room and headed through the empty dining room on his way to the bathroom. Besides the small table and small refrigerator in the empty kitchen, the house was emptied of all its furniture and possessions and reason being, last week Zulu showed the house to a middle-aged couple from Greece who fell in love with the house after doing a walk thru. They were in the process of completing the paperwork of the real estate transaction and having the lawyers close out on the deal. That would take a few months to complete and while everything was taking place Zulu would be relaxing at him and NyJewel's new domain of paradise in the Bahamas.

Since Zulu found the buyers for him and NyJewel's house his mission was almost complete in Buffalo. The other half of his mission of counting the re-up money and delivering it to Canada would be complete in no time, and then he just had to wait for Killa to get in touch so he could shoot Killa the rest of his money. Afterwards Zulu would be on the first flight up in the sky to Nassau.

Zulu hit the bathroom and splashed the toilet with his urine feeling like he just got finished working overtime at a 9-5. His fingers were numb and he was burned out. Whoever said hustling was easy was lying. Zulu then began rinsing his hands and glanced in the mirror noticing the bags pulling on his eyes. Since he dropped Killa off a few days ago he hadn't been able to sleep peacefully. Ever since earlier in the day when he starting counting the re-up money, which was more money than he ever counted by himself, paranoia disturbed the stability of his mind and kept him thinking of everything from what if the cops rushed the house to what if someone ran up in the house to rob him. Even though he had his

9mm Sig Sauer and a Mac-10 within arms-reach in the living room, Zulu was still scared with all that money in the house. It was going to be one hell of a night trying to sleep with over a half a million-dollars strait cash.

He dipped out the bathroom and hit the living room and began neatly stuffing the stacks of money in a large Timberland suitcase. After stuffing and securing the money in the suitcase Zulu fell back onto the air mattress inside the living room. With the Mac-10 by one side of the air mattress, the 9mm under his pillow, and his arm on the suitcase which was on the other side of the air mattress, Zulu shut his eyes feeling excited, nervous, scared, and extremely tired. His mind was so overwhelmed within a blink of an eye his hyperactive mind drifted into a restful sleep world before he knew it.

Zulu awoke the next morning feeling completely rejuvenated and mentally replenished. His rest was so pleasant his spirit felt super as he sprung to his feet taking in the activating rays of sunlight beaming through the closed blinds. He felt great and was ready to make his power moves in the world just like the powerful sun made all life move in the world.

Cream and Hawk pulled up into Zulu's driveway and tapped the horn twice. Zulu grabbed the Mac-10 and crept to the side door and opened it. He stuck his head out into the driveway observing Hawk standing at the back of the house clutching a 45 automatic.

"Come on its all good out here baby boy," Hawk alerted looking around the backyard before he skated to the front of the house checking the street out front. "Hurry up lil bro." Even though no one was rushing to die by coming at the Get Rich Crime Family, with any type of large bank being moved around there had to be extreme security measures. The streets were always watching and there was always someone who wanted to play the hungry big bad wolf and take the next hustlers' bankroll.

"Cream this shit heavy as fuck come and help me," Zulu told Cream who was standing by the trunk of the car in the driveway. Cream then ran inside the house and gave Zulu a hand pulling the suitcase from out of the house before they tossed it into the trunk.

Cream then jumped behind the wheel of the money car while Zulu and

Hawk jumped into the Acura TL parked in Zulu's driveway. Cream pulled out first with Zulu following behind. They followed Cream to a duplex house in Shoshone Park on the Northside. They pulled into the back of the duplex where Sun-Z stood out back with Lil Flip and Crumbs.

They snatched the heavy suitcase from out of Cream's trunk then rushed into the house through the back door. Once inside, there were three more suitcases full of neat stacks of money. In total it was four suitcases totaling 4.8 million dollars. It seemed so unreal but it was really real as silence filled the room and everyone stood breathless unable to find the words to express this moment of success.

"Yo I can't believe this shit," Lil Flip broke the silence happy like a little boy in a toy store before he started rapping. *"Ever count a million cash...and that's not what's even in the stash...the sight of all these stacks got my gut bubbling with gas...who said this street money aint fast...I push the Lambo while burning the L like a candle...all this money a young nigga don't even know how to handle."*

"You a dickhead yo." Crumbs responded laughing with everyone else. Sun-Z then grabbed a roll of plastic which he rolled across the living room floor. He then took a box cutter and began cutting the plastic into 5 foot sheets where the money would be placed, wrapped up and taped, then stashed in the secret compartments of the vehicles driven to Canada.

While everyone helped to securely wrap the money they inquired about Killa. Killa was in Canada and just waiting for his flight. He had a long journey back to Nigeria but it was well worth it. Killa refused contacting anyone because the phones were probably tapped. In Killa's situation no news was the best news. So until Killa made it back home to the Mother-Land no one would hear from him.

The Get Rich Crime Family had reached the top. Their street dreams had materialized and was sweet as the crisp smell of money filling the air. For the riches gained they lost almost half of their friends. Paying dues and taking losses was an inevitable feat to endure to obtain riches. Were the street riches even worth it they thought to themselves.

"Why the whole crew couldn't be here at this stage of the game?" Crumbs asked helping Hawk tape up a bulk of money wrapped in plastic. It seemed everyone stopped what they were doing and in silence contemplated the harsh reality.

"It's the name of the game," Sun-Z sat against the wall gazing up at the ceiling. "You can't win without losing…it's fucked up but its how shit is."

"Yeah it's like B.I.G. said," Hawk added, "Mo money mo problems."

"The King of NY never lied," Cream replied hunched over a bulk of money, "We didn't have none of the stress and drama we got now when we was little niggas on the corner…word up this shit crazy."

Zulu sat back in silence starting to feel a twinge of fear in his gut thinking of everything. And for some odd reason Yemaria's admonition of trouble ahead began to make Zulu worry about his future. Zulu then jumped to his feet and slid into the kitchen where a bottle of Jack Daniels sat on the counter. He poured himself a double shot and guzzled the fiery whiskey to burn the knot of tension he felt.

"*Arrrgggh,*" Zulu blew the steam from his system after gulping the whiskey. He then took a deep breath feeling the shivers as the liquor lightened his burdened soul. "Alright let's go." Zulu shouted feeling better as he stepped back into the living room to help finish securing the money.

They finished securing the money and then placed the money in separate cars in the back parking lot behind the house. They then transported the money to Earl's Auto Mechanic Shop where the money would be secreted into the hidden compartments of three different vehicles.

Zulu and Sun-Z sat up at Earl's while everyone else ran to grab a bite to eat. While Zulu and Sun-Z sat outside the shop kicking it, the butterflies began swarming in Zulu's stomach again. He didn't know if it was the money which had him nervous or was it Yemaria whose voice he kept hearing in his head. While Zulu sat in deep thought thinking, Sun-Z was dwelling in the universe of his own mind as well. A moment of silence then crept between them before Sun-Z came out of his zone.

"Yo Zulu I wanna kick it with you about something heavy when we come back from Canada." Sun-Z gave Zulu a grave look.

"What's good why we gotta wait until we come back from the Can if it's heavy like you saying?"

"Let's just hit the Can first we gotta be focused on this business…it can wait."

"Come on big bro I got a lot of shit on my mind already and I don't need to be trying to handle business wondering what's so serious…I don't like wondering about shit," Zulu was hoping Sun-Z wasn't feeling salty about the incident that transpired which caused Iyana to leave him. "If it's that serious spit it out now because tomorrow not promised," Zulu took a deep breath getting ready for the worst.

"Man lil bro," Sun-Z peered down at the ground, "This just between me and you because its too much shit going on and everybody don't need to know this."

"Aw come on yo," Zulu knew it and felt it as he watched Sun-Z angrily shake his head, causing Zulu to get on point.

"Man lil bro I feel like muthafukas think we sweet…ever since they knocked Dolla and Mel-Cash off muthafuckas been trying to play us."

"What the fuck is you talking about," Zulu wondered if Sun-Z was speaking indirectly about Zulu having to let a shot off to keep Sun-Z from killing him, NyJewel, and Iyana. "Who trying to play niggas?"

"The pigs Zulu," Sun-Z had the look of death in his eyes, "Them fucking pigs trying to finish us."

"What." Zulu scrunched his face up in confusion. "The cops our enemy but what the fuck going on in yo head…tell me what the fuck going on."

"You don't see the shit with Killa…they allowed a body to get put on Killa…ever since the war with 12th Street Black Bull and Gonzalez been acting like they own us…and you know what? They do…they got bodies on all us…from the shit yall did to that snitch Big Walt…to the shit on the west side…and now look at Killa…they got us fucked Zulu and it's only one way to get ourselves up out of this."

"This dude can't be serious…why the fuck he gotta see shit like this?"

Zulu grabbed his head feeling like his death sentence was just signed. Sun-Z had a point and a real serious point. No matter how crooked the cops were, they were still cops and for cops to snitch on criminals it wasn't snitching because from jump they were cops, crooked or not. If a crooked cop found himself in a jam he would sing quicker than an amateur on American Idol. The situation with Killa was crazy and made Zulu feel Sun-Z had a serious point.

"So how the fuck you think we can get ourselves out of this shit with them?" Zulu asked.

"Lil bro you already know...you the only one left with the heart to do what need to be done and that's why I told you and no one else."

"I know you not thinking what I'm thinking?"

"That's why I love you Zulu." Sun-Z smiled, "You already know what we gotta do...we gotta knock Black Bull and Gonzalez off...we can't let em live because I got a feeling they gone tell on us and have us fucked like Killa."

"Come on bro you bugging I'm not killing no cops." Zulu jumped out his seat looking at Sun-Z like he asked him to find a way to the planet Pluto.

"Why...you scared to bust yo gun now."

"Hell no nigga."

"Well when we get back me and you putting that work in."

"Hell no I'm going to the Bahamas...I'm not fucking with you...you losing yo mind...them cops aint telling on us about no bodies because they helped us...they just as fucking guilty."

"I'm not chancing it Zulu...them pigs gotta die...who give a fuck they cops they bleed just like us...we knock them pigs off like we do anybody else."

"Bro I'm not killing them cops I'm going to the Bahamas."

"I wish Killa was here to help me handle this problem.... you can't run from yo problems you gotta handle the shit first then you slide...what good would it be to be down there worrying yo whole life if them pigs gone throw you under the bus and rat you out...you aint gone never be comfortable and at peace...the only way you gone be able to enjoy yo self is if them pigs dead and we aint gotta ever worry about them telling on us."

"This dude too fucking smart for his own good...it's like he crazy dumb

and just paranoid...I'm getting away from this nigga a.s.a.p." Zulu couldn't believe this but Sun-Z was speaking the truth. If Zulu truly wanted peace and wanted to leave the streets he would have to eliminate any enemies who could jeopardize his future safety and freedom.

"Listen lil bro as soon as we get back and break everything down we gone handle them pigs and then I slide down to the islands with you...me and Iyana gonna make it work out...she want us to move down there with you and NyJewel."

"Sun I got this gut feeling like something ain't right...ever since I dropped Killa in Lockport I been having this feeling like it's time to chill and fall back before shit get ugly for every last one of us."

"Them pigs the only ones who can make it ugly for us I'm telling you Zulu...once we handle this we gone be good."

"Man I don't know...but before I dropped Killa off we went to see his Nana and she was telling us some shit about what's ahead of us."

"Yo we don't deal with that spooky voodoo shit," Sun-Z twisted the cap off his Orange Crush Soda pop and took a guzzle. "It's yo mind making you paranoid...and fear attract trouble...don't let that voodoo shit spook you out and scare you...God gave you the power to control yo destiny and we in control of our lives...that's why we gotta handle that situation...don't be scared you know what we gotta do."

"This nigga talking about me being paranoid...he got some fucking nerve...I'm trying to be cautious. Then he bringing some God shit up...this nigga really losing it."

Zulu took a deep breath and sighed deeply before falling back into the chair outside the mechanic shop. He peered up at the Smurf blue sky with its fluffy cumulus clouds and told Sun-Z, "Never was I scared...I just think you trying to do too much...we shouldn't even be making this move to Canada right now...we got this shit with Killa going on...this shit too crazy...we should chill big bro and let the pressure die own...we should hit the islands and chill for a few weeks."

"*Haaaa*," Sun-Z laughed. "You feel a little pressure and now you wanna fall back…we gotta eat and keep eating…those islands making you lazy and turning you soft…you a wanna be on the beach nigga now."

"Now you tryna play me."

"Come on and don't lie lil bra…you was down in the Bahamas with Ny and my wife…you aint try having no threesome with them two big booties in them bikinis on the beach?"

"What the fuck type of drugs you on yo," Zulu felt his stomach now doing somersaults. What the hell was Sun-Z going through? He was starting to think that everyone wasn't right and everyone was against him. "Really big bro…how could you even think of some shit like that?" Zulu asked tensing his face in disbelief and feeling insulted.

"Let me stop playing with yo emotional ass baby boy," Sun-Z massaged Zulu's shoulder playfully. "I know you wouldn't violate our loyalty…take a fucking joke sometime this shit too serious we need a joke here and there."

"I don't find none of this shit funny…I just wanna get the fuck outta here yo…this shit is crazy."

"Listen lil bro I know we been through a lot the past year and we still going through shit…but this the game and you can't stop playing with that determination and dedication because a few technical difficulties…problems gone always exist we just gotta handle them…and always remember you gotta have friction in order to move forward…in life and in this game you judged by how you perform under pressure…you gotta have challenges to know your strengths…and even though we got some pressure and shit not going smooth we can't stop hustling and putting that work in…we just gotta be smart and on point that's it…get it together we got business to handle…it's time to play ball now…and when we get back we handling that situation with them pigs so be ready." Sun-Z rose to his feet watching Zulu zone out. Sun-Z then slid inside the shop to check on the cars.

Zulu gazed up into the sunlight and let his mind drift away like the clouds floating. This was way too much for Zulu and it seemed like Sun-Z was on a warpath. Zulu was tired and needed to fall back to clear his head of all the frustration, drama, and negative energy the streets flooded him with. The game was only played to get rich and even when the riches were acquired all the riches of the world couldn't solve none of the problems of life that ruptured the natural peace of the soul. Zulu never knew that this is what the game led to. After all the pleasure comes the pain and the reality was the fact that this is the life he chose so he had to roll with the punches; Do or Die.

"It's either be true to the game or go out like a lame...damn," Zulu thought to himself feeling his spirit get aroused by a visual energy that made him see Terror, Dolla, and Mel-Cash surrounding him and barking, *"Stop acting like a bitch ass nigga...stop being scared...this the life you chose because you built for this...you don't put yourself through nothing you can't handle...you a real nigga down to yo bones and soul...and it aint over till you reach the finish line."* It was more than a daydream. It was like a vision and a spark of motivation.

"Everything should be finished in about a half hour," Sun-Z bounced out the shop observing Zulu jump out of his seat with a vibe of confidence.

"Let's get this show on the road big bro," Zulu shouted feeling the electricity in his body amp him up.

"What the hell you had to drink?"

"A drink of Life...and we aint make this far to stop now...we gotta keep going and do it for the homies who aint make it...let's go."

"That's the Zulu I raised," Sun-Z and Zulu shook hands as they stood at the garage doors to the shop. "Let's make this shit happen."

....

It was about six in the morning and a mild chill hung in the air as the photon rays of the sun evaporated the morning dew. The crew had just finished breakfast at a 24hrs Denny's on Sheridan Road and now it was time to hit Canada.

Zulu, Cream, and Hawk each jumped behind the wheel of the three money cars and Sun-Z jumped in a Misty Grey Denali truck which was clean as its shiny exterior and interior. Sun-Z pulled out first being followed by everyone else. They drove down the deserted Sheridan road where the huge parking lots to the department stores and shopping malls were mostly empty besides merchandise and food trucks and the vehicles of employees in the lots. This was a good sign of no undercover agents being on their tail. Still staying a few steps ahead of the feds, Sun-Z pushed it down Sheridan to the I-190 while everyone else took different routes to get to the I-190 which lead to the three bridges that connected the US Buffalo-Niagara region to Canada. Sun-Z was the first to hit the expressway and see if they were being followed. Having the eyes of a falcon he knew they were good as he checked his rear-view.

Zulu's paranoia finally subsided but he still made a few stops at two gas stations to be extra cautious. Zulu then jumped on the expressway and slowly cruised thru the early morning rush where workers from Niagara Falls and surrounding areas were heading into downtown Buffalo to start their shifts. Zulu then slid into the exit lane leading to the Peace Bridge where a string of tractor trailers hogged the bridge while slowly pushing forward.

"Booth #4," Zulu reminded himself as he pulled in the lane heading to booth 4. Booth 4 was a booth being worked by a toll attendant who was being paid by the drug connect Marcel Francois. Marcel Francois had a toll attendant on each bridge who would easily let specific cars pass thru. Zulu made these crossings all the time with tons of money undetected thanks to Marcel's power. Even with border patrol agents scrambling in and out of toll booths inspecting vehicles and racial profiling everyone but whites, everything was always sweet.

Thanks to George W. Bush homeland security was tightening the policy on international border crossings day by day since 911. And in 2003 with the Iraqi war firing up, officers of homeland security seemed to be launching a war on American citizens, especially Black Americans and dark complexioned foreigners. The constitutional protections citizens once enjoyed were now in the garbage with no civil rights it seemed.

Zulu slid to booth 4 while bopping his head to the *Tom Joyner morning radio show on Buffalo's WBLK 93.7.* Zulu approached the toll booth flashing his license at the older pink face man with salt and pepper hair. The toll booth attendant winked his eye at Zulu and quickly asked Zulu's citizenship and destination. Before Zulu could even respond, the man told Zulu to have a nice day and waved Zulu forward.

"You too my man," Zulu responded slowly pushing the wheel up onto

the bridge and pass the Border Patrol Office where several border patrol vehicles
were parked. Zulu noticed traffic was at a standstill like a tailgating event at a
football game. While Zulu slowly moved forward he was in awe thinking of
Marcel Francois' powerful connections on the border. That was international
power hustlers from the block could never imagine. Marcel Francois earned that
power through 10 years in prison trying to bride a border patrol official. With his
dedication and diligence in the game, it paid off and Marcel achieved his goal he
set out to accomplish. This was the life hustlers and gangsters lived for.

"This what the game about," Zulu told himself lightly stepping on the
gas pedal as traffic eased forward. Zulu then became shocked as he learned what
the traffic jam was about. Several border patrol agents walking bomb sniffing
dogs stepped through traffic while dogs sniffed under vehicles. *"This some
bullshit,"* Zulu growled watching the officers stop at certain vehicles mostly
driven by middle-eastern and dark complexioned people. This was racial
profiling at its best.

An officer stepped to Zulu's passenger window suspiciously eyeing the
interior before telling Zulu to roll his window down. He then asked Zulu his
reason for coming into Canada.

"My girlfriend lives here…what's the problem?"

"Pull over." The officer gave Zulu a demanding look that would make
most people uncomfortable.

"Just wanna slow my day up," Zulu ranted while letting a few cars pass
before he swerved over to the Border Patrol Office at the foot of the bridge.
Several officers were escorting mostly yellow to black men, women, and
children inside and there was a sprinkling of whites being scrutinized as well.

Everyone was escorted inside and made to sit in a large waiting area.
The area was bright and new with its eggshell white interior. Young to middle
aged Caucasian men and women sat behind desk questioning everyone who was
supposedly a possible terrorist. After about thirty minutes of waiting Zulu was
called to a desk where he was questioned about who he knew in Canada, where
did he work at back in the states, did he have a criminal history, blah blah blah,
and then, what was in the car.

"Nothing but my luggage." Zulu answered with a frown.

"We need your car keys so we can conduct a search of your vehicle."

"Hell no is you crazy…you got a warrant," Zulu informed before he was told to go back to the waiting area. Zulu stormed back to the waiting area vexed and feeling racially discriminated against. A few minutes after sitting down, an older and seasoned looking officer told Zulu to follow him. He led Zulu to an office and quietly slammed the door.

The man introduced himself as Mr. Savoy then offered Zulu some coffee. Zulu let Mr. Savoy know he didn't want any coffee he just wanted to leave and go see his girlfriend. Mr. Savoy then demanded the keys to Zulu's vehicle. He politely told Zulu he had two choices. Either give up the keys or they will confiscate the keys and the car then run it through the X-ray. It was Zulu's choice.

"I choose to call my lawyer because yall violating my constitutional right to privacy…I'm not even under arrest so y'all violating my search and seizure rights as well."

Mr. Savoy then laughed before speaking into the radio strapped on his shoulder. He then pointed for Zulu to look at the picture on the wall of the ruling Queen of Canada.

"First off you're on Canadian waters as we speak…you are not home in the United States where your constitution protects you from illegal search and seizures…you can thank your President Mr. Bush because we are Homeland Security and our job is to prevent terrorism in your homeland and here in Canada…and we have the full authorization from your government and our Queen to take extreme measures in keeping our border safe."

"Dude whatever yo name is you can't be serious," Zulu fell back in his seat not understanding much of what Mr. Savoy said. "I'm not no fucking Arab I was born in America and I don't know shit about Islam, bombs, or none of that shit you talking about…let me call my lawyer or a Canadian lawyer…you not searching my vehicle because you aint even got probable cause or had a reason to pull me over…this bullshit…yall let all the white people pass but pull me over…yall some racist muthafuckas."

"No we're not racists we're officers for homeland security and we have a right to interrogate whoever wishes to cross our border," Mr. Savoy stated before there was a knock on his door. He then stood up as two officers stepped inside. Mr. Savoy and the two officers then led Zulu out of the office and took him downstairs to a cell block where it was about twenty cells and like a little Asia. From Arabs dressed in their Islamic garbs to Hindus and Pakistanis with long beards and turbans on their heads the cells were packed with a concert of different languages being spoken.

Besides the weird smell of the middle-eastern detainees, the cell block and cells were the cleanest Zulu ever seen. They were new and still smelled like fresh paint with the tan walls and Emory green cell gates. Zulu was then searched and made to empty his pockets before he was shoved into an empty cell. Besides the wooden bench which was also the bed, there was a steel toilet with a sink on top. It was bigger than the average 6x9 cell and much space for Zulu to pace the floor as he walked back and forth tuning into the hundreds of thoughts racing thru his mind. Every second and minute felt like a journey through the whole universe as Zulu's thoughts collided with his emotions making him feel uneasy.

Two long hours later and about a thousand paces stepped in the cell, Zulu finally sat on the bench hoping they didn't discover the hidden compartment. He then began thinking about the others and hoping they made it across.

A heavy-set lady with a freckled face and short hair then approached Zulu's cell and stood at the gate. She was dressed in a brown skirt and blazer and she held a file in her hand.

"Good morning Mr. Stevenson."

"Aint nothing good about this morning and can you tell me what's going on…why they got me detained here and why I aint get to make a phone call or been able to contact my lawyer?" Zulu pushed up on the cell gate.

"Well first your gonna have to answer to the D.E.A for the boatload of money your trying to smuggle into this country."

The words of Yemaria begin ringing in his head, *"You bwoys have trouble ahead."*

"Fuck." Zulu threw himself off the gate and began pacing in circles. "I don't know what you talking about miss but I need my lawyer…I need the phone a.s.a.p."

"You're gonna get a phone call and speak with your lawyer as soon as the U.S. Marshalls transfer you back to Buffalo."

"Man what the fuck…what the fuck they coming to get me for?" Zulu stopped pacing the floor feeling his heart which was heavy as a ton of bricks.

"You bwoys have trouble ahead."

"Leave me the fuck alone Yemaria," Zulu blurted out loud causing the lady to look at him like he was crazy.

"Mr. Stevenson I don't know the scope and detail of your situation but did you know you are under investigation by the United States Government?" The lady asked watching Zulu become horrified and look like he just seen a ghost. "And I all know is that the D.E.A and F.B.I told homeland security that they had to turn you over to their department because you're an American citizen under their investigation and they have jurisdiction over you."

"Juris what?" Zulu slowly stepped to the gate not believing what he was hearing. All he could think of was how he failed to follow his gut instinct and unfortunately Yemaria's warning.

"Why the fuck didn't I follow my instinct…why?" Zulu stood motionless staring through the cell gate at the lady's feet. "Fuck…I can't believe this shit."

The lady then got Zulu's attention and handed him some paperwork detailing the confiscation of the car and the undisclosed amount of money that would be turned over to the US Government. The paper further stated that Zulu was indefinitely banned from Canada forever, signed by the majesty of the Queen.

"Fuck you and Canada bitch," Zulu yelled tossing the papers in the cell. He fell back onto the bench feeling sick as he dropped his head onto his knees. He was being turned over to the Alphabet boys. If the crew didn't get snatched up yet, he wished he could contact them and tell them to leave everything and break out. Zulu thought about Killa realizing he left just in time.

"I told Sun-Z dumb ass we should chill and just go to the Bahamas…I swear to God that nigga really stupid…think he know every fucking thing," Zulu rambled to himself standing up and pacing the cell again. About three hours later and a marathon of pacing steps in the cell, two officers came and opened Zulu's cell. They cuffed him and shuffled him through the cell block then upstairs to the waiting area where three U.S. Marshalls in their men in black suits awaited him. The Marshalls received a file from Mr. Savoy and before they left Mr. Savoy had some last words for Zulu.

"Well Mr. Stevenson…may your constitutional rights help you in your mighty legal troubles," Mr. Savoy snickered like a red devil.

"Fuck you you racist bastard."

"Move it," One of the Marshalls pushed Zulu forward as they escorted him outside to a black Suburban truck with black tinted windows. Zulu was placed in the backseat with one Marshall while the other two jumped in the front seat. They threw on the police lights and headed back across the bridge to the USA.

Zulu sat in the backseat in cuffs peering out the back window like a tourist happy to enter America. He eyed the city skyline of Buffalo as they slid off the bridge and for the first time in a long time he was happy to be coming back to the horrible place he called home, but then again he felt sick knowing he was about to enter a world of hell. As he sat amongst the Marshalls he didn't know what to expect or what charges he was facing. One thing he could feel was that it was over and this would probably be his last time in the free world.

"Can yall crack the windows so I can get some fresh air…feel like I'm gone throw up," Zulu humbly asked feeling his head and stomach swirling while taking in his last sight of the city which raised him and taught him the game he was probably about to get life in the feds for.

"Well young man," The Marshall driving cracked Zulu's window then stated, "You're in your twenties and depending on if you co-operate or not will determine if you can get out when you're an old man or if you'll die in prison as an old man."

"Death before Dishonor," Zulu mumbled to himself deeply inhaling the smell of Lake Erie and the chemicals from the factories along the west side expressway before they entered downtown. "Damn…I should've died with Dolla and Mel-Cash because this can't be life."

Zulu was taking to police headquarters downtown where he was allowed to contact Leonetti before he was to be interrogated by homicide detectives. He was shuffled into an interrogation room and uncuffed before being told to sit at a table. The table was old, tattered, and scribbled on by suspects since time immemorial. There was even dozens of cigarette burns on the table and there was no telling how many tears the table soaked up from the crying suspects who sat at the table.

"Hello Mr. Stevenson," A short stout Caucasian detective entered the room along with a black detective who looked extremely mean but was quiet and well conserved. The white detective looked like the typical detective who been on the force for years and his whole life revolved around chasing and interrogating criminals. He had a bald head with hair on the sides and he reeked of coffee and cigarettes. He dropped the file on the table as he dropped into the seat across from Zulu. The black detective stood by the door in silent mode like he was a guard. The white detective then pulled out a pack of Kools and asked Zulu if he would like one. Zulu wasn't a smoker but he needed one.

"Ok first," The Detective introduced himself as Detective Boch while handing Zulu a cigarette then giving him a light. He then began sifting through the file in front of him and said, "Tell me about your buddy ah…Jahtu…the Kadari guy whose wanted for the homicide…where is he?" Detective Boch asked while sifting through photos in an envelope.

"I tell you about my Lawyer…that's it," Zulu blew cigarette smoke up into the air wondering about Killa. Killa would be up in the air and heading over the Atlantic Ocean to his destination in Abuja, Nigeria in no time.

"Come on guy and tell me where's your buddy hiding because you're in a world of shit," Detective Boch pulled out a few photos from the folder and tossed them in front of Zulu. Zulu peeked at the photos then frowned as he glanced around the room un-phased. The pictures were images of slain murder victims Zulu didn't give a damn about and the reason being, they were pictures of Megalito, Kato, Old School Al, and members of 12th street. "Listen your indicted by the federal government and a county grand jury is indicting you on several homicides as well…that's not starting with the ass hole full of other charges your facing…talking is the only thing that can help you at this stage." Detective Boch observed Zulu puffing on the cigarette in his own world as he glared up at the ceiling watching the smoke rise.

"Lawyer…L-A-W-Y-E-R. Leonetti."

"Your lawyer isn't gonna be able to help you…only you can help yourself by talking to me…and you can start by explaining where your friend is hiding and why you guys killed these people," Detective Boch scooped up the photos laying on the table and placed them back in the folder. He then tossed two other photos into the center of the table.

Zulu wasn't even trying to look at the photos. It was one thing to inflict pain on other human beings. When it came to murdering another human being and it wasn't for a divine cause, the weight of guilt was heavy on the conscience when there was introspection with the soul. To be confronted and reminded of the gruesome horror one committed against another human soul by viewing the damage done, made the God within make every killer become spiritually devoured in his own guilt. This was the judgment only the God within could order. Police knew this psychological fact and used it to their advantage.

Zulu was ahead of the game and knew not to face his own demons so he refused to even lower his gaze to the table and look at anymore death he had caused. The pictures of the bloody and bullet riddled bodies of 12th street members was enough. Zulu didn't need no more surprises of victims of violence him and his friends committed. It was real and the past was creeping up on the present moment. What's in the dark was coming to light and Zulu felt his days of light were over. Homicide and violence alone got criminals lights knocked out in a court of law and with violence and drugs being the charges Zulu was facing, it was over and he was about to be thrown into a bottomless pit of darkness. He was sure to die ten times in a prison cell before he seen the white tunnel of light that lead to eternal rest.

"Fuck." Zulu thought to himself pulling deeply on the cigarette. "Damn."

"Listen dont make your life harder than it is," Detective Boch shouted smacking the table forcefully then sliding the pictures closer to Zulu. "Plenty of guys like yourself work with us to get themselves out of these type of jams."

"Haaa." Zulu laughed evil eyeing Detective Boch who thought he was scaring Zulu. Zulu wanted to put a bullet in the detective's head and take a picture of it so he could happily look at it while he spent life in prison. Zulu hated how cops stood behind their badges and acted like they were superheroes. "You wouldn't survive a day in my hood without yo badge…most of you cops would never even come on the east side without yo badge and gun…you a real coward," Zulu said before unconsciously catching a glimpse of the two photos he was trying to avoid eye contact with. At first Zulu just glanced at the photos while his mind was elsewhere.

"Nooooooo." Zulu screamed out loud feeling his soul shake something terribly as he took in the horrible sights of Mel-Cash's charbroiled body and Dolla's bullet pierced head. Zulu felt like his own soul got snatched from his body as he jumped out of his seat and stumbled back into the wall staring at the table hypnotically.

The black detective grabbed Zulu but Zulu roared like a Lion as he pulled away from him. Detective Boch then ran around the table to help the black detective restrain the wailing Zulu.

"Get the fuck off me…get the fuck off me," Zulu shouted as other detectives rushed into the room.

"We got this under control," The black detective advised as him and Boch restrained Zulu.

"I'm good just let me go…just let me go," Zulu asked lowering his voice. "I just need to breathe…please."

"Alright now control yourself," The black detective nodded a warning finger at Zulu.

"Are you ready to talk now," Detective Boch asked watching Zulu walk in circles holding his head in confusion.

"You piece of shit cops gone throw my friends deaths in my face trying to break me," Zulu asked becoming weak in the legs as he fell in the chair and put his head down on the table thinking about his last time with Dolla and Mel-Cash. Zulu sat with his head on the table hearing Yemaria's voice reverberate in his spinning head. The room seemed to be rotating when he lifted his head. Why? Why was life coming at the Get Rich Crime Family so tragically? It wasn't raining, it was a monsoon flooding the world of the Get Rich Crime Family.

"If I'm under arrest can I please go to my cell," Zulu asked, feeling the weight of turmoil in his mind and soul causing him to feel lifeless and devoid of all energy before lowering his head to the table and closing his eyes. He needed to rest literally.

Detective Boch scooped up the photos then him and the black detective left the interrogation room to get a cell ready for Zulu. The black detective then returned about 20 minutes later to hear Zulu snoring. He banged the table and rocked Zulu awake, then motioned for Zulu to follow him as he held the door for Zulu. He escorted Zulu down the corridor and took him to the booking center. Zulu was handcuffed and made to sit on a bench outside a crowded holding cell where other arrestees were housed.

Zulu fell onto the bench and leaned his head against the brick wall closing his eyes. His life was a real nightmare and he'd rather be sleep and living in the virtual reality of his dream world. Hopefully he could dream of something beautiful because this was ugly. Zulu dosed off once again like he was at home in bed. His senses were oblivious to the shouting of arrestees in the cells, the numerous officers and arrestees strolling pass him and the ringing phones and voices of the police dispatchers. Headquarters was busy like the stock exchange.

Zulu was in a deep sleep when he felt someone shaking him awake. Zulu opened his eyes and thought he was dreaming. It was Gonzalez looking into Zulu's face as Zulu opened his eyes. Zulu felt even sicker and wondered was he in the deep trouble he was in because Black Bull and Gonzalez probably told on the crew about the murders. Zulu felt his energy rise as he went to grab Gonzalez but his hand was cuffed. He wished he would've listened to Sun-Z and they could've killed the cops sooner because 9 times out of ten the cops already told.

"Wake up man," Gonzalez shook Zulu again as Zulu lifelessly peered into Gonzalez' face without blinking. Zulu was so zoned out he didn't even realize Gonzalez began suspiciously looking around and un-cuffing him. The secretaries were busy on their phone lines while officers were busy fingerprinting suspects and taking mugshots.

"Listen Zulu walk strait out of here and don't look back...when you hit the streets just run...run far away from Buffalo...find a way to get out the country because it's over for everyone...the Feds nabbed everyone...go...get outta here."

Zulu was puzzled rubbing his wrists as Gonzalez removed the cuffs. Zulu's mind was moving so fast it didn't seem real and he thought he was dreaming as he continued blindly staring into Gonzalez' worried face while rubbing his wrists.

"Get outta here now...go...hurry," Gonzalez shook Zulu out of his daze, "Walk out and when you hit the street take off running," Gonzalez stated watching Zulu hop off the bench and began strolling towards the front exit where officers were walking handcuffed suspects inside.

Zulu strolled forward with his eyes steadily ahead peering outside beyond the doors realizing this was real and not a dream. He was scared and excited. Scared he may not make it to freedom which was a few steps ahead and excited just because he should be. This was the shortest but longest walk ever. Zulu's nerves trembled as he kept his steady pace towards the door remaining calm praying he made it outside to freedom.

Gonzalez stood watching Zulu quickly stroll down the hall before Zulu stepped through the doors into the night air of freedom. Gonzalez smiled as he then headed to the Captain's office where he was summoned and ordered to turn in his badge and gun. After that he was to head to the Police Commissioner's office where he would be read his rights and put under arrest. Gonzalez was facing so many federal and state charges he could give a damn about the charge of helping a suspect escape, Gonzalez took his charges like a man. Black Bull on the other hand felt so guilty and couldn't stand up to his actions, he would go on the run but several days later he would be captured and provide information on every unlawful act him and Gonzalez committed since the beginning of their career together, not to mention the criminals they protected. What a shame.

About 20 minutes after Zulu escaped from headquarters, Detective Boch returned to the bench Zulu was handcuffed only to learn from a suspect charged with stealing copper that a Spanish cop un-cuffed Zulu and told him to run.

Zulu bounced out of headquarters under the full moon with an appreciation for not only oxygen but for freedom itself. Zulu was so tensed and out of it the air invigorated his life-force like he was under water all day. He calmly walked down the block but at a fast pace pass all the unmarked police cars parked on the street. He hit the corner then slowly skated up the block so he didn't draw attention to himself in this part of downtown where there were many court buildings and government offices. He ran onto a street where there was a huge church and a commercial building which was closed. Zulu then took off 100 miles and running like a slave heading to the Promised Land. He dashed through a parking lot to a restaurant before coming out onto a strip where there was an alleyway. He flew thru the alleyway which took him several blocks down near the Theatre District by Main Street. He then slowed down and walked thru the Party district on Chippewa street and once he hit a quiet street he went back to sprinting several more blocks before he spotted a construction site. He dipped thru the gate and spotted huge steel beams to a new building under development. There were piles of dirt, stacks of bricks, portable commodes, and a few front loader trucks scattered around the site. He scanned the site for anyone lingering around and spotted no one, he then dipped inside a bulldozer which sat behind a tall stack of cinder blocks.

He sat in the bulldozer gluing his eyes on the entrances to the site praying no cops came swarming in. At the same time, he kept his ears tuned into the multiple sounds of cars, music, and voices of people on the streets surrounding the site. Every few minutes or so, he would hear police sirens either heading to the party district or probably racing from headquarters. Every time he heard any sound associated with police, he just knew they would be swarming the site any minute.

The anticipation Zulu was experiencing inside the bulldozer was torture. It was a good thing he wasn't claustrophobic because he would've probably died from his speeding heart rate. His nerves were jumpy and he felt like he was being bit by a thousand mosquitoes. He had to get out the bulldozer and away from downtown. It's been about an hour since Zulu been in the bulldozer and by now, every cop in western NY was on the prowl for Zulu. He was determined to get away from downtown but where could he run to and who could he run to. Everyone was literally either dead or in jail. NyJewel was way in the Bahamas.

"Who who who," Zulu searched his disheveled mind which was going crazy and unable to think. "Think think think…just breath be calm," Zulu stated searching his pockets which were empty. They confiscated all his belongings earlier so Zulu had nothing.

"Fuck." Zulu muttered looking down disappointedly and noticing glimmers of light on the floor of the bulldozer. It was change and about a few dollars' worth. "Oh yeah, I can call Prince." Zulu told himself scooping up the change then cautiously climbing out the bulldozer while scanning the surroundings. Zulu exited the site peeping up and down the block looking for a payphone while swiftly walking. He walked two blocks before spotting a payphone at a gas station across from a high school.

"Come on come on Prince," Zulu threw the quarters in the phone and began dialing. The phone rung twice before a disconnected service message spoke on the other end. When Prince heard the news earlier which was all over the local news channels, Prince terminated his phone service just in case his phone was tapped and went into hiding since the Feds liked charging people for old crimes.

"Aw come on Prince," Zulu softly mashed the receiver down before trying the number again and receiving the same message. "Help me God please help me." Zulu laid his head on the phone feeling hopeless before the best thing he ever thought of entered his mind. The thought of Destiny alone was like life to a dying man.

Zulu dialed her number and she answered on the first ring but she was speaking to a customer on her headset at her marketing job. Zulu listened to her professionally try to market a product before she told the unconvincing prospect to have a nice day.

"Sorry about that whose calling?" Destiny finally spoke into the phone.

"Destiny it's me," Zulu screamed excitedly. There was a pause and it took Destiny a minute to catch her breath and respond.

"Oh my God Zulu." Destiny stated unbelievably.

"Sweetheart I need you like never before and like right now."

"Zulu me and Desiree coming to court tomorrow for you and Hawk."

"No Destiny I'm not locked up I'm on the run and I need you right now."

"Oh my God," Destiny whispered looking around making sure none of her co-workers heard her. "Where are you?"

"I'm downtown by Elmwood and Tupper I need you to get here quick."

"I'm on my way Zulu."

"Ok I call you back in 15 minutes." Zulu hung up the phone and scanned the surroundings before dipping out the phone booth. He spotted an older man who was casually dressed and staggering into a building down the block.

Zulu headed that way and upon approaching the older man Zulu could see the man was so drunk he could barely stand. Zulu became the man's crutch and helped the man into the building.

"*Hey there youngster,*" The older man slurred with an eastern European accent as he threw his weight onto Zulu. Zulu walked the man inside the building and sat him on the steps in the hallway.

"Damn old head you saucy as hell," Zulu carefully sat the man on the steps smelling the booze and nice scented cologne on the older man.

"Hey," The older man became loud while pulling out a lighter and a pack of Marlboros, "Me wife's sauce is de best," The man stated before drooling on himself and dropping his chin onto his chest, "But she not cook me anymore of her sauce..why..why she no more..that winch..you must tell her for me..I want her sauce…" The man mumbled before passing out while sitting on the steps.

Zulu took a cigarette out of the pack and lit it. He then wondered if the older man had a cell phone but then again it wouldn't be a good idea to call Destiny from the phone. Zulu stood there in the hallway for about 20 minutes before sliding outside and finding a pay phone next to a store next to the building. He dialed Destiny and she was about 5 minutes away. Zulu knew he couldn't stand around outside so he gave her a location which was a parking lot serving a few bars. Zulu skated down the block to the parking lot noticing everyone was drunk and not paying him any attention. Zulu dipped thru the swarms of rowdy college students and hit the parking lot peeping Destiny pulling in on the other side.

"Thank you God!" Zulu told himself while jumping inside her car.

"Oh my God Zulu," Destiny hugged and squeezed him tightly while in tears. "What is happening to yall this is sad... yall was all over the news...what is going on."

"Listen I don't know just get the fuck outta here," Zulu yelled while scanning the parking lot.

Destiny cautiously rolled out of the parking lot and drove Zulu away from downtown as he reclined way back in the passenger seat. In tears, Destiny then explained how she witnessed on the news Sun-Z, Cream, and Hawk were arrested in South Buffalo at a warehouse where they were in the middle of receiving a large shipment of drugs from an un-identified Canadian man. The cast also spoke on how Zulu was caught trying to transport over a half of million dollars across the peace bridge. Destiny then explained how the Feds raided Desiree and Hawk's house and confiscated their cars as well. The show was over.

"What the fuck," Zulu grabbed his head grievingly frustrated. He knew the feds had to raid his empty house where he had a couple of thousand dollars stashed and Killa's large sum of money. His house was off limits because they would surely be there waiting for the fugitive. Zulu wasn't even chancing going to Destiny's. He didn't know where to go or what to do. He had no money no nothing. With NyJewel thousands of miles away he had to figure out some way to stay low until NyJewel could come to his aid.

Zulu couldn't believe this. In one day, he went from being on top of the world with hundreds of thousands, to feeling like the dirt of the world and being broke. Right now he had nothing. He was a fugitive on the run and even the air he breathed wasn't guaranteed. This wasn't life at all Zulu thought to himself.

"Listen Destiny I know I hurt you in the past but I really need you. I have no one or nothing. All I have is the clothes on my back."

"Zulu I do anything for you," Destiny softly touched his hand while she gripped the wheel. "I don't have much but you have me and whatever I can help you with.

"I'm gone need a motel room for a few days until I can think something out."

"Ok Zulu," Destiny stated driving Zulu out to Depew, NY where she rented Zulu a kitchenette room for a week. Destiny was like an angel with wings who took Zulu up out of this world of hell. Destiny grew spiritually and found the glory of the God within her spirit to forgive Zulu for the past. And while Zulu hid out in his motel room Destiny brought him breakfast and dinner on a daily along with her consoling company.

A week had passed and Destiny extended Zulu's room from one week to two. On the 14th day when it was either extend the stay or check out, Destiny's paycheck was not only short because she was constantly taking off to help Desiree with the baby while Desiree was back and forth downtown visiting Hawk and seeing lawyers, but Destiny was fired from her job since she had too many family emergencies in a matter of two weeks. Destiny was giving her last paycheck and told to file for unemployment if she couldn't find another job.

Zulu felt so bad because there was nothing he could do for Destiny. He felt so incompetent and he felt like a heavy burden on her which ruined her life. Destiny had nothing to do with the streets but the harsh reality of the streets affected her life in a serious way.

Destiny may have lost her job helping her fugitive ex-boyfriend and her thug-loving sister, but Destiny was a thorough and ride or die Sista who was ready, willing, and able to be there in times of crisis. She couldn't afford to keep Zulu hidden at the motel any longer, but she had her home and home is where the heart is. So back to the hood Zulu went hiding with the first love of his life.

CHAPTER 22

Members and associates of the notorious Get Rich Crime Family were snatched up by the Feds and being detained in a Federal Detention Center in downtown Buffalo. By the luck of chance, Lil Flip and Crumbs slid pass the watchful radar of the authorities. They were still on the streets but scared to death and laying low.

Up inside the detention center's Fox Trot floor, inmates crowded around the T.V. in the dayroom as a news flash appeared on T.V. It's been almost three weeks since Zulu been on the run and over five weeks since Killa been on the run. Killa was back in the Motherland laying back in Nigeria while him and Zulu's faces were being flashed during every news segment. Cream tuned in to the T.V. while inmates got hyped at Zulu's escape from custody and Killa's escape. There were the bold informant ones who would step to Cream inquiring Zulu's and Killa's possible whereabouts. Cream would remain silent while ice grilling the nosey inmates even though he was happy Zulu and Killa was free. Since Sun-Z and Hawk were on different floors, it was only one Prisoner Cream cared to associate with and hold dialogue with about such serious issues.

Cream stepped away from the T.V. and headed to a table in the back of the Pod. An inmate sat at a table by himself studying a chessboard. He was in his late thirties and had smooth sandy brown skin and to have been locked up for almost a year, he was well groomed. A pretty boy in his looks but his penetrating eyes spoke of strength and power. And he was powerful. He was a king amongst Killers in the streets. And he was well acquainted with the Gangsters from the A-Squad like Sun-Z and Hawk. This was Ra-King Allah, known as Ra or Ra-King.

"Cream what up with you?" Ra-King asked keeping his studious eyes on the chessboard as Cream approached the table.

"Zulu and Killa still out there," Cream dropped into the seat across from Ra-King.

"*Hmm.*" Ra-King nodded his head thoughtfully still focusing on the chessboard.

"What you thinking bout Ra?"

"Do the math right," Ra-King finally lifted his eyes from the chess board and focused on Cream. "Only thing uncivilized about being on the run is how these devils gone put pressure on any and everyone who know and associate with Zulu and Killa, basically all yall peoples gone get harassed by these devils. These devils don't like no one beating them or escaping from they grip."

Ra-King paused observing Cream give his full attention. "It is what it is though…and if Zulu and Killa make it to they destinations they gone be legends in my eyes," Ra-King smiled and shook hands with Cream. "Word up…any real G who beat these devils or escape them is a legend on the level of the Most-High…and it's only one legend who on the level of the Most-High when it come to beating these white devils."

"Who that be?"

"Hmm," Ra-King closed his eyes while smiling like Cream was slow for not knowing who was the best to ever do it. *"Frank Matthews…The Black Caesar…a black man who the Italian Mob wouldn't even fuck with..Frank Matthews was.the best and a real legend in the streets of New York City and all over the country."*

"Yo I'm telling you Ra if my niggas ain't get caught yet they not gone catch them I'm telling you…I know Zulu on them islands by now and I know Killa been back in Nigeria…I know it."

"I hope so Cream because yo," Ra-King's smile faded and a look of sorrow covered his face, "I hate to say it but yo…with all the publicity yall got with them bodies, the crooked cops, and the major weight yall got knocked with and then Zulu and Killa escaping these people only gone make it worse you feel me…these devils hate seeing a Black Man get out of they grip." Ra-King took a deep breath sighing with grief like he was in Cream's situation. Ra-King was facing 40 years himself if he blew trial for conspiracy to purchase 35 kilos of cocaine from the D.E.A. His drug-connect whom he was copping from for years set Ra-King up with the D.E.A. His connect was file as a dumpster in Chinatown. Ra-King had loopholes in his case so he had light at the end of his tunnel. Now the Get Rich Crime Family, the only light they would see is probably electricity from the chair. Their situation was ugly.

"Cream I aint trying to make you stress no more than you are…but them people gone try to make an example out of yall…and truth be told…I hope Zulu and Killa do beat these people because somebody need to."

Cream massaged his forehead thoughtfully knowing it was the truth. With over seven counts of murder, distribution of narcotics across international waters into the U.S., and possession of over 100 kilos of cocaine and over 25 kilos of heroin, Cream needed to worry about his defense strategy instead of Zulu and Killa's escape strategy. The federal and state authorities in Western New York were about to have a field day of modern lynching the Get Rich Crime Family.

Recreation was called so Cream and Ra-King hit the gym to meet up with Sun-Z and Hawk. When they entered the gym Hawk was waiting at the pool table looking stressed out and he was stressed. Hawk was stressed because of Sun-Z's madness. Everyone knew Sun-Z was a mess since the war with 12th Street and now he was becoming a wreck. Hawk was so stressed he wouldn't even mention the madness wrecking Sun-Z's mind. Instead, Hawk racked up the pool balls to play Ra-King while telling Cream that Sun-Z was literally going crazy. That's all Hawk could say. When Sun-Z's unit finally slid into the gym, Sun-Z came through and gave Ra-King dap before telling Cream to spin the gym with him. Sun-Z and Hawk refused to acknowledge each other but instead ice grilled each other.

"Yo Cream I'm telling you that nigga losing his mind," Hawk yelled to Cream as he walked off with Sun-Z. "The nigga crazy and think he never wrong."

"What the fuck is he talking bout Sun-Z?" Cream was puzzled as him and Sun-Z slid onto the basketball court.

"Listen Cream I'm gone be strait up with you no chaser," Sun-Z stated in deep thought as him and Cream dipped around inmates standing on the side lines. "I don't think Zulu on the run Cream," Sun-Z said looking straight ahead.

What?" Cream was caught off guard and stopped in his tracks with his face twisted. "Then what you think?" Cream was confused as Sun-Z took a seat on the bleachers and took a deep breath before he explained what he thought.

Sun-Z pointed at Zulu's paranoia and fear the day before they made the move to Canada. Sun-Z on his high brain wave of intelligence believed that everything with the crew was set up too perfectly for things to crumble the way things did. Everything was in order. They had an airtight system of shipping money into Canada and shipping drugs back into Buffalo. From the toll booth attendants letting vehicles slide through to the trucks shipping the drugs, everything was tight. Then with two veteran detectives on their payroll feeding them info, they were two steps ahead of law enforcement. At least that's what Sun-Z thought. He should've known better. His pride and ego made him feel his wise and intelligent thinking built one of the most sophisticated networks that couldn't be busted by the feds. Sun-Z was drunk on his own power and intelligence.

Sun-Z's pride and ego was also challenged and he felt less than himself ever since the night he fought with his wife and NyJewel, and then Zulu had to intervene. Sun-Z blacked out that night but he remembered what happened clearly and instead of accepting his guilt, he felt defeated and was seeking to redeem himself. From wanting to kill the police to what he now had on his mind, it was all about making himself feel good over the pain of guilt and shame. Even with his wife running away to the islands with NyJewel, deep inside Sun-Z faced an insecurity of trust. That insecurity of trust came out as a joke when he made the comment to Zulu about having a threesome with NyJewel and his wife. Sun-Z didn't realize it, but the pressure was causing his mind to not see things clearly. Being that Sun-Z's pride and ego was hurt, he unconsciously made himself believe he wasn't the one who was wrong about anything, and now it was time to point the finger and at who?

Sun-Z would tell no one how the thoughts of Zulu having threesomes with NyJewel and Iyana in the Bahamas flooded his brain circuits even though he didn't believe it. The mind play tricks a lot, and Sun-Z truly believed Zulu's fear is what got Zulu arrested at the border. Then he further believed that Zulu's fear caused Zulu to break down and open his mouth about the whole operation. From Black Bull and Gonzalez' role of providing info to the crew down to the warehouse in South Buffalo where the drugs from Canada was delivered. The way Sun-Z seen it, Zulu was scared to murder the police so he hurried up and snitched to prevent doing it. Zulu basically wanted to protect the cops and keep them from getting murdered. The way Sun-Z seen it, there was no way Zulu could've escaped from police custody. Zulu was in witness protection and the authorities had the media making it look like Zulu was really on the run.

"Zulu police and I'm telling you…the nigga ain't right."

"Yo I don't know if you sniffing some of that shit they got on yo unit or what but you bugged the fuck out," Cream flipped in a rage and began pacing in circles in front of the bleachers while Sun-Z sat. Hawk and Ra-King then stepped up. "Yo Hawk this nigga really insane…I never knew this nigga was that crazy…he fucked up in the head." Cream stated disbelievingly.

Hawk and Ra-King stood beside Cream shaking their heads disappointedly at Sun-Z as he sat back on the bleachers with a look of firmness. He was sticking to his belief like it was solid reality.

"I can't believe the shit I just heard," Cream refused to even utter the words of Zulu snitching.

"Come on the nigga had to snitch," Sun-Z stood up. "Leonetti said they was holding Zulu at headquarters and by time he got there Zulu was gone…come on yo that's some bullshit about him escaping…he not Wesley Snipes who can escape from US Marshalls…that's Hollywood…and he definitely not no fucking Frank Matthews...believe that shit if yall want to."

"Yo Sun-Z I'm gone keep it G with you," Hawk placed one of his feet on the bleachers and gave Sun-Z a cold stare. "Since we was kids I never once disagreed with you on anything because you was always a great thinker and leader…I never…never ever told you you was wrong about anything..never…but right now," Hawk pointed his index finger at Sun-Z while biting down on his lip, "You wrong homie and I don't even know how you could entertain a thought like that."

"Word is Bond to the Father Allah," Ra-King cut in, "Sun-Z you should know better and Know the Ledge (Knowledge) and not fall off the edge into the white devils trick-knowledge…this is how they divide our people and conquer us…they cause us to tell lies on each other so we can fight and kill each other…come on Sun…you supposed to Knowledge before you Wisdom (Think before acting and speaking) and you never think bad about yo brother until reality manifest itself in black and white."

"I aint feeling this dude and he got me so sick," Cream was vexed looking onto the basketball court. "The only way shit like that should come out yo mouth is if you seen it in black and white…and that you will never see and Hawk gone verify that…Zulu gone die before he snitch...fuck is on this nigga mind."

"This nigga know Cream," Hawk punched his hands in anger reminding everyone how Desiree came on a visit speaking in code about Destiny having her boyfriend back. "Just stay the fuck away from us Sun-Z…because in a minute we all gone be suspect to you…in times like this we gotta stick together and we can't let no pressure break our sanity…at times like this we can't let internal issues break us…it's times like this we really need to be strong mentally and emotionally...and right now Sun-Z…you not showing strength and you the one not to be trusted…we out yall." With that being said, Hawk, Cream, and Ra-King dipped off and left Sun-Z in his own world of twisted reality.

....

It was now five weeks since Zulu been on the run and it was getting financially harder day by day for Destiny to provide for him and herself. Zulu was able to contact NyJewel once but he learned from her that the Feds contacted Leonetti inquiring about her since she was the legal owner of several business establishments that were financed by the Get Rich Crime Family. NyJewel was an entrepreneur and Realtor who had good standing in Western NY so the Feds spared her the money laundering charges she could have been facing. But then again, Leonetti warned her to stay away from the states until the case was over because the powerful and dirty Feds could indict anyone, even a hamburger. It was nothing for the Feds to formally charge someone. With that revelation Zulu had to be extra cautious contacting NyJewel because the Feds could be laying in the cut hoping she led them to Zulu. NyJewel being on top of her game and a solid woman wasn't scared to make it happen for her Man. She had a close friend

who worked at a D.M.V office in Rochester, New York, and that special friend
was going to get Zulu some I.D. so he could board a cruise ship heading to the
Bahamas.

So until that move came through, Zulu just had to stay under the shell.
But for the time being, ribs were touching and bills needed to be paid for
Destiny, Desiree, and the baby. Destiny lost a good marketing and sales job as a
result of her leaving work and taking off to mainly help Desiree and the baby
during this crisis, the streets had a way of ill affecting a law abiding citizen's life.

The feds not only raided Desiree and Hawk's $ 350,000-dollar house out
in suburban Orchard Park, but they confiscated all the money stashed away and
they were filing seizure of property papers to seize the house. Desiree was a
mother of a newborn but the Feds didn't seem to care. And since the Feds
snatched everyone, Desiree spent most of her days at lawyers' offices filling out
paperwork to keep her house, seeing Hawk's lawyer, and visiting Hawk. Her life
now revolved around the legal system and not being a mother to her child, a duty
Destiny took on.

The situation was hard on everyone. It was hard for those locked in the
cage and even the women who supported them. Destiny spent most of her days
watching the baby while Desiree handled legal issues. Destiny couldn't leave the
baby with Zulu while searching for a job because if police found Zulu and the
baby, the police would be more than happy to send the baby to child welfare
hoping to have the baby placed in foster care. Destiny refused to let that happen
so she was ruff riding it till the end with her sister and her fugitive ex.

One day after Desiree had a visit with Hawk at the Federal Detention
Center, Desiree had a discussion with Zulu and Destiny in regard to her living
situation. Desiree explained that it was probably a good idea to sell her and
Hawk's house even if the Feds didn't seize it, because there was no way she
could keep up with the taxes and other expenses attached to the lavish house.
Desiree then asked Zulu about a specific house on North Parade Avenue near the
Buffalo Science Museum. The house was a nice two story house owned by the
crew and the house was actually a stash house not too many people knew about.
Desiree wondered if she and the baby could move there since that house was the

only one that didn't get raided like the other houses the crew owned.

"Hold on Desi," Zulu had an eager look of interest and surprise on his face, "That house ain't get raided?"

"Na but they raided all yall other spots...and I ride by the house every day on my way here."

"Take me there now A.S.A.P," Zulu demanded hoping no thieves and burglars beat him to the punch because last Zulu remembered, it was a couple of bricks in the stash.

Nightfall hit. Desiree pulled onto Northampton Street which sat a block over from North Parade. Zulu jumped out the wheel and hit the backyard to an abandoned house. He leaped over a five-foot fence and landed in the backyard to the stash spot. A 1999 Jeep Grand Cherokee was parked in the yard which was one good sign. Next, Zulu glanced at the back windows of the house. They were all closed and shut tight, another good sign. Zulu then snatched a blue city garbage can and slid it under the back window. He whipped out a screwdriver and a hammer to pop the window out. He then climbed thru the window and the ADT alarm system tripped and began beeping. This was the third good sign that no one had been in the house.

Zulu had thirty seconds to disarm the alarm before it started screaming and not only alarm the neighbors but sent a signal to the nearest precinct. Zulu raced to the hallway with so much excitement and nervousness it took him a few seconds to remember the code. He deactivated the alarm then slid downstairs into the basement. He went to a vent duct connected to a furnace and began unscrewing the vent praying that the bricks were still here.

"Yesss," Zulu observed the mini duffel bag in the vent then snatched it and unzipped it. It was five kilos wrapped in green wax paper with clear tape on them. "Thank you God," Zulu thundered zipping up the bag and tossing it on his shoulder.

He felt happy because these keys of cocaine were the keys to his freedom. He raced upstairs and grabbed a scale and several boxes of Ziploc and sandwich bags from the kitchen cabinet. He then hit the bedroom and went to the closet. He stepped inside and reached up on the door frame and retrieved a

Smif-n-Wesson 380 caliber handgun. He threw it on his hip and broke out through the side door after resetting the alarm.

With Zulu laying down in the backseat Desiree pulled into Destiny's driveway and pulled all the way into the backyard. Desiree and Zulu then entered the side door and crept down into the basement. Zulu busted one brick open and weighed up 125 grams of the yellow tinted cocaine with pearly flakes. He placed it in a sandwich bag and double wrapped it. He then gave it to Desiree along with instructions on who to go see.

About one hour later.

Desiree waltzed into the *Fountain Blue Lounge* on Kensington Ave, home of the Hyena Crew from Bailey Avenue. Like the eyes which rolled round and round watching her, Desiree gyrated the hips on her slim legs as she strutted to the sounds of *Lil Mo and Fabolous' hit song Superwoman*. The hustlers and divas figured she was there to shut it down the way she pranced in them Gucci pumps. Desiree had a family depending on her so she had no time for partying, but money and sex was so appealing, she would flaunt her sex appeal because sex attracted money. It was strictly business on her mind and people could tell from the way she ignored the money splurging men who offered her drinks when she took a seat at the bar.

She ordered a shot of Hypnotiq before removing her Gucci frames and scanning the faces of the people sitting around the bar. While waiting for her drink she then searched the faces of the people sitting at the tables by the bar before peering into the back table section by the small dancefloor and kitchen.

Desiree received her drink and paid for it while keeping her eyes on the four men at the back table huddled up talking. It was Munchie and G-Boy and nine times out of ten they were discussing business with the two men they sat at the table with over shots of liquor.

After about 15 minutes passed and she was on her second drink, the two men exchanged handshakes and hugs with Munchie and G-Boy then broke out the bar on a mission. Desiree then calmly slid off her bar stool and nonchalantly stepped through the crowd and headed to the back of the bar. As she neared the back section, three promiscuous dressed females tipsy off the liquor bumrushed Munchie and G-Boy's table attracted to the gold jewels with the iced out Jesus pieces they were rocking.

One of the females gave G-Boy a hug while he was still seated and suffocated his face with her voluptuous double D's while she caressed his intricately designed French braids. The other female planted her backside in Munchie's lap while the third female stood by the table grooving to the music.

Desiree stood at a distance and turned away not appearing to be desperate like the hoochie mommas. Desiree stood by the jukebox sipping her liquor while slow grooving and checking out the song selection. Then after a few minutes she glanced over at Munchie and G-Boy and caught eyes with the both of them. They both then whispered to each other then said something to the females at their table. The females curiously looked around the bar before breezing from the table and hitting the bar for more drinks. G-Boy then waved Desiree over. She slid to the table clutching her purse like her life was inside of it.

"I knew you be back for some of this good dick and bankroll I got," G-Boy stood up to hug Desiree. "So you ready to stop playing house now that yo man gone huh?"

"Nigga please," Desiree gave G-Boy a quick hug then tried pulling herself away from him but G-Boy snatched her close to him and gripped her ass. "Stop it get off me Thomas you play too much." Desiree yanked away from G-Boy shouting his government name. These two had a history Desiree wouldn't dare let repeat itself.

"You know you want me stop fighting yo pleasure," G-Boy released Desiree shooting a smile at her revealing a mouth full of platinum grills. "You aint doing nothing but depriving yo self."

"Anyway what's up Munchie?" Desiree slid over to Munchie who stood to embrace her.

"You tell me what up," Munchie motioned for Desiree to sit after hugging her. "Yo I'm sorry to hear what happened in yall hood…we been wondering when you was gone come through and let us know how them boys doing…you know we fucks with the Get Rich Crew…whatever they need we got em."

G-Boy then leaned across the table close to Desiree's face and whispered, "And I been fucking with you before you turned Ms. Wifey…you know I'm still here for you."

"Boy let it go that was back in high school…we grown now and I would never do the things I did when I was younger…I was a senior and you was a freshman…no way…I moved on to bigger dick and more money Thomas," Desiree shot back in response rolling her chinky eyes at G-Boy.

"Whoa," Munchie busted out laughing peeping G-Boy turn fiery red feeling his ego get knocked down. G-Boy was in love with Desiree back in the days but she was too fast for him and she dumped him for the older hustlers who was who dumping bankrolls on her.

"Bitch I know you aint trying to play nobody because once a hoe you always a hoe…you played yo housewife role for a few years but now yo man gone and look at you…you up in my world…what the fuck you in my world for…you trying to sell some pussy…because niggas don't buy pussy no more…I got too much free pussy to spend money on sex," G-Boy snatched his shot of henny then threw it back.

"That's why I stopped fucking with you back then because you was too immature, you should know I never was a bum bitch selling pussy…I just know how to get mine like a lot of bum niggas and bitches wish they could…and you need to respect a bitch like me who know how to hold shit down for her man when he down and out…do you got a thorough bitch like me that's gone hold you down? I was probably the only real bitch you ever had and you ain't learned nothing because you still don't know how to respect a real bitch…don't judge me because the law I live by is too real for you to understand, I got a family depending on me and I got real niggas I gotta hold down so you need to respect me because I'm here to see yall so I can do what I gotta do for my peoples."

"Damn G-Boy she right," Munchie was more understanding and empathetic. He could respect where Desiree was coming from. "That's some real shit Desi and being that I fucked with the peoples however we can help them we will."

"How much money you need fuck all this beating around the bush shit?" G-Boy thought he really had Desiree figured out. He was just a Thug who didn't give a damn about a hoe. He pulled his bankroll out of his pocket and began peeling hundreds and dropping them onto the table. "What you need a few geez?" G-Boy asked still being judgmental not realizing Desiree's agenda.

"I came here to handle business with yall I aint got my hand out."

"I knew it," G-Boy snickered at Munchie, "You want us to run train on you for this money…you willing to work for it…an even exchange huh?" G-Boy blurted still dropping hundreds on the table. "You can't even handle my dick and now you want both of us." G-Boy smiled watching Desiree twist her face at him in disgust.

"Ugh you such a turn off and you lucky I don't feel like fighting because them fighting words coming at me like that," Desiree rolled her eyes at G-Boy then turned to Munchie.

"G-Boy chill you bugging yo," Munchie tapped G-Boy and told him to put his money up and to show Desiree some respect. G-Boy just couldn't get over the heartbreak she put him through. Munchie knew this was a serious matter and G-Boy had to put his emotions to the side.

Desiree had a look of determination in her eyes and she was sincere about some type of power move. "Talk to me Desiree…yo peoples sent you here so what's up. What kind of business you wanna talk about?" Munchie asked with his undivided attention.

Desiree looked over her shoulders and around the back of the bar suspiciously. The music was loud and everyone was in their own groove besides a few females with their eyes glued on G-Boy scooping his money up off the table. Desiree then leaned halfway across the table and whispered, "Zulu business."

Munchie and G-Boy both looked at each other, then at Desiree, then back at each other like she just mentioned Osama Bin Laden's name.

"Where he at?"

"He good yall aint gotta know all that…just know he got a couple of bricks and he need yall to help me move em."

Munchie and G-Boy twisted their faces in confusion. What the hell was Zulu's crazy ass up to Munchie and G-Boy thought to themselves. Zulu escaped from the police after him and the crew got knocked with over 100 bricks and Zulu was still on the run hustling and in the possession of bricks. This was crazy. Who the hell was Zulu connected to they thought. Or did Desiree just happen to come across some work the feds didn't find and she was using Zulu's name so Munchie and G-Boy wouldn't walk her for the work? Desiree observed the perplexed look on their faces and knew they were skeptical.

"Listen I aint trying to set yall up to get my man out of jail and Zulu not working with the police," Desiree stated taking a sip of her liquor and feeling their vibe of paranoia. Desiree then explained how Gonzalez helped Zulu escape from central booking at headquarters. She even told them how the Feds didn't raid one of the stash spots and that's where Zulu got the bricks from.

Desiree then glanced around the bar once again before reaching across the table and grabbing Munchie and G-Boy's hands, "I got 4 ½ ounces in my purse that Zulu want me to give yall to cook up so yall can see how good it is…we really need yall help…we still owe the lawyers and we broke…the feds took everything…yall not doing this just for me but this for everyone…please."

"How the hell you know you not being followed and you leading the Feds to us since you brought them peckerwoods up?"

"Come on yall should know better and if the Feds was following me they would have got Zulu…they want Zulu not yall," Desiree responded still holding both their hands.

"But you hiding him and then you coming to see us that's heat we definitely don't need."

Desiree let go of both their hands. She was getting impatient. She understood their caution but they were underestimating the precautions Desiree was taking. "It don't take a rocket scientist to know that if the Feds knew where Zulu was at they would come and get him…but Zulu smarter than that and that's why he sent me…he not trying to bring any heat to yall," Desiree explained feeling her desperation turn to anger.

Munchie and G-Boy both sighed deeply knowing they were only called upon to give a helping hand to a fellow Thug in a time of need. Just like Zulu's hand reached out for them in a time when they were in desperate need. Munchie and G-Boy could never forget the time they were facing 4-9 years for a drug possession and gun charge that should have been thrown out from the jump since the gun and drugs were found in a yard two houses away from where they were standing. Their lawyer was basically lazy and gonna have them cop out to the 4-9 years since they had records and he felt the drugs and guns belonged to them. It was Zulu who turned them on to Leonetti and fronted them three ounces out of Big Walt's work. The answer spoke for itself and Munchie and G-Boy were thankful Zulu made a move for them which kept them from going up creek to the system.

"Damn this shit crazy…they got my nigga on the run." G-Boy shouted over the music.

"Hell yeah this shit crazy," Munchie added.

"Aww come on yall—yall on some bullshit," Desiree was tired of begging out of desperation let alone taking the disrespect she took from G-Boy. All she was trying to do was feed the family. She was there to do business and provide a good product in exchange for cash. That was fair trade welcomed around the world universally. Munchie and G-Boy wasn't being fair she felt. Desiree looked into their hesitant faces and barked, "Don't be fronting on my brother because he in a jam right now…if Zulu aint have these problems yall would be running to him…and yall know Zulu aint gone forget who shitted on him."

"Yo all that uncalled for…we aint never say we not gone help yall…you bugging with all that slick shit you talking…anyway lets handle this business…we wanna see Zulu too if that's possible…that's our fucking brother and we would never turn our back on a real nigga like that…we just being on point so we don't get jammed up...that's all."

Munchie and G-Boy understood how much they were needed in this time of crisis. The Get Rich Crime Family was destroyed and everyone dependent on them was suffering, and Zulu while on the run was *N.O.R.E*; a nigga on the run eating and still trying to hold things down and keep up the support for the whole tribe. Munchie and G-Boy's respect for Zulu's strength and power to persist in a critical time like this was truly honored.

"Come on let's go check out this raw flake you got for us."

"I thank yall so much and Zulu love yall for this," Desiree hugged Munchie and G-Boy before they slid outside to Desiree's car where she gave them the coca that was in her purse.

The next day Desiree was driving Zulu over to Phyllis Street off Bailey Avenue to meet with Munchie and G-Boy. They cheffed up the 125 grams and made it do its magic. Now they needed to holla at Zulu and see him face to face to not only pay him for the 4 ½ ounces and show a nigga on the run eating some Thug Love, but they were gonna purchase a kilo and a half of that 87% pure cocaine.

Zulu and Desiree sat in the plushed out upstairs apartment with Munchie and G-Boy while *B.E.T.'s 106 and Park* flashed on the 62" screen of the Plasma T.V. Zulu and Desiree looked like a *Bonnie and Clyde* sitting together on the leather sofa in front of the T.V. counting up the thirty-six thousand dollars they received for the brick and a half plus the three thousand dollars for the 4 ½ ounces.

"Yo Zulu good looking out for this bro."

"No I thank yall for coming thru for ya boy," Zulu shot from the sofa while Munchie and G-Boy stuffed their weight in a bookbag then sprayed down the table and began cleaning it.

"Zulu they was scared acting like some crabs," Desiree was seriously joking, "I had to tell G-Boy you gonna whip his ass like you used to do back in the day."

"Desiree you lost yo damn mind," G-Boy stopped wiping the table down and looked at Zulu and Desiree smiling, "Zulu know I aint no lil nigga no more...aint that right big bro," G-Boy still acknowledged Zulu as a big brother even though they were A-Alike in the streets and held each other in high esteem and regard. Zulu was a few years older than them but they were equals.

"You know I fuck with yall boys don't pay Desi no mind she just crazy as hell." Zulu replied.

"Yeah I was crazy for fucking with you back in high school Thomas," Desiree stated remembering how she used to get clowned by her friends for being a senior in a relationship with a freshman.

"Stop spitting my government name Desiree," G-Boy barked, "And age aint nothing but a number...you know my mental was way advanced and I was rolling with Big Boys like Zulu," G-Boy got back at her stepping into the living room slapping hands with Zulu.

"Yeah yall already know outside my circle yall the only niggas I really fucked with...yall always kept it gangster and showed love," Zulu's tone of voice and big brother status captured everyone's attention as he spoke, "Right now it's a fucked up time for my hood and I appreciate yall coming through because my days is numbered out here...until it's over I just need yall to hold me down in this clutch...yall know I wont let no heat come yall way...I man up to my own shit so yall good."

"No question Zulu you already know we got you," Munchie swung over to the sofa and sat down. "Everybody go thru these jams and it's all about the people you got supporting you...we here for you bro...word up."

This was all Zulu needed for the time being. He was now just waiting for NyJewel's D.M.V. connect to come through with his new I.D. so he could get to Florida and board the Carnival Cruise ship heading to the Caribbean. Time wasn't moving fast enough but he seemed to have everything in motion. Only mission he had to accomplish now was getting in touch with Lil Flip and Crumbs who were somewhere in the city hiding. With no connect and drugs, Lil Flip and Crumbs were going to be soon starving but Zulu was going to find a way to reach out to them and leave them with the rest of the bricks so they could bounce back on their feet and get rolling. Now, everything was all about timing and how Zulu executed his plans, because if the hands of time worked on Zulu's side, Zulu would be in paradise with NyJewel in a matter of time.

....

Cream stood at the window in his room-cell letting his eyes affix themselves on the throngs of people outside on the street below. His room window offered a picturesque view of the structures hovering above Delaware Avenue and Niagara Square in the heart of downtown Buffalo. Cream wondered would he ever have a taste of freedom again as he watched the lunch hour people purchase foods from the food vendors on the corner outside the courthouses on the street. He then realized that the power and money he had in the streets held no weight when it came to the power of the government as he scornfully watched the white bureaucrats dressed in their expensive suits stroll in and out of City Hall and the court buildings in view from his room window. The government could snatch freedom from people easier than a swift hand could squash a mosquito. As the tinted room window with bars on it separated Cream from the outside world of freedom, Cream knew that thinking of freedom was not a reality since he was caged in the feds with no bail.

Outside Cream's room cell Ra-King flew into the unit stimulated after his visit. Ra-King knocked on Cream's slightly ajar door with urgency as he slowly entered observing Cream peering out the window daydreaming.

"I got a message from the free-cipher (Free-World) my G," Ra-King stepped inside and sat on the metal stool mounted on the floor in front of a small desk. Cream anxiously spun from his window and stepped to Ra-King with his eyes and ears open wide.

"Munchie and G-Boy just came thru to check me," Ra-King glanced back at the room door making sure it was closed then whispered as Cream stood several feet away, *"They broke bread with Zulu."*

"Worrrrd...what's good with him?"

Ra-King then explained the business that was conducted and how Zulu was trying to get in touch with Lil Flip and Crumbs before he slid to the islands. Munchie and G-Boy was then going to keep things rolling with Lil Flip and Crumbs. The game couldn't stop. Munchie and G-Boy had a decent connect to keep things afloat for Lil Flip and Crumbs so the ball could keep bouncing.

"Yo I respect Zulu to the fullest Cream...he basically trying to make sure the game still alive for yall before he slide and make moves...that's real G shit Cream, he making sure his peoples right and exact before himself…" Ra-King gestured his hands like he was giving a speech. "Everything looking good on the outside besides this unfortunate situation…but you know I got Munchie and G-Boy plugged in with my Dominican peoples so yall hood could bounce back while yall fighting this case…it aint over…yall just gotta weather this storm in here and get that nigga Sun-Z to stop being paranoid."

"Yo Ra good looking yo word up," Cream shook Ra-King's hand and embraced him with a hug, "I knew my boy Zulu was gonna make it happen and not let us down like the nigga Sun-Z was thinking…Zulu gone die before he go out like a sucka…that's word on Dolla and Mel-Cash…my G official."

"And oh yeah," Ra-King began laughing, "Munchie said they gotta get Zulu a haircut before he slide because he look like a black savage from the Caucasus mountains yo…" Ra-King and Cream both shared a laugh stepping out of Cream's room heading to Rec.

Upon stepping into the gym rec, Cream and Ra-King peeped Hawk standing by a pool table joyfully clutching his pool stick. Hawk was in good spirits and smiled like he wasn't a prisoner but a person enjoying life in the free world. Desiree had deposited twenty-five hundred dollars in his account as well as Cream and Sun-Z's he just found out when he got off the phone with her. Hawk didn't know how she came up on the large sum of money but he knew she was playing super-woman and holding things down. Hawk really became excited once Ra-King explained the situation to him. Desiree was being the boss chick she was by helping Zulu keep the game rolling. The Get Rich Crime Family was facing more pressure than the bottom of the sea but Zulu and Desiree was making the light of hope resurface because perfect performance is demonstrated under pressure.

Sun-Z on the other hand was still allowing his emotions and crushed ego to guide his intelligence. Instead of being happy for Zulu being on the run eating and holding it down for the crew, Sun-Z was in a world of misery and couldn't find happiness in the fact of Zulu being free while he was locked down. Sun-Z felt what Zulu was accomplishing was impossible and instead of giving Zulu props, Sun-Z became critical. It was ridiculous. Sun-Z's mind began to deteriorate from the throne of power he once sat on and while he sat in the cage, the weakness of human nature began to eat him in shame. He felt miserable seeing Zulu on the run playing hero. Zulu would probably make it to the islands and be treated like a king by Nyjewel and Sun-Z's wife Iyana. Sun-Z should have been ashamed of himself for letting those thoughts penetrate his mind.

But as life teaches, *"There has never been a man of intelligence who was free from errors, and at one time or another, everyone is subject to error because man strives for perfection out of his imperfections."*

....

"Now Zulu I need you to throw three cups of water into this pot with two teaspoons of Old Bay," Destiny instructed Zulu as he helped her in the kitchen making dinner. Destiny was in the soulful mood of love as she cheffed in the kitchen while jamming to the sounds of *Sunshine Anderson*. She was blessing the steak, crab legs, vegetable Alfredo, and homestyle muffins she was making. It was feast time for Zulu, Destiny, Desiree and the baby Divine Princess Satori because any day Zulu would get the phone call for him to snatch his new I.D. and head to Florida to board the cruise ship. Anyway would be their last time together so they were cherishing these last moments.

Once dinner was made Desiree sat up the table and made healthy plates for everyone. Graces and thanks were uttered, glasses of wine were raised, and then the nutritious elements of Destiny's lovely food was harmonizing their stomachs. The food was so mouthwatering and delicious everyone ate without talking, only humming and nodding to each other on how good the food was. It was a heart touching moment and they wished they could have more moments like this without the present predicaments. They all finished their meals hoping this wasn't the last supper.

"Zulu you know I'm gone drag Destiny and the baby down to them islands to see you brother," Desiree stated over her glass of Chardonnay as they all sat stuck at the table in front of their empty plates. "I need to tan myself anyway."

"Girl you already dark," Destiny remarked eyeing Desiree's dark peach skin tone.

"Yall know wherever my home is is yall home too."

"Zulu is you sure about that?" Destiny asked indirectly hinting at NyJewel.

"Let me tell you something love," Zulu leaned over to Destiny who sat next to him at the table. He softly grabbed her hand and peered into her beautiful face with intense sincerity. "I always loved you Destiny…and the way you held me down in this situation make me love you even more…there's no one or nothing who can come between us, change us, or dictate our relationship to each other…I thank you so much and I don't even know how to ever pay you back besides showing you kindness and love no matter where I'm at or whoever I'm with," Zulu manifested giving Destiny a soft kiss on her cheek.

"Aww," Desiree sat across the table blushing, "That was cute…yall should make a baby with them feelings," Desiree joked observing a warm expression on Destiny's face.

"I thank you too Desi…I don't know what I would've done without yall…and not for nothing...yall know yall the only family I had when my moms died…I appreciate yall from the bottom of my heart…I really do." Zulu expressed feeling Destiny squeeze his hand affectionately.

"Brother stop you gone make me sad," Desiree rose from her seat and swung over to Zulu and hugged him. She then stood by his side and told him, "We gone always be family Zulu…I don't care what happens between you and Destiny or who you be with…you was always the brother I never had and nothing will change that," Desiree poured herself another glass of wine. "Now if yall will excuse me I'm going upstairs to put me and the baby to bed." Desiree sipped her wine before grabbing the baby and swinging upstairs.

Zulu then helped Destiny clean off the table before they hit the living room to watch *D.M.X and Aaliyah's Romeo Must Die*. Once they finished watching the flick, Destiny grabbed a photo album from off the entertainment stand and slid back to the couch. Destiny didn't realize it because she was a little tipsy from a few glasses of wine but she dropped herself right onto Zulu's lap as she opened the photo album. Images of their younger days reflected in the pictures and rewinded their minds back down memory lane.

They both felt that warmth their hearts felt when they were younger, a time when their love wasn't tainted by pain and heartache. The time before Zulu fell in love with money and the streets wasn't his main focus. It was a pure feeling of tender love they felt beating in their hearts as they studied the pictures with deep concentration. It was a feeling of two separate souls connecting with each other and becoming one. It was a unity that was beyond the motion of time. It was the force of love which had no beginning or ending. It knew no barriers because it transcended all obstacles. It was an excitement that sparked a joy. And even when there was pain there was the sweet feeling of forgiveness. They sat in each other's embrace peering into the reflections of the pictures while their souls felt that intertwining connection they always felt with each other. Nothing else mattered as their minds and spirit generated an energy they both felt radiating from each other.

"Zulu what happened to us?" Destiny softly asked laying her head on Zulu's shoulder while still sitting in his lap. "It's like we forgot what we always had and what we wanted for our future."

Zulu sighed deeply realizing he got what he wanted from the streets but not the spiritual happiness he once yearned for with Destiny. He satisfied himself by fulfilling his street dreams but he was still empty inside and felt terrible, not to mention his legal troubles and dead friends.

"Remember we just wanted to be happy Zulu…just me and you with kids…a house of our own…with love and happiness," Destiny smiled remembering the vows they made in the park as kids. "You were gonna be an Astronomer and I was gonna be a Physician, remember Zulu."

"Wow," Zulu busted out laughing thinking of their childhood dreams and aspirations, "Back then that's all that was, was a dream…my life was doomed with this reality since day one and even though I ain't follow that path, I lived better than most."

It was sad to say but it was reality. It was the rich white privilege frame of mind that ruled society and made it hard for blacks, Hispanics, and poor whites to achieve these goals. It was hard for low income inner city youth to achieve childhood dreams when their main focus on life was about day to day survival and how to eat at the present moment. In the concrete jungle of the ghetto it was about daily survival and making it through the day. When most inner-city youth reached puberty, the poor socio-economic conditions of their environment made it hard for them to concentrate on the long term and higher goals of education and living a civilized life. Most have to deal with broken homes, drug abusing parents, violence, and the many other social ills and conditions of poverty which make many youths take the fastest way out of the wretched conditions they find themselves in. Crime is the fastest way out of poverty in the ghetto. Sad but true. There is no excuse for ignorance which is why many suffer in that life of crime. Unfortunately the life of crime is the easiest and quickest way for the poor to eat which is why the youth and most people in general run into that life blindly hoping to make their situation better even though the end result is worse than ever. It's the illusion of Maya as the Buddhist calls it. Zulu and many others living in this world of the rich slave makers of the poor were victims of a system that created these societal ills that forces many to run into the life of crime just to escape poverty.

"Yeah I remember them goals we had Destiny when we was kids," Zulu responded to Destiny's question while softly pressing his lips on her forehead as she lay her head on his chest, "It was easy back then for us to want those things because we was kids and didn't have the stress on us."

"What stress Zulu?"

"Life Destiny…look at how hard it was for us…I didn't ask to be in the streets…I really wanted to be an astronomer but ain't nobody buy me a telescope to study the stars…and ain't no one encourage you to be a health physician."

"Those are excuses Zulu…we have the God-giving ability to achieve whatever we put our minds to…look at our Ancestors who were in slavery…they never let the roadblocks they were facing stop them from achieving their goals in this racist society…we have to strive just like they did and we got it easier now because we can read and write and choose the careers we want, they didn't have those opportunities Zulu but they still made their lives better…and they made life better for us so we can be more than what we are."

"Here you go with that Black Pride shit…that shit sound good but do you remember the times I had to go out in the blizzarding snow to shovel just so I could buy us something to eat better than oodles and noodles…or what about when I had to stand out in the cold and hustle just so I could buy you them warm Guess boots so you could walk to school warm in all that snow…13 year old shouldn't have to live like that but it's real…I didn't ask for this life and ask to sell drugs…the shit just happened because the circumstances forced me to do it because that was the only option available to get us by…I played the cards I was dealt and I'm not ashamed of the life I lived, you can't knock a man for feeding himself the best way he know how." Zulu let his soul speak observing Destiny lower her gaze in acknowledgement to the harsh reality of their youth and life in the ghetto.

"It's just like the situation we got right now Destiny…you lost yo job due to a family emergency and now it's hard for you to even find a job that's gone pay yo bills like the last job…but look what I did…I sold some drugs and now you got enough money to pay yo bills for at least a year without stressing about where yo next check gone come from. I didn't ask for this neither did you," Zulu barked leaning forward and grabbing his bottle of Remy Martin from off the coffee table.

"Zulu I'm sorry," Destiny noticed a look of pain flash on Zulu's face and it wasn't from the liquor he guzzled. It was the pain of the lifestyle that kidnapped him and his friends and turned them into drug dealing murderers.

Zulu then slid Destiny from off his lap and rose from the couch. He paced the living room in circles before stopping and glancing in the mirror on the living room wall. His eyes reflected a soul steeped in the dark mire of pain. The glow of light the eyes took in had vanished from Zulu's vision. He looked into his face and felt lifeless besides the pain he felt inside.

"I love you Zulu and I'm scared," Destiny stood behind Zulu and wrapped her arms around him. "I'm scared to see you leave me because I don't know what's gone happen Zulu," Destiny murmured getting teary eyed. "I feel it's my fault for letting the streets take you away from me…and now I don't know what I'm gonna do without you."

Zulu slowly spun around and faced Destiny. They held each other tightly while Zulu whispered in her ear, "Don't be stressing and worrying about me because that's gone stress me out…I need you to be strong just how you was strong when we broke up…when I leave you gotta worry about yourself Destiny…you a survivor and no matter what happen to me I want you to be strong and live yo life because you deserve to be happy."

"No Zulu," Destiny's emotions flared up thinking of Zulu's situation. The tears flowed as she squeezed him with all her might not wanting to let go. "I can't be strong knowing your life is in trouble. How can I have peace knowing the only man that ever loved me besides my dad is in trouble with his life…I can't take this lightly because I don't know how to."

The soul of a woman's love was like a beautiful baby. It was soft and tender and a joy nothing could match. Zulu knew his fate was sealed and he accepted the fact that he may spend the rest of his life in Prison if he got caught. The fate of prison didn't really bother Zulu considering the fate of his friends and everyone else he knew in the streets. Everyone had to suffer the consequences of their actions. Zulu understood this and was man enough to man up to his actions. What was crushing his soul was feeling the pain of Destiny's sweet soul cry for him. This was one of the most unbearable moments of his life. His soul felt burdened from the pain he caused her throughout all the years. It was like a son driving his mother crazy to her death bed. Zulu felt the guilt of crushing Destiny's soul. It was like her soul only came to earth to unite with his soul but he was pulling away from her and she was going to break down for losing her other half.

"I'm sorry Destiny," Zulu let his soul cry out tears from his eyes, "I love you and I'm really sorry for not being the man you needed me to be…I swear on my mother's grave I'm sorry for not being here for you like you truly needed me…I'm sorry…I know I messed my life up and I gotta face it someday, but just because my life is fucked up don't mean you gotta suffer too…I swear-," Zulu gently touched Destiny's chin and lifted her head so he could look into her eyes, "No matter what happens…you will make me so happy if I know you will be strong out here when I leave…promise me…because I will never be alright knowing you not good…it's not about my life, it's about yours and I just need you to know you gonna be good without me."

"Yes Zulu…yes," Destiny answered with the sound of sweetness in her voice like a little girl.

"That's what I wanna hear," Zulu kissed Destiny softly on her lips. They kissed slowly and with passionate meaning. Zulu then lowered his hands to her butt and softly caressed it. Zulu then pressed her warm body against him and grinded his stimulated and erect sex organ against her crotch. It's been so long since he had sex he felt backed up like a prisoner ready to explode a lifetime worth of imprisoned sperm.

"No Zulu no," Destiny snatched her tongue from out of Zulu's mouth and pulled away from him. Zulu grabbed his bottle of Remy and swallowed like a fish before skating after Destiny who stepped across the living room fighting her urge not to give in to Zulu.

"Come here love," Zulu grabbed Destiny's hand as she tried pushing him away. Destiny loved Zulu with all her heart but her love was beyond sex. Destiny may have been tipsy and caught in the moment, but her moral conscience caught her and brought her to grips. If she was to let Zulu inside her the joy he would arouse in her would only crush her even more being that she could never have him the way she wanted him since his fate was sealed by trouble, not to mention he was sharing his life with NyJewel. It was best to keep the closed wounds closed and not open them back up.

Zulu on the other hand was saucy off the liquor and his sex drive was doing over 220 mph like a Lamborghini the way his erection was. Destiny's round rump was looking like a heart of love in her terry cloth shorts and Zulu lusted her throbbing nipples in the tight tank top she was wearing. It's been almost two years since Zulu felt Destiny's insides and he had to get a taste because it would probably be his last. If Destiny wasn't going to give it up Zulu was going to take it like it was his.

"Come here and stop pulling away from me you know you love me and want me," Zulu snatched her and pulled him close to her.

"Zulu stop," Destiny pleaded as Zulu hugged her tightly and began to stick his tongue inside her mouth. Destiny tried turning her face away from him but Zulu grabbed her face and held it while he forcefully shoved his tongue deeper into her mouth.

They then stumbled backwards and fell onto the couch while Zulu struggled to kiss Destiny. Destiny pleaded with the drunk and aggressive Zulu as he lay on top of her sticking his tongue in her mouth. Zulu then removed his hands from her face and slid them down to her shorts while pressing his body weight down on her. Destiny tried squirming from under him but Zulu wasn't letting her go nowhere as he clamped down on her while yanking her shorts down then unbuckling his pants.

"I love you Destiny stop this why you making me take it," Zulu whispered loudly using one hand to whip out his hard pole and guide it onto her tight lip-locked loving.

Destiny was like a virgin her loving was so tight and Zulu was like an animal ripping his penis into the screaming Destiny. Her vagina hasn't had the real deal in so long it kinda hurt her insides feeling Zulu's full package enter her.

"*Stoppp.*" Destiny screamed while Zulu lay on top of her humping like a wild animal. Destiny begged and pleaded for him to stop but Zulu blacked out. His mind replayed all their sensual moments of sex and his penis was missing the loving that once belonged to him. Zulu rammed Destiny's insides like this was his last time.

Destiny wiggled and tried pushing him off her to no avail. She did everything in her power but it was helpless as he lay on her with half his strength holding her down and the other half ramming her insides. He huffed and puffed as he relinquished all his power. Destiny just gave up resisting and let the beast go wild. She looked into Zulu's eyes and seen something she never seen in Zulu before. The streets had destroyed the Zulu she was once in love with. The streets created a beast she came to realize while looking into the lifeless face of the man she once loved but now hated as his animal instinct took advantage of her.

Desiree just happened to wake up and heard Destiny screaming when

Zulu first penetrated Destiny. Desiree jumped out of bed feeling tipsy and not knowing what was going on. She instinctively looked at her baby who was sleeping next to her and upon seeing the baby was alright, Desiree rushed downstairs fearfully praying the police didn't kick in the door to snatch Zulu. Desiree made it half way down the stairs and stopped in her tracks on the landing in the hallway when she heard the grunting of Zulu.

"That's what I'm talking about brother…give Maya Angelou that righteous loving she been missing," Desiree thought it was funny before she noticed a teary-eyed Destiny staring into space and laying on her back motionless while Zulu was humping like he was trying to literally go up into Destiny's womb. "Oh my God," Desiree covered her mouth now realizing why Destiny was screaming.

"*Arg…oooh…damn, I missed you so much Destiny…I love you,*" Zulu exploded his seeds of life deep inside Destiny before dropping his head next to her. Zulu and Destiny was unaware of Desiree standing at the top of the stairs looking on in shock. Zulu then tried kissing Destiny but mentally she was elsewhere. She was no longer aware of what Zulu was sexually doing to her. Zulu noticed she was unresponsive with her open eyes so he pulled himself from off her and slowly got up.

"Yo what the fuck sis," Zulu looked up and caught eyes with Desiree. He then pulled his pants up quickly and skated to the bathroom. When Zulu returned to the living room a few minutes later, Destiny was crying in Desiree's arms as they both sat on the couch. Zulu sat on the couch next to Destiny and gently touched her shoulder. Destiny jumped up screaming and cursing at Zulu with the glare of hurt in her eyes like a pure woman who been violated. Zulu rushed over to her trying to console her.

"Why…why…why," Destiny pounded on Zulu's chest as he held her. "Why did you do this to me…you don't love me…you changed and you not the person I loved…you a stranger…I don't know you…why…why did you take him away from me God…why," Destiny screamed swinging her arms while Zulu held her and tried restraining her. Destiny felt like the man she once knew and loved was no longer in Zulu's physical body. Who was this animal occupying the physical shell of the man she once loved? Who was this animal who lived a life of death and had a fate of being captured and thrown in a cage like a beast in the jungle?

Zulu's soul fell from the heavenly realm of purity the Creator created the Black Man in. The life of violence and the wickedness of this modern-day world brought out the worst in the human soul. This was like the Angel's fall from pure heaven to the file environments of the earth. The whole situation of Zulu's legal trouble was hell on earth, but throughout this hell, Destiny was the one soul that gave Zulu a spark. The spark was the divine spark of life and love that was so invigorating to his dead soul, it sparked so much life and energy in Zulu that he was flooded with an ocean of testosterone, arousing his animal self to gratify itself with her loving pleasure which made him feel alive again.

"I'm sorry Destiny I didn't mean to--," Zulu tried explaining but Destiny broke loose from him.

"Stay away from me I don't know you...why did you let this happen God...you let the streets take him...why God," Destiny screamed before Desiree intervened and began to take Destiny upstairs.

"Zulu let me calm her down she gone be alright," Desiree explained marshaling Destiny upstairs.

It was never the money that Destiny wanted. It wasn't the excitement of being in love with a Powerful Thug that made her feel happy and secure. The negative energy of Death and misery wasn't what she wanted in life either. Destiny only wanted the pure love of Zulu's heart. The love the Creator created all human beings with. Destiny finally came to realize that Zulu was an animal in physical form. His mind, heart, and soul was imprisoned by the lower nature of man which was responsible for the evil of the world. God created the Black man to live as a reflection of God, not an animal. This is what slavery, the streets, and white society made the Blackman forget as a Divine Being.

For the next few days Destiny locked herself upstairs in her room and stayed away from Zulu like he was contaminated with Ebola. Destiny would say nothing to him and acted as if he was a ghost that didn't exist. It was like she really believed Zulu wasn't Zulu and a stranger occupied Zulu's body.

Zulu tried apologizing to Destiny and seeking her forgiveness but Destiny was crushed because Zulu was like a walking dead man and it was too painful for her to see him living like that. As much as his soul was entrenched in the darkness of the world, only Zulu could forgive himself through the communication with the Divinity deep within his soul. Zulu's energy was negative and Destiny had to get away from Zulu and his world of trouble. Destiny felt it tugging at her soul and trying to pull her into that dark world of grief.

Desiree then informed Zulu that Destiny was going to leave the house and stay elsewhere until Zulu was able to leave the country. Desiree explained Destiny's pain to Zulu and also how Destiny felt violated by Zulu taking her by force and dumping his seeds into her pure womb. Desiree explained how Destiny was even more devastated at the way Zulu ruined his own life.

"How the fuck she gone say I raped her...that's my ex and we still love each other," Zulu explained to Desiree.

"Zulu I know yall love each other and it is what it is...but you just have to understand that we as women sometime don't understand how rough it is for yall men...the things yall go through make us suffer...I'm fortunate to understand as a woman because I'm from the streets...that's the only reason I can bear with this life...but all women not built to bear the burdens of the streets and Destiny is one of them...all my sister want is to be happy...the street glory of the cars, nice clothes, and the money doesn't satisfy her like love...all women want love, but some settle for the material things instead because not too many men know how to love a women...but no matter what, deep down inside all women want is the spirit of a man to love us and make us feel complete."

Desiree was able to bring Zulu's mind to a level of understanding the pain of women. Zulu caused Destiny a lot of pain not intentionally. It was just his lifestyle of being a Thug which caused Destiny so much pain. Zulu finally realized for once in his life how much pain he caused her. Destiny lost her job and livelihood because of her love for those in the streets. Even by her sheltering Zulu from the law she was living like she was a fugitive herself and depriving herself of happiness.

Desiree on the other hand was just down for the cause and her spirit understood the streets. Destiny was just a precious flower that needed to be tendered. Zulu finally realized he was killing her softly. Zulu had to do something right in his life once and for all. He would no longer disturb Destiny's peace and take his world of grief elsewhere.

It would only be a few days before NyJewel's connect from the D.M.V came through and Zulu would hit the finish line. So until he was able to make it to the finish line he would go back to the Thug Life world he loved so well. He went to the only true and living Thugs he knew he could count on in these troubling times; Munchie and G-Boy. Up in one of their honeycomb hideouts Zulu would lay low until his time came to flee the country and not look back.

CHAPTER 23

The fiery flames engulfed the paper as it burned in the ashtray sitting on the table between Lil Flip and Crumbs. They both peered into the fire watching the letter disintegrate into ashes. The letter was from inside a Federal Detention Center and it was in a cell where the mind guided the hand to express the thoughts scribed on the burning paper. What was scribed on the paper was devastating and extremely incriminating, not to mention unbelievably ridiculous. Before burning the letter Lil Flip and Crumbs examined it like it was hieroglyphic writing. They read it over and over again in silence trying to understand if what they were reading was real. Shit is really real their souls made them realize as their minds analyzed the letter and the facts surrounding the circumstances the letter described.

They were being put up against one of the greatest challenges any man could face. It wasn't that they couldn't carry out the actions that were needed to be carried out. It was the reason and the consequences their actions would bring. It was real. It was so real the vibration of their spirits was piercing each other as they peered into the fire burning the paper.

Lil Flip dropped his head onto the table while Crumbs flung his head back on the chair and gazed up at the ceiling. They sat in silence for what seemed like forever before Lil Flip decided to roll up a blunt of some bombastic weed that was medication for the soul. After rolling the blunt Lil Flip flicked the lighter to lite it while watching the fire and paper evaporate into vapors.

"I feel sick yo," Lil Flip finally spoke after he took a deep pull on the blunt then exhaled the earth's essence, "I don't even wanna smoke no more yo…I feel like I might throw up," Lil Flip muttered passing the blunt to Crumbs.

"Yo fam," Crumbs inhaled the blunt methodically letting the smoke seep from his mouth then sucking it back through his nostrils. "We caught between a rock and a hard place for real. Damn if we do damn if we don't…we fucked no matter what."

"Dude," Lil Flip disputably gazed at Crumbs, "Do you realize what the fuck we caught up in…whoever thought the game would come to this…this shit a little too much for me…especially being that we don't really know what the fuck going on."

"What if we don't do the shit and then shit hit the fan and we get jammed up…"

"This is fucked up yo…I never thought shit would come to this."

No one never knows what tomorrow will bring even though plans are made for the future, and in the wicked streets things change amongst friends and family before they can even realize it. Just like no one knew how Sun-Z flew the kite and the kite had intentions to change the game for better and worse. Jail never stopped Bosses from calling shots on the outside and Sun-Z was making moves on the inside to make sure Lil Flip and Crumbs would now be the bosses of the Get Rich Crime Family and eat like Thanksgiving. Lil Flip and Crumbs just had to secure their freedom by covering all loose ends since the game was turning sour.

Sun-Z may have lost some mental stability due to the war and his insecurity and envy towards Zulu, but he was a natural master mind and knew how to utilize whatever resources he had available even in the worst of situations. Since Zulu got everything set rolling with Munchie and G-Boy, Sun-Z and Ra-King networked on a business merger to keep the streets on lock while they sat in the cage. One hand washes the other. Munchie and G-Boy could keep Lil Flip and Crumbs flooded with work and Lil Flip and Crumbs would share the Get Rich Crime Family's clientele with Munchie and G-Boy. This was a supreme power move that would benefit everyone even those sitting in the cage.

Sun-Z seemed to have his sanity back and was back on the throne minus the character flaws he displayed, he was back on his level and thinking clearly. Everything was good. It was just one thing mentioned in the letter that troubled Lil Flip and Crumbs. It was a dark and deadly secret, and what's in the dark comes to light and when the four devils of the human mind are not checked by the God in the human soul, them four devils will come from the darkness of the mind to cause hell in the physical. Sun-Z was using straight trick-knowledge to achieve his agenda based on ill intentions. It was strait wicked and deceptive intelligence.

Lil Flip and Crumbs had to head uptown to Bailey Avenue and click up with Munchie and G-Boy who was hiding Zulu. Zulu not only had the bricks for Lil Flip and Crumbs, but this would be Lil Flip and Crumbs last time being with Zulu. This was going to be an everlasting memory for everyone, especially Munchie, G-Boy, Lil Flip, Crumbs and Zulu. This was like the crossroads where everyone's struggling destiny intersected in a world of heaven or hell, right and wrong, and it was the power of the choices one made to follow either the right path which got one across the crossroad into heaven, or the wrong path which kept one stuck at the crossroad in confusion living in hell and misery.

....

Zulu laid up in a plushed out Bachelor pad in the Bennett Village apartments on E. Amherst Street which was about 5 minutes from the Buffalo Zoo. The Bachelor pad was immaculate and laced with the luxuries of modern technology and comfort. From wall to wall plush carpet to the built-in salt water fish tank in the wall, to the Plasma T.V. mounted on the wall with the surround sound stereo and theater system, to the King sized Serta mattress swathed in silk sheets, Munchie and G-Boy sure knew how to entertain their guest. They even had a private barber come thru and chop Zulu's wig piece and give him a splendid wave cut which made Zulu feel and look like a brand-new man. The icing on the cake topped with the ice cream was the two sexy stallions Zulu was blessed with. Two sexy ladies would keep Zulu company while he barricaded himself in the bachelor pad until it was his time to bounce. They treated Zulu like a king cooking, cleaning, and giving him the sex it was a possibility he may never have again if he was caught by the feds. At first Zulu was reluctant on having the young women for his pleasure since his mind was only focused on his escape. Zulu didn't trust if the females would run their mouth about being with the legendary Zulu. Zulu should have known that Munchie and G-Boy knew better. They would kill or be killed before they let anything jeopardize Zulu's freedom and safety. The two lovely companions they blessed Zulu with were from Cleveland and they were paid more money than the law was offering for Zulu's capture.

Munchie and G-Boy even dropped some philosophical game on Zulu about being a nigga on the run. Zulu's goal was to hit the finish line but he had to weigh all possibilities. It was a possibility Zulu might not make it to the finish line. Therefore, Zulu needed to enjoy every moment and minute of his free life like it was his last because his situation wasn't promised. He was a national fugitive and there was a million eyes looking for him. Enjoy and eat the cake since he had it, and that's exactly what Zulu did with the two sexy ladies he had.

While Zulu camped out with his two sexy companions he let his animal nature gratify itself to the fullest. He ate like a bear, drunk like a fish, and humped like a dog since his days was numbered. The days were rolling by fast but not fast enough. It was on Zulu's fifth day hiding out in the bachelor pad when he contacted NyJewel inquiring about his I.D.

NyJewel was more anxious and impatient than Zulu as she cried into the phone. She was a hot wreck day by day and felt she was losing herself worrying. She couldn't live comfortably at all let alone eat or sleep not knowing what was going on with Zulu. Zulu assured her he was safe he just wanted to leave the states. Zulu also reminded her that the only way he could escape was if NyJewel stayed focused and calm. They waited patiently for almost three months so a couple of more days couldn't hurt.

....

It was Friday night and Bailey Avenue was jumping with the activity of bar hoppers flooding the bars lining the live strip. Munchie, G-Boy, and their goons from the Hyena crew posted up on Munchie's Pearl White Escalade Truck and G-Boy's smoke Blue GL 450 Benz truck in front of Bailey's Bar and Grill which was the livest bar on the strip.

Outside the bar they mingled with a swarm of scantily clad ladies while sipping liquor and shooting the breeze like players do. This is what the Hyenas called *The Ride of Life*. Get money and get fly. Bust your gun for a little fun and party with the ladies to relieve the stress when you on the Ride of Life. Even though they devoted most of their energy to work and play, they kept their minds ready for war just like now.

Regardless to the live activity and commotion taking place on the strip,

G-Boy and another individual was peeping everything moving thru the strip and anyone moving thru the crowd on the corner. They spotted a black on black Grand Prix with tinted windows spin the strip several times driving slowly. At first they figured it was some individuals deciding on what bar to go to on Bailey Avenue, but when the Grand Prix slowly bent the corner at the bar they were standing in front of, G-Boy peeped two individuals laid back in the Grand Prix as they passed him and pulled onto the side street. The Grand Prix pulled down the block away from the bar and pulled over. G-Boy skated over to Munchie to put him on point. The Hyenas had so much beef they had to stay on point and be paranoid just to stay alive.

"Yo yo come here I gotta holla at you," G-Boy pulled Munchie to the side and spit in his ear. "It's two cats in the Grand Prix and they pulled down the block, we gone slide down there and you already know...if we gotta get busy we gone hit the cut and meet you on Berkshire."

"You already know I'm on it," Munchie shot back then had everyone clear the corner before he jumped in his Escalade.

G-Boy and his man crouched low while creeping on the sidewalk alongside the cars on the side street. A few kids were on the street playing and one thing about growing up in the hood, people knew when it was about to go down, it was like a natural hood instinct of sensing danger. The kids knew it was about to be hell on Stockbridge Street so they quit playing and dashed to their porches as G-Boy and his man crept through the block with their hands on their hips. Even the grown folks sitting on the porches enjoying the night air rushed inside refusing to catch a stray bullet.

G-Boy and his man were about 4 cars away and across the street from the Grand Prix. The Grand Prix's engine was still running and the driver still had the car in drive because the brake lights were on. The passenger door then slowly opened and a skinny Man with a curly afro crawled out the car scanning the block like an outsider would.

"You back the nigga down who just got out the wheel and I'm gone hit the driver," G-Boy whispered as they ducked behind a car two cars behind the Grand Prix.

"I think that's them niggas from Zenner Street."

"We splash em first and ask questions later…let's go," G-Boy stated sprinting into the middle of the street aiming his pistol at the driver door while his man was a few seconds from getting the drop on the man who was standing outside the car at the passenger door.

Crumbs peeped G-Boy and his man spin from behind the car and hit the street. A revelation flashed swiftly in his mind. In a milli-second he realized Sun-Z set him and Lil Flip up to get killed. Damn. Sun-Z thought Lil Flip and Crumbs were snitches since they didn't get indicted with the rest of the crew. This thought flashed in Crumbs mind but with a natural reaction and a force from within to keep on living, Crumbs dropped on side of the car to take cover before the guns blazed. While Lil Flip sat in the driver seat he didn't know what was going on as Crumbs ducked while yelling his name.

"Flip duck Sun-Z set us up."

"Yo hold on," G-Boy yelled stopping in the middle of the street a breath away from opening fire on the driver side of the car. "Crumbs and Lil Flip?" G-Boy shockingly yelled lowering his gun as his man pumped the brakes on his Jordan's.

"Yeah it's Lil Flip and Crumbs what the fuck yo," Crumbs was still ducking behind the car gripping his pistol.

"Yo what the fuck wrong with yall little niggas we was bout to air yall niggas out," G-Boy quickly threw his gun back on his waist feeling his adrenaline suck his breath away making him breathless. "Yo we got too much beef in these parts for yall to come through like that, we thought yall was some niggas from Zenner street we beefing with."

"My bad we aint know," Crumbs hopped up still clutching his pistol as he stood on the other side of the car.

"Yo what the fuck," Lil Flip was slowly exiting the car. "Yall niggas aint playing around here."

"Yall niggas spinned the block mad times so we was gone swiss cheese yall."

"Hell yeah why yall aint jump out on the block that's what you do when you wanna live," G-Boy told them giving dap to Lil Flip. "I'm G-Boy this my Man Blammy right here."

"Yo we aint know if it was a good time to holla at yall with all them chicks around."

"Nigga money over bitches we get to the money first and don't nothing stop us from getting to the money."

"Hell yeah that's what I'm talking about," Crumbs spun from around the car and gave G-Boy and Blammy dap. The four then strolled back down the block to the bar and Munchie was pulling back up in front of the bar.

"Yo yall young niggas got a lot to learn if yall gone roll with the Hyenas," Munchie was seriously joking leaning against his Escalade, "Zulu spoke highly of yall but yall little niggas moving like yall ready to die coming through like that."

"Yo that was our bad."

"Yeah it's all good but fuck all that…Zulu told us all about yall and we gone get this shit popping," Munchie responded.

"Yeah we been waiting on yall boys," G-Boy advised Lil Flip and Crumbs, "Zulu got something special for yall too...he gone get yall boys right before he slide on some real nigga shit you heard."

"And Zulu gone be happy as fuck to see yall."

"Yeah we gone be happy to see Zulu too," Lil Flip and Crumbs depressingly stated giving each other a worried look before scoping out a flock of gorgeous ladies stepping into the bar.

"Yall like that huh?" Munchie observed the hunger of lust in their eyes. If only Munchie really knew Lil Flip and Crumbs wished they could party with the ladies instead of handling what was ahead.

"Yeah the ladies tight but we need to see Zulu and get them bricks, niggas is starving, fuck these hoes," Crumbs stated with his game face on point.

"We can take care of that after we see Zulu…and we gone see Zulu after we chill and have a few drinks."

Lil Flip nodded in agreement feeling a little uneasy as Munchie and G-Boy led them into the bar. Over glasses of Dom Perignon the Hyenas had a toast with Lil Flip and Crumbs. Despite the misfortune, it was time for more success and for life to be better than ever. They lounged in the bar for a while engaging in the usual street talk while letting their eyes watch the swirling hips of the ladies on the dancefloor. The four then dipped from the bar and jumped into G-Boy's Benz truck.

Munchie and G-Boy had Zulu stashed away at the Bachelor pad which was only 10 minutes from the bar but they had to take extra precautions whenever they went to the pad. They would never drive straight to the pad and they would always switch two to three different cars before they hit the pad. They had to be on point because this was the feds they were watching out for. Munchie and G-Boy loved Zulu like a brother and they would do all in their power to make sure Zulu was good on their watch.

G-Boy drove away from the bar and hit the streets driving all around the city as him and Munchie expressed their Thug Love for Zulu. Lil Flip and Crumbs could feel the same emotion for Zulu deep in their soul but Sun-Z came out of left field and was the only person who found the force of evil in his soul to feel otherwise about Zulu.

G-Boy pushed it through the city observing the night life while also making sure they weren't being followed by the Feds. The town was jumping and the freaks were out under the moon and party people were crawling all through the streets. Lil Flip began to feel like these same streets where everyone had fun and partied was pure evil. It was an evil Lil Flip and Crumbs had to battle in their own souls. An evil that made people in the streets kill the life that God created and kill the life they love. It was Pure Evil. Crumbs on the other hand was ignoring his conscience and appearing like everything was alright.

As G-Boy pulled up at clubs hollering at the ladies and saluting other Thugs in that lively mood, Munchie observed Lil Flip in the back seat under a spell of distress. He had that look on his face people have when their loved ones are in trouble and it may be their last time seeing their loved ones. Lil Flip looked sad but Crumbs was bopping to the music and rapping along.

"Yo G-Boy we aint being followed," Munchie stated as they pulled from in front of a club, "Lets get these boys to Zulu because they looking twisted....

you know how we felt seeing Alley go on the run…let's get these boys to they big bro."

"We got yall," G-Boy shouted blasting the music while pushing the pedal to the floor while *Nas' song "Life We Chose,"* blasted through the speakers putting everyone in a zone thinking of the life they chose.

Who knows what's in the hearts and minds of men but the Creator? Lil Flip and Crumbs had some troubling things on their minds which had them in a state of confusion and depression. They were confused because Sun-Z wanted what no one else wanted. This was depressing and Lil Flip and Crumbs felt their loyalty to the game was being tested. One thing they knew is they had to make a decision about this life they chose. It was either play the streets risking their life with prison and death but hoping to get rich, or go home, find a 9-5 and enjoy freedom while their pockets were slim. This was the crossroads. Crumbs knew what he wanted. He wanted them bricks Zulu had for them and he would do whatever to have more than the crumbs he had all his life. Lil Flip on the other hand felt otherwise seeing the misfortunes of the game and knowing the destruction that may lie ahead.

G-Boy pulled into in the Camelot Court apartments in the University Heights section of the city and parked his Benz truck. The four then jumped in a Buick Regal and headed to the Bennett Village to see Zulu. 15 minutes later they were slowly rolling down an alleyway behind the Bennett Village apartments. G-Boy quietly pulled the wheel behind one of the two story townhomes. They all slid out the car with G-Boy in the lead with his pistol out on alert for enemies and police. They crept halfway down the dimly lit alley pass several of the buildings before they approached the house Zulu was in.

Munchie led Lil Flip and Crumbs thru the backyard of the building while G-Boy stood in the alleyway making sure no one was creeping on them. Once the trio entered the house G-Boy then sprinted inside right behind them being sure they weren't followed. They entered the gloomy apartment where T.V light flashed revealing Zulu and his two concubines cuddled on the leather sofa watching *Eddie Murphy's animated sitcom The PJ's.*

"*Yoooo,*" Zulu shouted from the living room hearing Munchie and G-Boy stepping thru the kitchen disturbing the night silence with their boisterous yapping.

"We got a surprise for you bro bro," Munchie hit the dining room light.

"*Oooh shit,*" Zulu shoved the ladies from off him and jumped off the couch in excitement. He was so happy to see Lil Flip and Crumbs he rushed them and hugged them both at the same time.

"Damn big bro what's the deal?"

"Man you already know...how yall holding up out here?"

"Man," Lil Flip and Crumbs both shook their heads gazing down at the floor while thinking to themselves, *"This shit can't be real...this can't be life."*

Lil Flip then raised his eyes to Zulu and said, "Man big bro...I don't think shit gone ever be the same...ever."

"It may not be the same with yo fam gone," G-Boy cut in while grabbing some water from the refrigerator, "But you can make shit better if you go hard...it's either go hard or go home the game don't ever stop."

"Hell yeah the game is made to be played," Munchie added before the fellas all seated themselves in the living room. The females wrapped themselves in the covers and slid upstairs leaving the fellas to themselves. Munchie then pulled out a box of Garcia Vega blunts and a half ounce of blue skunk. G-Boy then slid out the kitchen with a liter of Henny XO and several cups.

"This for you Zulu," G-Boy held the bottle in the air after pouring everyone a shot, "And for a new alliance with Lil Flip and Crumbs...we gone make it happen for those who wont be able to enjoy this success."

"Salute," Everyone returned the cheers.

"Yall boys don't know how blessed I feel to spend these last moments with yall," Zulu told Lil Flip and Crumbs with a sincere smile on his face. "Yall the last two surviving from the hood...yall boys better be thankful yall still out here...everybody from the hood gone except yall and yall homies...damn."

"This shit can't happen." Lil Flip thought to himself guzzling his shots and interacting with everyone.

"Man yall boys looking stressed it's gone be good for yall," Zulu snapped Lil Flip and Crumbs out of their mental world of hell. "Yall just gotta stay focused and learn from our mistakes…yall can make it happen out here as long as yall stay focused."

"This shit serious out here Zulu…this shit real as hell and if I gotta do what I gotta do it better get greater," Crumbs dropped his head peering at the floor knowing that he haven't sold all of his soul yet, but if he followed Sun-Z's order, he would be trading in his soul for all the riches and evil of the world if he did what Sun-Z wanted.

"I don't know what this shit about anymore," Lil Flip stated wondering how did everything come to this moment. "This street shit so deadly and on some real shit…if I would've known this is what my life was gone turn out to be I wouldn't have fucked with this shit…this shit is ugly yo…you can't trust no one out here…no one…this shit make me feel sick." The guilty conscience began to eat at Lil Flip causing him to speak indirectly. Crumbs then shot a convincing look at Lil Flip like you better shut your mouth.

"I know how you feel lil bro…this shit don't make you happy at all…we was happier when we was kids we just aint know it," Zulu sighed deeply throwing his head back and peering up at the ceiling thinking of his past. Back in the days when as kids they were innocent with no stress or worries. It was all fun and games from playing football to wrestling and playing with G.I. Joes. Life changed so much since then. Zulu wished he could rewind the tape of life just to save his friends from dying and going to jail. He would rewind the tape so they all could choose a different direction which didn't lead to the Dream of Death. Man only lives once and the clock of time goes forward and never backwards. Whatever is done under the sun cannot be taken back. This was a reality Zulu knew he had to live and deal with. We only have one life to live and should live it in the most productive way with no regrets.

"Yeah we played the cards we was dealt even though it seemed like a bad hand," Zulu gazed upon everyone's face, "Damn near everyone dead-Dolla, Mel-Cash, yall homie Black Boy-, everybody else literally in jail…it's like before this street shit we was really good in life…we all only hit the streets to make a little money…but then that little money turned to needing more money and before we even knew it everything changed and it was like the streets was the only thing we knew that could make us happy…we be winning until this shit happen…but if we think of it…who really winning when everyone either end up dead or in jail?"

"Nigga what," Munchie got hyped and jumped up, "Zulu once you get that I.D. and slide to the Bahamas you gone be the winner…you gone hit them islands and look back at this shit like you did it…and aint nobody gone be able to say Crime don't pay because my nigga Zulu made it pay…word up," Munchie slid over to Zulu and slapped his hand several times. Munchie was amped up and motivated by Zulu's power move.

"Hell muthafucking yeah…everybody gotta die anyway so you might as well enjoy the life you was giving," G-Boy added lighting his blunt, "This the life we chose and we in too deep to start wanting a different life and trade it all in…yall know it don't work like that…Once you sell yo soul to that first drug sale and squeeze that hammer and taste the blood and power, you bust that nut in yo Thug Soul and give birth to a life we call what Munchie?"

"The ride of life we living…drug flipping…luxury living…dodging prison…romancing these women, playing this game and always winning."

"That's what I'm talking about," G-Boy and Munchie were slapping each other's hand while jumping up and down like they just won the Super Bowl. "Nigga the game gone keep rolling no matter what happen and it's all about who can keep rolling with the punches the game throw at you…only when the casket drop do the game stop…prison definitely don't stop the game so you gotta play it till it's over…this all niggas like us know…what else we gone do…this what life gave to us to play so we gone play it hard and play till we can't play no more."

It was sad but true. They all came too far to turn back the hands of time. They all corrupted their souls to the point they felt it was natural to feel the criminology of the heart. It was crazy and the tragedy of the street life befalling them wasn't natural at all and was not what life was supposed to be about. The tragedy of the street life only existed because they lived that lifestyle of death and knew of no other way to live. As young black men in this materialistic world they never knew a spiritual life of love, peace, and happiness. Ever since

Africans were snatched from the Motherland and shipped to the wilderness of North and South America in chains, the only life Black people ever experienced was that of blood, sweat, and tears, and it seemed only materialism could provide the happiness to their scourged souls. Black people were separated from their homeland where they knew Peace and Harmony. Before Europeans came to Africa, Black People lived according to nature and honored the life the Creator of the Universe created. But being in America Blacks were alienated from their divine culture and lifestyle of righteousness and taught a new way of life by the wicked white slave masters who raped, murdered, and stole land. These actions of the white slave masters were criminal acts which Black people soon began to imitate. *Black people were reduced to the level of beast as the Supreme Court Judge ruled in the Dredd Scott case.* Once freed from slavery everything revolved around material wealth since these were the rewards of the American Dream. Black people forgot about spiritual happiness. And in this day and time, most black men try accumulating wealth through the life of crime because it makes them feel above the white man who kept his feet on their necks for hundreds of years. In the life of selling drugs Black men rule themselves in their own economy and were equal to the white elite ruling class if not above them. And since Black people were denied the God giving right to education for hundreds of years by the threat of death, most Blacks got into a life of crime since that seemed the only option. But where there is a problem there is a solution. This cycle of destruction facing the Black Race could be reversed and turned to a cycle of life, love, peace, and longevity. It would take a lot of spiritual cleansing and the desire to live righteously for a change to take place.

Just like the power of righteousness and the God Conscience was striving to cleanse Lil Flip and Crumbs' soul from the wicked seeds Sun-Z planted in their minds. Sun-Z flew the kite ordering Lil Flip and Crumbs to get the bricks then murder Zulu because Zulu was a snitch. This was an ugly situation that harassed their souls ever since they read the letter and now sitting in Zulu's presence, their souls was in a hell hole being picked at by the devil's pitchfork. They sat here in the presence of their big brother with intentions on murdering him based on Sun-Z's unproven accusations of Zulu being file. Lil

Flip and Crumbs struggled to see foulness in Zulu for a justification to murder him but they couldn't. They felt the Power of Thug Essence emanate from Zulu as they sat in his presence. Sun-Z with his deceptive intelligence was using trick knowledge to master and manipulate Lil Flip and Crumbs because they were vulnerable and young. Lil Flip's soul was struggling do the right thing while Crumbs soul was more easily influenced to do what was treacherous.

It was like a war of Armageddon taking place within Lil Flip and Crumbs spiritual universe. Their mind and souls were battling for the right decision to make as they sat in the living room with Zulu, Munchie, and G-Boy. Through deceit Lil Flip and Crumbs appeared to be enjoying their final moment with their loved one but deep down inside it was a struggle that felt like death itself, a feeling only the feeling itself could understand.

"Yo check it out though," Zulu looked over at Lil Flip and Crumbs. "I known yall boys all yall life and I know yall always looked up to me like a big brother…yall even followed my steps…I aint trying to be no preacher and lecture yall but yo," Zulu closed his eyes and took a deep breath to feel his insides with the life of air since he was so tensed. He breathed in and out like he was relieving a burden from his soul then continued speaking, "I know I showed yall crazy negative shit out here in these streets…but if I never told yall anything positive I'm gonna tell yall now because it would crush me to see yall die in these streets or go to prison for life…I would feel responsible because I know yall look up to me to the point I probably could've kept yall out the streets…but if yall feel the way yall feel follow ya heart…if yall tired of this street shit get out while you can before it gets ugly…you don't have to end up like me and the rest of the crew…I don't even know what the future hold for me on some real shit…yall still got a chance at life…it's a reason yall aint get caught up with us and yall should take this opportunity to do something different because if yall stay in the game yall know what the outcome gone be...feel me."

Lil Flip and Crumbs knew it was the truth but they were too prideful and Thugged out to admit the truth. They both blew the tension from their souls knowing it was over for them. Their souls were too entrenched in the dirt of the streets and they felt their conscience could never be cleaned. Just how their conscience was making them realize their ill intentions and true motive for sitting with Zulu. This was the most painful spiritual moment any Man could face.

Zulu poured his heart out to them while they were contemplating his murder. This was the vilest emotion they ever experienced. How could they ever live peacefully with their souls after this moment? How would Zulu feel if Zulu knew they were going to bite him in the back like a slimy snake once they had a chance? Their souls were doomed and they were knee deep in the mud. The only way out for them was death because their souls would never be the same after this moment.

"Zulu it's like G-Boy said," Crumbs spoke unable to make eye contact with Zulu, "I'm too deep in the game to change…my mind already been made up."

"This the only life I know," G-Boy confirmed, "I'm gone get my money and die in these streets with my gun like Black Boy…I live like a G and I'm gone die like a G. Word to Black Boy," G-Boy raised his blunt in the air.

"Rest in Peace to all the real G's," everyone shouted raising their blunts and liquor in the air.

They all let the night roll on getting intoxicated and keeping Zulu company. Zulu knew this would be his last time seeing them all. He poured his heart out and told them all he hoped they could get out the game while they still had a chance. They were young, black, hood rich and probably not under federal investigation. If they knew what was best they would take the hood riches they had and journey to an exotic place like Brazil where their money would have them on the level of a Black King. To stay in the streets forever was to wait for trouble to come at them. From experience Zulu learned the hard way that it was best to bounce when trouble wasn't in the picture. The game was played to win and staying in the game forever wasn't how to win. Every man makes their own decision and in the streets the game was played to keep chasing the rush, that's why most decided they couldn't leave the game because there was no rush like the game.

The ether blue starry sky began to fade to a purple. The night was almost over and in a minute the light would replace the darkness as birds would sing in a new day. For the last time Zulu broke day with his Thug Family and now it was time for them to depart.

"We love you Zulu," Lil Flip and Crumbs both hugged Zulu but were unable to keep their gaze upon him, "We gone miss you Zulu."

"I'm gone miss yall too…just be safe out here and remember what I said."

"Zulu," Lil Flip looked deeply into his eyes, "Don't trust no one out here Zulu…watch everyone and I mean it…don't trust no one Zulu…people not right out here and I think I'm getting out Zulu."

"No question baby boy, I wish the best for you…just do the right thing with them bricks and that's enough for you to get out this shit…word."

Crumbs gave Lil Flip another ill look like he wanted to kill Lil Flip. Crumbs then finally glanced at Zulu. This would be Crumbs last time seeing Zulu alive and he wanted his mind to have the image of an alive Zulu and not the image of a bullet riddled Zulu that would haunt the little bit of conscience he still had in him.

"Love you Zulu, good looking for everything," Crumbs uttered his last words to Zulu. Everyone skated from the apartment before daylight appeared. Munchie and G-Boy then hit Lil Flip and Crumbs with the bricks from Zulu then sent them on their way. The alliance was set and the plan was to get money, but Lil Flip and Crumbs knew they had a critical decision to make.

"Why you was looking like you was about to put Zulu on point or some shit…I already see you don't feel how I feel," Crumbs barked on Lil Flip as they drove down the street, "I made my mind up and I'm gone get it done…it's either do or die...this the game."

Lil Flip remained silent peering out the car window observing a bum stand over a trashcan rummaging through a McDonalds bag. Lil Flip felt like shit. He felt worse than the bum in the garbage can, but through the miraculous reality of Divine intervention, Lil Flip felt the Creator of the universe deep within his soul make him realize his divine nature of righteousness.

"We not murdering Zulu…it's not right…Sun-Z not right…aint none of this shit right Crumbs."

"Hold on," Crumbs swerved the wheel over to the curb and put the car in park, "Fuck you mean this shit aint right…we got three bricks in our possession…we back…and if we knock Zulu off Sun-Z giving us everything…we gone be running the whole hood…and now we clicked up with the Hyenas…we gone run the city and be rich…this what I been waiting for all my life."

"Dude Sun-Z gone get us killed…he don't give a fuck about us…he want us to kill Zulu for some bullshit…Zulu aint no snitch and I know it…Munchie and G-Boy know it…dude if we kill Zulu don't you know Munchie and G-Boy gone kill us…they love Zulu like we do…but that shit don't even matter…I can't kill my friends…come on yo…money not stronger than the love I have for my friends…Sun-Z not right and I'm not doing this."

"So what the fuck you gone do with yo life…you gone stop selling drugs and get a job? Tell me…because if we don't knock Zulu off Sun-Z gone get it done and then have us knocked off."

"I don't know what I'm gone do but I know I'm not doing this," Lil Flip looked deeply into Crumbs soulless eyes and said, "You can have them bricks and everything else that come with this…I'm not mad at you Crumbs, I'm not destroying my life or no one else's anymore…I wanna live…I wanna live to see something good in life and not this."

"Yo you can't be fucking serious dude," Crumbs pulled his pistol out. "Nigga you gone walk away from something we started together…you a weak nigga…we been in these streets together since day one and you think you just gone walk away from this shit that easy and leave me out here dolo…hell no…what you gone do go to church and tell the preacher about all the shit we did…fuck no nigga…it's death before dishonor…nigga the streets gave me everything I ever had that was of value…my own mama told me I wasn't shit and she never did shit for me…it was the streets that took care of me and I'm gone stay true to the streets because they been true to me."

"Crumbs man," Lil Flip focused deeply on his best friend's eyes trying to reach him. Crumbs wasn't there it seemed like. "I don't want this no more and I'm out…I'm out…I hope you understand me…but if walking away from the streets gonna keep me sane and let me keep the peace I do have in my soul…that's what I'm gonna do…I'm out," Lil Flip began opening the car door.

"Muthafucka where the fuck is you going?" Crumbs banged the butt of his gun on the steering wheel. "This ain't no fucking *Boyz N the Hood* nigga…you not getting out the fucking car." Crumbs yelled in a rage as Lil Flip slowly opened the car door. "Close the fucking car door before I clap yo ass Flip."

"Look at what this shit done to you…for money you would kill yo own people."

"I don't wanna hear that shit…don't get out the car because I can't let you walk away knowing what you know," Crumbs began to level his gun as Lil Flip slowly raised himself out of the car. "I'm telling you don't make me do it yo."

"I'm gone Crumbs," Lil Flip stepped out the car looking up at the sun rising above the houses on the street. He made a righteous decision at the crossroads and he used the power of the indwelling divinity in his soul to overcome the wickedness within. He felt his soul coming back to life just as the sun climbed out of the dark skies. He slammed the car door shut and stepped onto the sidewalk still gazing into the life of the sun as he walked away. Lil Flip never even knew Crumbs jumped out the wheel yelling because the magnetism of the sun had a grip on his dark soul bathing it with light. Crumbs aimed the pistol at the back of Lil Flip's head as he slowly walked down the block looking up at the sun.

"Yo stop before I clap you…stop," were the last words Crumbs uttered before he pulled the trigger.

"Boom," the slug spit and blasted an inch away from Lil Flip's head. Lil Flip was experiencing a withdrawal of his consciousness from the physical realm. It was like he was in a deep daydream and he was unaware of the physical world. When the slug flew pass his head, his mind came back to the physical. He spun around and looked at Crumbs who stood several feet away behind the car aiming the pistol in his direction. Crumbs busted off another shot which splashed Lil Flip in the shoulder. Lil Flip stumbled backwards feeling his adrenaline activate him. He spun around and took off running as Crumbs began dumping slugs at him. Lil Flip made it about five houses away before a slug caught him in the back causing him to fall. Crumbs began to run down the block and finish him but a lady on her way to work was standing in her driveway screaming. Crumbs jumped in the wheel and peeled out heading back to the Bennett Village to finish his mission.

....

After hitting Lil Flip and Crumbs with the bricks Munchie and G-Boy were headed to an afterhours spot in the Riverside section of town. The ride of life never stopped for the Hyenas and any chance they had to party they would whether it was rain, hail, snow, or earthquakes, it didn't matter the time of day.

G-Boy stopped at a red light feeling his tiredness kick in while waiting for the light change. He struggled to find the strength to keep his fluttering eyes open. The light turned green and G-Boy didn't budge. He dozed off again.

"Yo wake yo ass up nigga," Munchie tapped G-Boy after a car honked its horn.

"Oh shit, my bad bro," G-Boy opened his eyes and mashed his foot on the gas feeling his second wind. "Yo I'm ready let's go see these hoes I need a head shot to wake me up for real yo."

"Man whatever just get us there." Munchie responded before G-Boy dozed off again but this time they were in traffic. "Yooooo," Munchie yelled jerking the steering wheel over when G-Boy shut his eyes and almost side swiped a parked car. G-Boy opened his eyes in shock as Munchie gripped the wheel from the passenger seat.

"Yo what the fuck just happened."

"Nigga fuck that pull over you gone get us killed in this car."

"Yo I'm good I dosed off I don't know what I was thinking," G-Boy rolled his window down sucking in the morning air while stretching his eyes wide open. He scooted forward in his seat and got himself together as he pulled up at a stop sign.

"Hell no G-Boy…fuck that after hour spot…it's no way we driving way over to Riverside with you dosing off…I'm too tired to drive…fuck that let's just go back to the hood."

"Yeah you right yo," G-Boy slowly pulled off from the stop sign. "Let's just go chill with Zulu since we aint that far from him."

"That sound like a plan," Munchie stated keeping his eyes focused on G-Boy as they headed back to the Bennett Village.

……………………

Crumbs pulled into the alleyway behind the Bennett Village and parked on side of a garage. He jumped out the wheel deeply inhaling the revitalizing energy for his miserable soul. Crumbs' was in a zone so tensed he could barely think nor feel anything as he crept down the alleyway to Zulu's building.

Inside the house Zulu was pacing the floor feeling the pains of anxiety flood his system. He couldn't wait to leave and be in paradise with NyJewel where he could relax. Then at the same time he felt sad he had to leave the only life he knew and the only people he knew. Zulu then heard an unfamiliar knock at the back door which threw his mind in shambles. He quickly scanned the living room and dining room checking to see if maybe Munchie and G-Boy left their keys because they never knocked. Since Zulu been hiding there, no one ever came by. Here it was a little after six in the morning and the only people outside were club hoppers, drug addicts, stick up kids, and the feds who loved raiding spots at the wee-hours of the morning.

Zulu snatched his pistol when he didn't peep any house keys lying around that Munchie and G-Boy might have left. He then slipped into his shirt and jumped into his sneakers. Zulu tip toed to the living room window checking the scene out front on the street. It was all clear. He then crept to the kitchen where the back door was and crouched low peeping out back.

"What the hell?" Zulu's fear vanished upon seeing Crumbs standing at the back door looking kind of hyper and talking to himself. Zulu quickly opened the door with his pistol in his hand saying, "Man you had me shook as hell…I thought the Feds was here to get me."

Crumbs opened the screen door thinking to himself, *"I wish it was the feds at this door instead of me too...I cant believe what I'm bout to do."*

"So you don't wanna see yo big bro leave huh man? Where the fuck Lil Flip at?" Zulu began sliding back through the kitchen as Crumbs stepped inside remaining silent. "I'm gone miss yall boys word up." Zulu was now entering the dining room where he sat his pistol on the table. Zulu then slid back to the refrigerator, grabbed a bottle of Orange Juice, then began to step out the kitchen and head back through the dining room. Crumbs wasn't a stranger so not once did Zulu look back at Crumbs as Crumbs stood in the kitchen behind Zulu.

"Click clack." The sound of metal inserting a slug into the chamber of a gun was the only response Zulu got from Crumbs.

Growing up in the streets and playing with steel all his life as a gun clapper, Zulu was a soldier who knew his weapons like a musician knew the sounds of his instruments but sometimes your eyes and ears could play tricks on the mind. Like the saying goes, *"Believe half of what you see and none of what you hear."* Zulu slowly spun around with the bottle of orange juice in his hand to see if his senses were deceiving him. He felt it before he even turned around and when he caught sight of Crumbs gripping the steel with trembling hands he couldn't believe it, it was real.

"Yo what the fuck is that for?" Zulu blurted in confusion.

Crumbs was gazing pass Zulu into the living room while unsteadily aiming the canon at Zulu's melon. He couldn't look into Zulu's eyes as he stated, "I'm sorry Zulu," a tear formed in his eyes as Crumbs gasped for air in his tight throat, "Sun-Z called this...I don't really wanna do it but I got to."

"Nigga what?" Zulu tensed his face still in confusion before realizing his own people were going to kill him, and kill him for what? Zulu was standing right near the dining room table where he laid his gun a few seconds ago. It was right in arms reach and he could easily grab it and blast Crumbs because Crumbs was overcome by the force of guilt puncturing his soul and he was shaking uncontrollably. Somehow Zulu became suspended in time and stood motionless as he looked upon the death headed his way. Zulu felt the hands of fate snatch everything from out of him as he instantly dwelt on this harsh and soul crushing reality. It was a blow to the breath of life the Creator blew into every living soul.

In this split second of introspection which transcended all time and space, Zulu felt like he was sitting with the Black Creator (Ancient of Days) in the realm of Eternity which was all in the mind. Everything in the universe came at Zulu full speed as he stood face to face with death.

Crumbs just stood there shaking while Zulu's eyes seemed to look through Crumbs. It was like everything Zulu ever lived for added up to this moment. This moment where his spirit and soul felt like it was journeying through the ancestral hall of judgment where his conscience was the judge. All the pain and joy, the good and the bad he experienced, the right and wrong he done all seemed to flash across his mind's eye as his two physical eyes focused on the black hole of death Crumbs unsteadily pointed at Zulu's existence.

Zulu didn't even recognize Crumbs. Zulu was so drawn up into the mental and spiritual realm all Zulu could see was a blurry form in front of him that was there to send him back to the black essence of the universe. This was Zulu's destination of life and Zulu knew with everything in his soul that this is how it was supposed to go down and nothing could stop it. Not even Zulu snatching his gun and busting back could stop the fulfillment of the Creator's plan. Zulu stood tall, head high with the fiery flame of God in his eyes piercing Crumbs tormented soul which was burning inside. Crumbs was so scared and felt the force of the Creator penetrating his soul, Crumbs was sweating profusely feeling like he was about to have a heart attack.

Zulu's mind was absorbed by the spiritual realm and he accepted his fate like a man, he didn't care for the opportunity he had to save his life by reaching his hand a few inches over to the table. He could've snatched his gun and flamed Crumbs before the scared and trembling Crumbs even realized what happened since Crumbs couldn't find the power to pull the trigger and kill Zulu.

The back door then opened and that's when hell opened its gates of fire. It happened quickly and no one knew what was transpiring as the commotion unraveled. Munchie and G-Boy was caught completely off guard observing Crumbs standing in the kitchen aiming the cannon at Zulu. They both were tired and under the influence of liquor and weed so their intoxicated minds were cloudy. Upon stepping into this scene their minds swiftly sobered up and they impulsively became alert, feeling activated to shoot first and ask questions later as they snatched their guns from off their hips and aimed them at Crumbs. They didn't even recognize Crumbs whom they just left about 30 minutes ago. This was one mind boggling event that had everyone twisted.

"Boooom," the force of the gunshot was a vociferous thunder that frightened everyone. Time stopped as the boom slowly reverberated. Everything was like slow motion and suspenseful and it was like Crumbs watched the bullet burst out the barrel of his gun and travel through time before it reached its destination. He never meant to pull the trigger. He was just so panicky and on the wave of fear while he had the gun aimed at Zulu his finger twitched when Munchie and G-Boy burst in, causing Crumbs to accidentally pull the trigger.

Zulu smiled observing the flash and feeling the force of death speeding in his direction as the hollow tip bullet zoomed towards his cranium. Zulu witnessed everything. He witnessed the innocence of his childhood. The street dreams. He felt the love for Destiny and the passion for NyJewel. He felt the anger in life. He tasted the death in life. He heard the wisdom. He observed everything his soul needed to experience on the physical plane before it was time to return back to its essence of the Creator.

It was time to go back home to the Most-High. He seen it all and done it all. He even witnessed the last moment of his life there in the Bennett Village. He observed Munchie and G-Boy fly into the kitchen with their guns drawn and run down on Crumbs. This was it Zulu realized before the bullet pierced his cranium and shattered the vision of his mental.

Everything quickly transpired and Munchie and G-Boy opened fire on Crumbs who froze up after he accidentally pulled the trigger. Crumbs still had his gun raised in Zulu's direction as slugs pummeled into his body. He attempted to spin and aim his gun at Munchie and G-Boy but they were spitting rapid fire as they stormed into the kitchen. Slug after slug banged Crumbs as he stood on his two feet wobbling from the force of destruction. The guilt of his soul was more painful than the slugs. The slugs seemed to not hurt Crumbs physically as he stumbled back onto the kitchen sink groaning with his gun in the air. Munchie and G-Boy dumped a barrage of slugs into Crumbs before he finally fell down to the kitchen floor still shaking.

"Oh shit, what the fuck just happened?" Munchie grabbed his head in shock standing amongst the tragedy. Munchie then noticed Zulu's hand twitching. "Zulu...fuck." Munchie rushed over to Zulu and knelt down cuffing Zulu's splattered head in his lap. "Zulu don't die bro...please don't die...G-Boy why we leave him here alone...aww shit yo."

"You piece of shit muthafucka," G-Boy stormed over to Crumbs who was on the floor shaking and coughing up blood trying to speak. "You dirt bag ass little nigga."

"*S-s-s-sun-z*," Crumbs began choking on his blood. "*He-he-put-put-the hit on Z-Z-.*"

"Fuck you nigga," G-Boy exploded placing the barrel of his gun on Crumbs' bloody mouth and squeezing the trigger. G-Boy then skated over to Munchie who held Zulu. "Damn Zulu...what happened my nigga? Damn...why they kill my dude."

"He aint dead G-Boy we gotta get him to the hospital." Munchie observed Zulu's hand still twitching.

"Yo sun...look," G-Boy was only being real, "Zulu gone yo...look at him yo...my nigga gone." That's when Zulu's hand stopped twitching.

Munchie then gazed down into the lifeless shell of Zulu which leaked blood into his lap. Munchie and G-Boy then gazed into each others' eyes letting their souls express what words couldn't express. Another Real Nigga was murdered because of treachery and betrayal just like their best friend Black Boy was murdered. What was the game coming to they wondered as they carefully lay Zulu's head on the floor staring at Zulu's lifeless shell.

Munchie then ran upstairs to snatch the two females who were hiding in the closet scared to death and terrified. It was no time for the females to get dressed so they snatched a few things and skated downstairs where G-Boy was wiping down the tables and anything else him and Munchie may have touched. They had the females cover their eyes as they led them outside but before Munchie and G-Boy exited the house they took one last look at Zulu.

"Damn...Rest in Peace...we love you my G...we love you."

CHAPTER 24

The double homicide that occurred on E. Amherst and Hill streets in the Bennett Village made local headlines and was the top story in Western New York. It was a shocking story that sent a message to hundreds of youth on the streets of Buffalo. Even though Killa escaped the authorities and made it back to the Motherland, he still had his own demons to face. The life of a Thug had no exit and no one could escape the Karma of life. Zulu's death was a testament to the street reality because even though he was an armed and dangerous fugitive who was able to evade Federal Authorities, Zulu couldn't evade the bullets which caught up with him before the Feds did.

The news of Zulu's death was like a bomb that devastated the grimy streets of Ruff-Buff. Rumors began spreading how the Hyena Crew murdered the remaining members of the Get Rich Crime Family so they could take over E. North. The streets were talking but nothing was factual. The ones who knew the truth were behind the walls of incarceration.

Inmates and Prisoners were entrapped by cement walls and steel barriers but the speed of sound seemed to penetrate through prison walls faster than the ear could hear. When things jumped off in the street, word seemed to reach the belly of the beast just as quick as it hit the street corner. The rumors were crazy in the streets and in jail. Inmates anticipated when the Get Rich Crime Family would hit Ra-King since they were all locked up together. People were always waiting and hoping to see some action in jail. Most people didn't really know the situation so they were assuming and hoping for something that wouldn't happen.

Ra-King received the visit from Munchie and G-Boy and he couldn't believe the situation. Crumbs not only flipped out and shot Lil Flip, but he killed Zulu on Sun-Z's order. Ra-King analyzed the situation realizing justice was going to get served. Sun-Z pulled a file move and was going to get it Ra-King told himself. Ra-King pushed up on some scalpels from a female nurse he knew and he was gonna rip Sun-Z to pieces like a Ginsu knife rip up a turkey on Thanksgiving.

Ra-King felt humiliated and disrespected because Sun-Z played him. For the first time in his life of helping people, Ra-King felt regretful for using his power to help another accomplish their goal. Sun-Z manipulated Ra-King and jeopardized the lives of Ra-King, Munchie, and G-Boy. Crumbs could've killed Munchie and G-Boy in that situation. The situation was ugly but could have been uglier. If Cream and Hawk believed the Hyenas killed Zulu and Crumbs, Ra-King's life would have been in danger inside the jail. Sun-Z played with high explosives this time and caused earthquakes that shook everyone's foundation. Sun-Z went to far this time and he needed to be taken out of his miserable mind. Justice was about to be served.

After receiving the scalpels from the female nurse in the infirmary, Ra-King skated back to his unit and up to Cream's room-cell. Cream lay on his bed gazing up at the ceiling.

"I got em baby boy," Ra-King slid inside Cream's room and closed the door behind him. "Here you go." Ra-King pulled out the scalpels as he dropped onto the stool at the desk.

Cream sat up in his bed and took a scalpel. In silence, Cream studied the scalpel thinking to himself. He lost all his friends. He lost every one of them except Prince, Lil Flip who was still alive and recovering from his gunshot, Terror who was a vegetable and better off dead, and Killa who made it to Nigeria. Cream was truly devastated and didn't care for life anymore. With the tragic and harsh reality they were all dealt, Cream would accept life in prison or death with no emotional sensitivity. He experienced it all and there was truly nothing else for him to experience but death.

"It doesn't seem like this shit even real," Cream finally spoke as he sat at the edge of his bed still scoping out the scalpel. "I swear this shit all a dream because aint no way we supposed to be experiencing life like this…this shit can't be real Ra-King."

"It's real as this fucking jail we in and the time we facing…it's real baby boy and it aint a dream it's more like a nightmare."

"Why life so harsh for us…it's like she don't let no one escape…nobody make it out…why...and then Zulu…come on yo…that's fucked up…why they do that to my friend?" Cream asked as if he was communicating with the Creator of the Universe who provided the wisdom to all questions one asked.

"Cream listen to me Sun," Ra-King held a steady gaze upon Cream as he sat on the stool gripping the scalpel. "When you on top of yo game in them streets and you staying afloat above them sharks, moving swiftly amongst them wolves and you show power to the gorillas, only those who close to you can take you under…this is the self hatred that black people were indoctrinated with during slavery…it's fucked up but this how shit is."

"This nigga had my man killed though…he had him killed yo."

"Listen Sun-Z so smart and deceitful he probably thinking yall gone feed off the rumors and hit me…he not gone expect for us to know what really went down…he not gone even expect for us to hit him the way we gone hit him."

"Ra you got a chance to win at trial and get back home…me and Hawk got this."

"Like I said before Cream this shit became personal," Ra-King rose to his feet sticking to his guns, "Just how Zulu was yo heart, Munchie and G-Boy my heart…them my little bros and without them I got nothing but myself…when that shit went down…they could've died with Zulu…Sun-Z put everyone in danger let alone he got Zulu killed…I can't sit back on this and I refuse to…I see you in a minute when they call rec." Ra-King stated spinning out of Cream's room.

Rec was called and Cream and Ra-King hit the gym ready to paint it red as their hearts pumped the vengeance of anger and death. The gym was filled to capacity as usual and the basketball games were in full throttle running full court. Cream and Ra-King hit the back corner on side of the bleachers where there was a heavy bag and speed bag along with a pull up and dip bar. This is where Sun-Z and many other inmates spent their time keeping their bodies' physically fit relieving stress from their minds by working out.

When Cream and Ra-King stormed through the crowd standing at the pull up and dip bar Sun-Z was nowhere in sight. They then posted up in the corner heatedly looking around the gym before Hawk crawled from beneath the bleachers with bloodshot red eyes. Hawk was already in position waiting for

Sun-Z to jump on the pull up bar. Hawk was on point and ready to slash Sun-Z's

jugular vein open with the gem star razor he took out of a shaving razor. Hawk

had death in his red eyes and he wondered what caused Sun-Z to lose it to the

point where he had Zulu killed. Hawk was aware of Sun-Z's situation with Iyana

and how she left him and fled to the islands with NyJewel. Hawk knew that

affected Sun-Z seriously even though Sun-Z played it cool like it didn't.

Knowing Sun-Z all his life Hawk knew his friend. Sun-Z was insecure. He was

so insecure that any little challenge to his power made him feel less than a man if

he didn't prove he could handle it and there was no one above him. It was just

like the war with 12th street. Sun-Z would go to extreme measures to prove he

was king above all. When Hawk analyzed the situation with Sun-Z and Zulu

stemming from the incident that caused Iyana to leave Sun-Z, Hawk realized that

Sun-Z had Zulu killed because his pride was assaulted and Zulu seemed to be

above Sun-Z.

"I can't believe this snake," Hawk blasted as they stood by the heavy

bag. "It's nothing left to say besides the fact that I'm--," Hawk clenched his fist

and bit down on his lip, "I'm gone kill my best friend and I wont regret it…I

wont and I'm not…he killed what we all loved…he deserve to die and I'm gonna

look him dead in his eye…he gone know he was wrong before I kill him…he

gone know."

Sun-Z may have lost it, but like every killer who had a conscience he

knew what he did was wrong. There was no justification for Zulu's murder and

he was sick to his stomach. For days Sun-Z barricaded himself in his cell

mentally and spiritually in the bowels of hell. He committed several murders in

life which were justified being that it was his enemies whose breath he snatched

away. Having Zulu's breath snatched away had no divine justification and every

time Sun-Z inhaled the breath of life the Creator placed in all life, Sun-Z found

himself curled up over the cold steel toilet throwing his insides up. For days he

sat in his cell throwing up all the filth, guilt, and spiritual weakness that filled his

soul. Sun-Z couldn't believe he had Zulu killed because he was so consumed in

his own world of power. He couldn't see anything but what his power drunken

mind allowed him to see. He never felt so stupid and miserable in his life. He lost friends, riches, his freedom, and he lost his wife. The only thing he hadn't lost thus far was the air he was breathing and that wouldn't be for long because he wanted to die so he didn't have to face the demons terrorizing his soul.

....

The Atlantis Royal Towers in Paradise Islands, Bahamas, climbed high up in the sky overlooking the island. The night sky was so clear it seemed like the stars could be touched while standing on top of the Atlantis Royal Towers. It felt like one was literally on top of the world. NyJewel stood on top of the hotel but she didn't feel like she was on top of the world as she peered up into celestial night sky questioning the Creator of the universe. She wondered why some people didn't have a chance for Happiness in life and others did. Why were some people cursed with poverty and crime while others were blessed with wealth and happiness? Why was life so cruel to some and beautiful to others? Her questions went unanswered as she peered up into the heavens. It really didn't seem to even matter any more because the reality of the situation was that her life been all about struggle no matter what. The strength she used to stay above the negative conditions of her environment was for what? The knowledge and education she acquired was for what? The material wealth she gained was for what? What is the reason for this life she wondered? Why did the Creator create us and bring us here? People are brought into the world just to suffer she realized.

"What kind of God are you?" NyJewel peered deep into the blackness of the night sky. "If you're the most-high and so powerful why do you let some of us suffer? Why do you bring children into the world to suffer and die? Why do you allow good people who believe in you to suffer and horribly die? Why? Why?" NyJewel cried her soul out seeking an answer. "Why did you bring me into this world God? Why did you bring me here just to punish me? Am I not worth your love God?" NyJewel asked before she lowered her gaze from the stars and overlooked the island.

The lights of the hotels, casinos, and restaurants lit up the island revealing the creative abilities of man. The palm trees, the beaches, hills and the winding roads were a harmonious expression of the beauty of the Creator's power of Creation which was for Man and Woman's use. The natural scenery of the island alone was a reason to love being on God's green earth. But with the weight of the tormenting agony on NyJewel's soul, she would rather die since all she strived for in life only brought grief and pain.

NyJewel stepped to the ledge of the roof realizing that whoever and whatever the Creator of the Universe was, the Creator created her for this moment in life because everything else in life behind her lead to this moment she was willing to take. The adrenaline rush and happiness she felt standing on the ledge ready to fall to her death was indescribable. She forgot about all the stress, worries, and past wrongs. She felt a freedom from all things that was a hinderance to the peace within the soul. Her soul felt light as a feather and she felt like she could fly from the madness of this world. She was ready to jump to her death so her soul could be released from the bonds of the physical world of pain and suffering. She was ready and deep within she could feel a heavenly force she never felt pulling her towards the essence of life. She could feel her mind slipping into the essence of life which was the source and beginning of all life and existence. It was now she felt the Creator of the Universe communicating with her and motivating her to draw near the center of her soul where she could find the light of peace. This moment of NyJewel's life was the best moment ever and now she realized why people were brought into this world. She inhaled deeply and closed her eyes before she braced herself to take the leap of faith off the tall building. This was it and she was ready to end her suffering. She leaned forward feeling the force of gravity welcome her, and right as she could feel herself fall forward Iyana snatched her back from the ledge.

"Ny noooo," Iyana used all the strength she never knew she had to yank NyJewel away from the ledge as they both fell back onto the gravel filled roof. Iyana held NyJewel in her arms as she cried. "Its ok sis...I got you and I'm here...it's gonna be ok sis."

"Iyana why is it like this? Why? I don't know what to live for anymore."

"You have to live for the power of God in your spirit sis...the blessings in life come from us overcoming struggle...you can't give up Ny...this is why God created us and gave us the power to be strong when it's hard...God wouldn't put us through anything we can't handle because we got the power to overcome any adversity…we have to be strong and earn God's blessings sis…God's blessings only come as a reward for us being strong in the hardest of times sis…we can't give up because we have the power of God in us to overcome any adversity."

Iyana's words of power were the truth which was the foundation of life. Life was ordained by struggle because the Creator of the universe created the human soul with more power than the sun and there were only challenges to bring out the best of the human potential. Just how the Black race experienced the horrors of slavery and survived what no other race could survive. The life of struggle faced by those in the ghetto could be overcome if there was a desire to live better by utilizing the Creative Power to change self and the environment. There was no reason to have power without struggle and all struggles could be overcome. The Black race was and is a testament to the power of the soul to overcome all adversity.

One struggle that couldn't be overcome was Sun-Z's misery. As he stayed in his cell starving himself and feeling the wrath of misery rattle his soul, his spiritual energy became drained from the secretions of the stress hormones flooding his system. He just couldn't find the energy to live anymore. He allowed his soul to be captured by the vicious dragon lurking in the darkness of his soul which caused him to live in a rage. He lost himself after the war with 12th street and became engulfed in the mind of madness. After Zulu was murdered, Sun-Z finally realized he lost his soul and his life-force was too weak to live since he became a soldier of death.

About a week after Zulu was murdered, a deputy found a pale skin Sun-Z lying in his bed under the covers resting peacefully. The stress and misery blocked his energy channels and disrupted the flow of his life-force causing him to die from a severe stroke. The power of his mind was used for destruction and it was the destruction of his own soul which destroyed Sun-Z. R.I.P. OG.

CHAPTER 25

Two years later.

Destiny rested her backside on a beautifully designed quilt watching her 18 month old son play with her niece. Destiny's baby boy became the light of her dark world and the love of her life. When Zulu was murdered Destiny felt she was the blame. It seemed like all through life she let Zulu run to the streets which destroyed him. After Zulu's death she felt like it was her fault for not using the power of her love to keep him in her world of peace which is the safest place for man; a woman's love. She felt miserable until she discovered she was blessed with Zulu's seed in her womb. Zulu may have given Destiny a world of pain, but the greatest gift he had given her was their Sun. With a seed from Zulu Destiny knew she now had a divinely inspired reason to live. She had to live to nurture her seed to grow beyond the dirt of the earth and blossom into that of greatness.

Just looking into her Sun's gleaming eyes made Destiny happy about life and now she had no regrets because she would groom her Sun into perfection so he could be better than his father. At times she wished Zulu was alive to see his Sun and share the wisdom of his experience with his Sun. No matter what Destiny was thankful. The Creator may have taken Zulu away from her but the Creator gave Destiny a part of Zulu that was pure and in essence a reflection of Zulu and Destiny.

"He looks so much like Zulu," NyJewel crept up on Destiny and sat on the quilt. "He's so handsome."

Destiny smiled watching her Sun chase her niece Divine Princess Satori around Zulu's tombstone before telling NyJewel, "And he can't sit still like Zulu either."

"I can see that."

"I'm gonna teach him to not follow the path of his father and the life of destruction our people live…I wish I could have stopped Zulu from living that life."

"It's not your fault Destiny," NyJewel gently rubbed Destiny's back consolingly, "It's not in God's plan for us to direct the course of anyone's life but our own…we just have to be a positive example for these babies to follow and show them a different path…God made life like a school where we all have to learn for ourselves…we just have to learn what is right and do right to teach these kids the right way."

The thought of watching her baby grow to be a civilized and strong black man with the knowledge of his true self who would raise a righteous family brought joy to Destiny's heart.

"And Destiny I'm here to help you in anyway."

"I thank you so much NyJewel."

....

Under a sun which shone it's blazing light onto Akodo Beach in Nigeria, Killa lay back in his beach chair sipping his Star Lager beer in deep thought. Akodo beach was one of Nigeria's hottest tourists' attractions hosting many beach recreations for tourist but hundreds of years ago, many African Ancestors left this beach and others in chains heading to the western world as slaves never to return home. Killa followed the journey of the Ancestors across the Atlantic but he made it back home. He escaped the grip of the American government. And as the pounding waters of the Atlantic Ocean pounded the beach, thoughts in Killa's head pounded his brain. The waters of the beach were clear and Killa seemed to look into the water seeing his life reflect. Life has been one helluva journey for Killa but he made it to his destination. He had nothing to complain about considering he beat the odds against him.

Killa peered up into the sun gazing deeply into the bright radiance of the source of all energy. Just like the sun-gazers of the ancient land of Africa took in the sun's illustrious energy, Killa felt an illumination in the darkness of his soul. The spiritual energy of the Motherland had a magnetic pull on the human soul that gave all humans a glimpse of the divinity of the human soul. Killa committed a lot of wrong in his life but he finally felt the urge to do right as he peered up at the sun being thankful to the Creator of the Sun and all life.

"I wanna thank you Oludamare (God)…you blessed me and allowed me to make it through that fire…all my friends are with you now…and the rest are in the beast (prison) living in hell…I thank you Oludamare (God) for watching over me…and for that I owe you…I owe you my life…you brought me in this world and I'm sorry for not living for you…I didn't know because I was living that life… but now that you put me through that fire and allowed me to make it out I realize I owe my existence to you Oludamare, the creator of the heavens and earth."

....

Prince pushed Terror in his wheelchair through the crowded and noisey visiting room at the United States Penitentiary Lewisburg; The Big House. Prince found a table and seated himself with Terror sitting beside him. The world was dead to Terror as his senses no longer provided external information to him. Terror would just stare into space and see what no one else could see. He was better off dead most would say, but Prince and Yemaria refused to let the doctors pull the plug on Terror. Prince and Yemaria made a sincere devotion to do all in their power to not only take care of Terror but they would strive to bring Terror back. God is the spirit in Man which keeps Man activated with life, therefore nothing is impossible to accomplish in life and being that Terror was still breathing despite his brain mis-function, Prince was gonna strive hard to resurrect the God within Terror just how Lazarus was resurrected.

"Terror look," Prince tapped him and began pointing at Cream who stepped into the visiting room in his beige prison suit. Terror just looked on in his unresponsive state as Cream walked up smiling.

"Terror," Cream shouted reaching down to hug him. Terror's mouth twitched but he didn't move as Cream hugged him then knelt in front of him. "Damn bro," Cream struggled to hold back his tears. It was sad seeing a friend in such a state. They were young men who caused so much hell in life this is what their Karma brought in exchange for their actions. "Prince damn yo…damn…"

"I know Cream it's hard…I dealt with it every day…not a day goes by I wish we didn't have to suffer the way we do…but you know I come to realize that the Creator put some of us through the fire so others can learn from the misfortunes others been through…I did the knowledge to the bible the other day and I was reading Genesis and the Lord told Abraham that his seeds would be slaves for 400 years and they would suffer but afterwards they would come out of their suffering with great rewards."

"Prince I feel you but how the fuck is Terror gonna enjoy anything? And how the fuck is me and Hawk gonna enjoy life when we got life in here with no parole...how Prince?"

"This is the consequence of your actions Cream...but your experiences and the things you did which got you life in prison could save other young black men from jumping into the streets and getting killed and spending the rest of their life in prison...you made a decision to chase that dream of death and this is what it brought you...even though you locked up you still have life and the breath of the Creator is in you...there's nothing stronger than the soul of a Black Man...the Black Man and Woman survived one of the most devastating and human tragedies to every suffer humanity; Slavery. Chattel slavery at that...and just how our ancestors survived them horrors for over 400 years you gone survive this prison sentence...you just have to share your knowledge and wisdom of the horrors of them street dreams with the youth because if brothers like you don't, our youth will blindly get in the streets to chase the American Dream which is only The Dream of Death for our Black Nation."

Peace

The Get Rich Crime Family's story is over but the game

don't stop. Munchie and G-Boy's journey on the road

to the riches is still popping. Get ready for

Chasing Cheese in the Rat Race.

In stores and available online

www.sekhemasaru.com.

Acknowledgements

To the Creator of the Universe whose most Ancient name is Amon-Ra. Dua Netcher. Imhotep to all the Divine Ancestors whose blood course through my veins. Thank you for my Old Earth (Mother) and Old King China Man (Father) for being the vehicles Amon-Ra used to bring me into the physical realm. Thanks' for everything Ma and good looking on the Knowledge of Self and the jewels you bestowed upon me Dad. R.I.P to all my Grandparents. To the beautiful Queen Earth (Steph) who brought forth my two beautiful seeds, thank you with Supreme Love for allowing me to resurrect and be a Father. To the Wisdom Black Barbie (NaKesha) thank you for all your support Sweetheart. Peace to the Father Allah (Clarence 13X) and the Nation of Gods and Earths. Salam Alekum to the Nation of Islam. And Universal Peace to all the holy African Shrines and any movement that strives for the upliftment of the black race and the whole human family of the planet earth.

To the Lockwood's, the Phillips, Addison's, Daniels, the Ivory's, Davis' (R.I.P Cousin Ant), the Bishops, Coopers (R.I.P Mike), Singletary's (R.I.P Lee), the Taylors, The Rose (R.I.P Uncle Sam) family, the Bonners (R.I.P Aunt Yvonne), the Walkers (R.I.P BW), to Aaron Jackson and his family, the Henderson's (R.I.P Aunt Cynthia), the Barclay Family and all the other family members and it's too many of yall. R.I.P to Abu Bilal (Uncle Willie Ray) Bird Dog (Uncle Berney), RIP to James Griffin and Al "Butch" Smith.

To my older brothers Buff and Todd. Cousin Puff (Sean K). To my brother and a-alike Vinny who took the place of my best friend and co-d Baby John (RIP). Good looking Vinny because without your critique this project wouldn't be as great. Peace Allah. To the foundation: Ross, Les, Rez, King Gooba (Boo), Teddy Loc, Juve, Big Boo (Lavon), Cousin Pen and Sabota, Man-Man (Cortez), Snacks, and Peace to the God Dakim. To my Uncle Joop and my downtown Family. To a Pure Comrade from day one; Deuce King, Peace to the whole Pure Movement and AK Reed. To Gully Dee and Be Great Clothing. Peace to the God Eternal Life Allah (Boo-Boo) and the real niggas from them Genesee Blocks. To my day one PNC's from Kensington & Suffolk who still alive; Page Cracks (The God Divine Justice), Boon, Baby Ray, Fat Mike Beaseley, Finbuck, 2 Cent, Fudge, Man-Z, and Goldie. To Dino and Jermain in Atlanta. To my nephews Minnesota Fats, Poobie and Devin. To Pop Dog, Ru, Monkey Trouble, Bobo, and Ray E. Fat Rita. To C-Note, B. Coop, 12 Gage and J-5. To Marcus the Darkest. Ern-Ski, Petey, Pee-Wee, Buck, Nee Poo, Ant Clark, Hot Rod. My G Castleberry. To Uncle P's Barbershop, my crew from Profile on Bailey Ave, and Big Jay and the ChoppaFella Fam. To Mario Burks, Chris Parker & Big Vinny. Peace to the Gods Kendu, Black Seed, and Juggernaut Messiah in Rochester. Eric and G. Lewis. Peace to the God Motion, Buzz and Fugi. To Tate, Dre, and Born Master. To cousin Goog, Nephew, Twan and Tocara. Peace to the God Magnetic (Johnny Vaughn), Len-Dog and Marty. To a friend whom I send blessings, Laquenta. Pusa what up sis. To Shatonya (Rip Ms. Tracy). To my sistrens Teirra, Toya, AJ and Chells. To Lovey, Chauncey (Season), Fugi and T. Jones down in Charlotte. To a beautiful and single mother, Ms. Irene Coleman. For my Old Players K. Battles, Helluva Boo and George. Peace to the Gods Born Reality and Saladin Q. Allah up in The Falls. Peace to the God Equan (Rudy). To Guy, Mel, and Juney from the Flip Side of Bailey Ave. To Kito Smith and Jamar Jones. To Jodi and the Zoo crew from Delavan and Courtland. To the old school Marshall & Bardol crew (Cal, Fruit, Toot, Moe, and R.I.P Uncle Sid). To Skip and Gortho from 10th street. To the Gangsters dead and gone from Central Park, The Fillmore Shakedown Crew, Sycamore & Woltz and all them vicious blocks on the east and west side of Ruff-Buff.

To my west coast fam: My Big Sis Freda. Cousin Booter, Nikki, Linique, Coco and Kevin. To my Harlem World and Boogie Down Bronx family: Uncle Ant and Aunt Shirley. Uncle Scat, Big Bro Sha and Cousin Pork. Peace to the Gods Mzee Nkosi and Divine (L. Thomas). To Lashawn Holmes and little Ty. To Al, the older God La-Sha and the Vogelsang Family. RIP to the Older God Lord Prince from the Bronx. To the living Legend and OG Tito Johnson. To Ant Live and R.I.P to a true G; Scotty Ragland from Harlem. (I thank the Ancestors for Scotty because he told me I was a Young Sage (a Wise Person) and he seen something in me I didn't see in myself at the time. Dua Netcher). Peace to the God Un, Glory (Deville) and Dre from Mount Vernon. To my BK fam: Scoot, Kasim, Grim and Beast. Peace to the God Father Ka CM B-Unique God Allah from Bed-Stuy. To cousin I from Brownsville. R.I.P Cree from Brownsville. To DJ Flash International from LI. And Peace to the God Allah Adams who is a great author of many works.

To all those I grew up with on them Bailey Blocks and everyone I broke bread with in them Ruff-Buff streets. To all the real G's I graduated Gladiator School with (Coxsackie, Comstock, Washington and Green) and everyone else in them NY Prisons and the Feds. Free the Older God Malik Allah from Jamaica Queens who been locked up in the NY prison system for almost 50 years as of 2017. Free Cousin Boonchie, my nephew Donnie, Ty Kimble, Ken Ben, Andre Vernon, Little Meatwhop, Cousin E from Cornwall street, Machiah from Ferry and Wohlers, big cousin K-Wan from Harlem and all the other real headz sitting in a cage.

There have been many great people who contributed and still spark my growth and development. If I didn't mention your name don't take it personal because I am only human but you are in my heart forever.

Peace.

A list of books for spiritual growth

Breaking the Psychological Chains of Slavery by Naim Akbar
From Niggaz to Godz by Akil
The African Origin of the Major World Religions by Dr. Yosef Ben Jochanan
The African Origin of Civilization by Cheik Anta Diop
The African Presence in Early Asia & Europes by Ivan Van Sertima
Destruction of Black Civilization by Chancellor Williams
Tree of Life Meditation & Metu Neter vols 1-5 by Ra Un Nefer Amen
The Making of the White Man by Paul Lawrence Guthrie
The Science of Self and When the World was Black by Supreme Understanding Allah
Introduction to African Civilization by John G. Jackson
The Black Man of the Nile and his Family by Dr. Yosef Ben Jochanan
From the Browder File and Nile Valley Contributions to Civilization by Anthony Browder
The Isis Papers by Dr Francis Cress Welsing
Spiritual Warriors are Healers by Mfundishi Jhutyms
The African Origin of Biological Psychiatry by Dr. Richard King
The Psychodynamics of Black on Black Violence by Dr. Amos N. Wilson

Made in the USA
Monee, IL
25 August 2020